Understanding and Preventing Community Violence

James F. Albrecht • Garth den Heyer
Editors

Understanding and Preventing Community Violence

Global Criminological and Sociological Perspectives

Editors
James F. Albrecht
Pace University
New York, NY, USA

Garth den Heyer
Arizona State University
Phoenix, AZ, USA

ISBN 978-3-031-05074-9 ISBN 978-3-031-05075-6 (eBook)
https://doi.org/10.1007/978-3-031-05075-6

This Springer imprint is published by the registered company Springer Nature Switzerland AG
The registered company address is: Gewerbestrasse 11, 6330 Cham, Switzerland

This book is dedicated to police officers across the globe, who continue to make personal sacrifices to ensure that society remains safe and secure and particularly to those who have lost their lives while nobly serving their communities.

"Blessed are the peacemakers, for they shall be called the children of God."

Matthew 5:9—King James Bible

This book is dedicated to my two children, Jimmy and Kristiana, who continue to provide me with continuous motivation through their unlimited sense of curiosity and their enthusiasm for life and learning.

James F. Albrecht

This book is dedicated to my two grandsons, Liam and Joshua.

Garth den Heyer

Preface

Essentially every documented law code has decried that violence perpetrated against others is immoral and illegal. Whether that violence is physical or sexual, or whether it results in injury or death, humanity has acknowledged that this misbehavior cannot be tolerated by individuals or by society as a whole. However, for centuries an injury caused to another could be settled through agreements between the families of the parties involved. If the respective parties could not settle the matter, then the family of the injured could invoke an injury of kind nature upon the family of the perpetrator. It is only in the most recent stages of human history that the state has taken upon the role of adjudication and punishment for violence targeting others.

Violence targeting an individual or the community at large has negatively impacted many societies across the globe and has done so for not only decades, but for centuries. Once people were drawn to areas that later developed into industrialized metropolitan centers, overpopulation created a sense of anonymity for those predisposed to criminality. Communities could no longer rely on themselves or their sense of cohesion to deter crime or hold individuals accountable. With the dawn of the nineteenth century, the responsibility for preventing violence and other criminality had fallen upon the public policing entities that evolved in the 1820s. After London developed a metropolitan police department under the guidance of Sir Robert Peel, that model was copied in Boston, Philadelphia, New York, and many other high-population centers in Europe and the United States and later was implemented in most countries, states, and cities across the globe.

For almost two centuries, the common government tactic for deterring violence and other street crime involved the presence of a uniformed police officer. And the traditional response when violence and criminality took place was to reactively respond and document the incident in a report, leaving the matter to police investigators to explore further. This was generally not effective nor efficient. It was not until 1994 that law enforcement strategies were dramatically re-engineered and took on a proactive enforcement-oriented approach. These actions could be considered revolutionary and did result in significant crime reductions in the respective jurisdictions that now relied on statistical analysis, crime mapping, enhanced intelligence gathering, the strict enforcement of quality of life and disorder infractions, and strengthened inter- and intra-organizational cooperation and collaboration. What is now referred to as the "Compstat" era has involved the commencement of technology playing a larger and more critical role in policing and law enforcement and the more effective measurement of organizational performance.

In order to better understand community violence, it is pertinent that associated criminological theory be examined. Originally, a scientific approach concluded that criminality was based on biological or genetic factors. As such, certain individuals were considered as being genetically inferior and basically evil. Later, a more judicious approach concluded that humans acted of free will. As such, and from the perspective of the criminal justice system, most criminals act rationally and intentionally and are therefore personally and criminally liable for their actions. Rational choice theory delineated that individuals will weigh the rewards of a criminal act against the likelihood of apprehension and punishment. In more general terms, if they think that they will "get away" with it, they will engage in that criminal act.

In line with the rational choice theory, the routine activities theory proposes that three primary factors contribute to the potential commission of a crime: the location, the perpetrator, and the victim. When considering all dynamics, the perpetrator will prioritize targeting the "easiest" target in a location that offers the least likely opportunity for detection and apprehension. By introducing an option that will obstruct any of the three factors, the probability of the crime will be diminished. For example, by adding sufficient lighting or opening the area to natural surveillance, a location could be made more safe and prevent a criminal act from taking place. As such, situational crime prevention and crime prevention through environmental design are two potential options to reduce the likelihood of criminal activity.

Another plausible theoretical explanation for engaging in violent criminality relies on social learning theory, which postulates that many criminals learn from others that opting to engage in crime is acceptable and "profitable." Peer associations and family experiences may support this ideological position and both have proven to be strong influential factors in continued and recidivist illegal activities. As a result, many criminals have become convinced that engaging in crime and even committing violence have become a rewarding "career option" for them individually.

Some more sociologically inclined theories have taken a larger societal perspective and have extolled that it is civilization itself that has created discrepancies in opportunity, perhaps based on race, ethnicity, social position, and/or minority status. With this obstacle to personal and community success in mind, some individuals or similarly impacted groups have opted to participate in criminality as the only means to achieve any sense of success and even survival. This theoretical position is supported by both strain theory and criminal race theory, among other sociological explanations.

So while generally the criminal justice system globally operates under the assumption that individuals undertake illicit and violent actions of free will, attempting to prevent crime and violence appears to be a more complex endeavor. While the police and the criminal justice system are often viewed as the primary mechanisms for crime and violence control, it is obviously important that government officials effectively address such issues as actual or perceived inequality and develop options that open sustainable opportunity for all individuals and people. This includes viable initiatives to promote and ensure stable and improved physical, mental and emotional health, education, employment, financial stability, and promotional advancement.

It should be obvious that the police and the criminal justice system play significant roles in crime and violence prevention and control. One the other hand, society in general has a larger social and interrelated set of responsibilities that must be considered and addressed in an effort to deter the desire for participation in illicit activities and the acceptance of criminal misbehavior as a societal norm. On a positive note, the incorporation of technology into crime control and suspect detection and apprehension strategies has proven to be a major development for law enforcement organizations globally. In addition, police administrators are consistently re-evaluating agency policy, procedure, and protocol to address community feedback and public criticism. As such, contemporary law enforcement and the entire sphere of criminal justice have become persistently evolving fields of public service.

The goal of this book will be to comprehensively examine the causes of community violence and serious acts of criminality and to thoroughly evaluate society's response, specifically by law enforcement and criminal justice actors, to these illicit misdeeds and often horrific acts involving misbehavior, immorality, and deviance. The global nature of the chapter contributions should provide a broad spectrum of perspectives and additionally prove to be enlightening and thought-provoking to any curious individual, but more so to criminal justice and government leaders, policymakers, researchers, academics, students, community representatives, and concerned citizens.

Professor of Criminal Justice and Homeland Security — James F. Albrecht
Pace University
New York, NY, USA

Contents

About the Contributors

Magne V. Aarset Magne V. Aarset is educated in Mathematics, Mathematical Statistics, Music, and Psychology at the University of Oslo in Norway. He has broad industrial experience from working among others in different branches, including the European aerospace and the Norwegian insurance industries, and lecturing/ research experience from the Norwegian University of Science and Technology (NTNU) and BI Norwegian Business School. He is now employed at NTNU and at Terp, a company producing a-books, that is, electronic textbooks adapted to the reader. His main field of research is within psychometrics and machine learning.

James F. Albrecht James F. Albrecht is a professor in the Department of Criminal Justice and Homeland Security at Pace University in New York City. Jimmy received a prestigious Fulbright Fellowship in 1998 and worked as a professor at the National Police College of Finland. He is also the recipient of a 2013 Embassy Policy Specialist Fellowship (USDOS/IREX) and was tasked with conducting research and making recommendations to improve law enforcement effectiveness and legitimacy in Ukraine. Police Chief Albrecht served in the European Union Rule of Law Mission (EULEX) in Kosovo (former Yugoslavia) as the Head of the EULEX Police Executive Department, in charge of criminal investigations and coordinating international law enforcement cooperation and intelligence analysis from 2008 through 2010. He had previously served in the United Nations Mission in Kosovo Police from 2007 to 2008. Jimmy is also a 23-year veteran of the NYPD who retired as the Commanding Officer of NYPD Transit Bureau District 20, tasked with the prevention of crime and terrorism in the subway and commuter transit system in New York City. He was a first responder and incident command manager at the September 11, 2001 terrorist attack on the World Trade Center and developed the counter-terrorism strategic plan for the subway system in the borough of Queens, New York City.

Abisoye Priscilla Aremu Abisoye Aremu is a human resource professional with keen interest and professional training in security, situational awareness, profiling, and intelligence analysis. Abisoye has a rich experiential blend of a Bachelor's degree in Sociology from the University of Ibadan in Nigeria, combined with professional certifications in Human Resource Management and Professional Leadership and Strategic Management. Through this and other exposures, Abisoye has a deep passion for security studies involving human resources and development. She recently completed her one-year compulsory National Youth Service Corps commitment at the Barricade Executive Protection in Abuja and is also a leading coordinator at the 'Now Experiencing a Touch' (NEAT) Foundation.

Amos Oyesoji Aremu Professor Oyesoji Aremu teaches Psychology in the Department of Guidance and Counseling University of Ibadan, Nigeria. He is a Commonwealth fellow and a visiting research fellow at the Institute of Criminal Justice Studies, University of Portsmouth, United Kingdom. Professor Oyesoji Aremu has to his credit over 80 books and other publications. In addition to his commitment as an astute academic, Professor Oyesoji Aremu has a wide administrative and managerial experience in the university system. Professor Aremu is a member of various local and international learned societies, such as the Counselling Association of Nigeria, the Nigerian Psychological Association, the International Police Executive Symposium, and the British Society of Criminology, and a fellow, Commonwealth Scholarship Commission. In 2007/2008, he was awarded the prestigious Commonwealth Academic Fellowship by the Commonwealth Scholarship Commission at the University of Portsmouth, United Kingdom.

Christiaan Bezuidenhout Christiaan Bezuidenhout holds the following degrees: BA (Criminology), BA Honors (Criminology), MA (Criminology), DPhil (Criminology), and an MSc in Criminology and Criminal Justice from the University of Oxford. He is attached to the Department of Social Work and Criminology, University of Pretoria UP, where he teaches psychocriminology, criminal justice, and contemporary criminology at undergraduate and postgraduate level as a full professor. He has supervised several postgraduate studies. Psychocriminology, criminal justice (policing), and youth misbehavior are some of his research foci. During his academic career, Christiaan has had numerous scientific articles published in peer-reviewed journals and has authored chapters in several books. He has also acted as editor-in-chief for various scholarly works. He was awarded the 2019/2020 University of Pretoria Institutional Community Engagement Award. He has assisted the South African government in the development of different crime prevention initiatives. He serves on the South African Police Service (SAPS) Tertiary Institutions Cluster for Training as well as Research. Christiaan does court work as an expert witness and he was the president of the Criminological Society of Africa (CRIMSA) from 2015 to 2017. He is doing research at East Carolina University (ECU) in the United States as part of his Fulbright Research Fellowship regarding the role of females in law enforcement.

Salih Hakan Can Dr. Salih Hakan Can began his career in law enforcement in 1984 as a Police Chief in the Turkish National Police. Upon graduation from the police academy, where he obtained a Bachelor of Science degree in Criminal Justice and Law, Hakan was promoted to ranking officer and worked in many divisions, including Interpol, Narcotics Investigations, and Financial Crimes. As part of Turkish National Police international police collaboration, he worked or joined law enforcement operations in Germany, Spain, the Netherlands, Switzerland, Russia, Azerbaijan, Kosovo, Bosnia, Bulgaria, Romania, and Albania. He received his Master's from the University of North Texas and a PhD from Sam Houston State University. While he was working at the Law Enforcement Management Institute of Texas, he established a program called "Incident Command Simulation," which received funding and great recognition from the US Department of Homeland Security. Hakan works on multiple projects with the United Nations, the Interpol, the National Sheriffs Association, and the International Association of Chiefs of Police. Dr. Can has had numerous books and journal articles published.

Durmus Alper Camlibel Durmus Alper Camlibel is Associate Professor of Criminal Justice at the University of Wisconsin, Oshkosh. He received his PhD in Political Science from Claremont University, California. Dr. Camlibel is also a former police superintendent, who served with the Turkish National Police from 2001 to 2018. He participated in United Nations and European Union projects in counter-narcotics trafficking and has presented his research at several national and international academic conferences. Dr. Camlibel teaches courses in introduction to policing, police deviance, police administration, introduction to criminal justice, crime prevention, terrorism, narcotic and drugs, and the senior capstone seminar. His research interests include inmate violence, police stress, police service delivery, drug abuse, terrorism, and ethnic conflict.

Ebrima Chongan Ebrima Chongan is an experienced policy advisor with a demonstrated history of working in the government administration industry. He possesses strong analytical skills and is competent in government, international relations, policy analysis, and criminal law. Ebrima is a strong community and social services professional with a Bachelor of Laws (LLB) focused in law from London Metropolitan University. Ebrima served in the Gambia Police Force as Assistant Inspector General and played a major role in the re-organization of the Gambia Police Force (GPF) when it was merged with the defunct Gendarmerie by developing a Five-Year Strategic Development Program.

László Christian Hungarian Police Brigadier General Christian is the Deputy Director for Education at the National University of Public Service in Budapest, Hungary. Laszlo is also an associate professor at Pázmány Péter Catholic University within the Faculty of Law and Political Sciences. He is the Head of Department for Private Security and Local Governmental Law Enforcement at the National University of Public Service in Budapest, Hungary.

W. Bradley Cotton Brad Cotton was a police officer for the Brantford Police Service in Ontario, Canada for 28 years, retiring as a police sergeant in 2018. He went on to pursue a Master of Business Administration degree at the University of Edinburgh Business School. Brad is a consultancy managing member for public safety and business for WB Global Partners, serving both public and private organizations and industry in assisting in the development of effective agency strategy.

Rune Glomseth Rune Glomseth was educated at the Norwegian Police Academy in 1983 and holds a Master's degree in Public Administration. Rune also holds certifications in Law and Political Science. He has a broad background from various positions in the police across 38 years, now assigned as Associate Professor in Organization and Management. He works with Leadership and Management programs at the Norwegian Police University College. His research interests include management and organizational culture, police culture, and changes in the police and leadership skills in top management in the Police. Professor Glomseth has been responsible for leadership development programs at the Norwegian Police Security Service, the National Criminal Investigation Service, and in several police districts.

Ross Hendy Ross Hendy is Lecturer in Criminology at the School of Social Sciences, Monash University. His research focuses on the development of theoretical and applied perspectives of police and policing, such as practitioner behavior, police use of force, and the effectiveness of police intervention. As a former sergeant with New Zealand Police, he has worked with researchers to enhance their understanding of the police environment and the limitations of police administrative data, and to provide advice about real-world issues that criminal justice practitioners and policymakers face in the criminological and criminal justice environment.

Garth den Heyer Dr. Garth den Heyer is a professor with Arizona State University and a senior research fellow with the Police Foundation. He is also a contributing faculty member at Walden University and an associate with the Scottish Institute of Policing Research. He served with the New Zealand Police for 38 years, retiring as an Inspector and Manager: National Security. He also spent more than 20 months as a strategic advisor to the Regional Assistance Mission to the Solomon Islands. His main research interests are policing, militarization, service delivery efficacy, policy development, strategic thinking, and organizational reform.

Annalise Kempen Annalise Kempen obtained her BPol Science degree in 1993 from the University of Pretoria. She started working in the South African Police Service in 1994. She became the editor of *SERVAMUS* policing magazine in 2002, when the magazine was privatized and converted to a community-based safety and security magazine. Annalise is also the assistant editor of the *Just Africa* journal.

Ritesh Kotak Ritesh Kotak started his law enforcement career in Canada, where he coordinated the creation of the cybercrimes unit and the research and innovation portfolio focusing on digital transformation. Ritesh then transitioned to the private sector, where he worked with various Fortune 500 Tech companies on global projects related to cyber security, investigations, and next-generation Internet of Things (IoT) applications for the Smart Cities projects. In 2018, Ritesh was selected by Harvard University's Kennedy School of Government for their Emerging Leaders

Executive Program. In 2017, he completed an MBA from the University of Edinburgh and holds a BBA from the University of Toronto.

István Jenő Molnar István Jenő Molnar is presently an assistant lecturer at the National University of Public Service in the Faculty of the Department of Behavioural Sciences in Law Enforcement in Budapest, Hungary. István is also the Vice President of the 'For Safety and Livable Cities Association' and the Head of Strategy Department in the Ministry of Interior Secretariat of the National Crime Prevention Council.

Catherine Parent Catherine Parent, MEd, is a registered nurse (clinician), researcher, and educator regarding complex behavior issues and mental health. Cathy also collaborates with Richard Parent in policing projects. Together they research and co-author major reports concerning police-involved shootings, police and mental health, ethics in law enforcement, and community policing practices.

Rick Parent Dr. Rick Parent is an associate professor emeritus at the School of Criminology, Simon Fraser University, and a former police officer. His research interests include community policing, police ethics, and the police use of lethal force, including the phenomenon of suicide by a cop.

Randall Snyder Randall Snyder has served since 2000 with the Pinal County, Arizona, Sheriff's Office. He has worked as a patrol deputy, patrol supervisor, and criminal investigator in the Person's Crimes Unit. He has investigated numerous incidents of domestic violence, sexual assaults, crimes against children, and violent felonies. Snyder spent two years on the Arizona Internet Crimes Against Children Task Force, where he conducts investigations involving the online enticement and exploitation of children, and received the US Attorney General's Special Commendation Award for his activities in this unit. Snyder is a member of the Arizona Child Abduction Response team, and has conducted multiple trainings for this multi-agency team. He is a member of the International Association of Cyber and Economic Crime Professionals and the Arizona Criminal Justice Educators Association, and is a certified social media intelligence analyst. Snyder received both his Bachelor's degree in Justice Studies and Master's degree in Criminal Justice from Arizona State University and plans to continue his education after retirement from the Sheriff's Office.

Perry Stanislas Dr. Perry Stanislas is an international expert in policing and security issues specializing in complex organizational and service delivery matters. His specific areas of expertise include: organizational development and transformation, anti-corruption work, strategic planning and leadership development, carrying out systems reviews, and research. Perry is a highly regarded trainer and consultant and has worked in numerous countries around the world, to include: the United States, Nigeria, Gambia, Kenya, Dubai, and numerous Caribbean countries. Dr. Stanislas is a member of the International Police Executive Symposium and the Association of

Caribbean Criminal Justice Professionals (ACCJP). He is also an honorary member of the Caribbean Institute of Forensic Accountants and was a keynote speaker at the first Caribbean Law Enforcement Conference, sponsored by the Trinidad and Tobago Police Service in 2014. Dr. Stanislas was the Senior Policy Advisor for Bedfordshire Police for strategic development and organizational performance for over a decade, and the first person in the country employed in this capacity by a British police service. Dr. Stanislas's success in this role led to Her Majesty's Inspectorate of the Constabulary (Home Office) nominating him to become an instructor at the prestigious Bramshill Police Staff College, where he taught on the Senior Command and Commonwealth Senior Command Course for chief officers.

Theresa C. Tobin Theresa C. Tobin is Professor of Criminal Justice at Molloy College, Rockville Centre, New York. She has spent over three decades as a member of the New York City Police Department, rising to the rank of Chief of Interagency Operations. She has received numerous awards and honors, including the NYPD's Medal of Valor for her heroic actions during the tumultuous events on September 11, 2001. She is an active member of several boards and has been a keynote speaker at many conferences and workshops.

Chapter 1
Law Enforcement Response to Internet Crimes Against Children

Randall Synder

Introduction

The concept of violence is different for each person. For some, when the term is used, images of war are pictured. For others, it is physical injuries sustained, maybe in a fight or during the commission of some criminal act. But for others, the concept of violence may be much less noticeable, yet just as life altering. This is the reality for thousands of children each year who are sexually solicited, exploited, and abused online. These children fall victim to internet predators, men and women who obtain sexual gratification from children and seek their prey on social media, chat boards, and even online games. But what is the "violence" if the offense occurs in cyberspace rather than in person? Are these people engaging in fantasy? A harmless role play involving "chat" and "just pictures?" No. The emotional and psychological toll taken on these children is as devastating, and long lasting, as any physical marks or injuries. Children contacted by internet predators are introduced to sexual acts that are detrimental to their continuing development, often times enticed into engaging in sexual acts with others or themselves and provided sexual materials to groom them into creating sexually exploitive images of their own. Once this happens, the revictimization of knowing that their images are on the web, literally worldwide, and can never be erased or recovered leads to traumas that can last a lifetime. The violence perpetrated against them, in the mental and emotional manipulation, physical abuse, and long-term distress, is easily fit into the definition and conception of violence that online acts are neither victimless nor fantasy.

Since the beginning of time, people have committed sexual offenses against one another and have even offended against children. The oldest known criminal codes, the Code of Ur-Nammu and the Code of Hammurabi, both list sexual offenses that

R. Synder (✉)
Arizona State University, Phoenix, AZ, USA
e-mail: randall.snyder@asu.edu

J. F. Albrecht, G. den Heyer (eds.), *Understanding and Preventing Community Violence*, https://doi.org/10.1007/978-3-031-05075-6_1

would have been considered "criminal" for the times. Additionally, the Bible lists in the books of Matthew, Luke, and Mark the statement by Jesus that "But whoso shall offend one of these little ones which believe in me, it were better for him that a millstone were hanged about his neck, and that he were drowned in the depth of the sea" (Matthew 18:6, KJV). Throughout history, women and children were often seen as property, first of their father and then of their husbands. Sexual offenses were largely blamed on the victims, instead of the perpetrators, and even crimes against children were often blamed on the children. In several countries, this "ownership" of women and children is still an implicit, if not explicit, part of their social makeups, allowing for victimization to be unrecognized or not reported. It was not until the nineteenth and twentieth centuries that this right of possession began to change, in the United States and in many industrial nations, and for society to consider women and children autonomous people. With this change in the social value of women and children, views of their sexuality also began to change and allow for sex crimes to be better recognized and addressed.

During the so-called sexual psychopath era, ranging from the 1930s until the 1960s, the increase in public outcry against sexual offenses created a public discourse on a topic previously considered "too hideous to contemplate" (Freedman, 1987). The increase in attention by the media during this era resulted in a rise in reporting, and public awareness, of this issue. Seen largely as a psychiatric issue, legislative efforts were largely focused on incapacitation in mental facilities (Freedman, 1987). Since that time the concept of sexual offending, and the perpetration of sexual crimes against children, has had to evolve through media furor, social shifts in the concepts of obscenity, sexuality and even gender identity, and women and children being considered autonomous beings rather than "property." Additionally, the age of consent, when children are legally allowed to consent to sexual activity, still varies from jurisdiction to jurisdiction, ranging from as young as 12 in Angola and the Philippines to between 16 and 18 in most countries, including the United States (World Population, 2020). Considering sexual crimes have been around as long as recorded time; it should come as no surprise that in the twentieth and twenty-first centuries sexual offenses, especially those perpetrated against children, are not only disturbingly common but increasing in complexity and more difficult to detect, investigate, and prosecute.

Where sexual crimes were, throughout the nineteenth and twentieth centuries, largely concentrated on offenses perpetrated in person, the advent of the internet has created new and complex challenges to law enforcement. Changing social norms around sexuality, ages of consent, and the minefield which is social media only compounds the situation. Moreover, with so much attention focused on enforcing statutory rape laws, changing definitions of "rape" to be more socially inclusive, and addressing the problem of sex trafficking, sexual harassment, and sexual abuse by those in power, it is no wonder that internet sex crimes, sometimes perpetrated continents away, are largely misunderstood by the general public. Furthermore, the legislative acts that occurred prior to and in the early days of the internet were largely based upon faulty logic, misconceptions about these offenders and their victims, and a legislative process that cannot hope to keep up with the pace of technologies used to exploit and abuse the victims of these crimes. Internet-based offenses were often made to "fit into" existing legislation or were included in broader laws for which they weren't intended. When specific legislation was drafted for cyber-based offenses, often times it was outdated by the time it was formalized, and the need for revision to modernize it to current technologies was almost instantaneous. Additionally, case law, decisions by judges during litigation, is often based upon this obsolete legislation and frequently reflects technological ignorance on the part of the judiciary. When cases are presented in light of new technology, or situations outside the knowledge or scope of the original legislation, decisions for future enforcement are made on these rulings more so than the original laws. The impetus for many of the legislative acts being applied today on internet-related offenses began well before the internet was created. The concept of "obscenity" has been argued in the US court system since Miller v. California (1973), 413 US 15, decided what was considered obscene, and this concept is still applied today in determining what does and does not constitute pornography. Most recently, the PROTECT Act of 2003 allows for depictions, even animations, of what appears to be children to be charged as "obscene." While many state statutes do not mirror this directly, it impacts the way that child obscenity and the sexual exploitation and abuse of children is viewed, especially as it pertains to these acts conducted online.

But many of these earlier cases looked at the concept of "pornography" as it applies to obscenity and the consensual recording of sexual acts between adults. When minors are introduced, the nomenclature did not change, despite the vast difference in the concepts of both age and consent. While traditionally called "child pornography," even in legislative writing, the community of investigators, child advocates, and other professionals who work with this material are trying to change the nomenclature to child sexual abuse material (CSAM) or child sexual exploitation material (CSEM), for those images in which a child is being sexually abused or is engaged in some type of sexual conduct, as a means of better explaining the horrific nature of the materials (Greijer & Doek, 2016). In this writing, the terms CSEM and CSAM will be used interchangeably, despite the significant difference between the two.

So, what is the law enforcement response to these violent acts perpetrated across the internet? How are these crimes, both virtual and in person, treated by the criminal justice system? In the following pages, an examination of the various cyber-related crimes will be conducted, with examples from actual cases to support the concepts and pinpoint the investigative and prosecutorial roadblocks that had to be overcome. Discussions about the crime types, some of the legislation surrounding the crimes, and investigative hurdles will be presented. While many consider cybercrimes against children, especially possession of exploitive images "just pictures," it will be demonstrated that these crimes are significantly more violent and impactful to victims than the concept implies. The physical and emotional scars that victims of these crimes receive often last a lifetime. This is especially true when the victim is aware that the evidence of their victimization, the photos and videos produced and distributed online, will be forever available and utilized for the gratification of predators and their recurrent traumatization.

Sexual Exploitation of Minors

The sexual exploitation of minors is often referred to as "child pornography" and involves the possession, manufacture, and/or distribution of images and videos of a sexual nature that have a child involved. Depending on the jurisdiction, the age of consent within the jurisdiction is taken into account on whether the image is considered in a particular case, but most often any person, under the age of 18, depicted in the images or videos can be considered a minor for legal purposes. Some states, such as Arizona, have additional sentencing enhancements when the children are considered especially young, such as under the age of 15. These enhancements, dubbed "dangerous crimes against children," take the young age of the victim into account and enhance sentencing accordingly. Federal sentencing guidelines have similar enhancements. As it pertains to the charges of sexual exploitation of a minor, the US Sentencing Guidelines (USSG) § 2G2.1 indicate that the offense level severity is increased by four levels if the victim is under 12 years of age and two levels if between the ages of 12 and 16.

The first federal agency to investigate and enforce child pornography laws was the US Postal Service in 1977 (California Coalition, n.d.). At that time, child pornography was largely distributed in printed format, sometimes in "newsletters" or other publications between individuals who knew each other and, often times, had met. Because this means of distribution was slow, unreliable, and fraught with danger since the sender and recipient had to have intimate knowledge of one another to distribute these images, most child sexual abuse was perpetrated without photographic evidence or documentation. As the internet grew in size and popularity, images could now be distributed over greater distances and with greater security; however, the speed and size limitations of the early internet still made distribution difficult. The US Postal Service reports that "during the fiscal year 1997, 33 percent of child exploitation cases investigated by Postal inspectors also involved computers" (California Coalition, n.d.). By 2000, that number had grown to 77%. The US Postal Service indicates that between 1997, when they began keeping statistics, and 2000, they arrested 828 individuals and identified 370 children. Additional statistics regarding the scope of the problem are collected by the National Center for Missing and Exploited Children (NCMEC), who have become the national clearinghouse for child exploitation since they began collecting exploitation tips in 1998. NCMEC reports receiving nearly 75 million reports of child exploitation or other online abuses since 1998, with over 69.1 million files and over 19,000 children identified (NCMEC, n.d.). In 2019 alone, NCMEC received more than 16.9 million reports.

Today investigations into child exploitation are conducted by multiple federal agencies, including the Department of Homeland Security, the Federal Bureau of Investigation, and the Postal Service, just to name a few. State and local policing agencies are also involved, through the 61 Internet Crimes Against Children (ICAC) Internet crimes task forces around the country. These teams, including full- and part-time investigators, undertake both proactive and reactive investigations into the online exploitation of children. Working in both the open and dark webs, investigators are able to coordinate between state, national, and international boundaries with the goal of rescuing children and apprehending offenders. These agencies and task forces, in conjunction with NCMEC, work through all of the tips received, plus proactive investigations started by the individual investigators, to try and curb the exploitation of children online. Examples of proactive investigations include engaging in chats with offenders posing as either a child or another offender, monitoring peer-to-peer file trading networks, and even undercover operations using offender information to infiltrate known exploitation networks. Reactive investigations include such examples as responding to CyberTips from the National Center for Missing and Exploited Children; calls for service to patrol that require additional investigation, silent witness, and other tip line contacts; and even conducting investigations into tips passed on to public information officers or similar media connected individuals.

Additionally, the COVID-19 pandemic of 2020 caused a significant increase in reports of online sexual victimization. While the prevalence of cyber-related tips had increased significantly in the 2000s, significant spikes were especially observed during the pandemic. As reported in Bourke and Hernandez (2009), "The FBI's Innocent Images Initiative, for example, reported an increase of 2,026% cases opened, and a 1,312% increase in convictions or pre-trial diversions, between 1996 and 2005" (Federal Bureau of Investigation, 2006, p. 6). The pandemic made this even worse. According to a recent USA Today article, "Tips to the National Center for Missing and Exploited Children, the clearinghouse for such information in the United States, nearly doubled from 6.3 million in the first half of 2019 to 12 million through June of 2020. Reports of online enticement similarly spiked during that timeframe, from 6,863 to 13,268" (Racioppi, 2020). In early March 2020, when many US states were beginning to enforce lockdowns and stay-at-home orders, an average weekly number of reports to NCMEC were about 250,000. By early April, in the midst of the lockdown restrictions, NCMEC began receiving over 1 million reports each week, for a period of approximately 3 weeks, before lockdown restrictions began to expire and numbers began to slowly subside (personal correspondence). This indicates that not only were many more children online for extended periods of time because of lockdown and being out of school, but the number or perpetrators online for longer periods of time were making contact and committing more offenses.

With this comes the increased difficulty in identifying and locating both offenders and victims, as more social media platforms move to "safer" security, such as end-to-end encryptions, anonymized profiles, lack of user information collection, and greater availability on mobile devices. Combined with this came the switch in how devices connect.

To connect to the internet, whether using a phone, computer, tablet, or other device, one must have an Internet Protocol (IP) address. This is a series of numbers, originally in a quad-dotted format (IPv4, or Internet Protocol version 4) that defined the device to the downline service, essentially an "address" that allowed the query to be routed to the correct internet location and information requested to be routed to the correct intended recipient. With the quad-dotted format (i.e., *192.0.2.235*), there were approximately 4 billion possible addresses. In February 2011, the number of available IPv4 addresses ran out, necessitating the conversion to IPv6 (Internet Protocol version 6) format. This format uses octets, eight groupings of characters, both numbers and letters, separated by colons instead of periods (i.e., *2001:0db8:0000:0000:0000:8a2e:0370:7334*). Because of this increase in the address, the number of possible addresses increased exponentially. However, this did not mean all prior IPv4 addresses went away, merely that new addresses would be in the new format and old addresses still existed. This meant that a person connecting to the internet could have an Internet Protocol (IP) address in either or both formats and the downline application or site being accessed may or may not collect both addresses. Additionally, subscriber information may not be available from the internet service provider (ISP) for both formats, thereby anonymizing the user from law enforcement. While some of these hurdles have been overcome by law enforcement investigation tasked with identifying these suspects and victims, a few challenges still remain. Further difficulties in investigations arise with the inclusion of technologies like end-to-end encryption, where platform servers never "see" the information being passed between users. Technologies incorporated into certain platforms that automatically delete communications after a set time frame further work to obfuscate investigations and allow offenders a modicum of anonymity and deniability.

You may ask what types of crimes are being perpetrated online? While the number and types of cybercrimes are too voluminous to detail, and outside the scope of this particular text, a number of the most common internet crimes against children will be discussed. These situations of exploitation, including those who possess, distribute, and manufacture exploitive material, and the comorbidity of these offender types, and the hands-on offending that can also take place offline, are examined. Recent crimes, such as sexting and sextortion, will be explained and discussed, and the topic of sex trafficking and how this age-old crime has been affected by the cyberization of society will be reviewed.

Possession of Exploitive Materials

Case Study 1

In 2015, "D.C." was contacted by law enforcement after information was obtained that the subject was making images of child sexual exploitation materials available on peer-to-peer software. When contacted by law enforcement, "D.C." admitted to possessing over 200,000 images and videos of children being sexually exploited, which he claimed he had been collecting for at least 15 years. While D.C. was also distributing the images, because of the way that the peer-to-peer platform was designed, his primary motivation was in the collection and possession of CSEM for his own gratification. He had gone so far as to take the images and burn them onto disks so he could view them on a larger screen television in his living room, rather than the smaller monitor connected to his computer. "D.C." took a plea agreement and was sentenced to 12 years in the Arizona Department of Corrections for Sexual Exploitation of a Minor and after release will be on lifetime probation and subject to sex offender registration.

While in some of these cases possession is independent of distribution, some aspect of distribution is also typically present, whether intentional or not. Additionally, offenders who view child exploitation materials are not exclusive to internet offenses. Studies conducted on the co-occurrence of sexual abuse of children and the viewing of abuse materials online have found that co-occurrence was more common than previously believed (Bourke & Hernandez, 2009). With the proliferation of exploitation material online, it is not uncommon to find offenders with millions of files of exploitation material in their "library." Many offenders have extensive collections that encompass terabytes of data, and some have taken to using cloud storage options to maintain their collections.

However, these voluminous collections are contrasted by those who try to avoid "possessing" any images by deleting files after use. Some offenders have found that the ease of availability online makes it "safer" to download their desired content and then delete the files after use, to re-download the next time material is desired. This has led to the necessity for computer forensic examiners to search in the unallocated spaces on devices and led to challenges in the courts whether deleted files retained in "open" space on a computer are still "possessed."

Distribution of Exploitive Materials

Case Study 2

In 2015, M.B was using peer-to-peer file sharing programs to obtain, and make available for distribution, images and videos of child sexual abuse materials. During the course of the investigation, M.B. made available dozens of images and videos for distribution. M.B. was captured by multiple agencies' investigative tools making files available. At the time a search warrant was executed on his residence, M.B. was actively downloading and trading files. When he learned of the search of his home, M.B. fled from Arizona to Texas, where he was later apprehended. M.B. accepted a plea agreement to 17 years in prison, with lifetime probation and sex offender registration upon his release from custody.

There are many methods of distribution, and one of the challenges of identifying and locating those subjects who distribute files of child exploitation materials is the wide number of means to distribute. While the electronic and internet service providers have means of locating some distribution, resulting in the CyberTips that result in reactive investigations, proactive methods are also used. Outside of the dark web, where child exploitation is rampant but anonymization is a key aspect, many social media platforms provide a means of distribution. Investigators must find methods to infiltrate the platforms, often using undercover personas and accounts. Frequently these accounts, because of the limitations that are placed on investigators, have limited ability to infiltrate and are only able to be active for short periods of time. In some cases, the distribution of files to undercover investigators has helped net larger activities. While undercover investigations can be very successful, there are certainly difficulties in conducting these types of investigations, and the legal challenges are nearly as significant as the technical difficulties.

Peer-to-peer (P2P) platforms have provided a quick and easy method for the distribution of child exploitation materials. The platforms often allow for the transfer of hundreds, even thousands, of files, in a single transaction. Other means of distribution are through social media platforms, either individually file by file or through trading links to cloud storage sites where multiple files can be stored. Sharing links through chat rooms, social media posts, and even electronic bulletin boards like 4chan, Reddit, and 8chan becomes common and easy. Further, those who trade in these files have developed their own slang, codes, and acronyms to be able to speak to one another without broadcasting in plain language their desire and intents. Being able to read and decipher these codes, and keeping up as codes change much like modern slang language does, is one of the challenges of the investigators. Additionally, as more offenders are captured, and technology advances, more sophisticated offenders use additional safety measures to try and thwart investigations. While these methods vary from offender to offender, some commonalities are found in the investigations and must be overcome to successfully prosecute.

Notably, some offenders have compiled and share a "handbook," which instructs on the "best" means and methods of sexually exploiting and abusing children (Davey, 2020). This "handbook" helps provide information to predators on the best ways to groom their victims, platforms that are preferred for use, and even recommends ways to convince children to share images and videos of themselves online, recommending cyber exploitation over in-person meetings (ibid). The handbook, titled "How to Practice Child Love," is authored by a subject identified only as "The Mule." It is a 170-page book which states in the opening, "This is an education and a step-by-step guide for adults to engage and practice sexual relationships with underage children. The purpose of this guide is to teach adults how to safely and harmlessly practice sex with children, without hurting the child, by using advanced and well researched child psychology and pedagogy" (Mule, n.d.). The index includes such topics as "where do I find a child?" and "exploring the child's genitals" (ibid). Credits for some of the materials in the guide are given on the final page and include the source "HuntingHighNLow," which states "Extremely experienced child lover from out in the field still not caught after decades of hunting and dozens of little kiddie lovers and kiddie orgasms" (ibid). As is evident from these quotes, the individuals who engage in this behavior can be just as organized and dedicated, if not more so, than aficionados in any hobby or profession. This very dedication to engaging in the sexual abuse of children, and sharing methods to avoid detection, makes the job of law enforcement responding to these crimes that much more difficult.

Some social media platforms also lend themselves to easier distribution than others. Some platforms are better monitored internally than others. However, some have lax oversight by the designers, or operate outside the United States, where discovery is less likely. Additionally, those which allow for "private messaging," often including end-to-end encryption to avoid detection by automated means on the platform servers or manual monitoring by administrators, become havens for this type of illicit activity. When predators find a platform that they feel is easily used for their purposes, they commonly become hot beds of activity but, like any fad, can change rapidly or be regional in their popularity. Parents regularly ask law enforcement which sites their children should avoid so that they will be safer. Unfortunately the only commonality between these sites is that if children are on them predators will be too.

Case Study 3
J.G., an offender in Kansas, was in communications with an undercover investigator in 2016 on a popular social media mobile platform, when he unknowingly distributed images of child sexual abuse material to law enforcement. In the process, he bragged about additional crimes that he had committed, including the sexual abuse of two young children, an offense for which he was on pre-trial release. J.G. provided explicit information about his abuse of one particular child and provided "tips" for the undercover officer on how he might be successful in abusing a child. When the investigator learned about the crimes J.G. was bragging about, and that he was being truthful about the incident and not just fantasizing, the information was passed on to investigators and prosecutors in Kansas. At the time, J.G. was violating the terms of his pre-trial release, not only by possessing and distributing images of CSAM but also by being on social media at all. This revelation resulted in a revocation of J.G.'s pre-trial release, additional charges for the distribution of the images, and an eventual conviction and 20-year sentence for the distribution of exploitive images.

Manufacture of Exploitive Materials

There is certainly no debate that a person viewing and distributing exploitive files is harmful to the minors involved, as concepts of "supply and demand" take place and the continual revictimization occurs as victims know that their images are exchanged over and over. The Canadian Centre for Child Protection (2017) conducted a study looking at the effects of victimization on children who had been abused and exploited. Recurring trauma was reported by many respondents, including having strangers identify them from having viewed their abuse images (ibid). Far and beyond from the trauma of knowing that people are trading and enjoying their abuse is the trauma from the abuse itself. For this reason, those offenders who are manufacturing the files, committing the abuse that is then immortalized in the files that are passed online, are among the most reviled offenders.

In some cases, the manufacturing of images is done for the sexual gratification of the abuser. In other instances, it is a means to an end, used to obtain additional images from other sources and provide "bona fides" that they are not law enforcement to further engage in communications and trades with other abusers. Others, like Peter Scully, create the videos and images purely for monetary gain. Scully, once deemed the "world's worst paedo" (Sutton, 2018), was an Australian ex-patriot living in the Philippines. Scully was convicted of sexually torturing and abusing young girls, some as young as 12 months old, on webcams for a "pay-per-view" style show, earning up to $10,000 per view (Sutton, 2018). Scully was, in part, caught when authorities found traces of the payments made to Scully from a viewer in another country, and the financial trail was followed back to Scully. Scully was given life in prison by Filipino courts, who reportedly considered "bringing back the death penalty" specifically for Scully.

Whatever the motivation, the amount of exploitive material being manufactured continues to grow at an alarming rate. Brian Rich, with the National Center for Missing & Exploited Children reports, that in 1998, there were 3000 reports of CSAM (as cited in Keller & Dance, 2019). In a paper by the US Department of Justice, Center for Problem-Oriented Policing published in 2006 and updated in 2012, it was estimated that in 2001 there were over 1 million images of exploitive materials online, with the number increasing by 200 new images a day (Wellard, 2001, as cited in Wortley & Smallbone, 2012). However, we know that the growth of the internet has been exponential, and with it, the growth of child exploitation. By 2018, that number had gone to 18.4 million containing approximately 45 million images of exploitive materials (Keller & Dance, 2019). As more children are provided technology without oversight, more images are produced, and more children are exploited and abused.

Case Study 4

In 2015, information was provided to the National Center for Missing & Exploited Children that a subject identified as R.C. was manufacturing child sexual abuse materials and distributing the images via the internet. She was also discussing the idea of having a child for the sole purpose of sexual abuse, beginning at birth with several other individuals. R.C., in her communications, traded child sexual abuse materials with these men, one of whom was already a registered sex offender for prior offenses. She also manufactured child sexual abuse materials of a child in her care and transmitted those images to a suspect in England, M.A., who, in turn, produced sexual abuse images of a child in his care and sent to R.C. Information from these communications were relayed to authorities in England to identify and locate M.A. and rescue the child from further abuse. R.C. was sentenced to 30 years' confinement, with lifetime probation and sex offender registration after her incarceration. In England, M.A. was given a 17.5-year sentence after his actions were described as "grotesque" by the judge (Thorne, 2015). Four additional suspects were arrested and convicted for various child exploitation-related offenses associated with R.C.

Co-occurrence with Hands-On Offending

As seen in the last case study, as well as in the following case study, there are sometimes co-occurrences with hands-on sexual abuse a well as online sexual abuse. While many who possess and distribute CSAM materials do so without sexually abusing children themselves, or as a precursor to that abuse, there are also those who both collect CSAM material and sexually abuse children. Those offenders who are sexually predisposed to abuse children often find that the "audience" on the internet is highly receptive to the images and videos they produce. These productions of CSAM often work as a type of currency, especially on the dark web, where they can be traded for access to other offenders' libraries of material. In the "Butner" Study, it was found that comorbidity between hands-on offenses and possession of CSEM was significantly higher than previously believed. According to Bourke and Hernandez (2009, p. 185), "the combined group of 62 child pornography and interstate travel offenders perpetrated contact sexual crimes against 55 victims. After participation in the treatment program, these offenders reported perpetrating contact sexual crimes against an additional 1,379 victims." This would indicate that many offenders who offend with "just pictures" in reality pose a significant risk to children and offend in person at a much higher rate than arrest and conviction rates would indicate (Bourke & Hernandez, 2009, p. 185). Further, offenders in the study averaged 13.56 victims per offender. This has also been observed by the author, as the offender in Case Study 2, M.B., had allegations of hands-on offending brought to light by multiple juveniles in another state during the course of the investigation; however, the statute of limitations had expired in that state, preventing any criminal proceedings on those acts.

Case Study 5
In 2016, information was obtained from the National Center for Missing & Exploited Children that a subject, identified as J.C. (not associated with R.C. from above), was distributing images of child sexual abuse. Based upon the information obtained and provided to law enforcement, it appeared that J.C. was sexually abusing a child and trading the images of the abuse to others in return for other images and videos of child sexual exploitation materials from these other parties. An undercover officer established online contact with J.C., and it was determined that he had been sexually abusing a juvenile in his control for several years. He then began attempting to locate child sexual abuse materials online and located a subject identified as E.M. in Australia. E.M. agreed to provide J.C. with the names of additional contacts around the world that traded in child sexual abuse materials and traded images with J.C. In return, J.C. began sexually abusing a second child in his control, documenting it in photographs, and sending the images to E.M. Based upon the evidence located, information was provided to authorities in New South Wales, Australia, and E.M. was also contacted. E.M. took a plea agreement with Australian authorities for 2 years' incarceration. It was also discovered in the course of the investigation that J.C.'s live-in girlfriend was aware of the sexual abuse of the first minor and

facilitated the abuse. She was sentenced under a plea agreement to 13 years' incarceration and lifetime probation and sex offender registration. In the United States, J.C. rejected a plea offer and took his case to trial, where he was found guilty on all 19 counts of Sexual Exploitation of a Minor, Sexual Conduct with a Minor, and Child Molestation. He was sentenced to two consecutive life terms, plus 301 years in prison, followed by lifetime probation and sex offender registration if he is ever released from custody.

Beyond the sexual exploitation of minors through the various means described above, there are additional cyber offenses that are committed with and against minors. In some of these cases, the initial communications may be consensual by the minor involved, but in other cases, the actions may be forced or coerced or obtained through some fraudulent means. Sometimes termed "cyber voyeurism" or "cyber-exhibitionism" (Bourke & Hernandez, 2009), these are incidents where children are being accessed by their webcams or camera phones to view the children in stages of undress. Regardless of the level of the child's culpability in their victimization, the fact remains that any time a child has sexually explicit images or videos distributed, the potential for harm to the child, physically and emotionally, is present.

Sexting

Sexual crimes are obviously not only perpetrated against children; sometimes they are perpetrated BY children, termed peer-on-peer sexual exploitation (Greijer & Doek, 2016). Sexting is a phenomenon that can touch any age group and has become "popular" between children, teens, and adults. Among some studies it is believed that 22% of girls have sent or posted naked pictures (Guardchild, n.d.) and 29% of teens think sexting is expected in a relationship (ibid). While 80% of sexters are under 18, young adults are not immune (Frances McClelland Institute, 2011). Often, these acts are part of modern "dating" and have no further consequences than one person sharing intimate images and videos with a partner. When these acts go no further, rarely is there a concern or any involvement by law enforcement. However, when children are involved, even in seemingly consensual settings, the files frequently still fulfill the definitions of, and requirements for, criminal charges. To avoid teens being sent to prison, sometimes for extended periods of time, many states have enacted "sexting" statutes, allowing minors to send these images to other minors without the full repercussions that would be applicable if an adult was involved. Because much of the sexting is committed between juveniles, there has been significant debate among practitioners, the legal community, and academics about what the proper response from the justice system should be. Many states have created so-called "Romeo and Juliet" exceptions to these situations that prevent minors from being charged with the same offenses for possession, manufacture, and distribution of child sexual images when they are within the confines of "sexting" or relationship situations, especially when the minors are within certain age ranges. Of course, these exceptions only apply when the actions are consensual and kept within the confines of the "relationship" and the appropriate age ranges. Once a juvenile distributes the images in a nonconsensual manner, or obtains images of minors outside their peer range, many of the consequences are enhanced. Some states even allow for minors engaged in exploitive or abusive behaviors to be charged as an adult, removing them from the juvenile system and opening the child to consequences that an adult would face. However, typically, these images do not stay with the intended recipient. While the distribution of sexual images of children can have severe consequences, adult victimization can have significant consequences as well. A jilted ex can, and sometimes does, load these images onto internet sites, distribute them to the victims' friends or family, or even just share them with friends for "pleasure" or ridicule. Some sites specialize in this proscribed distribution, or mainstream sites like PornHub can host them. In some cases, "hacks" into cloud storage accounts have located and distributed these sexting pictures, often of famous people. Stars such as Anne Hathaway, Kristen Stewart, and Miley Cyrus have all been victims of this unintended release of private pictures. In each of these cases, legal action has been threatened, but generally, the damage is done as the images can never be fully removed from the internet.

Case Study 6

In 2014, R.T. was involved in a brief relationship with an adult female, in which sexual images of the female were obtained. When the relationship soured, R.T. retaliated against the female by creating posts on a popular classified website. Within the classified ads, R.T. posted the nude and semi-nude images of the female and listed personal information including her place of employment, social media information, phone number, and other items that would help people find her. R.T. then "invited" individuals through these ads to contact the female and attempt to engage her in sexual acts. After the victim was contacted both online and in person, she contacted law enforcement became involved. Though the ad was removed, R.T. reposted it several more times as each ad was reported and removed. R.T. was later convicted of computer tampering, though since that time many locations have created "revenge porn" statutes and "sextortion" or sexual extortion statutes to try and combat this sort of problem.

Case Study 7

In 2016, law enforcement was alerted by NCMEC to a subject distributing images and videos of child exploitation materials on social media sites. An investigation determined that the suspect was 15-year-old T.M. T.M. was contacted and found to possess numerous files of child sexual exploitation materials. Additionally, T.M. indicated that he had engaged in online communications with adults, trading images of himself, other minors he "sexted" with, and other images he found online, with these adults. The minors he had "sexted" with were not aware that their images had been distributed to numerous online predators, often in exchange for additional CSAM files, and there was no way to remove those images from their recipients, or the internet in general. Many of the additional images that T.M. possessed were of incredibly young minors, including preadolescents, and as a result, T.M. was charged as an adult for the possession and distribution of child exploitation materials. However, because of his age, the terms of the plea agreement were significantly lighter than they would have been if he had been an adult. T.M. accept a plea agreement to probation and sex offender registration.

In situations such as Case Studies 6 and 7, what starts as a belief by the sender that their images would only be viewed by the direct recipient, later distribution of those images, often to adults, puts those victims at greater risk of continued exploitation and abuse. What is initially presumed to be an "innocent" exchange with someone the victim trusts into their private images being distributed worldwide.

Sextortion

While sex crimes, in general, are some of the most underreported crimes, averaging less than 33% reported to law enforcement, those victims who are being blackmailed and extorted on top of the sexual victimization results in even less reporting. The fear of having explicit or embarrassing images exposed to friends and family, especially for minors, can lead to additional trauma and anxiety. A 2015 report indicated that only 16% of victims of sextortion reported the offence to law enforcement (Thorn and Bouché 2017). Victims of extortion report being afraid every time a message or notification comes across their device, trouble sleeping because their abuser would contact them at all hours of the day and night, and even thoughts of suicide to escape from the demands of the abuser. One victim, who was extorted for images and videos for a period of more than 2 years, reported that after her abuser released the files to the internet, she was harassed by a classmate who found her images online and threatened to expose her further if she refused to begin producing the images for him (personal communication).

Case Study 8
The transition of sexting to sexual extortion is another risk of this type of behavior. In 2016, this was demonstrated in the case of S.W., an 18-year-old man in Central Saanich, Canada. S.W. was found to be in communications with a 15-year-old victim in Arizona, United States, when her parents reported the incident to law enforcement. The victim advised that S.W. had contacted her on social media, and they had begun an online "relationship." During the communications, S.W. was able to obtain information about the victim, including her school name, "friends" lists, and other information that was later used to extort sexual images and videos from the victim. Using a consensual image "sexted" to S.W., he then began a campaign of threats and extortion to obtain dozens of additional videos and images. Fearing the release of the prior images, the victim complied until she was no longer able to keep up with the demands. The victim indicated that S.W. would contact her at all hours of the day and night, threatening her if she was unable to provide the requested images or videos in the time frame provided, even making her send pictures while she was in school. The victim indicated that the constant fear and threat of having to provide

these materials to S.W. nearly drove her to suicide, before she broke down and informed her parents about the situation. Through coordinated investigations with Canadian authorities, S.W. was contacted and found to have a total of 14 victims, ranging from 13 to 19 years of age. S.W. used fear and intimidation to extort the files from his victims and was reported by CBC News as "demanding nude photographs, later threatening to post them online if she didn't send him videos of herself performing painful sex acts, according to the sentencing decision. When she resisted, he replied, 'I hope this hurts you. Mabey it'll teach you to talk back or not give me what I want [sic].' He also threatened to travel to her home and sexually assault her" (Lindsay et al. 2018). S.W. accepted a plea in 2018 to 18 months in jail, 6 months conditional sentence, and 3 years' probation and addition to the sex offender registry.

Case Study 9
In 2019, the "long arm" of the internet was again demonstrated in the case of K.R-N. Investigators in Australia were alerted to a subject who had contacted two minors on a social media application. Through the conversations, it was found that the male subject had threatened the minors and obtained semi-nude pictures as a result of the threats. Australian authorities were able to obtain information that the suspect lived in Arizona. Through a coordinated investigation, the suspect, K.R-N., an 18-year-old male, was contacted and found to have engaged in threatening behaviors with over 20 girls as young as 9 and in at least 6 states and 2 foreign countries. K.R-N. used threats of physical harm to the victims and their families to extort some files, other victims he threatened to expose images that had been obtained to coerce additional images. K.R-N. was sentenced to 5 years' incarceration, with lifetime probation and sex offender registration.

Luring Minors for Exploitation

Awareness of luring crimes skyrocketed with the airing of the Dateline television show "To Catch a Predator" on NBC between 2004 and 2007. The host, Chris Hanson, was seen interviewing subjects who engaged in conversation with what they believed would be a minor and then traveled to engage in a sexual encounter with the "child," only to be met with the television crew and law enforcement. Similar types of investigations are routinely undertaken by law enforcement agencies in an effort to proactively identify those individuals who are predisposed to meet with children for sexual acts, without an actual child being involved. However, despite these proactive and often highly publicized efforts by law enforcement, and the media, many people still engage in activities online to locate and entice children into engaging in sexual acts. In some instances, offenders have made reference to the television show, either in their chats with the "child" or in later interviews with law enforcement, and their awareness of the possibility of getting caught. Some reported incidents have the predators traveling across state, and even national boundaries, to meet with what they believe to be minors for sex. Other times, the victim and offender are determined to be only a few blocks away from each other.

Case Study 10
One such subject, R.G., was identified in 2012 after his 15-year-old victim's parents learned of the behavior. R.G., who was married with multiple young children at the time, engaged in exploitive behaviors with the victim, including discussions of a sexual nature and enticing the victim to provide sexually exploitive images over text message. Eventually, the conduct led to meeting at a particular location to engage in sexual acts. At one point in the communications, the victim was unable to use her phone to communicate and began conversing through a friend's device. When the original victim was unable to communicate with R.G., he attempted to lure her younger friend into similar acts. When the victim's family reported to law enforcement, a subsequent "meeting" was once again set between R.G. and the victim, this time with law enforcement waiting at the location. R.G. was contacted by the law enforcement, and he admitted to the situation and later accepted a plea agreement to 24 years' incarceration, with lifetime probation and sex offender registration.

The increase of minors online has also increased the availability of sex trafficking using online sources to recruit the victims and solicit the purchasers of these crimes. The internet site Backpage.com was identified to be complicit in the trafficking of minors, resulting in its closure and being seized by federal authorities in 2018. The owners of Backpage, Carl Ferrer, Michael Lacey, and James Larkin, were all charged with various crimes related to conspiracy to facilitate prostitution, money laundering, and human trafficking, among other charges (Cassidy & Ruelas, 2018). Beyond the use of sites like Backpage to advertise those minors being trafficked, many social media sites are also used to locate the victims. Since 1998, NCMEC reports receiving more than 89,000 reports of sex trafficking through their CyberTip program. NCMEC likewise reports that the average age of a child reported missing and trafficked is 15, though other sources indicate an average age between 11 and 14 (Smith, 2013). Regardless of the age, sex trafficking is the twenty-first-century version of slavery, making an estimated $99 billion worldwide (Kelly, 2019), with an estimated 4.8 million victims of forced sexual exploitation (International Labour Organization, 2017 as cited in Safehorizon.org, 2017).

Sex Trafficking

Sex trafficking is only one of the forms of human trafficking that is occurring on a regular basis across the United States and around the world. Luring victims for domestic minor sex trafficking (DMST) occurs regularly online. In a 2017 study (Thorn.org & Bouché, 2018), survivor respondents indicated that 75% of them had been advertised online, and one in six of those trafficked were under the age of 12. The use of technology is prevalent not only in the "sale" of those minors involved in DMST but also in the initial grooming and recruiting. From the survivor insight study:

> Across the sample, most traffickers continue to meet and groom victims through face-to-face contact. However, respondents who entered the life in 2015 noted much higher uses of technology in this process. Across the sample, 84% reported meeting their trafficker for the first time face to face, but only 45% of those entering the life in 2015 reported meeting their trafficker face to face. The remaining 55% reported use of text, website, or app. Similarly, 85% of the entire sample reported their trafficker spent time with them in person to build a relationship. By comparison, only 58% of those who entered the life in 2015 reported time in person as the means for building a relationship. Of those whose trafficker used technology in this process, 63% reported communicating online and 25% reported communicating via phone call. (ibid)

Despite the multitude of ways in which children can be exploited and abused, both online and off, funding and staffing for investigations into these types of crimes have remained relatively unchanged since 2009, at about $70 million nationally (Ingersoll, 2020). This means that investigators are being forced to deal with more cases, with insufficient staffing, training, and equipment, and often have to prioritize only the most egregious cases. Prosecutions, while also increasing with the number of cases identified and filed, often must meet certain "threshold" amounts before they will be prosecuted. In several jurisdictions, "low-level" offenders are only given probation for their crimes and often reoffend multiple times before penalties become severe enough to warrant incarceration. Additionally, many offenders are receiving reduced sentences, early parole, and other limited sentences as society pushes for "nonviolent" offender to be released, more therapeutic alternatives, and even an acceptance of pedophilia as a "sexual orientation" (Seto, 2012).

To increase the enforcement of these crimes, and attempt to decrease the prevalence of these offenses, several actions must occur. First is the need for changes to the understanding of the acts, beginning with nomenclature and stereotypes. As noted before, the term "child pornography" is increasingly being replaced with "child sexual exploitation material (CSEM)" or "child sexual abuse material (CSAM)" in an effort to redirect the stigma of the material. When the term "pornography" is used, most people think of mainstream magazines, such as Playboy or Hustler, or adult sexual material online such as PornHub. That is, the term pornography invokes the concept of consensual sexual exploration by adults. The images and videos in CSEM are neither consensual nor oriented around adults; rather, they are crime scene photos of the sexual abuse and exploitation of children, under the lawful age of consent. Furthermore, the idea that these crimes involve "just pictures" must be debunked. Each child in these photos and videos is being sexually abused, and that crime is being documented for the sick goals of the consumers of such material. This documented evidence is no more than "just a picture" than a murder weapon is "just a tool." These are evidence of sexual abuse, just as a CCTV may record the perpetration of a robbery or assault.

Further, there is a need for a major paradigm shift in social thinking as it pertains to pornography accessibility online. The average age of a child coming across hardcore pornography online is 11, though it can happen at much younger ages (Steele, 2018). Sites like PornHub, RedTube, xHamster, and others allow young children to get an impression about what love and sex is, which is totally unrealistic to normal relationships, as many of these videos display idealized, fantasized, or fetishistic behaviors and portray them as "normal." As a result, we see that individuals who consume more pornography, and begin consuming from a younger age, tend to become desensitized to it and eventually move toward more unusual and deviant forms of sexual materials to obtain their gratification. Coupled with the oversexualization in the mainstream media of young women and girls, in advertisements, television, and movies, and the push for older women to appear "young" and "fresh," leads these men to seek out pornography that fits within this concept. Their path from pornography depicting "school girls" or "cheerleaders" to "barely legal," models who are of legal age but appear to be younger, to actual minors is a progression that many have taken because of this skewed desire to fit in with the "normal."

To date, there have been inroads made in an effort to reduce or prevent this behavior, but many of the actions come only at the expense of victimized children. Backpage.com, a site allegedly dedicated to allowing people to advertise goods and services for sale or rent, was found to be heavily involved in the sex trafficking trade, both of adults and children, and the horror stories that came from victims who had been "sold" on this platform continue to be told. While it was shut down by the federal government in April 2018 (Lynch & Lambert, 2018), Backpage isn't the only culprit. Craigslist, another online classifieds platform, suspended their "personals" section to try and prevent sex trafficking and exploitation. But not long after these changes occurred, other sites like Bedpage, touted as a clone and perfect alternative to Backpage, appeared, along with numerous others, hosted outside the United States, making enforcement difficult. Amendments to the Communications Decency Act of 1996 (47 U.S.C. §230) continue to be debated as they pertain to the responsibility of online platforms like Backpage to be responsible for the information posted by users. Because §230 states, "No provider or user of an interactive computer service shall be treated as the publisher or speaker of any information provided by another information content provider," essentially anyone posting exploitive images on a hosting site is considered responsible, but the site itself is not. This is what allowed Backpage to host the trafficking of children for as long as it did.

Additionally, public awareness to both child exploitation and the expose of sexual content without consent has led to other sites being affected. In December 2020, the online porn hosting site PornHub was featured in an exposé in the New York Times, indicating that the site, among other things, hosted videos showing women being raped and sexually assaulted while incapacitated or unconscious, hundreds of videos of underage children engaged in sexual abuse or exploitation, and thousands of search results that allegedly depicted young children being abused and trafficked (Kristof, 2020). As a result of this news article, many of the credit card companies associated with PornHub cut ties, making it difficult for PornHub to monetize their content, and as a result, pulled tens of thousands of the videos posted by "non-verified users" pending review (Heater, 2020). While these steps are laudable, the problem, much like the mythical Hydra, continues to rear its ugly head and multiply regularly.

Once the media stop sexualizing children, and glorifying "young" as the preferred sign of beauty, and greater restrictions are placed on sexual content online to prevent minors from accessing it, the demand for child exploitive materials will likely decrease. PornHub allowed search terms such as "youngAsian," "girlsunder18," and "14yo," common terms to locate child exploitation materials by ethnicity or preferred ages, which brought users tens of thousands of responses (Kristof, 2020). If these terms are ubiquitous enough to be found on a public site like PornHub, imagine how many users are searching for this type of content and being allowed to find something to sate that particular paraphilia or fantasy. The sexualization of children is not only found on the platforms that promote pornography or allow users to set "dates." Child sex dolls, anatomically correct and approximating children in size and sexual "maturity," even using real ~~live~~ children's pictures, obtained from social media, to create the facial likeness, have been found on sites like Amazon and Etsy (Lockett, 2020; Guirola, 2020; Child Rescue Coalition, 2020). These dolls, billed as a $559 "high-quality sexy dolly live dolls for men," closely resembled an 8-year-old girl (Guirola, 2020). Not only are these dolls legal in many locations, but for sites like Amazon to sell them further promotes the normalization and promotion of child sexual abuse and exploitation.

Dr. Gail Dines talks extensively about the "pornland" culture that has taken over much of mainstream society and led to the increase in child sexual exploitation. The use of "sex" to sell products, promote movies and television, and even entertain adolescents and young adults creates a desensitization to the suffering of children who are abused and exploited in an effort to attain the "ideal" relationship or sexual encounter hinted at by the media. When children are used in these ads and programs, the normalization of child exploitation, similar to the normalization of sexualizing women, occurs. As PornHub and other sites provide content designed to simulate children, or even offering videos with minors being abused and exploited, it causes people to believe that this is somehow acceptable or condoned because it is on a "reputable" site.

Going forward, we know that the internet will continue to define popular culture, provide avenues of communication previously believed to be science fiction, and allow people to access materials that were inaccessible to all but a small few. Because of these advances, we have to look toward the future for legislative options that will help protect children and victims of sexual offenses while not infringing on other's rights. Many of the legislative acts that defined sex crimes investigations and prosecutions since the 1980s revolved around isolated incidents that drew significant media attention, such as the murders, and subsequent legislative acts, memorializing Jacob Wetterling, Megan Kanka, and Adam Walsh, and dictated legislative acts that were largely ineffective when enforced against the larger body of sexual offenders. Many pieces of legislation, including, but not limited to, the Adam Walsh Act, created nearly unattainable conditions for sex offenders to follow and be able to comply with, limited the available housing for offenders, and regulated where they could and could not frequent, without empirical evidence to demonstrate the effectiveness of such legislation. Outcome studies have almost universally suggested the laws do not meet their goals of making communities safely.

Additionally, the moral panics created by these cases created myths about sex offenses and offenders that further drove bad legislation and led to controls that may actually be causing more harm than good when it comes to the monitoring of offenders, the ability to teach children how to stay safe and avoid victimization and prevent offenders from being rehabilitated and reintegrated into society in a meaningful fashion. While the intent of these legislative acts was well intentioned, with the goals of protecting victims, especially children, from sexual offenders, the reality is that these actions, driven by emotion instead of evidence, have not fulfilled their goals. Additionally, the advancing technologies of the internet and social media move at a pace that legislators could never hope to attain. To this end, more preventive measures must be considered. Including internet safety in schools, having sex education courses at appropriate ages that include discussions of online and in-home safety, and stricter parental controls on devices and sites to reduce underage accesses are all steps in the right direction. Parents, teachers, and those who work with children also need to be educated on the dangers that occur online and in the home, so their parental wariness is not solely directed at "stranger danger."

Finally, the prioritization of child safety, by society, lawmakers, and the judiciary, needs to include better funding for investigations involving child sexual abuse and exploitation; stricter laws involving the punishment of those who seek to, or are involved in, the sexual abuse and exploitation of children; and the cooperation of the tech industries to remove content from their platforms, prevent new content from being distributed, and assist in the identification, location, and prosecutions of those who manufacture and distribute this type of material. The fact that PornHub previously had no checks in place to allow child sexual abuse videos to be uploaded and streamed by users is an example of how trivially this topic has been addressed by the tech industry. Backpage may be gone, but numerous sites took their place, and even Craigslist has other sections of their classifieds where investigators have found coded messages trading in child exploitation and abuse.

As can be seen from the examples and information provided, the methods and means for sexually exploiting and abusing children, both online and in person, are varied and complex. As technology changes and industry moves toward more safety for the users, the abilities of law enforcement to prevent, detect, and apprehend offenders grow more difficult. Investigators must train regularly and continually make themselves aware of current trends and platforms to keep up with the offenders. Additionally, parents, educators, legislators, and the judiciary also require regular updates on the best means to keep children safe from predators. Finally, technology platforms should work to better prevent child victimization and increase surveillance of suspicious and illegal activities.

References

Bourke, M. L., & Hernandez, A. E. (2009). The 'Butner study' redux: A report of the incidence of hands-on child victimization by child pornography offenders. *Journal of Family Violence, 24*, 183–119.

California Coalition on Sexual Offending (n.d.). *U.S. postal inspector child exploitation fact sheet.* Retrieved from https://ccoso.org/sites/default/files/import/postal_inspectors_report.pdf

Canadian Centre for Child Protection. (2017). *Survivor's survey executive summary 2017.* Retrieved from https://www.nationaalrapporteur.nl/binaries/nationaalrapporteur/documenten/publicaties/2017/09/26/canadian-centre-for-child-protection-survivors-survey/Executive_Summary_Survivors%27_Survey_tcm23-281780.pdf

Cassidy, M. & Ruelas, R. (2018, April 12). *Former backpage CEO pleads guilty in prostitution, money-laundering case.* Arizona Republic Retrieved from https://www.azcentral.com/story/news/local/phoenix/2018/04/12/backpage-ceo-pleads-guilty-prostitution-money-laundering-case/513255002/

Child Rescue Coalition. (2020). A mother's story: Daughter's photo stolen likeness turned into a child sex doll.

Child Rescue Coalition. (n.d.). *A mother's story: Daughter's photo stolen & likeness turned into a child sex doll.* Retrieved from https://childrescuecoalition.org/educations/child-sex-doll/

Davey, M. (2020, May 13). Child abuse predator "handbook" lists ways to target children during coronavirus lockdown. *The Guardian.* Retrieved from: https://www.theguardian.com/society/2020/may/14/child-abuse-predator-handbook-lists-ways-to-target-children-during-coronavirus-lockdown

Dines, G. (2011). *Pornland: How porn has hijacked our sexuality.* Beacon Press.

Federal Bureau of Investigation (2006). Online pornography/child sexual exploitation investigations: Innocent Images National Initiative, available at: http://www.fbi.gov

Frances McClelland Institute. (2011). *From policy to practice.* Retrieved from https://mcclellandinstitute.arizona.edu/sites/mcclellandinstitute.arizona.edu/files/From%20Practice%20to%20Policy_Sexting.pdf

Freedman, E. (1987). "Uncontrolled desires": The response to the sexual psychopath, 1920–1960. *Journal of American History, 74*(1), 83–106.

Greijer, S. & Doek, J. (2016). *Terminology guidelines for the protection of children from sexual exploitation and sexual abuse.* ECPAT International. Retrieved from https://www.interpol.int/en/content/download/9373/file/Terminology-guidelines-396922-EN.pdf

Guardchild.com. (n.d.). *Teenage sexting statistics.* Retrieved from https://www.guardchild.com/teenage-sexting-statistics/

Guirola, J. (2020, September 2). *Mom fights to ban child sex dolls after daughter's likeness was used for one.* Retrieved from https://www.nbcmiami.com/news/local/mom-fights-to-ban-child-sex-dolls-after-daughters-likeness-was-used-for-one/2287435/

Heater, B. (2020, December 14). *Pornhub removes all unverified content, following reports of exploitation.* Retrieved from https://techcrunch.com/2020/12/14/pornhub-removes-all-unverified-content-following-reports-of-exploitation/

Ingersoll, A. (2020, February 5). *Child pornography prosecutions on the rise.* Retrieved from https://www.investigativepost.org/2020/02/05/child-pornography-prosecutions-on-the-rise/

International Labour Organization (ILO) (2017). World Employment and Social Outlook: Trends 2017, 12 January 2017, available at: https://www.refworld.org/docid/5878ac1b4.html

Keller, M. & Dance, G. (2019, September 29) The internet is overrun with images of child sexual abuse. What went wrong? *New York Times.* Retrieved from https://www.nytimes.com/interactive/2019/09/28/us/child-sex-abuse.html

Kelly, C. (2019, July 30). 13 sex trafficking statistics that explain the enormity of the global sex trade. *USA Today.* Retrieved 12/28/20 from https://www.usatoday.com/story/news/investigations/2019/07/29/12-trafficking-statistics-enormity-global-sex-trade/1755192001/

King James Bible. (2017). *King James Bible Online.* https://www.kingjamesbibleonline.org/

Kristof, N. (2020, December 4). The children of pornhub. *New York Times.* Retrieved from https://www.nytimes.com/2020/12/04/opinion/sunday/pornhub-rape-trafficking.html

Lindsay, W. R., Taylor, J. L., & Murphy, G. H. (2018). The treatment and management of sex offenders. In W. R. Lindsay & J. L. Taylor (Eds.), *The Wiley handbook on offenders with intellectual and developmental disabilities: Research, training, and practice* (pp. 229–247). Wiley-Blackwell. https://doi.org/10.1002/9781118752982

Lockett, J. (2020, December 8). Evil trade sick child sex dolls modelled on 14-year-old Instagram star sold on Etsy. *The U.S. Sun*. Retrieved from https://www.the-sun.com/news/1937982/sick-child-sex-dolls-teen-instagram-star-etsy-australia/

Lynch, S. & Lambert, L (2018, April 6). Sex ads website backpage shut down by U.S. authorities. *Reuters*. Retrieved from https://www.reuters.com/article/us-usa-backpage-justice/sex-ads-website-backpage-shut-down-by-u-s-authorities-idUSKCN1HD2QP

National Center for Missing and Exploited Children (n.d.). *Missing Kids*. Retrieved 1/4/2021 from https://www.missingkids.org/gethelpnow/cybertipline

Racioppi, D. (2020, October 26). 'People don't want to talk about it,' but reports of kids being exploited online have spiked amid coronavirus pandemic. *USA Today*. Retrieved 1/4/2021 from https://www.usatoday.com/story/news/nation/2020/10/22/coronavirus-child-abuse-nj-online-child-exploitation-reports-increase/6004205002/

Safehorizon.org (2017). Retrieved from https://www.safehorizon.org/get-informed/human-trafficking-statistics-facts/#description/

Seto, M. (2012). Is pedophilia a sexual orientation? *Archives of Sexual Behavior, 41*, 231–236.

Smith, L. (2013). *Renting Lacy: A story of America's prostituted children*. Shared Hope International.

Steele, A. (2018, June 5). *Pornography viewing starts as early as elementary school*. Retrieved from https://youthfirstinc.org/pornography-viewing-starts-as-early-as-elementary-school/

Sutton, C. (2018, June 14). Rot in hell world's worst paedo Peter Scully who filmed baby rapes, tortured kids and made them dig their own graves smirks at life in jail. *The Scottish Sun*. Retrieved from https://www.thescottishsun.co.uk/news/2782723/worlds-worst-paedo-peter-scully-who-filmed-baby-rapes-tortured-kids-and-made-them-dig-their-own-graves-smirks-at-life-in-jail/

The Mule. (n.d.). *How to practice child love*. Obtained from law enforcement sources.

Thorn, L. and Bouché, V. (2017). Survivor insights. The role of technology in domestic minor sex trafficking.

Thorn.org & Bouché, V. (2018). *Survivor insights. The role of technology in domestic minor sex trafficking*. Retrieved from https://www.thorn.org/wp-content/uploads/2018/06/Thorn_Survivor_Insights_061118.pdf

Thorne, L. (2015, June 23). Paedophile sexually abused girl aged 2 on webcam boasting 'Peppa Pig kept baffled child calm'. *Daily Mirror*. Retrieved from https://www.mirror.co.uk/news/uk-news/paedophile-sexually-abused-girl-aged-5932345

United States Sentencing Guidelines U.S.S.G. §2G2.1 (n.d.). Retrieved from https://guidelines.ussc.gov/gl/%C2%A72G2.1

World Population Review (2020). Retrieved 1/4/2021 from https://worldpopulationreview.com/country-rankings/age-of-consent-by-country

Wortley, R. & Smallbone, S. (2012). *Child Pornography on the Internet*. Problem-oriented guides for police, Guides Series No. 41. Retrieved from www.cops.usdoj.gov

Chapter 2
Violent Crime Among Children and Juveniles in Oslo in 2020: Policing Challenges, Responses, and Experiences

Rune Glomseth and Magne V. Aarset

Introduction

Violent Crime Among Children and Young People: A Complex Societal Problem

Crimes among young people in general and violent crime in particular are complex societal problems that constitute demanding challenges for both the society itself, the police, other public authorities, and especially their ability to cooperate. This sets heavy requirements not only on police leadership but also on public leadership as such. Both leadership and interorganizational collaboration are important to handle this problem.

Partnership in policing is thus a key factor in dealing with violent crime among children and young people. It is a complex and intricate societal challenge that makes it necessary for the police to cooperate with several societal actors (Crawford & Cunningham, 2015 in Fleming, 2015).

This type of crime requires public leadership to be understood as a collective form of leadership that deals both with leadership within and between organizations. There is a demand for both strong leadership and collaboration, which are key components in public leadership (Brooks & Grint, 2010).

R. Glomseth (✉)
Norwegian Police University College, Oslo, Norway
e-mail: rune.glomseth@phs.no

M. V. Aarset
Norwegian University of Science and Technology, Alesund, Norway
e-mail: maa@terp.no

J. F. Albrecht, G. den Heyer (eds.), *Understanding and Preventing Community Violence*, https://doi.org/10.1007/978-3-031-05075-6_2

Figure 2.1 shows the key actors in the work of preventing, dealing with, and restoring juvenile delinquency and violence among children and young people in Oslo.

The police cooperate formally and well with Oslo Municipality, the child welfare service, and the schools. In the long run, we believe that it will be necessary to strengthen cooperation also with youth clubs, with sports clubs, and with the parents of children and young people who end up in groups and commit various forms of crime, including violence. In our opinion, this must be a joint responsibility for the municipality, the child welfare service, the school, and the police.

Violent crime among young people can be described as a wicked problem (Rittel & Webber, 1973 in Grint, 2005 and Brooks & Grint, 2010) and also as an adaptive problem (Heifetz, 1994; Heifetz et al., 2009). This problem does in fact not have any simple solutions. It is complex and intractable and requires a leadership approach that is more creative and adaptive than ordinary routine (tame) problems (Brooks & Grint, 2010).

Understanding both the context in association with violence among young people and the root causes of this societal problem is crucial for police leaders as it is for cooperating actors. In this sense, the context sets the framework for the goals, priorities, and managerial measures taken by the police and other public actors individually and jointly to prevent, counteract, and deal with juvenile delinquency and violence among children and young people. There is thus an interrelationship between context and leadership. Bennis (2009) emphasizes the importance of leaders understanding and being able to master the context in which they are to lead. Kouzes and Posner (2016) claim that context matters.

"Organizational effectiveness is affected by situational factors not under leader control" (Vroom & Jago, 1988). Vroom and Jago also emphasize that "Situations shape how leaders behave" (in Schafer, 2013), which, according to situational

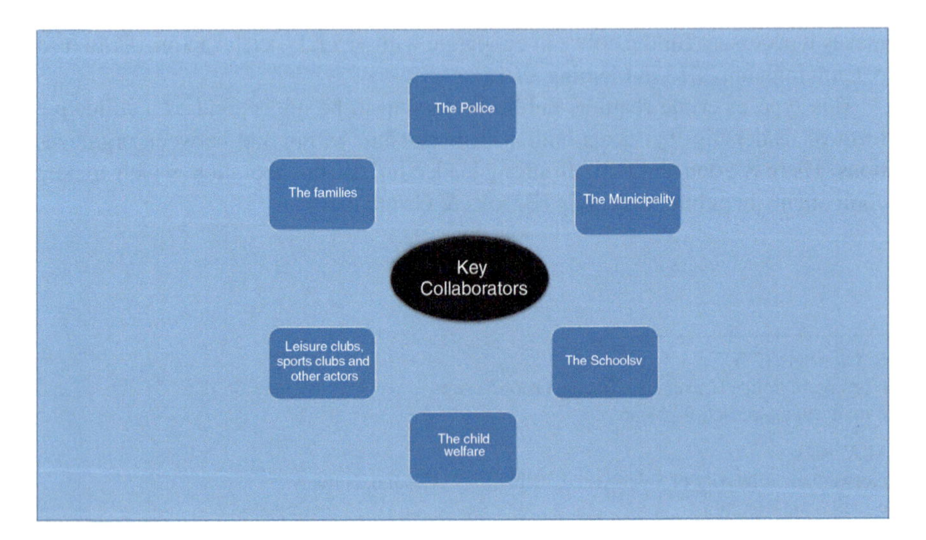

Fig. 2.1 The key collaborators

leadership theory (Hersey & Blanchard, 1969), is exactly what leaders should do, adapt to the situation. Tannenbaum and Schmidt (1958, in Schafer, 2013:14) also point out that "skillful leaders have been characterized not as those who use a fixed and rigid style, but those who can read circumstances and situations effectively so as to select the best approach to achieve a desired outcome."

We believe it is crucial for police leaders both to have a thorough and good understanding of the context and challenges they face and their causes. Such a good situational awareness is key in order to make the right assessments and thus choose their managerial approach to solve the problem in cooperation with their employees and other relevant actors.

The overall goal for effective public leadership is to create public value (Moore, 1995; Brooks & Grint, 2010; Renard & Reff Pedersen, 2017). Here, this means the absence or minimization of crime, and especially violent crime among young people, with respect to the consequences this may have for both the young people who commit violence, for the victims, and for the society as a whole.

In this chapter, we draw attention to *context*, *intervention*, and *results*. Our main focus is on the police's leadership style and the experiences drawn so far when it comes to violent crime among children and young people in Oslo. Our conclusions are based on registered crime, even though there may be significant dark numbers when it comes to most forms of crime, including violent crime among children and young people (Fig. 2.2).

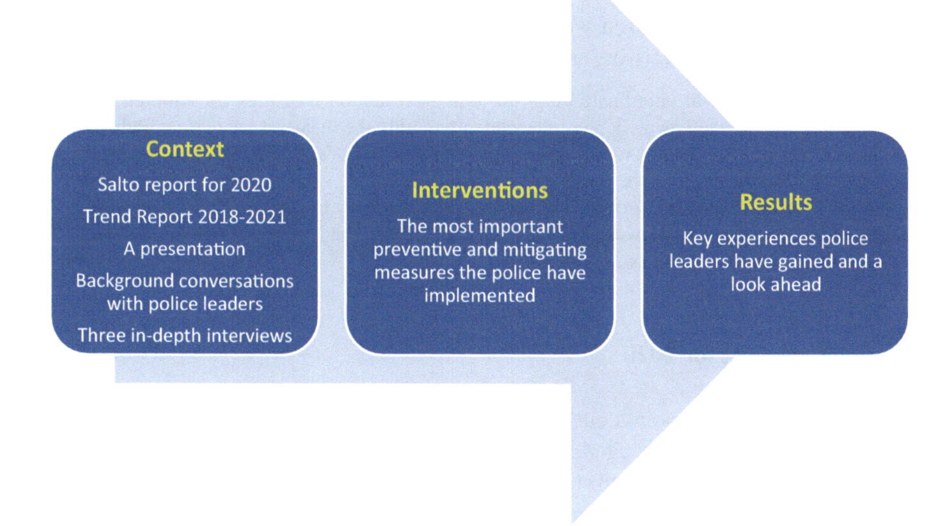

Fig. 2.2 Research design: chapter overview

The purpose of this chapter is thus to show how the police in Oslo assess challenges related to violence among children and young people and point out the most important preventive and mitigating measures they have implemented and what experiences they have gained so far.

We have tried to shed light on the problem, the measures, and the experiences from the perspective of leadership theory in general and police leadership in particular. Based on this study, we have also proposed a new overall model for police leadership.

Context: Crime Among Children and Young People in Oslo 2020

The Salto Model and the Salto Interagency Collaboration

A long-standing interagency collaboration has been established between Oslo Municipality and the Oslo Police District to prevent crime and drug problems among children and young people in Oslo. Since 2006, a so-called Salto report has been published annually, which objective has been to strengthen knowledge about crime and drug use among children and young people in Oslo. The slogan for this collaboration is "Together We Create a Safe Oslo."

We have studied the reports for 2018, 2019, and 2020. Here, we place the main emphasis on the Salto report for 2020, published in May 2021. In addition, we also use comments from a presentation that some of the authors of the report gave in May 2021.

On the Salto collaboration website, we can read about the Salto model and its overall content and objectives, as well as the form of collaboration:

> The Salto model will coordinate drug and crime prevention measures for children and young people, as well as work age-independently within the theme of hate crime, radicalization and violent extremism. The goal is for the municipality's children and young people to receive the right help at the right time, from an aid apparatus that cooperates well across agencies and professional groups. The sectors meet regularly to exchange knowledge and experiences, and get to know each other's working methods and cultures, so that it is easier to pursue targeted prevention.

The Salto Report for 2020

First of all, this report points out that in 2020, there was more than 97% of children and young people in Oslo aged 10–17 that was not registered with crime in Oslo. The proportion without registrations have remained over 97% for the last 10 years and even increased slightly from 2019. That is, the vast majority of children and young people in Oslo are law-abiding.

The number of young people (10–17 years) registered for repeated crime decreased from 188 in 2019 to 120 in 2020 even though the youth population in Oslo has increased by approx. 30 percent in the last 10 years. This is a very small proportion of the youth population which in 2020 was 53 833 people. Both the number of reported persons and the number of reports clearly decreased from 2019 to 2020.

The decline among those under 18 does not apply for the age group over 18 years. For the age group 18–22 years, the number of suspects and reviews has been relatively stable since 2015.

From 2019 to 2020, there was in Oslo a 30% decrease in registered reports of violence among children and young people under the age of 18. The main reason is probably the corona pandemic and that young people could not meet physically to the same degree as before. The report shows that the registered child and juvenile delinquency has clearly been affected by the pandemic, some crime categories more than others. The years from 2013 to 2019 all showed an increase, though, with the most evident increase in the years after 2015.

The numbers in 2020 are higher than in 2015 and 2016, and the proportion of suspects per 1000 inhabitants in the age group has the numbers from 2020 the fourth highest in the last 15 years (6.7 people per 1000 inhabitants). The decline in reports of violence in 2020 applies to the age group both above 10–17 and 18–22 years and below 15 years. The decline is significant for both girls and boys.

The proportion of children and young people registered with crime has been less stable the recent years, and about 60 percent of all criminal cases against young people under the age of 18 in Oslo concern young people who live in the east part of the town.

The Trend Report 2018–2021 from Oslo Police District

We have also studied the Trend Report 2018–2021 from the Oslo Police District. The following quote is from this report:

"A worrying development concerns the growth in reported violent crimes, including physical violence and various types of threats, coercion and personal attacks. The trend is international. Violence appears in a new form on social media, such as various types of personal attacks and 'character assassinations,' which are not necessarily unlawful yet.

The threat of attack has a socially controlling effect, limiting personal freedom and freedom of expression. Digital social control also works internally in criminal youth networks, combined with a violent romantic ideology conveyed on social media. The increase in violence is probably associated with several factors, including the spread of aggressive messages and incitement on social media, as well as structural factors such as social inequality, marginalization and the sense of powerlessness associated with technological restructuring.

There is the emergence of several volatile networks among young people on the eastern part of the town who commit different types of crime as robbery, violence and drug trafficking. Although crime among children and young people have been reduced over several years, and the majority of young people in the Oslo police district are law-abiding and committed members of society, there is an 'amp atmosphere' in several environments. Probably are the factors that affect the situation largely the same as with the emergence of networks.

However, digital communication and spread of provocations within and between environments are causes for more conflicts with fast escalation and for shifts in loyalty ties. The danger of pop-up crime is significant, and the crime rate is in many cases gross. The development is considered a danger signal for future crime and social marginalization. Increased activity in right-wing extremist circles is worrying. There is a danger of digital influence and pop-up forms of violence, including hate crime and extremist violence."

Some Identified Characteristics

Most registered young criminals are boys who live in eastern or downtown areas. They are Norwegian citizens, born in Norway with an immigrant background, and they start their criminal careers early. They are very mobile from an early age and rarely have "normal" upbringing conditions. The risk factors are plentiful and the protection factors are few.

Some of the main risk factors according to the presentation given by some of the authors of the Salto report are that these young criminals typical are coming from broken families, are exposed to crime, and have changed address a number of times. They have a low degree of mastery in school, spend a lot of time out in the public space, and have low participation in organized leisure activities. A large proportion of them have been under the care of the child welfare service.

As the parents often have their own challenges, there is significant lack of protection factors. There is overcrowding and poverty. The families they live in have many children and are characterized with communication challenges and a lack of general coping. Likewise, these families are characterized by significant socioeconomic differences from the average population of the city.

What It Takes to Succeed: Some Experience

The presentation mentioned above points out some important experiences. The children and young people must have their own motivation to change course. They need stable resource persons over time and help with physical or mental challenges. They also need to experience mastery. There is also a need for clear frameworks and clear demarcation as well as adding protection factors. The police have an important role, but a joint public effort through continued Salto cooperation is necessary.

Preliminary Research Questions

1. What developmental features are associated with violent crime among children and young people in Oslo in the period 2015–2019?
2. What are the main challenges that police leaders perceive when it comes to dealing with this violent crime?

3. What have been the police response and most important measures to combat violent crime among children and young people in Oslo?
4. What experiences have police leaders gained in dealing with violent crime among children and young people in Oslo?
5. What are the short- and medium-term challenges associated with violent crime among children and young people in Oslo seen by a selection of police leaders?

Our research has been performed within the following constraints. We have only been studying the following:

- Children and juveniles, i.e., the age group 10–17 years and the age group 18–22 years
- Inhabitants living in the following two police districts in the so-called Old Oslo, that is, the Oslo City Center (downtown area) and the Oslo East district
- Events occurred in the period 2015–2020

Furthermore, we have placed emphasis on Question 3, the police's response and measures, as well as on Question 4, the police's experiences so far.

Method

This preliminary case study is based on studies of relevant police presentations and reports on violent crime among children and juveniles in Oslo, i.e., the Salto reports and the Oslo Police Districts Trend Report 2018–2021.

The case study is also based on semi-structured in-depth interviews with a selection of three senior police managers in the Oslo Police District. The interviewees are strategic police leaders with responsibility for the police service in the Oslo City Center (downtown Oslo), the Oslo East district, and the police district's unit for joint prevention.

The interviews were conducted in part face to face and as online meetings in the period from early June to early August 2021. Notes were taken during the interviews. The interviews were transcribed, and a content analysis has been performed. Through this, we have identified key challenges from the police's point of view based on the abovementioned reports and their own practical experiences based on the measures the police have implemented to prevent, counteract, and deal with violent crime among young people in the two selected districts.

We have also been in contact with two researchers of police leadership to discuss the understanding of the phrase knowledge-based or evidence-based police leadership. In August this year, we were emailing with Maria Haberfeld, professor of Police Science, in the Department of Law, Police Science and Criminal Justice Administration at John Jay College of Criminal Justice in New York City, and Joseph Schafer, professor in Criminology and Criminal Justice, Saint Louis University, St. Louis, USA. From them we also got insightful input.

This case study has several limitations. It only covers two districts in Oslo, although these are the districts where this type of crime is most common. Only three interviews have been conducted, although these are with very central and senior police leaders. Therefore, this study must be perceived as a preliminary study that can advantageously be followed up in both breadth and depth.

Nevertheless, we feel that overall, the reports, the presentation, background conversations with police leaders, and the three in-depth interviews provide a relatively good insight into the context, i.e., the status of crime among children and young people in Oslo and the most important causes for this type of crime as Oslo municipality and the Oslo police see it.

We believe that this case study provides an interesting picture of this societal problem and how police leaders in Oslo understand it. The study provides concrete insight into what measures the police have implemented and what experiences these police leaders have had the recent years from senior police leader's point of view.

Leadership

Leadership Theory

We discuss police leadership through the following perspectives: police leadership as a contribution to creating public value and adaptive leadership theory as a mindset and a model for police leadership. Particularly, we focus on leadership while dealing with violence among children and young people which we consider to be a very complex problem, theory of situational leadership, and, finally, police leadership as a practice characterized by knowledge and exercise of discretion. We summarize these perspectives in a model presented in the end of this chapter.

Leadership is understood as an adaptable, relational, and collective process of how leaders work inside and across organizations to solve societal problems, and where different actors must interact to find relevant measures.

In the organizational and management literature, we can find a distinction between management and leadership; see, for example, Zalesnik (1977) in Jackson and Parry (2018) who suggested that leaders develop visions and drive changes while managers monitor progress and solve problems. Along the same lines, Bennis and Nanus (1985) argued that managers do things right while leaders do the right things.

Our view is inspired by Kotter (1990) in Andersen et al. (2017). He is regarding leadership and management as two complementary and dependent functions that leaders must master and be able to switch between. We therefore use the term leadership which includes both administrative, managerial, and relational functions (Kirkhaug, 2019). Mintzberg (2010) supports this view. He argues that there is a conceptual difference between the concepts of leadership and management but that this distinction has no bearing on the practical life of organizations.

Police Leadership: Creating Public Value

Section 1 of the Norwegian Police Act deals with the responsibilities and objectives of the police. This section of the law clarifies the police's (social) mission.

"The police shall, through preventive, enforcing and assisting activities, be part of society's overall efforts to promote and consolidate citizens' legal security, security and welfare in general" (Lov om politiet (politiloven) - Lovdata - LOV-2021-06-18-127 fra 01.07.2021).

Organizational and management researcher Mark Moore (1995) works with the concept of public value. He describes management via a strategic triangle consisting of three components: legitimacy, operational capacity, and public value.

The police's work to prevent, counteract, and deal with juvenile delinquency in the form of violence can well be explained with the help of Moore's strategic triangle. Operational capacity is naturally linked to the police's ability to prevent, counteract, and deal with this type of crime and to contribute to obedience to law, order, and security in various parts of the city. Legitimacy in this context is about the extent to which citizens, politicians, and the media perceive that the police have the competence and capacity to prevent, counteract, and deal with this type of crime, understood as the police's ability and performance to contribute to obedience and security for citizens.

In our opinion, legitimacy is basically about citizens' trust in the police and in the work of policing. The police create public value when they contribute to the social mission being taken care of and achieved to a degree that the majority of the population believes is sufficiently good.

According to Walsh and Vito (2019), leadership is the key force behind the creation of effective organizations. In policing, leadership can energize and become a dynamic force in the agency – invigorating change and sponsoring professionalization. Leadership is an activity and a resource that can only be partially linked to the position and degree in the police.

Leadership is a resource that is needed at all levels in police organizations (Fleming, 2015). Haberfeld (2013) defines police leadership as the ability of each police officer, starting with the first day on the job, to take control of the situation on the street. More precisely, police leadership is the ability to make split-second decisions and take control of a potentially high-voltage situation that evolves on the street, according to Haberfeld. She claims that police leadership is about the ability to take control.

Leadership is exercised both at the strategic level, at the middle management level, and in the front line. Effective leadership is an important condition for whether a police organization is perceived as legitimate among both internal and external actors. Effective leadership is also a clear prerequisite for police organizations to be able to function in an increasingly dynamic and complex landscape (Fleming, 2015).

According to Cordner (2016), police administration has two primary concerns: an internal one, the performance of management duties within police organizations, and an external one, the implementation of policies and programs designed to reduce crime and disorder and enhance public safety. He also states that in the twenty-first century, police administration seems to be getting more and more complicated and demanding.

In our opinion, police leaders are key players when it comes to the police's ability to create public value. They create public value together with their employees and the collaborating partners such as the municipality, schools, child welfare, and others. We agree that leadership is a resource that is needed at all levels in police organizations and that police leadership is a key force behind an effective police organization. Effective leadership is important when it comes to prevent, counteract, and deal with violent crime among children and juveniles.

Adaptive Leadership Theory in Police Leadership

So what is adaptive leadership? According to Heifetz (1994) and Heifetz et al. (2009), it is both not only a mindset, a theory, and thus a model for exercising leadership in general but also a practice and a framework for change processes. It is thus a concept for leadership where managers actively collaborate with employees and where problem-solving, learning, and development are central for organizations to adapt to changing environments and new challenges. Adaptive leadership is based on the premise that leadership is more of an activity and a process rather than individual personal capabilities (Heifetz, 1994).

Heifetz argues that there is first a need to distinguish between technical and adaptive problems. Technical problems or routine problems are characterized by the fact that there is a common agreement regarding the diagnosis of the problem and what measures are necessary to solve it among managers and employees. Adaptive problems are more complex. There is uncertainty, confusion, or disagreement about what the problem is and how to solve it.

Adaptive problems need a different kind of leadership than leadership to deal with technical and more routine and familiar problems. Adaptive and more complex and demanding problems mean that managers and employees must change and go beyond their usual way of thinking and acting. This distinction is well illustrated by the following question: Is this a routine problem that you have previously encountered and found workable solutions to (technical problem), or is it a new, more comprehensive and complex problem that you have not faced before and thus have no experience of solving before (adaptive problem)?

The process of adaptable leadership involves six stages when executing change in a complex, organizational setting making decisions and handling complex and non-routine problems. These include identifying the adaptive challenge, focusing attention on the problem to make stakeholders aware that change most occur, framing the issues in such a way as to sustain their attention, maintaining stress at a productive level to ensure continued efforts to handle the problem and towards change, securing ownership of both the problem and the solution from stakeholders themselves, and creating a safe environment for them by providing the resources.

We will argue that police leaders should use an adaptive mindset and the adaptive leadership model when they need to understand and deal with violent crime among young people. We believe this approach can be useful especially when there are several stakeholders and a need for partnership and interorganizational collaboration as in this case.

Police Leadership from the Perspective of Situational Leadership

The situational approach emphasizes the importance of contextual factors that influence leadership processes (Yukl, 2013). Yukl points out that major situational variables include the characteristics of followers, the nature of the work, the type of organization, and the nature of the external environment.

Kirkhaug (2019) shows that the situational approach related to leadership is concerned with being able to identify which conditions support and limit leadership and under which conditions different types of leadership are more or less effective.

Nye (2010) states that leadership is like power. It is a relationship. Furthermore, followers have the power both to oppose leadership and to lead. He further claims that followers empower leaders as well as vice versa. This means that leaders must adapt their leadership to those they are to lead and the situation they are in. Burns (2010) point out that to understand leadership requires understanding of the essence of power. We can see that there is a connection to adaptive leaderships and that there may be some overlap between these two theories.

According to Hersey and Blanchard (1969), different followers require different leadership styles. They suggest that a leader should adapt his/her leadership style to the individual followers' development level which should be characterized by their competence and their commitment.

Hersey and Blanchard identify the following development levels:

- The development level D1 of a follower is characterized by low competence and high commitment.
- The development level D2 of a follower is characterized by some competence and low commitment.
- The development level D3 of a follower is characterized by moderate to high competence and low commitment.
- The development level D4 of a follower is characterized by a high degree of competence and high degree of commitment (Fig. 2.3).

Furthermore, situational leadership theory is suggesting that the leader should adapt his/her leadership style with respect to a directive dimension and a supportive dimension. That is, an effective leader needs to evaluate the followers' development level characterized by competence and commitment and adapt their leadership style characterized by the degree to which they are directive or supportive.

Cordner (2016) presents situational theories of leadership. He claims that the situational model of managerial and leadership effectiveness suits well in any

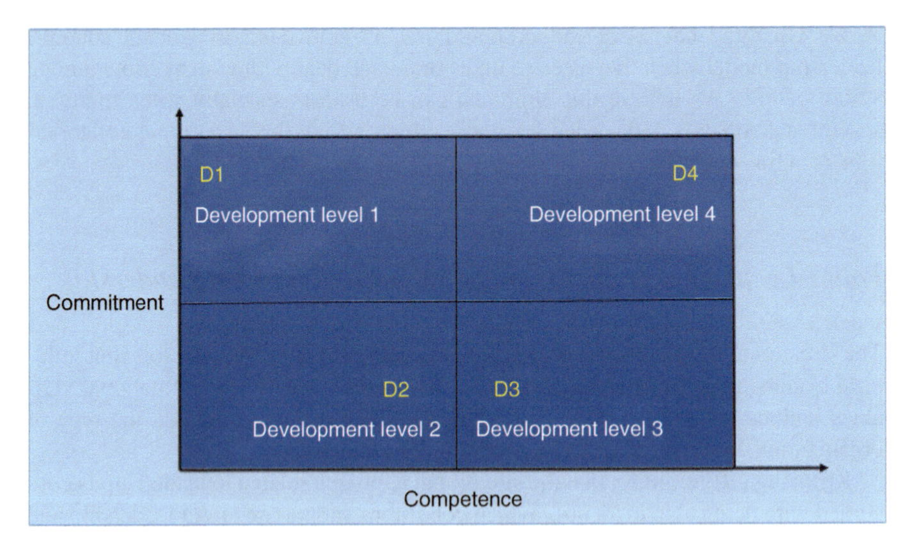

Fig. 2.3 Illustration of development levels among followers

organizations as well as in police administration. The kind of leadership that will be most successful will vary from one situation to another.

Haberfeld (2013) has a relatively comprehensive discussion of policing and situational leadership theory. She refers to research and writes that effective leadership styles will need to be flexible and to respond to the ever-changing reality.

Baker (2011) communicates strategic and situation-based leadership and claims that the combination creates a framework for decisions in both the short and long term. He writes that both approaches to leadership create a flexible basis and a roadmap for police leaders when it comes to effective leadership.

Schafer (2013) says that "what works" is almost never universal but instead a function of context, objectives, traits, and habits of the leader, characteristics and motivators for followers, and the environment within which leadership is taking place. He further claims that there is a dyadic relationship between leaders and followers, characterized by an ongoing influence loop between the two, and that this is an important point related to situational leadership.

The situational leadership model II (SLII) is illustrated in the model developed by Blanchard (1985) and Blanchard et al. (1985) in Fig. 2.4.

- The directing style (S1) is a high directive – low supportive style.
- The coaching style (S2) is a high directive – high supportive style.
- The supporting style (S3) is a high supportive – low directive style.
- The delegating style (S4) is a low supporting – low directing style.

As illustrated in Fig. 2.4, the situational theory model suggests that there is a one-to-one relationship between the development level of the followers and the leaders' style.

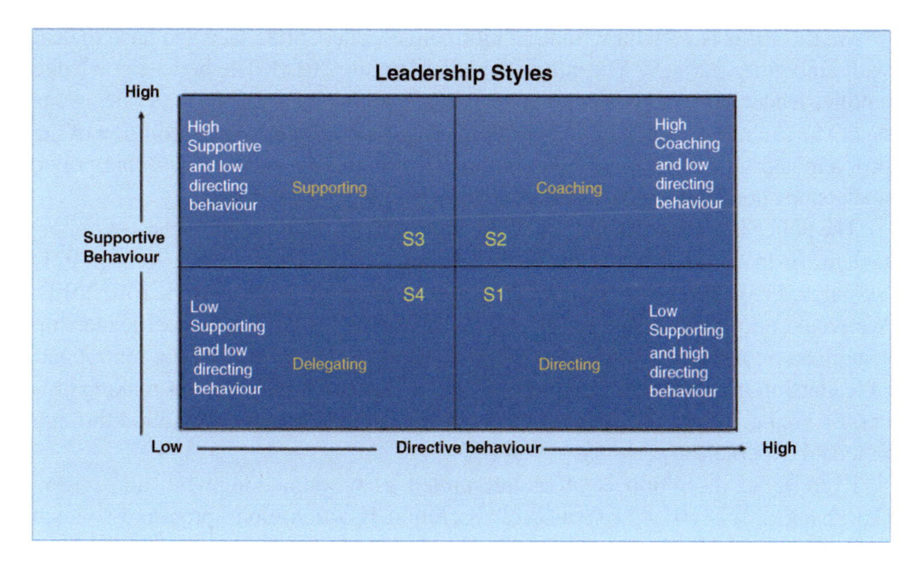

Fig. 2.4 Illustration of the situational leadership theory SLII

From a practitioner's point of view, situational leadership in the police is intuitively correct. Leadership behavior depends on what you lead, where you lead, and who you lead and of course the situation the police leaders and his/her coworkers face. For example, there is an obvious difference in leadership behavior of a first-line leader during a sharp operation and a police chief who must ensure that operations in a police district meet the budget and achieve their goals.

Police Leadership Characterized By Knowledge and Discretion

There is a move to develop a deeper evidence base in policing. The evidence-based policing movement seeks to infuse a greater degree of scientific evidence to support how police organizations operate. This can include not only crime-reduction efforts but also internal management and leadership efforts (Schafer, 2013). Contemporary police organizations cannot be lead, in any effective manner, without taking into consideration the best practices, based on the empirical research findings. It is about having the knowledge of the profession, about the profession, and what works and what does not and trying to incorporate knowledge-based practices into your policies and deployment strategies (Haberfeld, 2021).

Cordner (2016 p. 357) claims that scientists have established strict rules for linking cause and effect. Police administrators, however, must still make allocations and decisions, formulate policies, and implement strategies based on their best judgments of the effects of different actions. He also points out that these judgments should be backed up as much as possible by valid knowledge. Such knowledge results from research, experiments, and careful analysis.

We think this is very important. Senior police leaders often face and have to deal with ambiguity (Grint & Thornton, 2015 in Fleming, 2015). The better knowledge a police leader has of a problem, the context in which it appears, the better decisions he or she can make, which in turn could mean a positive effect on the solution of the problem and thus for the local community. Therefore, we want to state that police leadership should be evidence-based to the greatest possible extent.

The police is a front-line organization where discretion is mentioned as an important factor in the practice of the police profession (Klockars, 1985; Reiss, 1971; Skolnick, 1994; Manning, 1977; and Neyroud & Beckley, 2001 in Cockcroft, 2013). We would argue that discretion is also an important factor in practical leadership regardless of organization. We believe that the exercise of discretion is a central part of leadership in the police, especially related to decisions and decision-making processes. We believe that police leaders acquire skills in exercising discretion through practical experience.

Exercise of discretion is often interpreted as wisdom, judgment, and reason (Kirkhaug, 2017, 2019). Exercise of discretion is a conscious process in which deliberations or decision-making takes place on the basis of clear goals, but where the points of reference are weak.

Certain processes mean, among other things, that a leader is able to identify the situation he/she is facing, and whether there is a need for a lot or little exercise of discretion. Kirkhaug refers to Weick (1995) who uses the term sense making about processes that make it possible not only to perceive one's surroundings but also to communicate this perception to others. Filstad (2020) links sense making to leadership, more specifically to processes in which people interact and try to understand ambiguous conditions. She emphasizes that meaning-making processes are important when new conditions disrupt established ways of acting.

We perceive the exercise of discretion related to leadership as conscious and practical reasoning where the purpose is to make usable decisions. Leadership in modern police organizations is characterized by complexity, diversity, and paradoxes that leaders constantly face and must decide on. Violent crime among young people is, as has been pointed out earlier, complex, a so-called wicked problem which, in our opinion, requires both thorough knowledge and good exercise of discretionary leadership. Furthermore, we believe sense making is an important element in the decision-making process. Against this background, we would argue that modern and effective police leadership consists of a combination of evidence- and discretion-based exercise of leadership (Fig. 2.5).

Our model is inspired by Mintzberg's triangle of leadership as a practice, where he sees leadership as a combination and a function of craftsmanship, science, and art. Art adds ideas and integration. Crafts create connections on the basis of concrete experiences, and science brings order through systematic analysis of knowledge. He also points out that there is no optimal way to lead; it depends on the situation. We believe that police leadership can also be perceived as a practice that, regardless of level and function in the police organization, can be explained on the basis of the factors craft, science, and art (Mintzberg, 2010).

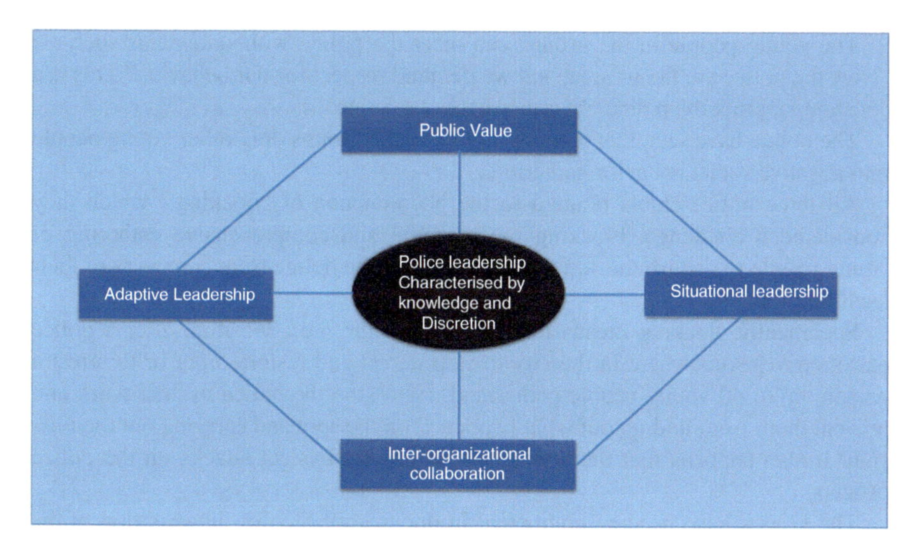

Fig. 2.5 Police leadership characterized by knowledge and discretion in dealing with violent crime among young people

Findings

Introduction

Through an analysis of the content of the interviews with the three police leaders, we have grouped the answers into four categories: challenges from the police leaders' point of view, the most important measures they have implemented, experiences they have gained so far, and finally some thoughts on future challenges and important priorities.

Challenges as the Interviewed Police Leaders Perceive It

The police leaders point out that there is a certain increase in crime among children and young people in Oslo. It is perceived that violent crime in this group increases somewhat. Several networks of young people have emerged.

There are several groups fighting for hegemony when it comes to drug sales within specific geographical areas of the city. They seek to achieve what the police call territorial control. This means that they perceive the areas as theirs. It also means that they see the police as foreign elements in "their" areas. In other words, the groups do not recognize the police's legitimate presence in the public space or as a natural part of the cityscape.

The young people in the groups can meet the police with statements such as: "Now the police are in our area, and we demand respect for our behavior." This is a development that the police obviously cannot tolerate.

The police have seen that leading figures in the groups drag other young people into negative social behavior and crime.

All three police chiefs pointed to the phenomenon of "flocking," which they considered a challenge. Flocking means rapid and comprehensive gathering of young people to disturb the situation and prevent the police from carrying out their legal mission.

Specifically, flocking means that in a short time, i.e., 3–5 min, after a police patrol arrives somewhere in the city to stop unrest and restore order or to arrest a person, up to 40 young people gather and try to stop the police in their work and prevent them from finding out what happened on the spot and carrying out the mission. It also happens that the young people go on physical attacks on the police officers.

The groups have become competent in documenting police intervention in the various areas. They use the telephone cameras to take pictures and film police activity and operations. They are very active towards the police and systematically challenge the police's legal authority for their activity in the districts concerned, especially Oslo City Center and Oslo East, which are the focus of this study.

In these youth environments, it has become common to bring and use a knife in the public space. Using knives as weapons is customary in youth environments. Violence and threats are part of the language and cultures of the groups.

The police have seen that young people who have perpetrated violence in the youth environments accumulate a form of violence capital. This is rumored and is suitable for making other young people feel fear and for controlling their behavior.

Violence in some youth environments poses a challenge to the subjective and objective sense of security in the population. Children are especially vulnerable to insecurity. In this way, this is in the core of the police's social mission.

The police have experienced that the mentioned youth environments only talk to police officers who carry out dedicated preventive work and not with the ordinary patrols. This has created a divided police service, which in turn entails challenges for police leaders.

The police leaders claim that the police have a relatively good overview of and control over the various groups and their activity, but this naturally requires continuous prioritization and follow-up and police resources.

Most Important Measures

The police work purposefully to keep an eye on and have sufficient knowledge of the various groups. They prioritize preventing new recruitment to the individual groups and the establishment of new groups.

The police emphasize a number of preventive measures. Prevention is the police's main strategy for the period 2021–2025. The police prioritize close and good cooperation with the City of Oslo, the city administration, and other public actors such as child welfare and schools. There is personal and close contact between the police and the municipality.

The police emphasize rapid investigation and rapid and adapted punitive measures and what they call a holistic approach. All cases of violence are investigated, even though it is known that the perpetrator is under the age of 15, which is the criminal minimum age in Norway. Priority is given to finding the perpetrator, his background, and the cause of the violent incident.

A security program has been established. That means that victims of violence are followed up in all cases. Specifically are all young people under the age of 18 who have been exposed to violence contacted by the police. This is to prevent victimization and for victims of violence to be exposed to violence again and to counteract revenge which has been a very common response to threats of violence and actual violence. The police establish a dialogue with the perpetrator and victim to prevent new violence after an episode of violence. Here, the police use relatively large resources.

The police have developed a security guide that aims to contribute to increased security in the public space.

The police prioritize being a professional actor online and thus be able to meet young people and the general population in this arena. The Oslo police are on Facebook, Snap, and Instagram. They are not currently on TikTok.

Zero tolerance has been introduced for violence against the police, teachers, other public actors, and coaches in sports clubs as well as leaders in leisure clubs. It is communicated systematically and demonstrated in practice that such behavior has consequences.

A pilot project has been carried out with action plans and close follow-up of 24 people from the criminal youth environment. This has had a good effect, and there are few relapses.

A concept called fair policing has been developed. It is an operational strategy that the police patrols must practice. It entails a mandatory action on the part of police officers towards the youth environments and how they should deal with the youth problems. As a basis for this operational strategy, an educational program has been developed that contains theory, experiential knowledge, and training. All operational police officers in Oslo undergo this training, which aims to professionalize the police's handling of juvenile delinquency, groupings, and violence among children and young people.

The police work against both individuals and groups. The approach pressures that the focus is person-oriented, local-oriented, and situational. The latter means that the police try to influence the development in the local environments, for example, the physical design of living environments, small schools with several teachers, and the composition of the population in different environments; in short, emphasis is placed on situational crime prevention.

The Police Unit East in Oslo has received a solid strengthening of staffing.

Some Important Experiences

The police leaders pointed out that there is a very small group of young people who are responsible for most of the juvenile delinquency. They emphasize that it is important to prevent young people in the environment from continuing to commit crime.

All three police leaders emphasized the importance of identifying the root causes of juvenile delinquency and also violent crime committed by children and young people.

By identifying and analyzing the underlying causes, the police, in collaboration with other public authorities and voluntary organizations, can implement effective measures against individuals, groups, and situations that together can help prevent and deal with juvenile delinquency in general and violent crime among children and young people in particular.

One of the police leaders argued that it is necessary to initiate research projects related to this form of crime and the underlying causes of it and to find good tools to prevent young people from ending up in unfortunate environments and developing antisocial and criminal behavior.

The police leaders believe it is important to work to maintain the police presence throughout the city and especially in the areas that are most exposed.

The police must be and be perceived as a natural part of all local communities, and not be a foreign element. It must also be ensured that the police become a close and accessible police force. It is also crucial to strengthen and maintain trust in the police.

They also emphasized that it is important to avoid the police being perceived as two different forms of police in the youth environments (preventive police personnel and ordinary patrolling police personnel).

The interviewed police leaders believed that the police must be aware of resource efforts and the tactical level of the task solution in the vulnerable districts.

The police must make wise considerations when solving assignments. This means that one must not develop a too sharp approach. Likewise, the consideration of effective assignment solution and intrinsic security for the police officers must also be taken into account.

The strategy from the police has, given the challenge, been not to overcheck geographical areas and the relevant groups. In addition, the police have been very careful to have a good legal basis for their activities/tasks. Finally, the police have emphasized talking to the young people and clearly justifying the relevant checks they carry out.

The police must talk to the young people and the youth communities. They must continue to justify and explain their activity.

The police leaders believe that in general it looks as if the implemented measures have had and have an effect so far.

One of the police leaders concluded that it is demanding police work to work against these youth environments. This means, for example, deciding whether the various meetings with the young people in the vulnerable local communities were in a control situation or a contact situation. The deviation from the police approach can be demanding. The actual encounters with young people who are active and threatening, sometimes with violence against police officers, can be challenging. He said that the work places demands on experienced and safe police officers. This type of policing was not as easy for newly trained police officers, he said.

Another of the police leaders pointed out that although the police and partners in other organizations have a relatively similar understanding of this societal problem and agree on the objectives of the joint work. There may be differing views on the choice and prioritization of instruments. This can be a challenge, and it must be handled.

Finally, one of these senior police leaders mentioned that the police should emphasize the perceptions of the population. The police can with advantage listen to and respect the views, assessments, and criticisms as well as input on the police's task solution and behavior.

A Short Look Ahead

Several of the factors mentioned in the previous chapter are factors that the police and the cooperating actors should be aware of in the years to come. The police leaders pointed out the need for and the benefit of the police cooperating in partnership with the municipality, the school, and the child welfare service. They also expressed the good forces that work well together and must work to strengthen and improve this relationship and cooperation.

They pointed to the need to ensure that resources are coordinated at an overall level between the collaborating organizations.

They stated that the work to prevent and deal with juvenile delinquency, including violence among young people, requires a knowledge-based approach both in the police work itself and in the management of this. This is to ensure a thorough understanding of the causes of violence, which measures have a lasting effect, how to ensure effective organizing of cooperation between the various actors and effective management of both the police and the cooperation.

Targeted research projects to contribute to both specific and comprehensive understanding of this phenomenon must be initiated in the years to come, said one of the police leaders.

One of the police leaders pointed out how important the work is to prevent and deal with violence among children and young people for several reasons. He expressed concern that this crime may contribute to stigmatizing young people and youth groups. He thought this could have very unfortunate consequences in the long run.

Another of the police leaders thought that in 10 years' time we would still see violence among children and young people in Oslo. He assumed that there would be an increase in violence and threats among children and young people in the future.

He further believed that there would still be a small group of young people who would be responsible for the largest proportion of crime, including violent crime (Fig. 2.6).

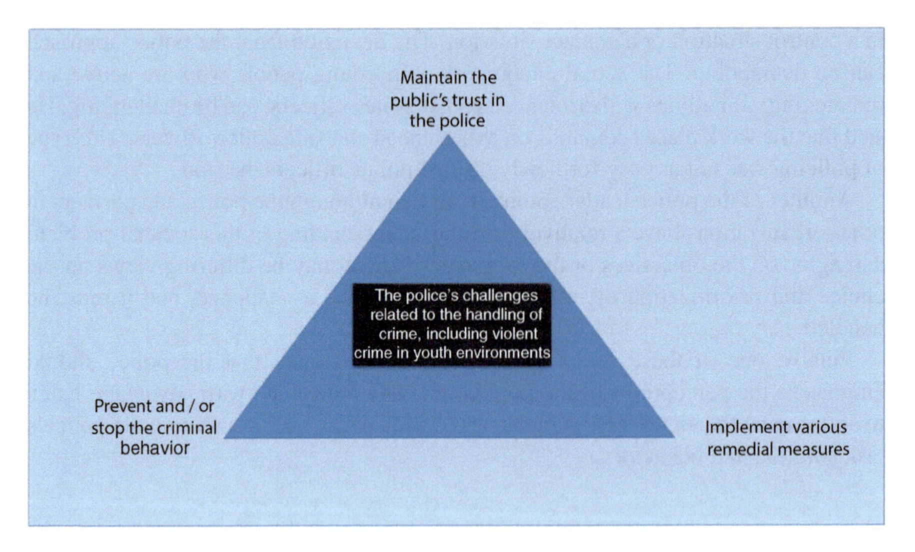

Fig. 2.6 Challenges related to the police's handling of juvenile delinquency

Conclusion

From this study, one can draw several lessons related to the police's prevention and handling of juvenile delinquency in general and violent crime in particular among children and young people.

Crime and violent crime among young people are complex societal problems that involve very demanding challenges for society, the police, and other public authorities and their ability to cooperate. This requires not only effective police leadership but also effective public leadership as such. Both leadership and interorganizational collaboration are important to handle this problem.

Based on an assessment of this societal problem, a review of theory, and the interviews with police leaders, we have developed a model for effective police leadership. It emphasizes that police leadership must be knowledge-based and discretionary in order to ensure that the police and the police's assignment solution contributes to public value. From this study, one can draw several lessons related to the police's prevention and handling of juvenile delinquency in general and violent crime in particular among children and young people. We consider police leadership as an adaptable, relational, and collective process that must be adapted to the situation leadership is performed, the tasks to be solved, and the employees and partners the police have.

The police leaders point to challenges related to juvenile delinquency and violence among children and young people, among other things, the establishment of groups fighting for hegemony when it comes to drug sales within specific geographical areas of the city. Associated with these groups, crime and violent crime occur.

The young people in the groups are persistent and challenging towards the police, which they regard as foreign elements in the areas that they regard as their own.

The police see the phenomenon of flocking when the police are to intervene in the environment.

The police must have a conscious strategy in dealing with the problem and these groups.

Preventing and dealing with violence among children and young people require a thorough understanding of the problem and the causes behind it. The handling requires the police to cooperate with other public actors.

The police emphasize a number of preventive measures. They emphasize rapid investigation. A security program is established, and a concept called fair policing has been developed. The police are focusing both on individuals, groups, and situational factors, and they consider the measures have had a positive effect so far.

We support the analyzes made both in the police trend report and in the Salto report, as well as statements from the three interviewed police leaders that one must understand the root causes of child and young people's crime and violent crime in particular. To find out more about these, we believe targeted research projects can be sensible measures. Here, there will also be a need for resources and societal prioritization over time to bring about a change in this problem.

This study must be considered as a preliminary and limited study. It has given a certain picture of the phenomenon of violence among children and young people in Oslo, the police's work related to preventing and dealing with the problem, and some police leaders' experiences in connection with this.

But there are more questions to ask and more answers to find to gain better knowledge about what works and how effective police leadership can contribute to solving this societal problem that does not only exist in Oslo.

References

Aarset, M. V., & Glomseth, R. (2019). Police leadership during challenging times. In J. F Albrecht, G. den Heyer, & P. Stanislas (Eds.), *Policing and minority groups* (pp. 29–53). Springer.

Andersen, O. J., Moldenæs, T., & Torsteinsen, H. (2017). *Ledelse og skjønnsutøvelse, analyse, intuisjon, forhandlinger*. Fagbokforlaget.

Baker, T. E. (2011). *Effective police leadership. Moving beyond management*. Looseleaf Law Publications, Inc..

Bennis, W. (2009). *On Becoming a Leader*. Basic Books.

Bennis, W. G., & Nanus, B. (1985). *Leaders: The strategies for taking charge*. Harper & Rowe. In B. Jackson, & K. Parry, (2018). *A very short, fairly interesting and reasonable cheap book about Studying Leadership*. Sage.

Blanchard, K. H. (1985). *SLIT: A situational approach to managing people*. Blanchard Training and Development. In P. G. Northouse, (2013). *Leadership. Theory and practice,* 6th ed. Sage.

Blanchard, K., Zigarmi, P., & Zigarmi, D. (1985). *Leadership and the one minute manager: Increasing effectiveness through situational leadership*. William Morrow. In P. G. Northouse, (2013). *Leadership. Theory and practice*, 6th ed. Sage.

Bowling, B., Reiner, R., & Sheptycki, J. (2019). *The politics of the police* (5th ed.). Oxford University Press.

Brooks, S., & Grint, K. (2010). *The New public leadership challenge*. Palgrave MacMillan.

Burns, J. M. (2010). *Leadership*. Harper Perennial Political Classics.

Caless, B. (2011). *Policing at the top. The roles, values and attitudes of chief police officers*. The Policy Press, University of Bristol.
Caless, B., & Tong, S. (2017). *Leading policing in Europe. An empirical study of strategic police leaders*. The Policy Press, University of Bristol.
Cockcroft, T. (2013). *Police culture. Themes and concepts*. Routledge.
Cordner, G. W. (2016). *Police Administration* (9th ed.). Routledge.
Crawford, A. & Cunningham, M. (2015). Working in partnership: The challenges of working across organizational boundaries, cultures, and practices. In J. Fleming, (2015). *Police Leadership. Rising to the top*. (pp71–95). Oxford University Press.
Filstad, C. (2020). *Politiledelse som praksis*. Fagbokforlaget.
Fleming, J. (2015). *Police leadership. Rising to the top*. Oxford University Press.
Glomseth, R., & Aarset, M. V. (2020). Politiets sentrale og lokale ledelse i krisehåndtering. In A. K. Larssen & G. L. Dyndal (Eds.), *Strategisk ledelse i krise og krig. Det norske systemet*. Universitetsforlaget.
Grint, K. (2005a). *Leadership: Limits and possibilities*. Palgrave Macmillan.
Grint, K. (2005b). Problems, problems, problems: The social construction of "leadership.". *Human Relations, 58*(11), 1467–1494. The Tavistock Institute.
Grint, K. (2010). *Leadership. A very short introduction*. Oxford University Press.
Grint, K. & Thornton, S. (2015). Leadership, Management, and Command in the Police. In J. Fleming, (2015). *Police Leadership. Rising to the top*. (pp 95–110). Oxford University Press.
Haberfeld, M. (2013). *Police leadership. organizational and managerial decision making process* (2nd ed.). Pearson.
Heifetz, R. A. (1994). *Leadership without easy answers*. Harvard University Press.
Heifetz, R., Grashow, A., & Linsky, M. (2009). *The practice of adaptive leadership, tools and tactics for changing your organizations and the world*. Harvard Business Press.
Hersey, P., & Blanchard, K. H. (1969). *Management of organizational behavior: Utilizing human resources*. Prentice Hall.
Jackson, B., & Parry, K. (2018). *A very short, fairly interesting and reasonable cheap book about Studying Leadership*. Sage.
Johannessen, S., & Glomseth, R. (2015). *Politiledelse*. Gyldendal Akademisk.
Karp, T., Filstad, C., & Glomseth, R. (2019). 27 days of managerial work in the police service. *Police Practice and Research, An International Journal, 20*(5), 427–443.
Kirkhaug, R. (2017). Lederskapsskjønn. In O.J. Andersen, T. Moldenæs, & H. Torsteinsen, (2017). *Ledelse og skjønnsutøvelse, analyse, intuisjon, forhandlinger*, Bergen, Norway: Fagbokforlaget.
Kirkhaug, R. (2019). *Lederskap, Person og funksjon*. Universitetsforlaget.
Klockars, C. B. (1985). *The idea of police*. Beverly Hills, CA: Sage Publications.
Kotter, J. P. (1990). *What Leaders Really Do? Harvard Business Review on Leadership, May-June, 1990*. The Harvard Business Review paperback Series. In O.J. Andersen, T. Moldenæs, & H. Torsteinsen, (2017). *Ledelse og skjønnsutøvelse, analyse, intuisjon, forhandlinger*, Bergen, Norway: Fagbokforlaget.
Kouzes, J. M., & Posner, B. Z. (2016). *Learning leadership, the five fundamentals of becoming an exemplary leader*. Wiley.
Kouzes, J. M., & Posner, B. Z. (2017). *The leadership challenge, how to make extraordinary things happen in organizations*. Wiley.
Manning, P. K. (1977). *Police work: The social organization of policing*. Cambridge, MA: MIT Press.
Mintzberg, H. (2010). *Mintzberg Om Ledelse*. L&R Business.
Mitchell, M., & Casey, J. (2007). *Police leadership & management*. The Federation Press.
Moore, M. H. (1995). *Creating public value. Strategic management in government*. Harvard University Press.
Newburn, T. (2005). *Policing. Key readings*. Routledge.
Neyroud, P., & Beckley, A. (2001). *Policing, ethics and human rights*. Cullompton, Devon, UK: Willan Publications.
Northouse, P. G. (2013). *Leadership. Theory and practice* (6th ed.). Sage.
Nye, J. R. (2010). *The powers to lead*. Oxford University Press.
Reiss, A. J., Jr. (1971). *The police and the public*. New Haven, CT: Yale University Press.

Renard, C. C., & Pedersen, A. R. (2017). *Når ledere skaber offentlig værdi. Seks fortellinger fra samfunnets maskinrum*. Nyt fra Samfunnsvidenskaberne.
Rittel, H., & Webber, M. (1973). Dilemmas in a general theory of planning. *Policy Science, 4*, 155–169. In K. Grint (2005). *Problems, problems, problems: The social construction of "leadership."* Human Relations, Vol. 58 (11): 1467–1494. The Tavistock Institute.
Schafer, J. (2013). *Effective leadership in policing*. Carolina Academic Press.
Skolnick, J. H. (1994). *Justice without trial: Law enforcement in democratic society*. New York: Macmillan.
Tannenbaum, R. & Schmitt, W.H. How to Choose a Leadership Pattern. Harvard Business Review 36, May-June (1958): 95–101. In J. Schafer, (2013). *Effective leadership in policing*. Carolina Academic Press.
Vroom, V. C., & Jago, A. G. (1988). *The new leadership: Managing participation in organizations*. Prentice-Hall. In J. Schafer, (2013). *Effective leadership in policing*. Carolina Academic Press.
Walsh, W. F., & Vito, G. F. (2019). *Police leadership and administration. A 21st-century strategic approach*. Routledge.
Weick, K. (1995). *Sensemaking in organizations*. Thousand Oaks, CA: Sage Publications.
Yukl, G. (2013). *Leadership in organizations* (8th ed.). Pearson.
Zaleznik, A. (1977). Managers and leaders: Are they different? *Harvard Business Review, 55*, 67–85. In B. Jackson, & K. Parry, (2018). *A very short, fairly interesting and reasonable cheap book about Studying Leadership*. Sage.

Reports

The Salto Report for 2020, Oslo Municipality and Oslo Police District, published May 2021 https://www.oslo.kommune.no/getfile.php/13406652-1622017924/Tjenester%20og%20tilbud/Politikk%20og%20administrasjon/Prosjekter/Salto%20-%20sammen%20lager%20vi%20et%20trygt%20Oslo/1%20Kriminaliteten%20i%20Oslo/Barne-%20og%20ungdomskriminaliteten%20i%20Oslo%202020.pdf
Sætre, M, Hofseth, C. & Kjenn, B.L. (2018), Stab for virksomhetsstyring, Oslo politidistrikt. Trender i kriminalitet 2018-2021, Digitale og lokale utfordringer – (The Trend Report 2018-2021, Oslo Police District, ISBN: 978-82-8228-031-0)

Interviews With

John Roger Lund, Assistant Chief of Police/Head of Unit East Oslo Police District
Robert Thorsen, Police Super Intendent, Head of Uniformed Unit, Oslo City Center, Oslo Police District
Rune Solberg Swahn, Assistant Chief of Police/Head of crime prevention, Oslo Police District, Crime Prevention Department

Emails

Joseph Schafer, email from him Thursday 05.08.2021 16:45 some comments on the theme knowledge or evidence-based police leadership
Maria Haberfeld, email from her Friday 06.08.2021 19:18 some comments on the theme knowledge-based police leadership

Chapter 3
Police Training and Use of Force: Methods to Reduce Violent Encounters

W. Bradley Cotton

Introduction

The greatest victory is that which requires no battle. Sun Tzu

Training is an absolutely critical element of anyone involved in law enforcement. Not just any training will do, it must be the right type of training. Training that is unrealistic and that focusses only on use of force, defensive tactics, driving, firearms and the physical elements of policing is, without question, all necessary but, on its own without other types of training to compliment it, can have disastrous consequences.

There are many books and seminars dedicated to training and officer survival. *The Bulletproof Mind* and *Warrior Mindset: Mental Toughness Skills for a Nation's Peacekeepers* are just a couple. These books and seminars by the same title have recently come under fire in the press for teaching militarised tactics to police officers (McLaughlin, 2020).

We much prefer framing in a different, more positive fashion. Author and former Navy SEAL Commander Richard Marcinko is quoted as saying "The more you sweat in training, the less you bleed in battle" (Marcinko, 1992). Officers need to spend the time learning how to deal with the myriad of situations they will encounter on the street, the vast majority of which will never end in a use of force of any kind. The Washington Post maintains an online database of all persons shot by police in the United States, based on media and social media reports in addition to submitted national statistics (Tate et al., 2021). According to their data, since January 1, 2015, 6005 persons have been shot (Tate et al., 2021). In that 6-year time frame according to the National Emergency Number Association, approximately

W. B. Cotton (✉)
University of Edinburgh, Edinburgh, UK
e-mail: bcotton@ed.ac.uk

J. F. Albrecht, G. den Heyer (eds.), *Understanding and Preventing Community Violence*, https://doi.org/10.1007/978-3-031-05075-6_3

1.44 billion emergency calls were received (Tate et al., 2021). That translates into a tremendously small percentage of calls that ended tragically. According to other data, of the 240 million emergency calls,[1] roughly 62.9 million became police/public contacts, and of those an estimated 337,590 had a use of force reported (Garner et al., 2018).[2] What is not addressed is the impact that those deaths had on the community. Interestingly, it's more than likely that many of those situations that do end in a use of force may not have needed to.

For decades we have heard media accounts of the "War on Drugs" and the "War Against Gangs". We have seen an increase in the militarisation of police in appearance, training and equipment. As a public, we seem to have been conditioned by the "War of Crime", but what we are finally coming to realise is policing is not truly like a war. That position is an outdated understanding of what and who police need to be in today's society and for today's community. Today, police need to be Peacemakers and Referees. Revisiting the Marcinko quote, we like the way that Norman Schwarzkopf put it even better, "The more you sweat in peace, the less you bleed in war" (Norton, 1991). Recognising it is another "war" reference; we are going to take some licence and propose the following as our desire for you to take away in this chapter:

> The more you sweat in training on peaceful solutions, the less *anyone* will bleed.

As we walk through this chapter, we will look at some of the traditional models and methods of police training. We will talk about de-escalation and pre-escalation, particularly as a response to incidents where persons are suffering the effects of mental illness or mental breakdown as they have such a significant impact on policing. We will also cover the use of dynamic simulation-based training as a tool to reduce violent encounters and briefly touch on the future of police training.

As you can imagine, the proper training of police officers is absolutely critical. Gone are the days of handing someone a badge, gun, baton and a set of handcuffs and pushing them out the back door of the station with instructions, "Don't get yourself killed and stay out of trouble".[3]

Today, depending on your location, fully training a police officer can require a degree of up to 3 or 4 years and demand much more than just use of force training (Dekanoidze & Khelhvill-Kyviv, 2018; Huisjes et al., 2018). Training can (and should) include courses on mental health, de-escalation, law, culture, ethics, ethnicity, diversity and more.

---

[1] We should note that this figure does not include officer or public-initiated contacts that occurred outside of the NENA system.

[2] As mentioned, not all states and departments have national reporting requirements (hence the Washington Post website creation).

[3] This first day was described to the author on his first day as an officer in 1991 by a soon-to-retire veteran hired in the late 1950s.

Stress Inoculation Training

One of the most important considerations of good training is the positive effects it can have on pre-event, event and post-event outcomes. This is generally referred to as stress inoculation training.

When one is inoculated or vaccinated, one receives a "little bit of the disease" that your body learns to fight off. Incorporating stress inoculation training in simulations allows the student to be safely exposed to different types of situations and experience emotional arousal while learning appropriate responses without being overwhelmed (Novaco, 1977).

When the human body experiences stress, many things happen physiologically. The degree of response is generally thought to be determined by how threatening the individual feels the situation is (Anderson et al., 2019):

> In a non-spontaneous threat situation, the threat is processed cognitively and physically, normally without difficultly. In a spontaneous, startled, fearful situation however, the amygdala, which is hardwired for survival, primes the body with adrenaline for an automatic response. The triggering of the amygdala is directly responsible for what many consider (post-incident) as irrational responses, such as panic, flight, freezing in place, aggressive actions that utilize untrained skills, repeating an action time and again (a motor skill feedback loop), or an inappropriate physical response. (Ross & Murphy, 2017)

Stress inoculation improves an individual's response to the stressors an individual may experience in a critical incident. It can have a very positive spin-off benefit of reducing the effects of the incident (post-traumatic stress disorder) (Ford, 2019). Many empirical studies have been undertaken that support the positive effects of stress inoculation training to reduce anxiety and enhance performance (Saunders et al., 1996).

Designing realistic scenarios that mimic real situations "…provides individuals with experience with minor stressors that fosters psychological preparedness and promotes resilience" (Meichenbaum, 2017). As a result, when designing scenarios and simulations, realism is a key factor for consideration to best prepare students for the realities of police work, and training must reflect the diverse situational demands faced in the field (Able et al., 2019).

Types and Lengths of Training and Use of Force Compared

The empirical evidence suggests the more educated officers are in police matters, the less they will use force (Rydberg & Terrill, 2010; Shjarback & White, 2016).

There is always a need for new police officers to be hired, and that need has become increasingly more pronounced over the last two decades. Police services around the world have commented on the difficulty they are having filling roles with qualified applicants that are indicative of the community (Rydberg & Terrill, 2010; Shjarback & White, 2016). This has led to a number of plans to try and fill ranks. It has also led to programs of training that can run very short. In Canada, typical training runs from 12 to 26 weeks before officers are sworn in. However, in Europe, many programs run 2–4 years and actually incorporate degrees focussed on the science of policing.

As mentioned earlier, not only do program lengths differ, but the subjects studied also vary greatly. In North America, there is a distinct focus on operations and tactics. The training tends to be much more militaristic and technical with a focus on weapons (lethal and less lethal), defensive tactics and officer safety. There is little serious consideration paid to diversity, ethnicity, mental health and de-escalation compared to the European schools which feature entire courses on police history, culture, diversity, mental health and more.

There have been many studies about the length of training programs and the impact that they have on the use of force. Numerous studies over the last few years appear to confirm that there is a nexus between use of force and education.

In addition to the studies by Rydberg and Tyrell (2010) and Shjarbak and White (2016), other studies further show positive results from officers who have degrees (Table 3.1).

This does not mean that higher educated officers are reluctant to use force or that those that are less educated are more willing, but what it does appear to reflect is critical thinking and the ability to apply knowledge and skills from other experiences and learning within the fluid dynamics of the different situations that officers face daily and the positive outcomes of better attitudes, higher levels of professionalism and lower use of force. Additionally, these longer courses serve to fill the police officer's personal "toolbox" with practical skills that they can apply in day-to-day situations.

The Toolbox

When we conduct training for officers (or anyone for that matter), we frequently refer to the "toolbox". What is the toolbox? It is a symbolic repository that each of us carries which contains the "tools" of our training and experience that we can pull out and use as situations demand.

Students are told that when you see a colleague do something that you like and that worked, put it in your toolbox to take out and try yourself. When you read or experience or learn something, do the same thing. You fill up your toolbox with

Table 3.1 Synthesis of early research into degree-educated officers in the United States

Research findings	Research authors
Police less authoritarian	Parker et al. (1976) and Roberg (1978)
Police less cynical	Regoli (1976)
Police have a more flexible value system	Guller (1972)
Police have improved attitude toward minorities	Parker et al. (1976)
Police more ethical and professional with less complaints	Roberg and Bonn (2004) and Lersch and Kunzman (2001)

Source: Rogers and Smith (2018)

tactics and skills that you can use to resolve situations. Some of these tools are experiential, and we can only decide on their effectiveness for us through using them in a real experience (either reality-based simulations or real life), but many of these tools can be taught (de-escalation and techniques for mental health intervention) in a classroom.

Example: An experienced colleague who was an extremely skilled negotiator attended a call during a domestic dispute between a husband and wife. He and his partner separated the pair, and he spoke to the husband in the family room. Within a few minutes, there was laughter and conversation coming from the other room. They dealt with the issues to the best of their ability de-escalating the argument. The officers got agreements that the husband and wife would stay apart until cooler heads could prevail and police wouldn't have to return. Outside they compared notes, and his partner asked about the laughter. The experienced officer had noticed a baseball game playing on the TV and used his knowledge of the game and teams to open communications and build rapport. This created an open doorway that allowed him to speak with the husband and help resolve the issues. Will this always work? No. Another colleague attended another dispute and noted the house was in a state of renovation. He too was renovating and tried to use that as a rapport builder. The problem was the dispute was about the renovations and his attempt at rapport building actually escalated the situation which took longer to resolve! He had no idea what the argument was about, but at least he was willing to try. The key takeaway here is ask questions to divine the nature of the incident and then use your toolbox to select something that might work. Had he done that, he might have been able to avoid the emotionally charged topic of the renovation and been able to create rapport using another.

De-Escalation and Pre-escalation

The subject of de-escalation has been receiving a lot of global press following the unjust deaths of a number of black, indigenous and people of colour in the United States and elsewhere. De-escalation is the practice of defusing potentially volatile situations, slowing things down and resolving them with minimal force. Pre-escalation is the use of tactics and techniques to prevent potentially violent events by recognising and removing trigger events that lead to breakdowns, particularly when dealing with mental health. Both types of training have a significant part to play in reducing police use of force.

Priming is the understanding that past experience forms a lens through which we see and react to current stimuli. By example, if you were once stung on the lip by a bee that had flown into your coke can while on a patio, you might be very cautious about drinking from a can outside ever again. In fact, you might be so cautious that you insist on your drink being in a glass.

Early studies in policing suggested that officers used experiential classifications to prejudge or predict future behaviour by individuals they were interacting with

(Klein, 2009; Muir, 1977; Taylor, 2020; Wilson, 1978). Obviously, there were many sweeping generalities that were made. While some may have some validity in certain circumstances, as police we have to be cautious about stereotyping and developing bias upon which we base our actions.

Damaging, sweeping generalisations have led to issues of systemic racism and inequality in policing practices, and these practices must be avoided at all cost. Each circumstance needs to be taken based on the evidence before the officer and not inferred evidence that may or may not be true and that the officer has no way of confirming.

It is when we look at the context of reducing the use of force that this concept becomes tremendously important. An officer responding to a "rough part of town" and a location "known to them to be frequented by gang members" for a call about a "subject with a gun" paints a very vivid picture for a responding officer. Studies have shown that information like this can have a significant impact on an officer's decision to use force having been subconsciously made *before they even arrive* (Luoma-aho & Canel, 2020; Taylor, 2020).

It's not an example of a subject with a gun but takes an officer dispatched to assist the fire department at a call involving a house fire. The dispatcher advises that the parents do not know where the children are and are concerned they are still in the house. The officer proceeds to the call at an exceptionally high rate of speed, approaching 180 km/h in an urban environment. The officer, a new dad himself, has formed such a convincing preconceived picture in his head about what is going on that he has difficulty separating from reality. He misses the fact that the fire department was already on scene and, due to the heightened arousal, misses the dispatched information that the children were located. How could dispatch have modified their information? Simply by changing call type and the order the information was broadcast. Had the call been put on as a traffic direction assistance call instead of an active fire, what do you think the result would have been? Would it have changed the level of arousal the officer felt? Most likely.

The same would be true of being dispatched to a "person with a gun call" versus a group of kids playing "cops and robbers" in the park. The same incident, if classified differently, will elicit a different response from the officers. In the first, the officer approaches, possibly gun in hand. Any furtive or quick movement by the subject could be met with lethal force. In the second, the officer is aware, still concerned about the possibility of a gun being present, but their level of arousal is lower and their response more balanced.[4]

The effect of dispatch priming on police use of force is only just beginning to be empirically explored, and the understanding we currently possess is in its infancy. We have briefly discussed it here because we feel the effects of dispatch priming can play a significant part in situation outcome and students need to be aware of the possibility of its role.

---

[4]This example is based on the 2014 shooting of 12-year-old Tamir Rice by Cleveland Ohio (USA) police officer, Timothy Loehmann (Stone & Socia, 2019).

Pre-escalation Tactics

There have been many recent studies of de-escalation training and its effect on use of force. However, another method of lowering the incidence of use of force is pre-escalation, pre-dispute or pre-intervention (International Mediation Institute, 2016).

Any practices of this nature seek to find ways to intervene before a crisis develops. Tactics could involve the design of spaces using Crime Prevention Through Environmental Design (CPTED) concepts to reduce the incidence of crime in a neighbourhood or space and the inclusion of teams like the Mobile Crisis Rapid Response Team ("MCRRT") or Crisis Outreach and Support Team ("COAST") which get to know those in the community suffering mental illness. Through their knowledge of the individuals, they get to know and understand their clients and what can trigger crisis events. An example would be the date a loved one committed suicide, or a friend died. These dates can prove quick traumatic and frequently coincide with crisis events for the subject. Often a visit from the team and some additional supports near or on that date can prevent a crisis from developing. Risk mitigation tables use community teams to intervene before crisis develops for those at acute risk and part of a community safety framework (Nilson, 2018).

Tactics also can include identifying and addressing the system issues and biases that could potentially create conflict, community partnerships, shared responsibility and team building to name a few. We strongly believe that appropriate training sets the stage for excellence in pre-escalation.

De-Escalation Tactics

To date there are few studies that have been done to gauge the effectiveness of de-escalation training (Sherman, 2020; Wolfe et al., 2020).

Additionally, no definition of de-escalation or de-escalation training currently exists in policing (Sherman, 2020). This does not mean that we can't engage in training to try and defuse situations.

The Oxford Dictionary defines de-escalation at a "reduction of the intensity of a conflict or potentially violent situation" (Oxford Dictionary, 2021). Any efforts police can take to reduce the emotional intensity of encounters would be considered de-escalating.

In an emotionally charged encounter, having the assistance of a hybrid police-mental health team like MCRRT or COAST would be ideal for any attempt at de-escalation. However, some police services may not have this capability. The Crisis Intervention Team (CIT) model and training for individual officers is only a week-long and could afford some significant understanding and translate into de-escalation in potentially violent situations (Robinson, 2020).

Time and distance are two factors that we often fail to take into account that form one of the cornerstones of de-escalation. One of the easiest ways to defuse and slow down a situation is to back off and slow down. This is an emphasis on CIT training and, when possible, can greatly diffuse a volatile situation (Pollack & Humphreys, 2020). Time and distance are generally things that the police have on their side. We usually have some ability to create distance and allow an individual time to calm down.

Academic evidence will come on the effectiveness of training like CIT, advanced mental health understanding, verbal communication tactics and the use of hybrid team in the process of de-escalation. Regardless, the process has value and has been seen by the author in the field to reduce use of force.

Breathing

De-escalation is also a matter to keep oneself grounded. Dynamic events can wreak havoc on the psychology and physiology of officers. As the levels of stress increase, respiration and heart rate start to climb. When they do, so do the effects of physical deficits in the officer's body. These motor and cognitive deficits alter perception, create tunnel vision and tunnel hearing and reduce fine motor skills. This is the fight or flight response we hear spoken of often. Fight, flight, posture and submit are the choices that we are faced within the face of a violent occurrence (Andersen & Gustafberg, 2016; Grossman, 2014).

Specific training that teaches officers how to deal with the effects of these stressors and minimise them is available. Systems such as iPREP or focussed breathing (combat breathing) have been empirically shown to reduce stress, improve cognition and help produce better critical decision-making and judgement (Andersen & Gustafberg, 2016; Hourani et al., 2011).

Tactical breathing, combat breathing or box breathing are techniques taught by many instructors up to and including the US Navy SEALs to control the physiological effects of stress and calm decrease sympathetic nervous system activity. It is as simple as breathing in for a count of four, hold for a count of four, out for a count of four and hold for a count of four. The technique will have a profound effect on one's ability to function in a dynamic situation (Andersen & Gustafberg, 2016; Finn, 2021; Grossman & Christensen, 2017; Rottger et al., 2020).

Dynamic Simulation-Based Training

Conducting effective training for police is not a simple task. Training has many components that need to work together to be effective for officers, especially when looking at reducing the amount of force being applied in situations.

Legal Framing

Before any action is undertaken, it is vital that the action is legal. This means that the officer has a lawful authority for the actions that they are about to undertake. Lawful authority is granted through the knowledge of the various laws and legislations that govern police actions. This includes local and departmental regulations and policies. Principle among these is the power of arrest granted by those authorities. This means that for a use of force to be legally undertaken, it needs to conform to the legislation, and that means that officers must know their authorities. Failing to know their authorities can lead to unlawful actions on the part of the police which at the low end of the scale would mean that a charge might be tossed out of court. An example would be an unlawful search in which the seized property is given back to the subject and the charges lost. The next step up could create bad case law that affects all officers in the jurisdiction. At the far end of illegal action is legal action against the officer from a criminal or even civil perspective.

Academic Framing

This can include legal framing, but it also goes deeper into the "why" police need to undertake the actions they do. The academic framing will include academic evidence, background and history. Academic framing can (and should) also include the culture, history, ethnicity and the subtle differences that make up the community as it is all relevant. If you think about legal framing as the "what" and part of the "why", academic framing supplies the other part of the "why" and the classroom part of "how" and "when".

It is also during the academic framing that we should be learning about techniques that will reduce the need for us to resort to force. This is the opportunity to introduce concepts of effective communication, first-contact approach, negotiation, pre-escalation and de-escalation. All of these concepts are necessary to reduce the need for police to use force. See the descriptive sections earlier in this chapter.

The rest of the framing is applied through physical training. Don't let the length of the legal framing and academic framing sections above lends to a belief that they are not at all important. They are absolutely vital to understand and minimise use of force.

Introduction of Physical Skills

During this phase of the training, officers are slowly introduced to the physical skill sets necessary to effect arrests and defend themselves and others.

Instructors should walk through the skill set with officers, describing what they want done and demonstrating it with other instructors and then students. Students will then be encouraged to engage with each other and move slowly through the new skill. It is crucial that new techniques are taught slowly to allow officers a chance to absorb the training and learn to facilitate the techniques:

> As a young recruit, sitting in a class, we were asked if anyone had ever taken any martial arts. I had taken a few lessons as a teen, and eager to please I put my hand up and went to the front of the room. I was asked what martial art I had taken, and I said that I'd taken some judo. The instructor stood facing the room and said, "Defend yourself." He turned and punched me, full speed in the face, bloodying my nose and bruising my lip. He made some derogatory comment about my skills and sent me to get cleaned up.[5]

[5] The author's experience at the hands of an "instructor" when he was a young recruit. Unfortunately, this method of teaching was all too common and resulted in many injuries. The event did nothing to teach me about defensive tactics. It did teach me some critical lessons about awareness, reactionary gap and not trusting that particular instructor. This is not how training should be conducted!

Proper instruction is about moving slowly, building skill and increasing confidence for officers. Officers need to be confident in their skills and abilities if they are to be successful on the street. It may seem pointless to learners initially but starting at 10% speed and intensity is a great way to test the mechanics of the motions, get comfortable with the techniques and build confidence. It is unwise and potentially injurious to have students go 100% on each other. As you will see, when students are given that opportunity, it is with safety officer, proper safety equipment and significant controls in place. Anything else is a recipe for disaster. Most importantly if students don't feel comfortable and confident in using techniques in the gym, they won't feel confident on the street. A lack of confidence in their abilities leads to force multiplication and the over-reliance on intermediary weapons such as a baton, conducted energy weapon or aerosol spray (e.g. oleoresin capsicum or mace). Taken to extremes, it can lead to an over dependency on the firearm and lethal means.

For illustration, we once conducted an experiment with a group of citizens who were taking part in a "Citizens Police Academy". Many comments had been made that indicated an overreliance on television and film as a source for their understanding. We set up a very scenario and issued volunteers some inert use of force options and a blank firing pistol. The scenario was a fairly straightforward one; an intoxicated and argumentative male is causing problems yelling at people. He has a beer bottle in his hand he is drinking from. It was interesting watching the half-dozen or so students interact with the instructor who was playing the part. Overwhelmingly, students drew their gun and pointed it at the male when he refused to listen. The male ended up being shot twice: once when he held his arms out and shouted and the other when he took a (simulated) drunken staggered step toward the student.

Clearly this was not a fair test for the students. They had been given no instruction and had to rely on their own knowledge to react to the stimulus presented in the scenario. The scenario was specifically set up to get the students to engage verbally. The instructor was not behaving violently. He was loud and obnoxious, but not threatening. The two students that did engage more appropriately were community college students who were taking a law and security program and who worked security part time, but even their approaches were far from perfect.

It may seem counterintuitive, but confidence in physical abilities can actually reduce more serious use of force, injuries and even the use of lethal force. If you are confident in your skills, that comes through when interacting with the public. A lack of confidence and skill can lead to the overreliance on tools or improper techniques when using tools which in turn lead to injury and death.

As much as students, some instructors and some administrators may want to see officers proceeding quickly through some kind of "officer training mill", rushing trainees (regardless of whether they are new cadets or seasoned officers), is never a good idea. Students must be successful in the relatively stress-free environment afforded by legal framing, academic framing and the introduction of physical skills *before* proceeding to any kind of simulation.

Simulations and Scenarios

In dynamic simulations, officers wear protective gear and are outfitted with training equipment that functions identically to what they carry on the street. Typically, dynamic simulations fall into two categories: closed dynamic and open dynamic. Closed dynamic have a specific skill to be demonstrated in a specific way. Open dynamic scenarios have multiple branches that the actors will follow based on what the officer does, where they stand, their approach, what they say and how they say it. As mentioned earlier, dynamic simulation training is most effective when it is the final part of a series of training that includes the following:

- The academics behind the correct procedures.
- Operational policies.
- Legalities.
- The mechanics behind accepted tactics and techniques.
- It has been practised at a slow pace in a rigidly controlled environment (closed dynamic scenarios).

Trainers are after success for their students to reinforce the good practices and demonstrate that the tactics work. The overall goal of any use of force training should be teaching students to resolve the situation using as little force as necessary.

Closed Dynamic Simulations

The next step in training is the application of the academic, legal and practical introduction in a carefully created, highly structured, instructor-supervised "scenario". Trainees are given very clear direction and walked through the lesson in a manner similar to below:

> Instructor to group. (A second instructor demonstrates on the role-playing instructor as the lead instructor speaks).
>
> When I blow the whistle, move quickly from this line to the X on the floor. Take a defensive stance and tell the subject they are under arrest and why. From there I don't want you to rush. Take your time and make sure you get this right. We can build on speed later. (The instructor who is playing the part of the student is proceeding slowly and deliberately). Have them hold their arms out away from their body and turn slowly in a circle. When they have turned completely, have them kneel down and cross their ankles and hold their arms out and back away from their body, palms face up. Move in on their left side on the 2 position. Before you make contact, load your handcuffs, ratchet facing out. Have them bring their hands together, back-to-back behind them. Quickly ratchet the handcuffs on, right wrist then left. Check the fit and double lock them. Once you have done that, you will instruct them to stand, make sure you maintain contact with them holding their left elbow with your left hand and the back of their left hand with your right. Once they are standing and we have checked the handcuffs and your escort position, the scenario is done.

It may seem simple, perhaps even overly detailed, but this is a representation of a closed dynamic simulation. These are simulations that are completely laid out with all the expected steps and learning outcomes forward facing for the student. If the student makes an error, they are corrected immediately and repeat the process until they get it right.

This is a safe place for the student to practice their skills and gain confidence. It can be very repetitive for instructors, but most will recognise the need and allow as much practice as reasonably necessary.

Closed dynamic simulations can be applied to practically anything, from the basic arrest above to use of force options and everything in between. These simulations don't have to be defensive tactic based. We have used them for everything from laying a spike belt to learning how to search a house. Again, use your imagination. Training shouldn't be boring for the students.

Open Dynamic Simulations

The chapter will centre around the use of open dynamic simulations to reduce officer use of force. While there may be a temptation to believe that "No officer should ever encounter something on the front-line that they have not seen at least once in training", that is likely not realistic. There are as many possible outcomes as there are individuals. It is however possible to give officers a wide, evidenced-based exposure to those scenarios that you are most likely to have occur in your community.

Example: The dispatcher advises assistance is requested at an apartment complex. A male with a severe mental crisis is holed up in his apartment with a knife. He has been threatening suicide. He also threatened his wife and small child who are now outside with a neighbour. He is alone in the apartment. On your arrival, you speak to the wife outside. She explains that he was injured almost a year ago and has been off work. He has been using prescription drugs for pain and was told today that his benefits for the injury are being cut off. While talking to the wife, the man comes out on the balcony shouting. You can see the knife in his hand. Attending inside with your partner, you can see the door to the apartment is open. The man is pacing back and forth yelling. He has the knife in his hand. When he sees you in the hallway, almost 20 feet away, he stops and glares at you. Speaking very calmly, he tells you that if you come in the apartment you will have to either kill him or he will kill you. There is no one in the hallway. What will you do?

This is an open dynamic scenario because it is fluid and active. Unlike closed dynamic simulations which are created to test or reinforce a specific skill, the open dynamic allows the officers the choice of making a decision and following that through to completion. These scenarios are generally played out with inert or training use of force equipment (blue guns) like pepper spray cans that contain water, plastic expandable batons and Simunition[6] firearms which fire paint projectiles.

[6] Simunition is the trade name of a popular firearm conversion platform that is designed for most popular pistols, rifles and shotguns used by police. The kits include different working parts, different barrels and specialised ammunition (blank and marker). They are considered significantly safer than many other options as the weapons cannot chamber or fire live ammunition.

These are culminating exercises designed to help trainees use new and established skill sets in a highly controlled environment. Every scenario or simulation is designed with specific training goals in mind and has multiple branches of action for the subject. The branches that the subject acts out are however not chosen by them but are a reaction to the actions of the trainee.

In the above scenario, some possible branches might be as follows:

1. Trainee stays in the hallway, protected by the doorframe, and begins to engage the subject with de-escalating talk.
2. Trainee stays in the hallway but stands in the doorway engaging with de-escalating talk.
3. Trainee stays in the hallway but does not use de-escalating talk and instead begins to yell commands to drop the knife.
4. Trainee enters the apartment but remains in the doorway.
5. Trainee enters the apartment but moves toward the subject.

You can imagine the possible outcomes in each of these scenarios. Take a few moments and write out your thoughts as to what could happen in each. What do you think the goal of this scenario was?

The first two outcomes will likely end with the subject putting down the knife, beginning to cry and being taken into involuntary custody for mental health review. The last three outcomes will generally not be positive. They will generate increased aggression. From the third branch on is where you see other training, like firearms and the communications that surround those skills taking precedence. There is a much higher likelihood in the last three branches of the scenario ending with the subject receiving a lethal force option.

In each of the branches, there are mini branches that can be followed. For example, if the trainee enters the apartment, hears the subject say something like, "I'll kill you if you come any closer!", and exits to engage from the doorway with de-escalating talk, the trainee needs to be rewarded for recognising the error and moving to correct it.

In this particular scenario, there were three goals. The first was to slow down and maintain reactionary distance. The second was to reinforce the need to verbally engage the subject and get them talking, making an attempt to build rapport. The third, equally (and arguably more) important goal was to reinforce an awareness of officer-induced jeopardy.

Officer-Induced/Officer-Created Jeopardy

This is a concept by which an officer actually creates a situation in which they are forced to defend themselves, often lethally (Garrison, 2018; Ijames, 2005; Jenkins, 2019).[7] Some examples would be being the sole officer to attend the drug house full

[7] At the time of writing, there were only 16 Google Scholar entries for "Officer Created Jeopardy" and only two for "Officer Induced".

of gang members to arrest one of them, entering a location that you don't need to enter (like the apartment scenario above), forcing a subject to attack or moving carelessly within a subject's reactionary reach. There has been little academic research done on the concept, but it is well known within training circles and most try to train to avoid it.

Courts in the United States have been split over the reasonableness of the use of force if the officers create the situation. Some have held that if the police created the situation that required them to use force, it is then prima facie unreasonable. Others have held that only the facts at the time the decision to use force was made are relevant. Regardless of the US Court's dichotomy, if there is a method we can use that will reduce the need to take a life, we are morally and ethically bound as peacekeepers to do everything we can to minimise the chance. The aftereffects of such an incident critically harm a community, hurt both families and officers and cause immeasurable damage to trust.

Designing Training Simulations to Reduce Use of Force

There can be a tendency in training circles to always be going for the big, impressive simulations. While there is nothing wrong with having larger group scenarios, we need to make sure that we don't get caught up in the "exotic" at the expense of the practical. We need to base our simulations on evidence, risk and community need.

Risk Matrix

A very simple risk matrix is pictured in Fig. 3.1. There are four categories of risk that we can consider when designing training.

1. High frequency/low impact: These tasks are the activities that we undertake hundreds of times a day. Walking into the station from our car. Searching the back seat after an arrest. Sitting in the car writing a report and having a coffee.
2. High frequency/high impact: These are situations which are frequent and carry a measure of great risk to us and those around us. Emergency response driving. Conducting an arrest. Doing a traffic stop.
3. Low frequency/low impact: These are tasks that we are asked to do occasionally that are generally very low risk. Manning a barricade at a fire scene. Helping out at a festival. Picking up an abandoned bicycle.
4. Low frequency/high impact: These tend to be either really major incident like a train derailment which involve multiple agencies, or they can be situation of exceptional danger for the police and public like an active shooter, high-risk takedown or a weapons call.

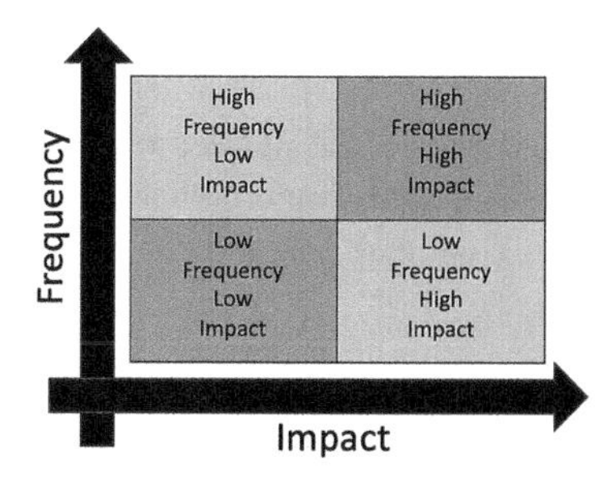

Classification of Operational Risks

Operational Risks are classified by two factors:

- Frequency – how often the event occurs
- Impact – the amount of the losses resulting from the event

Fig. 3.1 Operational risks. (Mulyana, 2012)

Risk is fluid and dynamic. As much as we want to try to manage all aspects of a situation, we can't. So, we train for the worst but expect the best. We need to train for the routine as hard as you train for the one-off events.

Let Go of Your Ego and Depersonalise

We are all human, and as such, we are all fallible. We will make mistakes. We will take things personally that we shouldn't. Sometimes it can be difficult to separate our emotions and our ego from the situation.

We have to learn that most people who react negatively to us as police or law enforcement don't have a problem with us as individuals; they have an issue with the institution of policing. As such, we can't take their words, actions and behaviour personally, but we sometimes do, and that can have dangerous consequences with respect to the use of force. Our sense of self-worth, self-esteem and self-importance can easily get tied up in the job. Cutting remarks, blatant disregard for authority or even personal attacks can all serve to deplete the ego and increase the likelihood of a more significant use of force response. The effects of ego depletion can even lead to officer-induced jeopardy as discussed earlier. Regardless of who you are, every individual's ego has limits that they can be pushed to before their ego is depleted (Staller et al., 2019). You have to realise three things:

1. Recognise your limits and when it's time to tap out because you are feeling the frustration.
2. Remember that it is most often not personal but against the office you hold.
3. Do not engage subjects in personal attacks; stay professional and focussed on the objective. If they have a legitimate gripe, acknowledge it. If it's not legitimate, defend it, but don't get into an argument.

Training Equipment

There is lots of cost-effective equipment available on the market to allow officers and students to train safely and effectively. That said, some dedicated equipment can be expensive. Padded training suits are a great addition and can allow trainees to use physical techniques with relative safety.

Inert Training Weapons

While it is permissible (and has been done!) to conduct a training course with "finger guns", it may not be the most realistic. Inert firearms, foam batons, water-filled sprays and similar devices are available. Like the padded suits, some can be expensive (Simunition gun conversion kits can be more expensive than the guns themselves), but they add an element of realism and feedback not possible any other way. Airsoft and paintball are other less effective options. It is ideal if these weapons fit in the standard carriers to help reinforce their use.

Helmets and Safety Glasses

These are essential for all taking part. Helmets should protect the head while allowing the student to see and hear clearly.

It is recommended that when scenario training, trainees and officers train in the uniform that they wear day to day with boots, vest (bullet resistant or stab/cut resistant) and their duty belt, to be as realistic as possible.

Goals of Your Training

First and foremost, what are the lessons you are trying to convey? If you are an instructor,

you need to be very clear about what it is you are trying to teach students. If you are the student, you need to understand the goals of the session. If you are in an administrative role, you want to ensure that the training that is being conducted meets your operational goals and is supported by evidence. If you are in a legal/liability role, you want to ensure that the training conforms to legal requirements and is teaching students lawful methods and tactics. If you are a civilian stakeholder, you want to ensure that the training emphasises safe outcomes with minimal force whenever possible. These are just a few possible groups of people who have an interest in police training. Each viewpoint is valid and needs to be taken into account. It is not enough justification to train for an event because it is cool, exciting or fun. Scenarios must have clear, evidence-backed goals that are being met.

The second most important goal of designing training is that the scenarios are winnable. Little is learned from scenarios that are unrealistic or that always "kill" the trainees. What is learned from a scenario involving aliens or a gang member in the trunk of a car that suddenly pops out in a traffic stop and starts shooting? As mentioned in the next section, evidence-based scenarios are by far the best for learning.

A note on "killing" trainees: We never allowed trainees to "die" in scenarios. Trainees were taught that all scenarios were survivable and that they were to continue regardless of what they felt their injuries might be. Again, this point is evidence-based on multiple cases of officers and subjects surviving being shot, stabbed or otherwise injured and continuing to fight, subdue the assailant and still go home.[8]

Evidence

What does the academic and researched evidence show needs to be conveyed in your community? Have you had a number of injuries that occurred while handcuffing? Then you likely need scenarios that include this element. Have you had an increase in the use of intravenous drugs and lots of used syringes being found? Then you may want to incorporate sharps[9] in a session on searching or have a syringe used as part of a scenario. Have you had an increase in a type of mental health calls? Then incorporate this specific type in your mental health scenarios.

There are many sources of data that you can pull from. Some sources will depend on your location, but typically the best places are calls for service, your situation table (if you have one), your local mental health unit, other support units and other police services and trainers.

Writing Scenarios

Following on the previous paragraph, once we know what we need to teach, we build our program around the need, beginning with the legal and legislative frameworks followed by the academic reasoning to give a sound foundation for what must be done to affect the most desirable outcome with the least force possible. Finally, we craft the scenario. It is important that all aspects are written down and followed for each repetition.

---

[8]A Google search of "surviving gunshot wounds" or "surviving being stabbed" will reveal many examples to support this both in the media and in academia.

[9]A sharp is anything that can stab, jab or otherwise puncture the skin. The term most often refers to syringes and medical needles.

Sample teaching plan	
Learning goals	A statement of what the goals of the exercise are. Generally (but not always) given at the start of the session
Safety instructions/ briefing	A rigid set of instructions to be followed by all participants. Safety words, proper practice, safety equipment. Breaching safety protocols endangers everyone and is taken very seriously. No live or real use of force equipment is ever allowed in the training area with few exceptions. (firearms allowed on the range for shooting, batons allowed for that portion of training on heavy bags, etc.)
Safety search	All members line up and are checked by at least two members (one of whom is an instructor) to verify no real equipment is present
General statement of simulation or scenario	Given to all students, generally at the same time. Explains the scenario and gives a chance to ask questions
Individual instructions	Given to trainee before they start
Detailed scenario	This is the part of the scenario that it is the responsibility of the instructors to follow. It is here that the branches and possible outcomes are written out. As previously mentioned, the goal is to use the appropriate (least) force necessary to successfully end the scenario. As you will see in the examples, levels of force can vary from verbal interaction to lethal force in the same situation depending on how the student reacts to the stimulus
Student debrief	It is here that the instructor, role players and the trainees have a chance to learn from what they did. They are given an opportunity to discuss what went right, what went wrong, how they could improve. They are also asked to articulate their choice of using force to the instructional team as they would in court. This further reinforces the need to understand their options and ensure that they have exercised good judgement in their response. Depending on the outcomes, learners may be given a chance to go again and correct minor mistakes. Major mistakes will go again. Never let a student leave on failure; they must have success with the techniques you have been reinforcing, or they won't use them in the field
Instructor debrief	Generally, at the end of the sessions. Like the student debrief, the good and bad areas for improvement are discussed and any issues that need to be tweaked. It is permissible to test your scenarios on volunteers before running them with the main group. This is a great way to share ideas and solicit feedback

The cases at the end of the chapter will give an idea of how you can maximise your training opportunities from very elaborate scenarios to very simple scenarios that require little by way of equipment.

Dynamic training scenarios with real actors and proper training equipment help to prepare officers for what they will encounter on the street. The training scenarios need to be representative of the actual situations being encountered in that locale. Training needs to be repeatable and consistent for all participants. It is also essential that the locations and actors are believable.

Simulation/Scenario Examples and Questions

These scenarios are abbreviated but give an example of what can be done easily. To be conducted in a training session, much more information would be given (safety instructions, equipment, etc.) as in the teaching plan in the previous section.

Citizens call regarding a female who appears intoxicated and is lapsing in and out of consciousness on a bench. Officers approach and interact with the female	
Goals	Verbal communications, de-escalation, pre-escalation, recognition of mental health crisis, knowledge of involuntary admission for mental evaluation, effective search
Branches	(a) Officers talk in a normal tone to female and approach – She talks to them and reveals she is despondent and suicidal over the loss of her mother. She wants to die and says she will kill herself. She has just shot up with drugs and was going to try and find more. When asked about weapons or things that could hurt her or the officers, she places the syringe on the bench (b) Officers talk aggressively – Female becomes aggressive and argumentative. Tries to walk away. Becomes increasingly uncooperative. Will not reveal syringe (c) Officers go hands on gently – Female will wake slowly and then start when she realises it's the police. See branches (a) and (b) (d) Officers go hands on roughly – Female is instantly defensive. If aggression continues will threaten with the syringe but not attack

A male is seen on a downtown corner. He is yelling at the air and swatting his arms saying "Get away! Leave me alone!"	
Goals	Verbal communication, maintain reactionary gap, de-escalation, pre-escalation, recognition of mental health crisis-psychosis, knowledge of involuntary admission for mental evaluation, effective search
Branches	(a) Officers approach, maintain reactionary gap (safe distance), engage male verbally asking what is wrong. Male keeps repeating about the giant bugs flying around him but is cooperative (b) Officers approach and are aggressive with their approach. Male escalates and yells louder, swatting the air more aggressively (c) If officers close the distance and don't leave enough room, the male will scream and swat at a bug on one of the officers. If the officers recognise the hallucinations and back off, the male will not pursue. If they don't and continue to close, he will continue to swat the officer (d) If the male goes hands on, he will resist only to continue swatting the bugs. He will not attack the officers. He will struggle but only with the goal of getting away to continue swatting the bugs

The above scenarios are simple enough to replicate and adapt. Again, we stress that the importance of the scenarios is to ensure that the officers resolve the situation with the least force necessary.

One favourite type of simulation was called the "Bag Drill". The trainee wears protective gear, training use of force equipment, and is hooded over their helmet with a bag they can't see through. The instructor wears a full contact padded suit. The safety officer stands in front of the student and instructs them to "react to your environment" when the bag is removed. The student can be moved, turned around and placed in different places. The suited instructor can engage physically, be verbal, use "lethal" weapons or do nothing and sit on the floor singing. The subject has many options within this environment and can engage from any location within the defined area. This type of scenario is very effective at making a student scan and critically assess the environment before reacting. You can easily run a single student through half a dozen simulations in a few minutes.

Culminating Scenarios

The following scenario is an example of a culminating scenario for trainees at the end of a week-long session. It brought together all the elements of the weeks training. It is a more complicated scenario, but it was tremendously worthwhile for the participants:

> Dispatch advises that smoke is pouring from an elementary school and shots are being fired.
>
> On arrival, police find fire and EMS taking cover behind vehicles which have been shot at. One firefighter has been hit and is being tended to by fire crews. Smoke is billowing from the windows of a classroom. Screams and shots can be heard inside the school.
>
> Police quickly get portable air systems (Scot Air Packs) from the fire department and move into the school in a "T" formation. They are met with a thick wall of smoke. Visibility is almost zero. A lone student runs screaming out of the smoke between the officers. They ignore her and continue moving down the hallway on hands and knees where the smoke seems a bit thinner, trying to see. Over the fire alarm, they can still hear sporadic shots and hear the screaming of children and what sounds like an angry male, screaming that he will "Kill them all!". They pass two motionless, small forms in the smoke before they pass a doorway to a classroom and suddenly can see a little better thanks to air currents. They stand up as a male adult, dressed all in camouflage and tactical gear emerges wielding an assault rifle, pointed down. The officers order him to, "Drop the gun!"
>
> The subject turns toward the officers and starts shooting at them, hitting two of them. All four officers return fire, rounds hitting the wall behind and the subject. The subject drops to his knees then collapses moaning. Two officers cover the hallways as one covers the subject and the fourth moves forward and after kicking the gun away, secures the subject with handcuffs.
>
> The officer does a quick search and goes over the radio, "Shots fired, subject in custody. He's hit multiple times. We're going to need EMS at some point we but need to secure the rest of the school and get the fire out." Another officer applies a dressing over the most serious wound while two officers scan the hallways for additional threats.
>
> There is a loud whistle followed by a shout of "Red!" The officers immediately relax and holster their weapons. The "subject" sits up.

Post-scenario

One of the officers looks somewhat shaken. "Everyone good? No injuries?" The instructor asks. Each shakes their head. The shaken officer, a 25-plus year veteran, shakes his head and mutters, "Wow! That was intense. I couldn't see a thing!"

These officers are sweaty, out of breath and bruised. Two are bearing the welts and paint left by Simunition marker bullets, a grim, but transient reminder of the hazards police can face.

The instructor leads a second group through the scenario which has a similar outcome but ends with an exchange of gunfire in a classroom where the subject is shooting at realistic cardboard target "victims".

Debrief

Both groups are simultaneously debriefed about what they did, what went right, what went wrong and how they feel they could improve. It is an iterative process of self-exploration that is guided by the instructional staff. The safety officer and the subject both offer their take on the response of the teams and solicit their feedback. Most are stunned by the complexity of the scenario which was created with the assistance of local fire who donated the air masks and live actors. One comments that they never thought they would ever use the air mask training that had been provided the year prior but were glad to have had it.

This type of scenario is a culminating event that brings together the training events of the week and features multiple facets. As we have demonstrated, scenarios don't have to be this complicated to be effective. You can do a lot very simply or you can make more complicated scenarios. It depends on your resources and your imagination. The most important point is, make an effort to be realistic and tie training to evidence creating a cohesive package.

Training and Technology

There will likely come a time when realistic virtual environments exist that are largely indistinguishable from the real world. Until then, dynamic simulation-based training is in no real danger of being replaced with video and virtual reality.

The goal of training is to impart the desired lesson on all students and to be as consistent throughout. Consistency is absolutely critical as each student, no matter the number, needs to have had a similar straining experience with as few variations from the lesson goals as possible. Deviations are quite unwelcome and could lead to dire outcomes for students, the agency or the public. It is possible to impart the knowledge on any number of students in a consistent fashion. It takes dedication, patience and an understanding of the potential consequences.

Virtual reality and video-based training have begun to make an appearance in the training arena. They do offer repeatability, accessibility and strict adherence to sets of guidelines but not without costs. Digital scenarios are not yet capable of responding outside of their parameters, engaging in conversation or understanding as humans do. Advances in technology with devices like Oculus Rift VR headsets, the "As Real As It Gets" (ARAIG) three-dimensional force feedback suits and 360-degree treadmills are making it possible to move and interact within a virtual environment, but the environments themselves and the characters within don't yet interact realistically (Laffan et al., 2020; McGregor & Bonnis, 2016). At best, these virtual training environments can supply some rudimentary branched closed dynamic simulations but play out more like a choose-your-own-adventure book than an open dynamic simulation.

Dynamic simulations remain the most realistic, cost-effective and versatile training tool for police services currently available.

Conclusion

This chapter has covered training and the use of force. The goal is to use the minimum force necessary to safely conclude the situation. Unfortunately, there will undoubtedly be situations that won't be resolved without force being applied, and, in some cases, that force may even have to be potentially lethal (as in the final example).

What has been stressed throughout and is reinforced now is that whenever possible, every effort must be made to use the least force possible before force is escalated. We need to gather as much information as time allows to make the best decision.

Every use of force incident will have an impact on a number of people: the subject receiving the force, the officer using force, the families of both the subject and the officer, the community in which the event occurs and the police service.

Following a program of training that includes legislation and legal frameworks, academic understanding of concepts and background and the application of this learning in realistic scenarios designed to consolidate the knowledge, trainees will learn to confidently apply new understandings and reduce incidence of higher levels of force.

Apply the Skill

Answer the following questions using your new knowledge of training to reduce use of force.

1. What is a closed dynamic simulation?
2. What is an open dynamic simulation?
3. How fast should closed dynamic simulations be performed?
4. Write out a detailed plan for a simple closed dynamic simulation involving a less lethal use of force tool (spray, TASER, baton etc.).
5. Write out a detailed plan for a simple closed dynamic simulation involving a non-use of force scenario (a house search, search of a person, etc.).
6. Write out a detailed plan for an open dynamic simulation.
7. What things must you consider when planning your scenarios?
8. Why is local knowledge of the community important to reduce use of force?

References

Andersen, J. P., & Gustafsberg, H. (2016). A training method to improve police use of force decision making: A randomized controlled trial. *SAGE Open, 6*(2), 2158244016638708. https://doi.org/10.1177/2158244016638708

Anderson, G. S., Di Nota, P. M., Metz, G. A. S., & Andersen, J. P. (2019). The impact of acute stress physiology on skilled motor performance: Implications for policing. *Frontiers in Psychology*, 10. https://doi.org/10.3389/fpsyg.2019.02501

Arble, E., Daugherty, A. M., & Arnetz, B. (2019). Differential effects of physiological arousal following acute stress on police officer performance in a simulated critical incident. *Frontiers in Psychology*, 10. https://doi.org/10.3389/fpsyg.2019.00759

Dekanoidze, K., & Khelashvili-Kyviv, M. (2018). *Police education and training systems in the OSCE region* (p. 164). National Police of Ukraine. https://www.osce.org/files/f/documents/f/7/423401.pdf

Finn, M. (2021, January 3). *How to reduce stress like a Navy SEAL*. Gear Patrol. http://gearpatrol.com/fitness/health-wellness/a325714/box-breathing-navy-seals/

Ford, R. (2019). *Impact of stress inoculating training on Police in aftermath of critical incidents*. 120.

Garner, J. H., Hickman, M. J., Malega, R. W., & Maxwell, C. D. (2018). Progress toward national estimates of police use of force. *PLoS One, 13*(2), e0192932. https://doi.org/10.1371/journal.pone.0192932

Garrison, A. H. (2018). Criminal culpability, civil liability, and police created danger: Why and how the fourth amendment provides very little protection from police use of deadly force. *George Mason Civil Rights Law Journal, 28*(3), 241–312.

Grossman, D. (2014). *On killing: The psychological cost of learning to kill in war and society*. Open Road Media.

Grossman, D., & Christensen, L. (2017). *On combat: The psychology and physiology of deadly conflict in war and peace*. BookBaby.

Guller, I. B. (1972). Higher education and policemen: Attitudinal differences between freshman and senior police college students. *Journal of Criminal Law, Criminology & Police Science, 63*(3), 396–401. https://doi.org/10.2307/1142063

Hourani, L. L., Kizakevich, P. N., Hubal, R., Spira, J., Strange, L. B., Holiday, D. B., Bryant, S., & McLean, A. N. (2011). Predeployment stress inoculation training for primary prevention of combat-related stress disorder. *A Training Method to Improve Police Use of Force Decision Making: A Randomized Controlled Trial, 4*(1), 101–116.

Huisjes, H., Engbers, F., & Meurs, T. (2018). Higher education for police professionals. The Dutch case. *Policing: A Journal of Policy and Practice, 14*(2), 362–373. https://doi.org/10.1093/police/pay089

Ijames, S. (2005). *Managing officer created jeopardy*. Police1. https://www.police1.com/archive/articles/managing-officer-created-jeopardy-t4w1PZChSkzfdf84/

International Mediation Institute. (2016, August 11). *Pre-dispute and pre-escalation processes to prevent disputes: A brief introduction*. International Mediation Institute. https://imimediation.org/2016/08/11/pre-dispute-and-pre-escalation-processes-to-prevent-disputes-a-brief-introduction/

Jenkins, B. (2019). *Canadian police tactical units: The normalization of police militarization or a pragmatic response to high-risk calls?* Master of Arts, Carleton University. https://doi.org/10.22215/etd/2019-13738

Klein, G. A. (2009). *Streetlights and shadows: Searching for the keys to adaptive decision making*. The MIT Press. https://mitpress.mit.edu/books/streetlights-and-shadows

Laffan, C. F., Coleshill, J. E., Stanfield, B., Stanfield, M., & Ferworn, A. (2020). Using the ARAIG haptic suit to assist in navigating firefighters out of hazardous environments. In *2020 11th IEEE annual information technology, Electronics and Mobile Communication Conference (IEMCON)* (pp. 0439–0444). https://doi.org/10.1109/IEMCON51383.2020.9284922

Lersch, K. M., & Kunzman, L. L. (2001). Misconduct allegations and higher education in a southern sheriff's department. *American Journal of Criminal Justice, 25*, 161–172. https://doi.org/10.1007/BF02886843

Luoma-aho, V., & Canel, M. J. (Eds.). (2020). *The handbook of public sector communication* (1st ed.). Wiley.

Marcinko, R. (1992). *Rogue warrior*. Pocket Books.

McGregor, C., & Bonnis, B. (2016). Big data analytics for resilience assessment and development in tactical training serious games. In *2016 IEEE 29th international symposium on computer-based medical systems (CBMS)* (pp. 158–162). https://doi.org/10.1109/CBMS.2016.64

McLaughlin, K. (2020, June 2). *One of America's most popular police trainers is teaching officers how to kill*. Insider. https://www.insider.com/bulletproof-dave-grossman-police-trainer-teaching-officers-how-to-kill-2020-6

Meichenbaum, D. (2017). *The evolution of cognitive behavior therapy: A personal and professional journey with Don Meichenbaum*. Routledge.

Muir, W. K. (1977). *Police: Streetcorner politicians*. University of Chicago Press. https://press.uchicago.edu/ucp/books/book/chicago/P/bo3645755.html

Mulyana, R. (2012, November 5). *Operational risk*. https://www.slideshare.net/abyanima/operational-risks

Nilson, C. (2018). *Community safety and well-being: Concept, practice, and alignment*, 9.

Norton, M. (1991). *Naval academy graduates get a Schwarzkopf send-off – Baltimore Sun* [News]. Baltimore Sun. https://www.baltimoresun.com/news/bs-xpm-1991-05-30-1991150152-story.html

Novaco, R. W. (1977). A stress inoculation approach to anger management in the training of law enforcement officers. *American Journal of Community Psychology, 5*(3), 327–346. https://doi.org/10.1007/BF00884700

Oxford Dictionary. (2021). De-escalation | definition of De-escalation by Oxford Dictionary on Lexico.com also meaning of De-escalation. https://www.lexico.com/definition/de-escalation

Parker, K. E., Anchor, K. N., Weitz, L. J., & Roback, H. B. (1976). Experimental application of behavior modification strategems toward changing ethnocentric attitudes. *Social Behavior and Personality: An International Journal, 4*(2), 187–192. https://doi.org/10.2224/sbp.1976.4.2.187

Pollack, H. A., & Humphreys, K. (2020). Reducing violent incidents between police officers and people with psychiatric or substance use disorders. *The Annals of the American Academy of Political and Social Science, 687*(1), 166–184. https://doi.org/10.1177/0002716219897057

Regoli, Robert M., (1976). An empirical assessment of Niederhoffer's police cynicism scale. *Journal of Criminal Justice, Elsevier, 4*(3), 231–241

Roberg, R. R. (1978). An analysis of the relationship among higher education, belief systems, and job performance of patrol officer. *Journal of Police Science and Administration, 6*(3), 336–344.

Roberg, R., & Bonn, S. (2004). Higher education and policing: where are we now? *Policing: An International Journal, 27*(4) 469–486

Robinson, L. O. (2020). Five years after Ferguson: Reflecting on police reform and what's ahead. *The Annals of the American Academy of Political and Social Science, 687*(1), 228–239. https://doi.org/10.1177/0002716219887372

Rogers, C., & Smith, B. (2018). The College of Policing: Police education and research in England and Wales. In C. Rogers & B. Frevel (Eds.), *Higher education and police: An international view* (pp. 87–106). Springer International Publishing. https://doi.org/10.1007/978-3-319-58386-0_5

Ross, D. L., & Murphy, R. L. (2017). Stress, perceptual distortions, and human performance. In *Guidelines for investigating officer-involved shootings, arrest-related deaths, and deaths in custody* (p. 322). Routledge.

Röttger, S., Theobald, D. A., Abendroth, J., & Jacobsen, T. (2020). The effectiveness of combat tactical breathing as compared with prolonged exhalation. *Applied Psychophysiology and Biofeedback*. https://doi.org/10.1007/s10484-020-09485-w

Rydberg, J., & Terrill, W. (2010). The effect of higher education on police behavior. *Police Quarterly, 13*(1), 92–120. https://doi.org/10.1177/1098611109357325

Saunders, T., Driskell, J. E., Johnston, J. H., & Salas, E. (1996). The effect of stress inoculation training on anxiety and performance. *Journal of Occupational Health Psychology, 1*(2), 17.

Sherman, L. W. (2020). Evidence-based policing and fatal police shootings: Promise, problems, and prospects. *The Annals of the American Academy of Political and Social Science, 687*(1), 8–26. https://doi.org/10.1177/0002716220902073

Shjarback, J. A., & White, M. D. (2016). Departmental professionalism and its impact on indicators of violence in police–citizen encounters. *Police Quarterly, 19*(1), 32–62. https://doi.org/10.1177/1098611115604449

Staller, M. S., Müller, M., Christiansen, P., Zaiser, B., Körner, S., & Cole, J. C. (2019). Ego depletion and the use of force: Investigating the effects of ego depletion on police officers' intention to use force. *Aggressive Behavior, 45*(2), 161–168. https://doi.org/10.1002/ab.21805

Stone, R., & Socia, K. M. (2019). Boy with toy or black male with gun: An analysis of online news articles covering the shooting of Tamir Rice. *Race and Justice, 9*(3), 330–358. https://doi.org/10.1177/2153368716689594

Tate, J., Jenkins, J., & Rich, S. (2021, September). *Fatal force: Police shootings database*. Washington Post. https://www.washingtonpost.com/graphics/investigations/police-shootings-database/

Taylor, P. L. (2020). Dispatch priming and the police decision to use deadly force. *Police Quarterly, 23*(3), 311–332. https://doi.org/10.1177/1098611119896653

Wilson, J. Q. (1978). *Varieties of police behavior* (Vol. 1). https://www.hup.harvard.edu/catalog.php?isbn=9780674932111

Wolfe, S., Rojek, J., McLean, K., & Alpert, G. (2020). Social interaction training to reduce police use of force. *The Annals of the American Academy of Political and Social Science, 687*(1), 124–145. https://doi.org/10.1177/0002716219887366

Chapter 4
Control Behaviours During Conflict Resolution Police–Citizen Encounters in South Australia and New Zealand

Ross Hendy

Introduction

This study of New Zealand and South Australian police officers informs two key areas of interest to officer practice. First, this research rekindles an approach to measure the coercive interplay between police officers and citizens during police–citizen encounters (PCE) taken by earlier social behaviourists and interactionalists (Braithwaite & Brewer, 1998; Sykes & Brent, 1983; Terrill, 2005). In measuring each chain of interactional behaviour, this research reveals—or perhaps confirms—that officers use verbal control behaviours far more frequently, and for a greater proportion of time, than physical control behaviours (i.e. physical force).

Second, such a finding informs a salient policy question of the impact of routinely arming police. While many national policing systems have progressively routinely armed their public policing agencies, a few western jurisdictions do retain routinely unarmed policing models (Hendy, 2020a). Advocates of routinely unarmed policing often propose that officers who are routinely armed with firearms behave differently from those who are not routinely armed. Often arguments predict that routinely arming police will inevitably lead to officers adopting the American 'Dirty Harry' caricature, where officers are morally content to use excessive force to achieve just ends (Klockars, 1980), whereas officers should follow the example of the virtuous unarmed British bobby PC Dixon of Dock Green whose maturity and dignity will afford a miraculous approach to disarm an armed person through gentle persuasion (Squires & Kennison, 2010). In other words, a new routinely armed policing agency will become one that relies on overpowering physical force to resolve conflict in place of gentle persuasive verbal communication. The present research provides an avenue to address this question. The careful observation and

R. Hendy (✉)
Monash University, Melbourne, Australia
e-mail: ross.hendy@monash.edu

J. F. Albrecht, G. den Heyer (eds.), *Understanding and Preventing Community Violence*, https://doi.org/10.1007/978-3-031-05075-6_4

comparison of officer behaviour from routinely armed (South Australia) and routinely unarmed (New Zealand) agencies provide an opportunity to explore how practice differs in two neighbouring policing jurisdictions. Can we observe an abundance of *Dirty Harries* in South Australia and can we discern differences in their use of control behaviours during police–citizen encounters with their *Decent Dixon* cousins from New Zealand? Such findings will be of interest to all policing scholars with an interest in police use of force and militarisation.

Control Behaviour and Coercion

It is accepted that in certain circumstances officers have the legal authority to control the physical movement of a citizen: a search, detainment or arrest (see *Policing Act 2008* [NZ]; *Search and Surveillance Act 2012* [NZ]). There is an abundance of policing literature that considers these control behaviours, such as those that explore why officers use force (e.g. Alpert & Dunham, 2004; Sykes & Brent, 1980; Worden, 1996), how officers use force (e.g. Alpert & Dunham, 2004; Alpert & MacDonald, 2001; Hickman et al., 2015; Kraska, 2001) and the role of police coercion (e.g. Muir Jr., 1977; Terrill, 2001, 2014; Terrill et al., 2003). In essence, the issues here lie at the intersection of the actions of a police officer to use 'control, coercion, or force' to achieve a policing process with those persons who decide to 'consent or dissent to' that process. In Anglo-American policing lore, this conversation is often muddied by the concept of 'policing by consent': the power of police to achieve police work through fostered cooperative relationships with the public rather than relying on the fear of consequences should they resist (Bowling et al., 2019; Keane & Bell, 2013).

Some scholars observe that the literature lacks robust theoretical explanations for police coercion and the use of force (Terrill, 2014). This is perhaps, in part, because of definitional inconsistencies with regard to coercion, force and excessive use of force (Geller & Toch, 1996; Klockars, 1996; Terrill, 2001). Predominant definitions in the policing literature consider coercion as a conflation of physical and verbal actions (Terrill, 2001). Muir (1977, p. 37) defines coercion as 'a means of controlling the conduct of others through threats to harm' and posited that police–citizen interactions are coercive relationships that comprise 'extortionate transactions'. Muir explains that extortionate transaction relies on a *victimiser* possessing extortionate power over a *victim* where the victim fears some level of injury from the victimiser and thus becomes the victimiser's hostage, and in order to prevent injury, the victimiser demands a ransom from the victim. In the case of a police–citizen encounter, the ransom is compliance. It is Muir's thesis that officers use the extortionate relationship as a principal method to control citizen behaviour.

But questions about why citizens follow, or indeed resist, police officer instructions during interactions are central to understanding police–citizen interaction. One avenue taken to explain citizen cooperation with police uses procedural justice theory (PJT). The central tenet of PJT is that the respectful and fair treatment of citizens by police officers facilitates their cooperation during and after police–citizen interactions. Such behaviour promotes a level of compliance with the law (Bottoms & Tankebe, 2012; Dai et al., 2011; Reisig et al., 2007; Sunshine & Tyler, 2003). Tyler's model of process-based regulation illustrates how 'process-based judgements' positively influence citizen-level cooperation and compliance. This, in turn, promotes positive acceptance of the legitimacy of regulatory authorities and compliance with regulation. A variant model of process-based regulation for policing incorporates public judgement of police legitimacy through the display of 'procedurally just' practices of officer decision-making and the quality of treatment of citizens by officers (Bottoms & Tankebe, 2012). Simply expressed: the quality of treatment by officers and the quality of officer decision-making during police–citizen encounters enhance citizens' obligation to obey the law and increase their trust in police officers, resulting in compliance and cooperation. Sunshine and Tyler argue that 'legitimacy is a social value that is distinct from performance evaluations' (Sunshine & Tyler, 2003, p. 534). As such, police–citizen relations can be influenced by a citizen's subjective assessment of the 'fairness' of their treatment by officers.

Hough et al. (2010) draw attention to the importance of cultural values when constructing understandings of legitimacy, noting Tyler's research that North American public perceptions of legitimacy are more aligned with fairness of the criminal justice system than its effectiveness (see Tyler & Huo, 2002). However, while Roberts' and Herrington's systematic review of procedural justice literature contends that procedural justice theory holds 'for the most part' (author's emphasis, Roberts & Herrington, 2013, p. 120) across different cultures and nations, they draw attention to several deviations. In Australia, for instance, procedural justice was found to be less effective in fostering cooperation among ethnic minorities than ethnic majority groups (Murphy & Cherney, 2012). A randomised control trial (RCT) by Mazerolle et al. (2012) of roadside alcohol breath testing in Brisbane, Australia, found that 'perceptions of procedural fairness, police respect, and trust and confidence in police, ... were all significantly higher' (Mazerolle et al., 2012, p. 17) when officers used a predefined script that incorporated legitimacy-enhancing statements. This contrasted with North American research that found that some procedural justice factors had limited impact on citizen behaviour during police–citizen encounters (Dai et al., 2011). Specifically, only the effect of officer demeanour and officer consideration of citizen voice showed an increase in citizen cooperation (for officers) and compliance. Dai et al. (2011) also found that qualities of police interpersonal treatment (care, disrespect, force) were insignificant factors in the explanation of citizen noncompliance. Perhaps most importantly, this study revealed that a citizen's 'irrationality' had a positive effect on citizen disrespect and noncompliance, which is consistent with other research on the effects of mental impairment and intoxication (e.g. see Reisig et al., 2004).

Conflict and Conflict Resolution During Police–Citizen Encounters

A difficulty of policing within democratic, pluralistic societies is the inherent risk that where there are competing groups, or indeed individuals, police action that advantages one party will disadvantage another (Herbert, 2006). Indeed, the 'taking of sides' places police in conflict with those who are alienated. This is apparent in the common law adversarial prosecutorial process: police act on the side of the victim and lead the prosecution of the suspect, but in advancing the victim's cause, police become adversaries of the suspect's cause. Deutsch's 'crude law of social relations' considers the impact of cooperative and competitive behaviour. He stipulated that 'characteristic processes and effects elicited by a given type of social relationship (cooperative or competitive) also tend to elicit that type of social relationship' (Deutsch, 1973, p. 365). In other words, cooperation among actors fosters further cooperation, whereas competition among actors breeds further competition. Deutsch explained that cooperative relationships emerge from the use of strategies of mutual problem-solving, persuasion and openness. Conversely, competitive relationships form if parties adopt strategies that involve power or use coercive tactics, threats or deception. Cooperative situations between actors arise from the *perception* that the goals of the actors are positively linked, whereas competitive situations arise when goals are incompatible and negatively linked (Braithwaite, 1998; Deutsch, 1973). In a policing context, it could be argued that officers alternate between behaving with predominantly cooperative behaviour (interacting with victims, complainants, community groups and informants) and predominantly competitive behaviour (interacting with suspects, offenders or groups who are in opposition to police goals and values). In simplistic terms, Deutsch's proposition was that cooperative actions breed cooperation and competitive actions breed competition: cooperation is to be encouraged and competition discouraged (Braithwaite, 1998). Competition leads to destructive conflict: a situation where conflict expands and escalates to the point where it becomes independent of the source of conflict. Deutsch suggests that a mutually cooperative approach is the most effective for combating and resolving conflict. But he also acknowledges the difficulty in resolving conflict in an asymmetrical relation. Deutsch also proposes that some behaviours encourage resistance or alienation: illegitimate actions, negative or inappropriate sanctions or influential behaviour that is excessive in nature.

Control Behaviour, Encounter Goals, Utterances and Strings

Sykes and Brent's (1980, 1983) applications of general systems theory to police–citizen interaction provide a framework to observe how coercive, definitional or imperative officer actions act as regulators of citizen behaviour. Their approach deconstructs interactions into utterances (a single action) and strings of utterances or behaviours. This approach aids the analysis of situational determinants of encounter processes and outcomes. For instance, strings provide an opportunity to analyse conversational transactions to investigate officer decision-making through the construction of officer–citizen interaction maps. Similar approaches have since been used to analyse police use-of-force transactions and measure the effect of one utterance on the outcome of the encounter (Braithwaite, 1998; Terrill, 2005; Terrill & Mastrofski, 2002). Utterances—and strings—have also been analysed to measure the effect of how the action of one actor affects another actor (Sykes & Brent, 1983; Terrill, 2005; Toch, 1969). Transactional frameworks have been used to explain models of interpersonal communication, but they are not limited to verbal exchanges: the 'listener's' body language is as important as the subject of the 'speaker's' verbal communication (Wood, 2010). As such, effective communication is a shared process; both the listener and speaker 'share the responsibility for effectiveness' (Wood, 2010, p. 24); or indeed as Sykes and Brent propose, 'both actors in a relationship share responsibility for how the relationship develops' (Sykes & Brent, 1983, p. 253). Toch's test of 'violent' police–citizen encounters revealed that citizens and officers were equally responsible for the tactics used by officers, since the behaviour of the citizen determined the police officer's response. Sykes and Brent, too, hypothesised that interactions between police and citizens are a 'process in which acts of each participant at each point in time are, at least in part, contingent upon past acts' (Sykes & Brent, 1983, p. 110). Sykes and Brent's typology of utterance actions includes *definitional* acts (those used by either actor to define or construct an understanding of the situation or topic of discourse), *controlling* acts (those that attempted to alter the behaviour of the other actor, such as physical actions, accusations, handcuffing or the use of weapons or making an arrest), *resistant* acts (actions used by actors when they refused to answer a definitional or controlling question) and *confirming* acts (such as acquiescence to control, following a direction (or order) or answering questions). Braithwaite (1998) used a similar approach when operationalising Deutsch's theory of conflict resolution. Utterances were coded using a model of five behavioural dimensions: *information exchange*, *legitimacy*, *power*, *coercion* and *antisocial strategies*. Braithwaite hypothesised that skilled officers would use cooperative tactics, rather than competitive tactics. This was on the basis of Deutsch's theory that cooperation breeds cooperation. However, the findings did not support the hypothesis: the officers who were identified as 'skilled' were more controlling than the control group (of 'average' officers) in using coercive and threatening behaviour. Braithwaite concluded that 'while it is *likely* that competition breeds competition, it is not *necessarily* so' (Braithwaite, 1998, p. 270).

Summary

The overlay of key theoretical concepts from procedural justice theory, Deutsch's theory of conflict resolution and Sykes' and Brent's application of general systems theory reveals the importance that communication between officers and citizens plays during police–citizen encounters. Each framework suggests that the outcome of a police–citizen encounter can be predicted by the quality of communicative exchanges between citizen and officer. The general systems theory approach provides a further framework to conceptualise how officers' use of verbal utterances and physical actions act as *control behaviours* to regulate citizen behaviour during encounters. Therefore, examining how officers use control behaviours should provide an opportunity for insight into officer practice and determine if there are observable differences in practice across police agencies.

Method

The data presented in this chapter draws on a wider study designed to compare routinely armed and routinely unarmed police officers during police–citizen encounters (see Hendy, 2018, 2020b, 2021b). New Zealand and the Australian state of South Australia were selected as research sites, since both jurisdictions employed police officers who were trained and permitted to use firearms as necessary. The South Australian officers were required to openly carry firearms at all times, whereas the New Zealand officers were routinely unarmed (i.e. they did not carry firearms on their person at all times) but had access to firearms if the circumstances permitted. While other jurisdictional combinations were possible (e.g. Northern Ireland/Republic of Ireland, Norway/Sweden, etc.), the Antipodean comparison appeared to be the most feasible for cross-national research, since both jurisdictions shared a common language, colonial histories (neither were established as a penal colony) and legal frameworks and both lacked the widespread systemic corruption endemic in other Australian police agencies (Hendy, 2021a).

Research Sites and Sampling

The research was conducted at two police stations over a period of 8 months: *South City Station* in a large metropolitan city in South Australia and *New City Station* in a large provincial city in New Zealand.[1] The study took an oversampling approach to maximise the potential number of encounters that might provoke conflict resolution behaviour from the officers. This resulted in the observation of 48 shifts at *New City Station* (42 evening shifts and 6 nightshifts) and 37 shifts at *South City Station* (33 evening shifts and 4 nightshifts) predominantly on Thursdays, Fridays and Saturdays. The time in the field amounted to 800 h. The researcher accompanied officers during a rostered shift (the time that an officer or a pair of officers were

[1] *South City Station* and *New City Station* are anonymised to maintain the confidentiality of the research participants.

rostered for duty) which was 8–12 h in duration. Officer participants were drawn from all seven general duties patrol (GDP) teams at *South City Station* and officers from the five public safety (PST) teams at *New City Station*. Despite the nomenclature, PST and GDP officers performed the same duties: they were 'patrol officers' whose primary aim was to respond to emergency calls for service and undertake proactive preventative action when required.

At the beginning of a shift, a patrol unit of two officers was invited by the researcher to join the study. If agreeable, officers were inducted into the research and briefed on the research protocols. The protocol included, among other information, that the purpose of the research was to observe how conflict was resolved by officers during police–citizen encounters. While officers had the opportunity to opt in prior to observations, citizens had the choice to opt out at the completion of an encounter.[2] The protocol sets out procedures for the researcher to observe and code in situ encounters between one officer and one citizen (O_1C_1), one officer and two citizens (O_1C_2), two officers and one citizen (O_2C_1) and two officers and two citizens (O_2C_2). Encounters with three or more citizens or three or more officers would not be coded. All incidents that the officers were dispatched to (or were self-initiated) were eligible for coding (there were no restrictions on the type of event), and encounters would only be removed from the dataset if officers opted out at the end of the shift ($n = 0$) or citizens did not opt in at the end of the encounter ($n = 2$).

Behavioural Typology

The in situ coding of police–citizen encounters used Braithwaite's (1998) operationalisation of Deutsch's 'crude law of social relations', previously used to examine conflict resolution behaviour used by police officers in South Australia (Table 4.1).

Data Collection

Participant behaviours were coded according to the modified taxonomy of Braithwaite's conflict resolution behaviours (see above) using Noldus' *Pocket Observer* v.3.2 (Noldus Information Technology, 2014b). This mobile application is designed to code behavioural interactions in the field and in situ (Noldus, 1991) and then synchronises to the desktop computer program *Observer XT* (Noldus Information Technology, 2014a) on return to the research office. *Observer XT* assembled each subject behaviour into a sequence called an event log. The event log

[2] This protocol was approved by the Cambridge University Institute of Criminology Ethics Committee. See Hendy (2018) for a detailed explanation of the opt-in/opt-out procedure.

Table 4.1 Braithwaite's taxonomy of conflict resolution behaviours modified by Hendy

Simplified	Original category	Description
Officer behaviours		
Information exchange	Informational seek	Questions that elicit information about the parties involved, events that have taken place or proposed solutions
	Information give	Information provided in response to a question
Verbal affirmation	Support statement	Statements that communicated empathy towards the citizen, positive reinforcement or compliments
	Accept statement	Statements that indicated acceptance of the citizen or agreement with the citizen
Verbal control	Control statement affect	Changing the affective state or emotional behaviour of the citizen
	Control statement conversation	Statements that directly controlled the flow of conversation
	Control statement environment	Statements that attempted to change the environmental setting of the interaction
Verbal refutation	Reject statement	Statements that the other party's position is not accepted
	Threat statement	Insulting or derogatory remarks that were more extreme than reject statements and statements threatening negative consequences or warnings about future behaviour
Physical control	Physical act	Any physical touching or handling of the citizen
Citizen behaviours		
Information exchange	Information seek	Questions that elicit information about the parties involved, events that have taken place or proposed solutions
	Information give	Information provided in response to a question
	Information refuse	Verbalised statement refusing to give information or no comment made in response to an information seek
	Information excuse[a]	Defensive statements that justified or provided excuses for citizen behaviour
Refuse verbal control	Refuse control	Actions, statements or behaviours when the citizen refuses or ignores the control statements behaviour used by officers
Verbal abuse	Verbal abuse	Verbally aggressive statements that were insulting, derogatory or undermining. Also included shouting or threatening statements
Physical abuse		Any physical action directed at or against officers
Officer and citizen behaviours		
Inactive		Present during the encounter but not exhibiting any of the above behaviours
Absent		Not present during the encounter

[a]Braithwaite named this behaviour "self-defence" but changed to differentiate from the physical action of self-defence
[b]Added by the author

contained a continuous sequence of behaviour data that included the subject identifier, the subject's behaviour and the start time of the coding entry. The subject–behaviour coding took approximately 1–5 s from the time the researcher observed the behaviour, decided on how to code the observed behaviour and selected the correct sequence of the application's subject and behaviour buttons. As the encounter had ended, a further input screen was displayed to record independent variables to the event log. Situational variables relating to the encounter and subjects were recorded on a second handheld device using the *Qualtrics Surveys* mobile application (Qualtrics Labs Inc., 2014). Variables included time, date and location details, event-type variables, occurrence variables and actions taken. *Qualtrics Surveys* functioned as a slave to the *Qualtrics Research Suite* website, transferring data directly to the Qualtrics website through the Vodafone data network.

Data Analysis

Observer XT summarised the time that each participant was coded as exhibiting a specific behaviour. This summary was used to provide two statistics. The first was the duration of each behaviour type coded during the encounter, shown as a percentage of the total behaviours used during the encounter. The second counted the occurrence of each behaviour type coded during the encounter. For the purposes of the analysis here, the duration of behaviours expressed as a percentage of overall behaviour type and the average frequency of occurrence of the behaviour type are compared between the research sites (i.e. *New City Station* and *South City Station*). The duration percentages are shown as a 'group' score. For encounters with two officers and one citizen (O_2C_1), each participant's behaviour percentage was divided by three. This allows for the three participants' behaviours to be expressed as a percentage, the sums of which would total 100 (the first column of Table 4.6). In the case of encounters with two officers and two citizens (O_2C_2), each participant's behaviour percentage was divided by four. (However, officer behaviours in Table 4.8 show a combined 'patrol behaviours' and 'citizen behaviours'.) The statistic in the second column of Tables 4.6 and 4.7 shows the average frequency of occurrence of participants' behavioural tactic per encounter. The average frequency is calculated by taking a count of each occurrence of a participant's behaviour from the event log and then dividing it by the total number of encounters in the dataset. These two statistics provide an opportunity to infer an understanding of participant behaviour during encounters.

Interactions Between Police and Citizens

The Dataset

The study comprised 278 encounters ($n_{NZ} = 136$, $n_{SA} = 142$), which included 'investigative' encounters (with people categorised as victims, witnesses, associates, bystanders and suspects) and 'enforcement' encounters (which included field arrests, field actions and field warnings). Categories were assigned at the end of the encounter according to officers' final classification. If the citizen played several roles during the encounter (e.g. a suspect, then arrestee), the encounter was coded according to the citizen's final role.[3] Encounters were almost equally distributed between enforcement encounters (n = 133, 48%) and investigative encounters (n = 142, 52%). The most frequent encounters were suspect encounters (n = 84: $n_{NZ} = 30$; $n_{SA} = 54$), followed by field arrest encounters (n = 56: $n_{NZ} = 34$; $n_{SA} = 22$) and victim encounters (n = 46: $n_{NZ} = 41$; $n_{SA} = 5$). Encounters at *New City* were longer in duration (M_{NZ} = 18:27; SD_{NZ} = 17:07; Mdn_{NZ} = 15:35) than those from *South City* (M_{SA} = 8:21; SD_{SA} = 8:17; Mdn_{SA} = 5:23). Arrest encounters were the longest (M_{NZ} = 25:05; M_{SA} = 15:56) followed by suspect encounters (M_{NZ} = 15:17; M_{SA} = 8:14). When compared with encounters involving a field warning (M_{NZ} = 13:08; M_{SA} = 6:11), encounters involving a field action were shorter at *New City* (*NC*) (M_{NZ} = 10:57) but longer at *South City* (*SC*) (M_{SA} = 6:55) (Table 4.2).

Encounter Initiation

There was a difference in the method of initiation between the two sites. Encounters at *NC* were most frequently initiated by citizen calls for service ($n_{NZ} = 98$), whereas encounters at *SC* were most frequently initiated by officer interventions ($n_{SA} = 94$). The frequencies of the second most common method of initiation were in reverse order: officer-led interventions at *NC* ($n_{NZ} = 21$) and citizen-led calls for service ($n_{SA} = 10$) at *SC*. On-scene citizen requests for service were prominent at *SC* ($n_{SA} = 17$) but not at *NC* ($n_{NZ} = 3$). Supervisor-directed encounters were prominent at *NC* ($n_{NZ} = 10$) but not so prominent at the *SC* site ($n_{SA} = 4$) (Table 4.3).

[3] The category of 'field arrest' was used when an officer believed there was sufficient evidence that a citizen was guilty of an offence and taken into custody. A 'field action' was used to when an officer had determined some degree of culpability or criminal liability on the citizen's part but the citizen was not taken into custody (such as when a citizen was removed from a place, prevented from re-entering a place or prevented from having contact with a person). A 'field warning' was used when an officer had determined a degree of guilt but chose to warn instead of arrest or other sanction.

Table 4.2 Frequency and duration of encounters

	New City, New Zealand					South City, South Australia				
	n	Mean duration (m:s)	*SD*	Median	Duration range (h:m:s)	*n*	Mean duration (m:s)	*SD*	Median	Duration range (h:m:s)
Investigative										
Victim	41	19:50	23:28	17:42	0:50–2:24:22	5	12:33	13:02	07:19	1:50–33:08
Witness	6	10:29	12:12	5:34	1:06–33:14	0				
Associate	3	9:23	3:42	9:14	5:46–13:10	1	5:57	–	–	–
Bystander	0					2	4:23	1:33	4:23	3:17–5:29
Suspect	30	15:17	10:27	13:46	0:52–38:44	54	8:14	9:29	4:14	0:24–48:45
Enforcement										
Field Arrest	34	25:05	16:31	22:21	8:21–1:38:34	22	12:56	9:40	10:47	3:16–34:26
Field Action	6	10:57	7:29	11:15	2:12–23:34	32	6:55	5:41	4:48	2:03–29:20
Field Warning	14	13:08	8:32	11:59	0:37–30:16	25	6:11	4:25	4:33	0:37–17:06
Other	2	22:30	10:36	22:30	15:00–30:00	1	2:29	–	–	–
Total	136	18:27	17:07	15:35	0:37–2:24:22	142	8:21	8:17	5:23	0:24–48:45

Table 4.3 Encounter initiation sources

	New City		South City	
	n	%	*n*	%
Dispatched (call for service)	98	72.1	22	15.5
Officer initiated	21	15.4	94	66.2
Supervisor directed	10	7.4	4	2.8
Request by another officer	4	2.9	3	2.1
On-scene citizens	3	2.2	17	12.0
Other	–	–	2	1.4
Totals	136	100	142	100

Encounter Event Types

Encounters originated because of different problems or purposes. The range of event types is shown in the Appendix. The table shows the frequency and event type of the encounters when they were categorised and dispatched to a patrol, assessed by the officers on arrival or when they commence an encounter, and then the category at the end of the encounter. Analysis of the event types reveals several differences between the two research sites. The first relates to the proportionality of non-dispatched encounters: at *NC*, 19% (n_{NZ} = 26) of encounters were not dispatched from calls for service, whereas at *SC*, 78% (n_{SA} = 111) of encounters were not dispatched. Consequently, the difference in the frequency of event type change between the research sites reflects the high incidence of non-dispatched events at *SC*. At *NC* the final event type differed from dispatch for 44% (n_{NZ} = 60) of encounters compared to 89% (n_{SA} = 126) at *SC*. Second, there is a difference in the most frequent event types at each research site. At *NC*, the three most frequent event types were domestic violence (13%), minor assault (13%) and investigative enquiries (7%). At *SC* the most frequent event types were disorder (21%), liquor offences (including breaching alcohol control regulations) (11%) and traffic offences (including both vehicle and pedestrian) (11%). Conclusions drawn from the comparisons should be treated with caution as the distribution of event types differed for each research site. The most frequent encounters were those comprising two officers and one citizen (O_2C_1) (n = 195: n_{NZ} = 83; n_{SA} = 112) and those of two officers with two citizens (O_2C_2) (n = 69: n_{NZ} = 47; n_{SA} = 22). Together these cases accounted for 95% of the dataset. The remaining permutations have been removed from the analysis due to their low count.

Officer Participants

The demographical characteristics of *NC* and *SC* officer participants were similar. The majority of officer participants were at the rank of constable and ranged in age from 21 to 59. There was a slightly higher proportion of female officers at *NC* (*NC* = 24.4%; *SC* = 19.6%) and of White/European officers at *SC* (*NC* = 91.1%; *SC* = 95.7%). The Mann–Whitney *U*-test found that the age range of officers was not significantly different in the two samples: U (n_1 = 45, n_2 = 46) = 13,065, two-tailed p = 0.079. On average, *SC* officers were involved in more encounters (M = 6.04, SE = 0.668) than in *NC* (M = 5.73, SE = 0.623). This difference, −0.310, was not significant $t(89) = -0.339$, $p = 0.994$, and the effect size was small, $r = 0.036$ (Table 4.4).

Citizen-Participants

There were variations in citizen demographics between the two research sites (Table 4.5). The *SC* sample comprised a higher cohort of suspects (37.1%) and enforcementees (49.6%) than the *NC* sample (17.5% and 33.9%, respectively). The *NC* sample had a higher proportion of victims (36.6%) and witnesses (6.6%) than the *SC* sample (5.7% and 0%, respectively). These citizen roles were attributed based on the final disposition made by officers. The proportion of citizen-participants' sexes was more balanced at *NC* (male = 52.5%, female = 47.5%), whereas at *SC*, there was a higher proportion of males (male = 81.1%, female = 18.9%). The apparent ethnicity of the citizens was predominately White/

Table 4.4 Basic demographic information of officers ($N_{NZ} = 44$, $N_{SA} = 40$)

		New City		South City	
		N	%	N	%
Officer rank	Constable[a]	44	97.8	40	87.0
	Sergeant	1	2.2	5	10.9
	Senior sergeant	0	0	0	0
	Inspector	0	0	1	2.2
Sex	Male	34	75.6	37	80.4
	Female	11	24.4	9	19.6
Ethnicity	White	41	91.1	44	95.7
	Māori	4	8.9	0	0
	Asian/Indian	0	0	1	2.2
	Other	0	0	1	2.2
	Aboriginal	0	0	0	0
Age range	21–29	11	24.4	5	10.9
	30–44	30	66.7	34	73.9
	45+	4	8.9	7	15.2

[a]The South Australian constable ranks have been grouped together

Table 4.5 Basic demographic information of officers ($N_{NZ} = 44$, $N_{SA} = 40$)

		New city			South city		
		N	Sample percentage	Census percentage	*N*	Sample percentage	Census percentage
Sex	Male	96	52.5		142	81.1	
	Female	87	47.5		33	18.9	
Ethnicity	Caucasian (White/ European)	148	80.9	83.2	129	73.7	83.8
	Māori	27	14.8	7.0	0	0	0.1
	Asian/Indian	5	2.7	2.7	6	3.4	8.1
	Pasifika	3	1.6	1.6	0	0	0.1
	Other	0	0	0	15	8.6	1.1
	Aboriginal	0	0	0	25	14.3	0.1
Age range	12–16	10	5.5		7	4.0	
	17–20	13	7.1		25	14.3	
	21–29	58	31.7		69	39.4	
	30–44	28	15.3		31	17.7	
	45–59	65	35.5		43	24.6	
	60+	9	4.9		0	0	

European at each site. Ethnicity at *NC* was Caucasian (80.9%), Māori (14.8%), Asian/Indian (2.7%) and Pasifika (1.6%), whereas the ethnicity at *SC* was Caucasian (73.7%), Aboriginal (14.3%), Middle Eastern (8.6%) and Asian/Indian (3.4%). The citizens' age range was 12–60 years or more. The Mann–Whitney *U*-test found that the age range of citizens in the *NC* sample was significantly older than the *SC* sample, U ($n_1 = 183$, $n_2 = 175$) = 13,065, two-tailed $p = 0.002$.

Encounters with Two Officers and One Citizen (O_2C_1)

O_2C_1 encounters comprised 83% of the dataset (n = 195) and were almost equally split between *NC* (n_{NZ} = 83) and *SC* (n_{SA} = 112). However, there were significant differences between the sites. The first related to the count of citizen-initiated events (including those dispatched as a result of a call for service) and officer-initiated events: more than three-quarters of events at *NC* were citizen-initiated (77.1%) compared with one quarter at *SC* (25.6%). It is likely that the disparity was a result of the mode of officer patrol. For *NC*, the most frequent event types were minor assault (12%, n_{NZ} = 10), domestic violence (12%, n_{NZ} = 10) and routine investigative enquiries (7%, n_{NZ} = 8.4), whereas at *SC*, the most frequent events were street offences including disorder (23.2%, n_{SA} = 26), pedestrian and traffic offences (12.5%, n_{SA} = 14) and liquor offences (10.7%, n_{SA} = 12%).

O_2C_1 behaviours observed during encounters are shown in Table 4.6. Analysis of duration and frequency is separated according to research site. The first analysis

Table 4.6 Behaviours during O_2C_1 encounters

Research site	*NC* (n = 83)		*SC* (n = 112)		*NC* (n = 83)		*SC* (n = 112)	
Mean dur. (mm:ss)	16:52		8:28					
Participants	O_2	C_1	O_2	C_1	O_2	C_1	O_2	C_1
Analysis	Duration of behaviours for participants expressed as a percentage of overall behaviour				Average frequency of behaviour occurrence per PCE			
Behaviours ↓	(67%)	(33%)	(67%)	(33%)				
Information exc.	30.63	27.07	26.88	25.81	8.65	6.53	7.29	6.59
Verbal affirmation	1.77	–	2.48	–	1.46	–	1.41	–
Verbal control	3.55	–	10.98	–	2.48	–	4.39	–
Verbal refutation	0.08	–	0.18	–	0.12	–	0.12	–
Physical control	1.11	–	3.53	–	0.49	–	0.99	–
Refuse verb. control	–	0.53	–	1.98	–	0.45	–	1.04
Refuse phys. control	–	0.16	–	0.26	–	0.07	–	0.08
Verbal abuse	–	0.48	–	1.35	–	0.37	–	0.72
Inactive	15.96	4.02	11.97	3.17	3.14	0.94	2.34	0.63
Absent	12.86	0.21	8.58	0.09	1.23	0.08	0.65	3.00

column shows the behaviour duration percentages in *NC* for each party across both sites. The second analysis column shows the average frequency of behaviour per encounter. The behavioural rows show the percentage and average frequency of each behaviour. The analysis table also shows the mean of encounter durations for each site. Within each site column, statistics for the two participant sets are shown: the first is that of the *patrol* behaviour (abbreviated as O_2) with the *citizen* scores adjacent (abbreviated as C_1). Encounters at *NC* were longer in overall duration than those at SC (M_{NZ} = 16:14, M_{SA} = 12:40); the difference was statistically significant $t(193) = 4.34$, $p = 0.000$, and it did represent a medium-sized effect, $d = 0.60$. The most frequent behaviour and that which amounts to the highest duration was *information exchange* for both encounter participants at both research sites. The next most frequent officer behaviours were coded as *inactive* and *verbal control* for officers.

Encounters with Two Officers and Two Citizens (O_2C_2)

O_2C_2 encounters were more frequent at *NC* than *SC* ($n_{NZ} = 47$; $n_{SA} = 22$) and accounted for 25% of the dataset ($n = 69$). The mode of encounter initiation differed significantly between the two sites. At *NC*, 85% of encounters were dispatched ($n_{NZ} = 40$), whereas at *SC*, 91% of encounters were officer-initiated or citizen street calls for service ($n_{SA} = 20$). The most frequent *NC* O_2C_2 event type was domestic violence at 17% ($n_{NZ} = 8$) followed by minor assault at 15% ($n_{NZ} = 7$), intimidation at 6% ($n_{NZ} = 3$) and civil dispute at 6% ($n_{NZ} = 3$). In contrast, the most frequent *SC* O_2C_2 event types were disorder at 14% ($n_{SA} = 3$) and theft at 14% ($n_{SA} = 3$), followed by suspicious behaviour at 9% ($n_{SA} = 2$) and liquor-related offences at 9% ($n_{SA} = 2$). The mean duration at *NC* was 21:38, whereas for *SC*, it was 7:18. The difference was statistically significant $t(67) = 4.03$, $p < 0.001$, $d = 0.44$ (Table 4.7).

A Comparison of 'Exchange' and 'Control' at South City *and* New City

Comparison between the research sites of the behaviours reveals variation in officer practice and citizen response in the dataset. The most prominent differences appear in the frequency and duration of *verbal control* and *physical control* used by officers during encounters. V*erbal control* behaviours at *SC* were almost twice as frequent (*NC* = 2.48; *SC* = 4.39) but three times as long as at *NC* (*NC* = 3.55%; *SC* = 10.98%). Similarly, *physical control* behaviours at *SC* were twice as frequent (*NC* = 0.49; *SC* = 0.99) but three times as long (*NC* = 1.11%; *SC* = 3.53%) as at *NC*. Variation in citizen behaviour between the sites can be seen in the average frequency and proportional duration of *refuse verbal control* and *verbal abuse*. In both cases, the average frequency in SC was twice that in NC.

Table 4.7 Behaviours during O_2C_2 encounters

Research site	*NC* (*n* = 47)		*SC* (*n* = 22)		*NC* (*n* = 47)		*SC* (*n* = 22)	
Mean dur. (mm:ss)	21:38		07:18					
Participants	O_2	C_2	O_2	C_2	O_2	C_2	O_2	C_2
Analysis	Duration of behaviours for participants expressed as a percentage of overall behaviour				Average frequency of behaviour occurrence per PCE			
Behaviours ↓	(50%)	(50%)	(50%)	(50%)				
Information exc.	25.55	28.22	20.50	27.03	12.62	12.51	6.59	8.09
Verbal affirmation	1.68	–	2.93	–	2.30	–	1.14	–
Verbal control	2.73	–	7.31	–	3.51	–	3.59	–
Verbal refutation	0.05	–	0.04	–	0.15	–	0.05	–
Physical control	0.40	–	3.87	–	0.47	–	0.68	–
Refuse verb. Control	–	0.61	–	4.16	–	0.79	–	1.41
Refuse phys. Control	–	0.00	–	0.00	–	0.09	–	0.14
Verbal abuse	–	1.03	–	1.68	–	0.85	–	1.00
Inactive	10.75	7.31	6.26	6.13	4.49	2.51	1.77	2.00
Absent	8.49	9.73	6.87	4.60	1.40	1.85	0.95	0.45

O_2C_2 encounters shared similar behavioural characteristics with O_2C_1 encounters. *Information exchange* was the most frequent behaviour for officers and citizens. But in the case of patrol behaviours, the frequency of *information exchange* at *SC* was approximately half the rate of *NC*. The disproportionality was less extreme when comparing the total proportion of time during the encounter; patrol *information exchange* made up a quarter of all encounter durations at *NC*, whereas it comprised a fifth of all encounter durations at *SC* (*NC* = 25.6%; *SC* = 20.5%). The frequency disproportionality may be a result of the difference in the mean duration of encounters: shorter encounters provided fewer opportunities for participants to change from one behavioural state to another. The second similarity with O_2C_1 encounters relates to the difference in the use of controlling behaviour. Like in the O_2C_1 encounters, *SC* patrols used *verbal control* more frequently and for proportionately longer during O_2C_2 encounters shown in the dataset. While the variance of frequency in O_2C_2 encounters is minimal (*NC* = 3.51; *SC* = 3.59), the difference in proportional duration is significant (*NC* = 2.73%; *SC* = 7.31%). Likewise, *SC* patrols used *physical control* more frequently and for proportionally longer than *NC* patrols in their respective encounters.

Further analysis reveals differences between the two research sites where behaviour *was* or *was not* observed. In Table 4.8, occurrence frequency of all control and

Table 4.8 Occurrence of control behaviours during encounters expressed as a frequency and percentage

			NC		*SC*	
Group	Behaviour	Type	n	%	n	%
O_2C_1	Verbal	Verbal control (officer to citizen)	61	73.5	93	83.0
		Refuse verbal control (citizen)	20	24.1	51	45.5
		Verbal abuse (citizen to officer)	14	16.9	35	31.3
	Physical	Physical control (officer to citizen)	14	16.9	40	35.7
		Refuse physical control (citizen)	2	2.4	7	6.3
O_2C_2	Verbal	Verbal control (officer to citizen)	34	72.3	19	86.4
		Refuse verbal control (citizen)	23	48.9	11	50.0
		Verbal abuse (citizen to officer)	12	25.5	8	36.4
	Physical	Physical control (officer to citizen)	5	10.6	5	22.7
		Refuse physical control (citizen)	2	4.3	2	9.1

all resistance behaviours during encounters is summarised, showing the count of encounters where at least one instance of a control behaviour (verbal or physical), refuse control behaviour or verbal abuse has been coded. This analysis shows the incidence of control and resistance behaviours across the O_2C_1 encounters (as a count and as a percentage). It is apparent that the occurrence of control behaviour was more frequent at *SC* than *NC*, but this may be due to the different distribution of event types. *Verbal control* was used during 83% of encounters at *SC* ($n_{SA} = 93$) and 74% at *NC* ($n_{NZ} = 61$). This was not the case for citizen behaviour: *refuse verbal control* and *refuse physical control* occurred at almost twice as many encounters at *SC* than at *NC*. *Refuse verbal control* occurred during 46% of encounters at *SC* ($n_{SA} = 51$) and 24% at *NC* ($n_{NZ} = 20$). Similarly, *verbal abuse* by citizens towards officers occurred during 31% of encounters at *SC* ($n_{SA} = 35$) and 17% at *NC* ($n_{NZ} = 14$). The occurrence of *refuse physical control* was relatively infrequent: 6% of encounters at *SC* ($n_{SA} = 7$) and 2% at *NC* ($n_{NZ} = 2$). Analysis of the occurrence of control behaviours during the O_2C_2 encounters shows similarities with O_2C_1 encounters. There is a high incidence of the occurrence of *verbal control* used by officers: 86% of encounters at *SC* ($n_{SA} = 19$) and 73% at *NC* ($n_{NZ} = 34$) compared with 83% and 74%, respectively. Similarly, the occurrence of *physical control* during encounters was twice as frequent at *SC* than at *NC*: 23% of encounters at *SC* ($n_{SA} = 5$) and 11% at *NC* ($n_{NZ} = 5$) compared with 36% and 17%, respectively. However, in the case of O_2C_2, the occurrences of physical control were about two-thirds that of O_2C_1 encounters.

There were differences in citizen behaviour between O_2C_1 and O_2C_2 encounters. In the case of O_2C_2 encounters, there was a higher rate of occurrence of *refuse verbal control*: 50% of encounters at *SC* ($n_{SA} = 11$) and 49% at *NC* ($n_{NZ} = 23$) compared with 46% and 24% of O_2C_1 encounters. There were also more O_2C_2 encounters with *verbal abuse*: 36% at *SC* ($n_{SA} = 8$) and 26% at *NC* ($n_{NZ} = 12$) compared with 31% and 17%, respectively, of O_2C_1 encounters.

Cross-National Comparison

The analysis of the usage of active conflict resolution behaviours of *NC* officers revealed that *information exchange* comprised 83% of the total duration of patrol behaviour during O_2C_1 encounters and 81% of O_2C_2 encounters. The same analysis of the active behaviours of *SC* officers shows that *information exchange* comprised 61% of the total duration of patrol behaviour during O_2C_1 encounters and 59% of O_2C_2 encounters. Proportionally, *SC* officers spent less time using *information exchange* during the encounters than *NC* officers. *SC* officer use of *verbal control* amounted to 24.9% in total duration for O_2C_1 encounters and 21.1% for O_2C_2 encounters. *Physical control* behaviour occurred in 8.0% of the total duration for O_2C_1 encounters and 11.1% for O_2C_2 encounters. While it can be concluded that *SC* officers in the research spent less time during conflict-prone encounters using *information exchange* (59–61%) between officers and citizens than *NC* officers (81–83%) and used more *verbal control* (21–25%) than *NC* officers (8.8–9.3%) and more *physical control* (8–11%) than *NC* officers (1.3–3%), the generalisability of these findings is limited due to the potential for bias associated with limitations inherent in research access.

Control Behaviours

Analysis of frequency data revealed variations in the use of conflict resolution behaviours by officers from *SC* and *NC*. These differences are summarised in Table 4.9. As with the caveat above, the reported ratios are of the average frequency per encounter of *information exchange* to *verbal control* and the average frequency per encounter of *information exchange* to *physical control*. Except for *NC* victim encounters, the ratios of both control behaviours (*information exchange* to *verbal control* and *information exchange* to *physical control*) were higher at *SC* than at *NC*. This pattern was consistent for both O_2C_1 and O_2C_2 encounters. These differences illustrate that while *information exchange* was the predominant behaviour used during encounters, officers from *SC* used controlling behaviour more frequently than those from *NC*.

Table 4.9 Ratio of the frequency of information exchange to verbal control and physical control

		NC		*SC*	
		Ratio	*n*	Ratio	*n*
Information exchange – Verbal control ratio	All O_2C_1 encounters	1:0.29	83	1:0.60	112
	All O_2C_2 encounters	1:0.27	47	1:0.54	22
Information exchange – Physical control ratio	All O_2C_1 encounters	1:0.06	83	1:0.14	112
	All O_2C_2 encounters	1:0.04	47	1:0.09	22

Discussion

The merit of measuring *all* communicative behaviour to provide a descriptive analysis of conflict resolution behaviour is evident in this study's findings. The predominant method of interaction between officer and citizen was the conversational-style information exchange. This was the case for both O_2C_1 and O_2C_2 encounters in the dataset. The use of *verbal control* by officers was frequent (>1 average frequency per encounter), and the use of *physical control* was infrequent (<1 average frequency per encounter). There was variation between the research sites in the use of *verbal control*. When examining O_2C_1 encounters, the average frequency of verbal control per encounter at *SC* was twice that (4.39) at *NC* (2.48). The duration as a percentage of overall behaviour was also different: 10.98% at *SC* compared with 3.55% at *NC*. This pattern was similar regarding physical control: the average frequency per encounter at *SC* was 0.99 compared with 0.49 at *NC*. The duration as a percentage of overall behaviour was 3.53% at *SC* compared with 1.11% at *NC*. This pattern was less apparent during O_2C_2 encounters. While the average frequencies of verbal control and physical control per encounter were similar between the sites, the duration as a percentage of overall behaviour differed. Verbal control amounted to 7.31% at *SC* compared with 2.73% at *NC*, with physical control amounting to 3.87% at *SC* compared with 0.40% at *NC*.

Differences Between the Two Research Sites

Several methodological explanations may account for the differences in use of control behaviours between the research sites. This could have been a result of the variance of encounter duration. Encounters in *SC* had statistically significant differences in mean duration. This may be because of the high incidence of non-dispatched encounters in *SC*. For an officer to initiate an encounter, they have identified suffi cient cause to affect an intervention such as an enforcement action. This contrasted with encounters originating from a citizen call for service; as in these cases, officers had to collect sufficient information to form a suspicion (i.e. investigate). Second, the mode of travel and geographical spread is likely to have influenced the distribution of encounter event types for each site. Officers in *NC* mostly used vehicular transport and therefore had a greater ability to travel outside the central business district. In contrast, officers from *SC* conducted foot patrols and were therefore limited to dealing with street offences.

One explanation for the variance in the frequency and duration of conflict resolution behaviours might be a result of legislative differences between the jurisdictions. In South Australia, police have a general power under the *Summary Offences Act 1953* [SA] S.74A to require a person to provide their name, date of birth, residential address, business address and location of any place that person works[4] where an officer has:

> reasonable cause to suspect—(a) that a person has committed, is committing or is about to commit, an offence; or (b) that a person may be able to assist in the investigation of an offence or a suspected offence. (Parliament of South Australia 1953, p. 8)

Consequently, many encounters at *SC* began with the officer asking for identification of the citizen, such as asking the question 'Do you have something with your name on it?' This style of communication was coded as *control statement conversation* or *control statement affect* (later conflated in the present analysis as *verbal control*) as it caused the citizen to present their identification or provide their personal details. In New Zealand, there is no such general power; the power to demand identification of citizens is limited to specific statutes (e.g. *Land Transport Act 1998* [NZ] or the *Sale and Supply of Alcohol Act 2012* [NZ]) and only of those who are suspected of committing offences. Similarly, there is no general power for those who are suspected of committing criminal acts (codified under the *Crimes Act 1961* [NZ]) or witnesses to any offence. Consequently, officers at *NC* gleaned details of witnesses or victims in a less controlling or direct manner to *SC* officers; posing questions such as 'What is your name?' without 'demanding' or 'requiring' the presentation of an item of official identification, the style of questioning at *NC* was more *definitional* regulation than *imperative* regulation (Sykes & Brent, 1980, pp. 184–185) and thus coded as information exchange. One hypothesis here is that *SC* officers were more attuned to 'demanding' citizen identification than *NC* officers. Unlike the officers at *SC*, *NC* officers did not tend to begin encounters with questions that related to identity; they tended first to advise citizens of the reason they were present and why they had been called. An alternative explanation for this variation might originate from the higher proportion of dispatched events (81%) attended by *NC* officers compared to that of *SC* officers (22%); knowledge of a citizen's name may have been given to officers prior to commencement of the encounter resulting in lesser necessity for *NC* officers to ask for identification at the beginning of encounters. Nonetheless, should the former hypothesis be correct, then this cross-national observation provides new insight into existing policing theory. Skolnick's theory of the police officer's working personality (2011) draws on how the social and occupational environment affects the officer personalities and how they behave in the occupational setting. Skolnick's chief influencers on personality are danger and authority, which are fuelled by police culture, social isolation and solidarity. However, the present research suggests that legal capacity may influence officer behaviour: the restriction or freedom to use legal powers to execute police processes affects how officers collect information and consequently interact with citizens.

Officers from *SC* made use of two other legal powers that were unavailable to those from *NC*. South Australia law allowed officers to conduct searches for

---

[4] The location of any place a person works is subject to suspicion of sexual offences relating to children (S.74A(4)(f)).

weapons in or near licensed premises (*Summary Offences Act 1953* [SA] S.72A, S.72B) and to use drug detector dogs in public places (*Controlled Substances Act 1984* [SA]). This legislation provides police with the power to conduct random searches of citizens in public places and venues. The 'stop and search' for weapons allowed officers to detain citizens at random to conduct a search for weapons using an electronic detector wand. Drug detector dogs were deployed in public areas, and an illicit drug 'stop and search' would commence if the detector dog gave a positive indication. Stop and search powers available to *NC* officers required a higher burden of suspicion. Searches for firearms or weapons required officers to suspect that the person was in possession of a weapon, whereas officers had to believe that a person was in possession of illicit drugs before a search (*Search and Surveillance Act 2012* [NZ]). Consequently, stop and searches for drugs and weapons at *NC* relied on some level of evidence, unlike the random searches at *SC*, and were thus less frequent.

Black (2010) suggests that 'law' is quantifiable. Legislatively, the thresholds to conduct drugs or weapons stop and searches were lower at *SC* than *NC* (due to the ability to conduct random searches), which appears to be associated with the frequency of stop and search encounters: it was 'easier' for an officer to conduct a search at *SC* than at *NC*. The application of Black's reasoning to the present research suggests that the quantity of law was greater at *SC* than at *NC*. Black proposes that 'law varies inversely with other social control' (Black, 2010, p. 6) and predicts that societies with higher levels of law have lower levels of other social controls. If one accepted that *SC* had a higher level of law than at *NC*, then the present cross-national research provided an opportunity to observe the influence of high law on officer behaviour. Thus, the present research might lead to a second hypothesis that a higher level of law is positively associated with higher levels of officer control behaviour.

A key difference between the two research sites related to the mode of patrol deployment. *SC* officers predominantly travelled to incidents within their patrol zone on foot as beat patrols, whereas *NC* officers were predominantly vehicle-based. This was a limiting factor for *SC* officers, as they were only able to attend events within 10–15 mins' walking distance from *SC* station. Similarly, the location of *SC* station—within the shopping and entertainment precinct—influenced the type of events available to contribute to the dataset. These were mostly disorder, alcohol offences and traffic offences, which mostly began at an outside location. Almost all *SC* encounters occurred at a public place (outside = 85.2%; inside = 13.4%) with only a small number of encounters occurring in private premises (outside = 0%; inside 1.4%). In contrast, *NC* officers had a wider geographic reach; they were not limited to events within walking vicinity of their patrol station, thereby being exposed to a greater frequency of domestic violence events, minor assaults and investigative enquiries. Another compelling disparity between the two sites relates to the quantity of officer-initiated encounters. At *SC*, 66.2% of encounters were officer-initiated, whereas only 15.4% of *NC* encounters were officer-initiated. The *SC* encounters related to liquor offences, disorder, traffic offences and suspicious behaviour events which were relatively minor and did not rely on a witness or victim to make a complaint. Terrill's (2001) analysis of encounters with suspects found that officers who were involved in self-initiated encounters were more likely to use verbal control than physical control. Physical control was more likely when officers responded to citizen-initiated encounters, since officers had anticipated the need to use physical control, according to the information available at the time, before the commencement of the encounter.

In all instances, the mean duration of encounters was shorter at *SC* than *NC*. At *NC*, arrestees were transported to custody by the arresting officers in a sedan patrol vehicle (where officers and citizens were able to freely continue to communicate), whereas at *SC*, arrestees were transported to custody in a secure 'cage' vehicle, unable to be in contact with the arresting officers. Consequently, coding of *SC* arrest encounters concluded when the citizen was secured in the cage vehicle, whereas coding for *NC* arrest encounters ended once the citizen arrived at the police custody centre. The same pattern, while not as extreme, was found in mean durations of the encounter types. Officers observed these offences in situ, and they were able to proceed without an investigation. It is probable that the difference in mean durations correlates with the high proportion of officer-initiated encounters at *SC*. As officers did not have to collect information to 'establish the facts' of an incident they witnessed, officers devoted less time (or in some cases no time) to the investigative phase and moved directly to the treatment phase.

The observation of the aforementioned situational and environmental differences points to the challenges with cross-jurisdictional (and indeed cross-national) research. Legislative, operational and environmental differences among the research sites reveal the challenges of staging comparative naturalistic enquiry on the most similar systems research design approach (Lamont & Boduszyński, 2020). As outlined, engaging with a research question relating to the armament of police officers necessitated a cross-national comparison. Indeed, the unsuccessful trial of routinely armed patrols by New Zealand police is testament to the political and operational challenges associated with the perceived increase in police militarisation (Hendy, 2021a; New Zealand Police, 2019). Nevertheless, such issues signal the complexities of how lay opinions are formed.

Reliability of Findings

Some citizen variables were different between the research sites, as was the distribution of encounter event types. As such, these analyses must be treated with some caution. Differences in the demographic variables between the two samples of citizen-participants may have affected the data collected during the present research. Terrill and Mastrofski's (2002) analysis of PCEs found that males, non-White people, poor and young suspects were treated more harshly by officers than suspects from other groups. Another study found a positive relationship between alcohol impairment and the use of force: Kaminski et al. (2004) found that perceived levels (by officers) of suspect judgement impairment increased the odds of the use of harsher levels of force. Their findings are consistent with the increased use of controlling behaviour in the present study. The *SC* citizen sample comprised a higher proportion of males (81.1%) than the sample at *NC* (52.5%). Likewise, the age range of citizens was statistically significantly different, with citizens at *SC* younger than at *NC*. There was also a higher proportion of citizens displaying signs of impairment due to alcohol intoxication at *SC* (67.5%) than at *NC* (30.6%). Officers at *SC* were interacting with more males, who were younger in age, and more frequently intoxicated, than the officers at *NC*. Sex, age and levels of impairment are relevant to the police use of force discussed in the literature.

Conclusion

During conflict-prone encounters observed in this research, *SC* officers spent less time engaging in *information exchange* with citizens than *NC* officers did and used more *verbal control* than *NC* officers and more *physical control* than *NC* officers. The present research could not attribute a single explanation for the disparity. While legislative differences between the two sites (such as the power to demand identification and conduct random weapons and drugs searches) are the most likely explanation for the increase in the frequency of controlling behaviour at *SC*, they do not account for the variation in the proportion of control behaviour. It is more feasible that environmental factors influenced officer behaviour. The *SC* station was positioned within the centre of a night-time entertainment district and catered to victims, suspects and offenders of alcohol-related 'street' offences: disorder, minor assaults, pedestrian offences and breaching liquor-free zones. Alternatively, the disposition and demeanour of citizen-participants may have affected officer behaviour. Citizen-participants at *SC* were younger in age, were more frequently of White/European ethnicity and had a greater proportion of males than those in the *NC* sample. As discussed above, citizens with these characteristics are more prone to experience police officer use of force. *SC* officers were not dealing with the same distribution of encounter event types as the *NC* officers.

This research has highlighted the benefits of incorporating verbal and physical control behaviours. While police agencies may methodically collect self-reported use of force data from officers, the omission of data on the use of control or coercive verbal communication, often absent from 'use of force reporting', prevents a comprehensive analysis of conflict resolution during officer–citizen interaction. Thus, the merit of the present study was that it measured *all* communicative behaviours to provide a descriptive analysis of conflict resolution behaviour. During the study, the predominant method of interaction between officer and citizen was the conversational-style *information exchange*. The dataset comprised events where *SC* officers used controlling behaviour more often and for a longer proportion of time during encounters than *NC* officers.

Legislation

Controlled Substances Act 1984 [SA]
Crimes Act 1961 [NZ]
Land Transport Act 1998 [NZ]
Policing Act 2008 [NZ]
Sale and Supply of Alcohol Act 2012 [NZ]
Search and Surveillance Act 2012 [NZ]
Summary Offences Act 1953 [SA]

Appendix

Table 4.10 Encounter event types at dispatch, arrival and end of encounter

	Dispatched				Beginning				End			
	NZ		SA		NZ		SA		NZ		SA	
	n	%	*n*	%	*n*	%	*n*	%	*n*	%	*n*	%
Arrest warrant					1	0.7	1	0.7	1	0.7	3	2.1
Attempted suicide	7	5.1	1	0.7	7	5.1	1	0.7	6	4.4	1	0.7
Breach bail	2	1.5			3	2.2	7	4.9	4	2.9	10	7.0
Burglary	2	1.5			2	1.5			2	1.5		
Civil dispute	2	1.5			3	2.2			3	2.2		
Court order	1	0.7			3	2.2			3	2.2		
Disorder	12	8.8	11	7.7	12	8.8	35	24.6	6	4.4	30	21.1
Domestic Incident	4	2.9	1	0.7	2	1.5	3	2.1	3	2.2	3	2.1
Domestic Violence	19	14.0			20	14.7			18	13.2		
Drugs (cannabis)							4	2.8			5	3.5
Drugs (not cannabis)							7	4.9			4	2.8
Drugs (search)							2	1.4			2	1.4
Enquiries					10	7.4			10	7.4		
Escort (custody)					2	1.5	1	0.7	2	1.5	1	0.7
Intimidation	5	3.7	1	0.7	5	3.7	3	2.1	5	3.7	2	1.4
Intoxicated person	3	2.2	1	0.7	4	2.9	4	2.8	3	2.2	5	3.5
Liquor offences			1	0.7			15	10.6	1	0.7	16	11.3
Lost property							1	0.7			1	0.7
Mental Health	1	0.7			1	0.7	1	0.7	2	1.5	3	2.1
Minor assault	9	6.6	3	2.1	12	8.8	5	3.5	17	12.5	2	1.4
Missing person	4	2.9	1	0.7	3	2.2	2	1.4	2	1.5	1	0.7
Obstruction					1	0.7	4	2.8	3	2.2	3	2.1
Offensive weapon	1	0.7			1	0.7	1	0.7	1	0.7	2	1.4
Preventative task	2	1.5			6	4.4			6	4.4		
Property damage	3	2.2	2	1.4	4	2.9	2	1.4	4	2.9	1	0.7
Public relations	4	2.9			4	2.9			4	2.9		
Serious assault	1	0.7	1	0.7	1	0.7	1	0.7	1	0.7	1	0.7
Sexual affronts	3	2.2			3	2.2	1	0.7	2	1.5	1	0.7
Silent emergency call	4	2.9			1	0.7						
Suspicious behaviour	3	2.9	1	0.7	3	2.2	9	6.3			7	4.9
Theft	6	4.4	5	3.5	7	5.1	5	3.5	6	4.4	6	4.2
Traffic offences	2	1.5			5	3.7	16	11.3	6	4.4	16	11.3
Trespass	3	2.2			3	2.2	2	1.4	4	2.9	2	1.4
Vagrancy			2	1.4			6	4.2			6	4.2
Vehicle crash	2	1.5			2	1.5			2	1.5		
Weapon offences	2	1.5			2	1.5			1	0.7		
Weapons search (random)							3	2.1				
Youth incident	3	2.2			3	2.2			3	2.2		
Nil offence									5	3.7	8	5.6
Not dispatched	26	19.1	111	78.2								
Total	136		142		136		142		136		142	

References

Alpert, G. P., & Dunham, R. G. (2004). *Understanding police use of force: Officers, suspects, and reciprocity*. Cambridge University Press.

Alpert, G. P., & MacDonald, J. M. (2001). Police use of force: An analysis of organizational characteristics. *Justice Quarterly, 18*(2), 393–409. https://doi.org/10.1080/07418820100094951

Black, D. J. (2010). *The behavior of law*. Emerald Group Publishing.

Bottoms, A., & Tankebe, J. (2012). Beyond procedural justice: A dialogic approach to legitimacy in criminal justice. *Journal of Criminal Law and Criminology, 102*(1), 119–170.

Bowling, B., Reiner, R., & Sheptycki, J. (2019). In B. Bowling, R. Reiner, & J. Sheptycki (Eds.), *The politics of the police* (5th ed.). Oxford University Press.

Braithwaite, H. (1998). *Behavioural tactics for the successful resolution of conflict* (PhD doctoral dissertation). Flinders University of South Australia.

Braithwaite, H., & Brewer, N. (1998). Differences in the conflict resolution tactics of male and female Police patrol officers. *International Journal of Police Science & Management, 1*(3), 276–287. https://doi.org/10.1177/146135579800100306

Dai, M., Frank, J., & Sun, I. (2011). Procedural justice during police-citizen encounters: The effects of process-based policing on citizen compliance and demeanor. *Journal of Criminal Justice, 39*(2), 159–168. https://doi.org/10.1016/j.jcrimjus.2011.01.004

Deutsch, M. (1973). *The resolution of conflict*. Yale University Press.

Geller, W. A., & Toch, H. (1996). Understanding and controlling police abuse and force. In W. A. Geller & H. Toch (Eds.), *Police Violence* (pp. 292–328). Yale University Press.

Hendy, R. (2018). *Procedural conflict and conflict resolution: A cross-national study of police officers from New Zealand and South Australia*. (PhD). University of Cambridge.

Hendy, R. (2020a). Effectiveness and efficiency: Oslo police officers' perspectives of the necessity and utility of temporarily routinely arming in response to a terrorist threat. *Policing and Society*.

Hendy, R. (2020b). Switching on, switching off: Reflections of a practitioner researcher examining the operational behaviour of police officers. *Police Practice and Research, 21*(1), 62–77. https://doi.org/10.1080/15614263.2018.1558585

Hendy, R. (2021a). Policing in New Zealand. In J. Mbuba (Ed.), *Global perspectives of policing and law enforcement* (pp. 245–263). Lexington Books.

Hendy, R. (2021b). Suspicious minds and suspicioning: Constructing suspicion during policework. *Journal of Organizational Ethnography*. https://doi.org/10.1108/JOE-12-2020-0056

Herbert, S. (2006). Tangled up in blue: Conflicting paths to police legitimacy. *Theoretical Criminology, 10*(4), 481–504. https://doi.org/10.1177/1362480606068875

Hickman, M. J., Atherley, L. T., Lowery, P. G., & Alpert, G. P. (2015). Reliability of the force factor method in Police use-of-force research. *Police Quarterly, 18*(4), 368–396. https://doi.org/10.1177/1098611115586175

Hough, M., Jackson, J., Bradford, B., Myhill, A., & Quinton, P. (2010). Procedural justice, trust, and institutional legitimacy. *Policing, 4*(3), 203–210. https://doi.org/10.1093/police/paq027

Kaminski, R. J., DiGiovanni, C., & Downs, R. (2004). The use of force between the police and persons with impaired judgment. *Police Quarterly, 7*, 311–338.

Keane, J., & Bell, P. (2013). Confidence in the police: Balancing public image with community safety – A comparative review of the literature. *International journal of law, crime and justice, 41*(3), 233–246. https://doi.org/10.1016/j.ijlcj.2013.06.003

Klockars, C. B. (1980). The dirty Harry problem. *The Annals of the American Academy of Political and Social Science, 452*(1), 33–47. https://doi.org/10.1177/000271628045200104

Klockars, C. B. (1996). A theory of excessive force and its control. In W. A. Geller & H. Toch (Eds.), *Police violence*. Yale University Press.

Kraska, P. B. (2001). *Militarizing the American criminal justice system: The changing roles of the Armed Forces and the police*. Northeastern University Press.

Lamont, C., & Boduszyński, M. P. (2020). *Research methods in politics and international relations*. SAGE Publications.

Mazerolle, L., Bennett, S., Antrobus, E., & Eggins, E. (2012). Procedural justice, routine encounters and citizen perceptions of police: Main findings from the Queensland Community Engagement Trial (QCET). *Journal of Experimental Criminology, 8*(4), 343–367. https://doi.org/10.1007/s11292-012-9160-1

Muir, W. K., Jr. (1977). *Police: Streetcorner politicians*. University of Chicago Press.

Murphy, K., & Cherney, A. (2012). Understanding cooperation with Police in a diverse society. *British Journal of Criminology, 52*(1), 181–201. https://doi.org/10.1093/bjc/azr065

New Zealand Police. (2019). *Operating procedures for armed response teams*. Retrieved from Wellington: https://www.police.govt.nz/can-you-help-us/armed-responseteam-trial

Noldus, L. P. J. J. (1991). The observer: A software system for collection and analysis of observational data. *Behavior Research Methods, Instruments, & Computers, 23*(3), 415–429. https://doi.org/10.3758/bf03203406

Noldus Information Technology. (2014a). Observer XT.

Noldus Information Technology. (2014b). Pocket observer.

Qualtrics Labs Inc. (2014). *The world's leading research & insights platform | Qualtrics*. Retrieved from https://www.qualtrics.com/

Reisig, M. D., McCluskey, J. D., Mastrofski, S. D., & Terrill, W. (2004). Suspect disrespect toward the police. *Justice Quarterly, 21*(2), 241–268. https://doi.org/10.1080/07418820400095801

Reisig, M. D., Bratton, J., & Gertz, M. G. (2007). The construct validity and refinement of process-based policing measures. *Criminal Justice and Behavior, 34*(8), 1005–1028. https://doi.org/10.1177/0093854807301275

Roberts, K., & Herrington, V. (2013). Organisational and procedural justice: A review of the literature and its implications for policing. *Journal of Policing, Intelligence and Counter Terrorism, 8*(2), 115–130. https://doi.org/10.1080/18335330.2013.821737

Skolnick, J. H. (2011). *Justice without trial* (4th ed.). Quid Pro Books.

Squires, P., & Kennison, P. (2010). *Shooting to kill? Policing, firearms and armed response*. Wiley.

Sunshine, J., & Tyler, T. R. (2003). The role of procedural justice and legitimacy in shaping public support for policing. *Law and Society Review, 37*(3), 513–548. https://doi.org/10.1111/1540-5893.3703002

Sykes, R. E., & Brent, E. E. (1980). The regulation of interaction by Police. *Criminology, 18*(2), 182–197. https://doi.org/10.1111/j.1745-9125.1980.tb01358.x

Sykes, R. E., & Brent, E. E. (1983). *Policing, a social behaviorist perspective*. Rutgers University Press.

Terrill, W. (2001). *Police Coercion*. LFB Scholarly Publishing.

Terrill, W. (2005). Police use of force: A transactional approach. *Justice Quarterly, 22*(1), 107–138. https://doi.org/10.1080/0741882042000333663

Terrill, W. (2014). Police coercion. In M. Reisig & R. J. Kane (Eds.), *The Oxford handbook of police and policing* (pp. 260–279). Oxford University Press.

Terrill, W., & Mastrofski, S. D. (2002). Situational and officer-based determinants of police coercion. *Justice Quarterly, 19*(2), 215–248. https://doi.org/10.1080/07418820200095221

Terrill, W., Paoline, E. A., & Manning, P. K. (2003). Police culture and coercion. *Criminology, 41*(4), 1003–1034. https://doi.org/10.1111/j.1745-9125.2003.tb01012.x

Toch, H. (1969). *Violent men: An inquiry into the psychology of violence*. Aldine.
Tyler, T. R., & Huo, Y. (2002). *Trust in the law*. Russell Sage Foundation.
Wood, J. D. (2010). *Interpersonal communication*. Wadsworth.
Worden, R. E. (1996). The causes of police brutality: Theory and evidence on police use of force. In W. A. Geller & H. Toch (Eds.), *Police violence* (pp. 23–51). Yale University Press.

Chapter 5
Technology in Policing

Ritesh Kotak

Introduction

Policing is rapidly adopting new technology to create efficiencies and be effective. Understanding the evolution of policing technology is important in understanding how the profession has developed to its current state and what it may potentially morph into. There is a misconception that technology is only related to complex software, mobile applications (apps) or computer-related advancements. This is not the case; technology is defined as, 'scientific knowledge used in practical ways in industry, for example in designing new machines' (Stevenson, 2010). This includes everything from protective equipment, use of force options to even the vehicle used in an operation. The use of technology is nothing new; in fact, it has been developing since the inception of the modern police service. Police services have adapted to using vehicles, radios and conducted energy weapons. As technology evolves so does the police service. If they did not adopt technology, then we would still see community call boxes, and police cars would be non-existent. However, in the last two decades, we have seen an explosion of high-technology advancements being adopted by police services. A big part of this is the fact that consumer and commercial technology has become readily available at affordable prices. Police agencies are made up of people who are using consumer technology in their personal lives; thus, they have been able to influence their services to adopt change. In most cases, these changes have had little resistance and have been accelerated by tragedies; on the other hand, technologies have also been resisted. Any change will create opportunities but also challenges. This chapter will look at technology from several different perspectives and explore what the future state may look like.

R. Kotak (✉)
Toronto, ON, Canada
e-mail: Ritesh@RiteshKotak.com

J. F. Albrecht, G. den Heyer (eds.), *Understanding and Preventing Community Violence*, https://doi.org/10.1007/978-3-031-05075-6_5

The Turn of the Century

Prior to 2001, the advancement of technology in policing was relatively slow; the focus was on digitizing records, search and closed-circuit television (CCTV) and getting connectivity to the police cars. The internet was becoming widely adopted in a consumer environment, and law enforcement agencies were contemplating how this could be leveraged for operations and the issues it may pose. However, the morning of September 11, 2001 changed the world in many ways. The tragedy in New York meant that nothing will ever go back to how life was before that morning. Under President Bush, there was an unprecedented amount of spending on security, technology and an expansion of the authority that law enforcement possessed (Bornstein, 2005). This moment is a pinpoint from when we started to see an exponential development in this area. Vendors started to build tools to enhance surveillance and detection, while the technology community, in general, started to grow and become powerful entities. Companies such as Google, Facebook, Twitter, Amazon and many others started to scale given the mere fact that devices were becoming cheaper, consumer preferences started to shift online, and there was ubiquitous access to the internet.

Since the attacks in New York on September 11, 2001, there was an emphasis on enforcement-related technology. Many would argue that a blank cheque was provided to agencies in preventing the next attack from occurring. The money funded numerous initiatives including multimillion-dollar projects on developing Real-Time Crime Centre's (RTCC) and the broad implementation of CCTV to investigative software that could ingest large amounts of data and try to visualize it on geographic information system (GIS).

Real-Time Crime Centre (RTCC)

A major gap that was identified due to the terrorist attacks in New York was an inability for first responders to communicate with each other and share data in real time. Interoperability, the ability to exchange data/information with other services, became a major priority. The current process lacked coordination and communication and needed to be revamped. The lack of sharing of data, resources and communications led to confusion and potential loss of life. To prevent this from happening again, many agencies used new funding to create a multi-agency coordination centre, where representatives from fire, EMS, police, the city and other agencies were present in the same site to allocate appropriate resources. They jointly supported the creation of a Joint Operations Centre at NYPD headquarters. In many jurisdictions, this was a siloed operation and uncoordinated. We learned how to leverage each other to create a more efficient and effective response. The development of the New York Police Department (NYPD) RTCC was estimated at a cost of $11 M (Gov Tech, 2006).

Any RTCC requires investment in creating a common operational picture. The Joint Operations Centre (JOC) created a common location for multi-agency collaboration. In addition, the staff of the RTCC can analyze and visualize on a computer screen all the calls for service at one address or neighborhood. Imagine if every agency had their own dashboard; it would be impossible to coordinate. To make this a reality, it requires information sharing at its core. This is achievable, but there are numerous challenges in achieving this level of information sharing. These challenges are as follows:

Trust/Culture

Agencies must trust each other to share information. A police agency may believe that certain information is classified as confidential and thus cannot be shared. This does not mean that no data can be shared, but only that specific piece of data must be withheld. Having a data classification can address this need from 'public disclosure' to 'top secret'. Arbitrarily stating all police data is confidential is not helpful and can become counterproductive. Not having any data classification is also not appropriate.

Data classification is essential, but the first step is not a technological solution but ensuring that trust exists between the parties, and fostering a collaborative culture with stakeholders will overcome these barriers.

Systems Need To Be Updated

There is a major misconception that a new system such as a Records Management System ('RMS') will solve your problems and ensure data sharing through integrated portals. As a policing leader, you must recognize that you are not building something new but onto something existing. This requires planning, and you cannot ignore legacy systems. These systems house important records and information. Unfortunately, there is no easy solution to this but to work with your vendors on integrating or migrating your previous data. The only solution may be manual entry or thinking of creative workarounds.

Joint Procurement

It does not make sense for every agency to procure their own Records Management System, communication systems, etc. There are economies of scale that could be achieved by procuring with partners and surrounding agencies. Many agencies have partnered together and created standards at the provincial or national level to procure certain systems from a single vendor.[1] It is important to understand that there are drawbacks to joint procurement such as a potential loss in autonomy to questions regarding the quality of the product. No decision will be perfect, but the benefits here may outweigh the drawbacks. Data sharing allows partners to communicate more effectively and efficiently while creating a jurisdictional standard.

Having a common operational picture will allow agencies to share information with each other while breaking their own silos. These silos will be not only external but also internal to the organization. Through the experience of many public safety professionals, a common finding is that such an exercise reveals and breaks down internal divisions. In policing, there are numerous different categories of jobs from the frontline detectives to specialized operations. There are community-related functions to covert ones that operate in secrecy. The truly secret operations (they do exist) are a small sliver of overall operations. This goes back to the issue of culture and data classification. Not everything is deemed top secret and can be shared only with a select few; the majority of the information especially in a police service is sharable with vetted partners.

If an RTCC is to be successful, then it must first address the internal challenges of silos and a resistance to change and then the broader external environment on working with partners in an open and collaborative way. Joint procurement and similar systems that can communicate with each other will only prove beneficial.

A word of caution, police investment in RTCC is important, but at the same time, technology will not solve your problem. For example, many police RTCC have implemented CCTVs/video surveillance, acoustic detection systems such as shotspotter and radiation detectors. The issue with having numerous different sensors and devices is the false positives. Video surveillance is one item that may have a lot of benefits if implemented correctly. Having someone watching cameras all day is ineffective and may not even prove to be a deterrent (Liedka, 2019). Law enforcement is examining and implementing facial recognition technology which is in its infancy. Acoustic devices are expensive and have not always been shown to be effective. Similarly, one can only imagine how false positives for radiation sensors could be set off when an individual has received any sort of radiation treatment. There are many impressive RTCCs in the global policing ecosystem, but what is necessary is that all partners are represented, that there is a transparent data flow, and that those potential issues, such as false positives and biases, are addressed.

Intelligence/Data Gathering

All police officers and leaders must be familiar with the data that is generated. This is an essential skill set to effective policing in this decade. This subsection will discuss the types of data which can be generated.

[1] Prime-BC was a joint initiative spearheaded by the Solicitor General of British Columbia, Canada, to create a provincial standard for Police RMS. Link to the Administrative Report to the Vancouver City Council https://council.vancouver.ca/991019/a12.htm.

Open-Source Intelligence (OSINT)

This is data that can be acquired by public means. The most common is searching keywords on social media or using a search engine to obtain information. However there may be limits to how this data could be used, acquired and leveraged in policing operations. Information may be available on everything from local newspaper stories, legal cases, corporate filings, name changes, loan applications to high school yearbooks. There may also be situations where images may be geolocated and indirectly provide location information.

Example: Alexander Sotkin, a member of the Russian Army who posted a geolocated image of himself on Instagram which showed he was in Ukraine when Russia was claiming that they had not crossed the border (Segall, 2014). A Russian spokesperson stated that these images were forgeries, but the data was captured using 'photo map' as Sotkin may have not disabled the function. In another example, in 2018, a secret flight to Iraq by the President of the United States was uncovered by a photographer simply taking a picture of a plane flying over his house which was posted on social media and deduced by cross-referencing flight information that it was most likely Air Force One headed to the Middle East (Gillespie, 2018).

OSINT can provide many clues on everything from criminal investigations to covert operations. However, it could also be used against police services. Nothing can be considered secret from the identity of officers to operations. Someone will be there to publish the data intentionally or unintentionally.

There are also DNA banks. Police services have used genealogy sites to submit DNA to find familial matches. We have learned that the Toronto Police Service leveraged a DNA bank to map the genealogy of a cold case involving the killing of a 9-year-old girl in 1984 (Dubinsky, 2020). Solving the homicide of a child is commendable; however, the use of a third-party DNA bank brings in serious questions on privacy and ethics and if police can legally leverage such investigative techniques.

Forensic Data

The use of forensic evidence is growing as more individuals own digital devices. Forensic artefacts are created whenever a user does essentially anything on a device from unlocking the phone to turning on the flashlight app. It can help with the retrieval of information to trace the movement of an individual. It can be performed on any device from smartphones to the GPS in your vehicle. Everything leaves a trace, and with the right skill sets and tools, it can be recovered. The forensic function is also becoming easier to perform at a cursory level. The notion of 'push-button' forensics will allow frontline officers to conduct basic searches, retrieve evidence and accurately preserve it.

The majority of forensic examination is time-consuming and requires a high level of expertise. This is an area that police services need to continue to upgrade and scale. There have been and continue to be serious discussions on the outsourcing of certain functions of forensic examinations. It is expensive to maintain equipment, train personnel and retain them within the organization. Services have also created partnerships with universities and even civilianized many of these positions. Regardless of the approach that an agency takes, do not underfund or neglect this element of the process.

A forensic examination is also becoming more difficult as encryption is difficult to break. If a device is encrypted, then prior to any forensic examination, it must first be decrypted. This is difficult and may even be impossible in some cases. In 2020, the FBI requested Apple to decrypt two iPhones for them that held evidence involving a shooting at a Naval Base which Apple has refused to do (Benner & Nicas, 2020). Eventually, the US government did gain access to the device, but this shows the difficulty that forensic examination will have and how time-consuming it could become. One must start to address these issues today to deal with the challenges of tomorrow.

Judicial Requests

Judicial requests are complicated and can take many forms from warrants, production orders to requests through international treaties.

This section is not an analysis of the geopolitical implications of technology and who has jurisdiction over a matter. The internet has created a borderless world where any user equipped with an internet-connected device can access information on servers located anywhere in the world. Physical objects are subject to duties and inspections, while humans are subject to border control mechanisms and extradition. However, with the internet, a company can be American, with servers in Europe serving clients in Australia. So, who has jurisdiction?

The jurisprudence in this area is limited, for example, in the *United States v. Microsoft Corporation*, the US government was seeking access to emails that were located on an Irish server. Microsoft challenged the decision which went all the way up to the Supreme Court. The decision was ultimately referred back to the lower circuit court who rendered the matter moot as the US government passed the *Clarifying Lawful Overseas Use of Data Act* or CLOUD Act (Daskal, 2018). This is the US government seeking information from a US organization. If the information is housed by a foreign entity, then the Mutual Legal Assistance Treaty ('MLAT') is the best course of action to obtain data stored on overseas servers. However, this is a long and difficult process. It requires your respected justice department and a legal request to a foreign entity. It may be that serving the company at their headquarters is not sufficient but instead serving the request where the data is physically housed. In order to do this, you must be aware of where the data is located, and this creates additional uncertainty. It is important to mention judicial requests in this section as it could house valuable data from emails, cell records, IP logs, etc. However, obtaining it may be difficult and create delays.

Next-Generation 911 (NG911)

The implementation of NG911 systems is a major undertaking by agencies across the world. The migration from house phones to cell phones created challenges but also opportunities, the ability to more accurately locate individuals and leverage the rich media functionality of smartphones. When every second matters, technology can greatly assist. We can order food on an app and track several metrics of our meal in great detail to the exact location of the driver and the estimated time of arrival based on traffic conditions to the type of car being driven. However, with policing it is nowhere near where it could be. The integration of smart sensors, social media and crowdsourcing can be leveraged to promote community engagement and 'Smart Policing'. Many 911 call centres are not capable of retrieving video. There are problems, however, in relation to the use of videos, the exposure to call-takers, the storage of data, and the provision of emergency services to the caller. This discussion is not a debate on if this is a practical use of the technology but instead a recognition that there may be ways to be creative and innovative in getting the right resource to the right person.

Imagine smart-connected fire extinguishers. The second they are used, a signal is sent to the local fire station to send a response. As an individual dealing with a fire, you may not have the ability to call for help, and when each second is critical, this becomes essential.

In the Netherlands, a crowdsourced NG911 system called ComProNet would publish the call for service and engage the community to send in images, messages and videos to a hashtag generated for the call (The Police Chief, 2011). This is the future, and it may be coming sooner than many expect, thinking about NG911 technology will be essential for future police leaders.

Predictive Analytics

Predictive analytics have been used in industries such as health care and retail, but now applications for public safety are being explored. Predictive policing, a term coined by Beck and McCue, seeks to essentially predict crime before it happens and lower recidivism rates (Beck & McCue, 2014). This relatively new concept is being introduced to public safety institutions as the newest crime-fighting tool to address delinquency and create safer communities. A few major police agencies within America have utilized the tools and reported on its success. However, many agencies are still sceptical of its effectiveness and cognizant of the issues that may arise.

The ability to predict the future has fascinated societies throughout generations. The idea of predictive analytics in policing was first popularized by Steven Spielberg's Hollywood thriller, Minority Report. A pre-crime unit was tasked with predicting crime before it happened and sent in officers to arrest would-be perpetrators. An article in The Guardian discussed how the movie, which introduced concepts such as pre-crime, was being explored in real life from using CCTVs in parking lots, to predict the likelihood of thefts based on walking patterns of individuals, to creating traffic systems to hinder house burglaries (Arthur, 2010). There are ample examples of how leveraging new technology can lead to better outcomes in policing; however, this idea, in particular, raises concerns around the topics of privacy, bias and human rights.

Algorithmic policing creates opportunities but also major challenges. The issue of predictions being based on incomplete and biased data further marginalizes particular groups. The data may yield an incomplete picture and false positives and violate an individual's civil rights. Any implementation needs to be thought-through and be transparent. At the end of the chapter, suggestions will be made on how to apply new technologies within policing.

A Push to Modernize

From 2015 to today, there has been a global push to motivate public safety agencies to modernize. As policing budgets globally become subject to increased scrutiny, there is a demand and pressure to modernize. Modernization does not mean simply substituting services that could have been done by an officer to an online form but instead a redefining of the entire task to create an additional value add.

The 'Connected' Officer

Officers have the option of not being tethered to a desk or vehicle anymore. Instead, they now can conduct their operations remotely. The concept of a 'personal area network' of the officer includes smartphones that may have access to note-taking apps, report-taking and internal searches. However, it does not need to end there as sensors on the use of force options can create a recorded alert along with smartwatches that measure heartbeat, steps and stress levels. Then there are smart glasses to smart vests that all have sensors with particular functionality.

The officer can now be connected and have access to vital information instantly. This type of technology may not be required for all members as a community officer may require certain features that differ compared to a tactical officer or plainclothes officers. The technology untethers officers and can benefit the officer and increase officer safety.

Body Cameras

Police services across the world are equipping officers with video cameras to record the contact that they have with community members. The objective is to increase transparency between police-community interactions. Yet, body cameras can also provide productivity as opposed to accountability. If the officer's personal area network is equipped with sensors on use of force and if a use-of-force weapon is taken out of a holster, the camera can start to record, alert supervisors and provide a direct feed to the RTCC. Another example is real-time language translation. Imagine a first responder attending a call for service where they don't speak the language of the individual, the technology can provide a real-time translation. It could also translate sign language. Imagine a situation where a mental health professional could be beamed in virtually to provide advice and converse with the individual in crises. Natural language processing and advancements in artificial intelligence allow for such innovation. As a police leader, shift the thought process on technology from accountability to productivity.

Automated Enforcement

As police agencies grapple with budgets, many have turned to automate certain operations such as red-light enforcement to detect vehicles that do not legally come to a complete stop to speed cameras that detect the speed of vehicles. Here speed measuring devices record the speed, and a camera with a built-in automated license plate reader records the vehicle information. An automated search of the registration generates a fine and is sent to the registered driver. Not everything can be automated nor should it, but it may be worth experimenting how automated technology could be used to increase public safety and compliance and promote community policing principles concurrently.

Drones or unmanned aerial vehicles (UAV) are also being used for different purposes such as accident reconstruction to search and rescue. This will be an area that will rapidly develop over the years and continue to generate value for a police service. A collision on a major highway can cause hours of delays. There are also a finite amount of human resources. A drone can quickly survey the area and create a 3D rendition in minutes that could be used to conduct an investigation virtually or at a later time. The weather elements of rain or snow can disrupt the scene so the faster the evidence can be preserved would benefit the investigator, accused and victim. Similarly, leveraging drones for search and rescue can provide several obvious benefits.

Online Services

The COVID-19 pandemic has accelerated the use of online services. Society is getting accustomed to utilizing online systems and apps. In most cases, there is a demand for such services, and police services must deliver. Failure to do so could have two consequences:

1. The increased need for human report takers for minor and non-criminal occurrences
2. Unreported crime

Not everything needs to go online, but providing a simple form where a community member can submit a report or look up relevant information is critical. Mobile apps and police service websites are resources that an individual will seek for information. This process could also be further enhanced with the use of videoconferencing systems especially as communities became more accustomed to the platforms. It could also promote access to justice and accessibility for individuals who may not have the ability to travel to their local police station. If done correctly, when someone uses a search engine to ask a question, a police site with accurate information will provide value to the requestor.

Another element is victim support. In 2015, the United Kingdom launched 'TrackmyCrime' (Ministry of Justice, 2015). The objective here was to allow the victim to essentially track the progress of the crime throughout its entirety, stay connected with the investigator and access victim supports. Online reporting and elements of it can positively enhance the experience for a victim who is suffering from a traumatic incident.

Virtual Reality Training

Training can really benefit from the use of technology. Video cameras can capture training for feedback purposes, and biometric sensors can provide insights on stress levels. This is just the tip of the iceberg. Virtual reality training has not been fully leveraged. The NYPD has been testing virtual reality in multi-payer simulations (Eyewitness News, 2019). These training exercises provide invaluable insights and can expose officers to different scenarios from an individual in crisis to practicing for a tactical entry. There have also been numerous devices created to add to the simulation from haptic vests that send shocks to the body when you have been virtually incapacitated to weaponry that feels and looks real. The technology will only get better and can be an invaluable tool. There have also been studies suggesting that virtual training could be used to reduce post-traumatic stress to first responders by placing them in stressful simulations to prepare for stressful real-world incidents (MCgregor & Bonnis, 2016).

In summary, modernization was pursued as a cost-effective exercise to reimagine the delivery of policing services. However, as students wanting to learn about the implementation of technology, it is important to understand the true motivation behind the technology. Is it used to substitute an already manual or static task or is it modifying the task altogether? For example, take the task of notetaking. Police officers take a copious amount of notes, and for the majority of them, they are handwritten into a physical notebook. There is no real way to share the information, protect access and have the ability to search the notes efficiently. The immediate next step is to augment notetaking with typed notes, however, where the real interest lies in the ability to use body-worn cameras or smart devices to auto-transcribe notes. The notes can be in multiple languages, immediately accessible, and can be shared in a safe and secure method. It also frees up the officer to be back on the road faster to resume patrol. There are several examples of such modernization, but it is important to not augment but completely redefine the task to derive value: incremental v. exponential.

Modern-Day Technology Issues

We have covered several different technologies and how they impact or will continue to impact policing operations. At this point, it is time to have a brief discussion on modern-day technology-related issues that a police service may face and should consider.

Cyber Everything

Cybersecurity is no longer something that is the responsibility of your information technology departments. It must be built into the cultural fabric of the organization. It needs to be a critical human resource function from hiring officers with basic competencies, continuous training and evaluations to every member of the service. Post-breach analysis has revealed how unsuspecting individuals can be targeted. The most dangerous operation that any member may do on any given day is open email. If the email is embedded with malware, this will infect networks and could access or worse alter data which diminishes trust with the public. Cybercriminals are working overtime to gain access to police data. Through social engineering attacks, ransomware or malware, they will disrupt operations.

The public is also being targeted. A police member swears an oath to serve and protect the community. That may have been in the physical world but now has converged to the virtual world as well. Cybercrime statistics internationally are constantly on the rise. As more of the population gets connected, more people will fall victim to these crimes. I would argue that the majority of crimes have some element of cyber attached to them either directly or indirectly.

Imagine a break-and-enter of a residential address. The accused may have targeted the address because of social media posts and used an online mapping platform to get an aerial/street view of the property. If a vehicle was used, then there would be information on the GPS, and the homeowner may have a smart doorbell that captured the accused. CCTV may have been present on the street or at the neighbour's premises. The accused may have coordinated the theft using an app on a mobile device and then sold items online. This has become a core competency for policing professionals.

Future crime will become more complex and further blur the lines between the physical and virtual worlds. Police services must become accustomed to conducting such investigations. This includes frontline officers. These investigations should not require specialized units and instead need to become decentralized. Logic dictates that if the crimes are becoming more digital, then through centralization of operations, you will quickly run into a capacity issue. These functions must be decentralized. Leverage the centralized resources for complex cases and to research trends and provide training on emerging issues to the membership.

The Impact of Artificial Intelligence

AI is going to be a massive disruptor for policing operations. We have discussed how natural language processing may be used in conjunction with body cameras to provide on-scene translation and how sensors can be leveraged to create alerts to how the potential of incidents could be detected and disrupted through predictive analysis.

The technology is evolving at a rapid speed, for this chapter to create an exhaustive list would not be possible. Every day there are new advancements in the AI space. This will continue to materialize, and a police service may be overwhelmed on how to implement new technology. The opposite response of not exploring it at all is a mistake as there is a benefit to the community. Instead of addressing different AI-related application, the rest of the chapter will focus on working through an example of AI technology – facial recognition.

Ethics, Law and Privacy

This chapter would not be complete without discussing the ethical, legal and privacy considerations when implementing new technologies internally or externally. The best method to provide insight into these sometimes-abstract concepts is through an example. The example will be related to the use of Clearview AI, a facial recognition platform that has been used by many law enforcement agencies around the world and then subsequently halted pending legal, ethical and privacy reviews.

There is little detail that has emerged on the inner workings of the algorithm (Hill, 2020a). However, here is what we do know. The application scraped publicly available data and indexed it via faces on their servers. Clearview then made the platform available to law enforcement and selected commercial agencies to test the platform. According to the founder, Mr. Hoan Ton-That, it took approximately 2 years to develop the platform (CNN Business, 2020). It can be safely assumed that the majority of this time was primarily focussed on two activities:

1. Scraping different online sources for photographs
2. Developing, training and resting a facial recognition algorithm

The images are all claimed to have been downloaded onto Clearview's servers when they were publicly accessible, and as such, no consent was required according to Clearview. On the onset, this creates several challenges:

1. Should the platform have obtained explicit consent for repurposing the data to a law enforcement platform?

2. Should a platform delete a stored image if it is deleted by the user on the host platform?
3. What if a user decides to make their account private or deletes their account?
4. What if a user is tagged by the algorithm but they are in the background of the photo (captured in transit)?
5. How can a user know what images of them are captured by Clearview AI and can they request deletion?
6. What if the image captured and indexed is obscene or involves a minor?
7. What happens with the images uploaded by law enforcement agencies to identify an individual indexed on the platform?

The ease to deploy these platforms with pre-generated facial recognition systems can be a benefit to organizations looking to leverage or commercialize platforms. However, similar to mistaken identity, a facial recognition match to a wrong individual could subject them to be targeted by law enforcement agencies. An article published in June 2020 by the New York Times claims that Mr. Robert Julian-Borchak Williams is probably the first victim of being wrongfully arrested because of a faulty facial recognition identification (Hill, 2020b). Mr. Williams was identified by the Detroit Police due to a third-party system that compared closed-circuit television ('CCTV') security footage. These images of a black male were wrongfully matched to Mr. Williams. Eventually, the Wayne County Prosecutor dismissed the charges, and, in a statement, the prosecutor stated the following, 'In the summer of 2019, the Detroit Police Department asked me personally to adopt their Facial Recognition Policy, declined and cited studies regarding the unreliability of the software, especially as it relates to people of color' (New York Times, 2020).

This brings up several legal issues that need to be addressed such as the bias in algorithms especially within communities of colour. If the accuracy of these systems diminishes based on race and other factors such as image quality and noise in the image, then this is troublesome for a law enforcement application.

A Concluding Framework

The implementation of any tool must consider the ethical, legal and privacy implications of the technology. The different factors of consideration are the following:

Consent

Is consent required? If yes, was consent clearly provided and has the consent been revoked? Consent is ongoing and can be difficult to ascertain in a digital context. Is the consent required to access, would a reasonable individual be aware of what they are consenting to, and is there any recourse of the individual? At this point, it is also important to note that the use of dark patterns in obtaining consent should be outlawed (Narayanan, 2020). A user should not be nudged towards providing consent; it should be a neutral process and free from manipulation especially if it involves public safety technology.

Data Source

Is the data lawful, how was it collected, where is it being housed? These are the fundamental questions and require research on the vendor and all the component parts. As law enforcement, they must be aware who will have access to their searches, where will the data be housed, will it be encrypted and is data that is inputted/uploaded retained on third-party servers. Traditionally, government agencies prefer keep systems on their premises, but given the costs to maintain such systems and the need for high-performance computing to run data-heavy algorithms, leveraging cloud-based systems has become accepted. This may prove to be more secure as detecting anomalies and having experts monitoring traffic would be the responsibility of the vendor. However, complacency will be detrimental as these systems are exposed to third-party vendors and network intrusions. This is not a chapter on cybersecurity protocols, but they must be contemplated and implemented within the use of law enforcement digital tools.

Security

Building on the previous point, the systems that house access to sensitive information such as biometrics must be secured. Security would include access control to the room/device/portals, audit logs and encryption of the data.

Legality

This seems simple but it may be overlooked. The question with software such as Clearview AI is not whether the 1-N matches could be used but, more importantly, is the platform even legal.[2] The initial collection of the images or the images within a private database such as Clearview may violate domestic law – possession of certain images, the breach of contract on violating Terms of Services of the scraped platform and the privacy-related requirements of consent. Finally, are there any con-

[2] There are two categories of matches, a '1-N' match or a "1-1" match. A '1-N' match is taking an image and searching a database for a match to identify an individual. A '1-1' match is used to verify an individual to an image; a common application is passport verification at points of entry.

stitutional elements such as civil rights violations in the use of the platform? Would the equivalent use of a physical object require a warrant? Would you as law enforcement need a production order to obtain an image on someone's Facebook profile? If the answer is yes, then using third-party platforms to circumvent this is inappropriate.

Privacy

At the very minimum, an independent Privacy Impact Assessment ('PIA') should be completed by a competent third party.[3] Daniel Solove, a privacy scholar, states six principles of privacy need to be assessed within each context:

1. An individual has the right to be let alone.
2. Shield oneself from unwanted access.
3. Not be done in secrecy.
4. Not subject individuals to lose control over their personal information.
5. The protection of their individuality and dignity.
6. Control over their intimate relationships or aspects of life (Nelson, 2011).

Surveillance tech that is warrantless is in direct contradiction to these principles. I propose that moving forward, each law enforcement agency should consider the above information. This should also not be done in isolation but be a transparent process. Any and all digital tools moving forward should go through an approval process prior to any implementation, followed by reviews every 12 weeks to ensure compliance and an external audit on all tools on an annual basis.

Approval Process

When presented with a new digital tool, the primary step is to ask the above questions related to consent, data source, security, legality and privacy. In addition, a PIA is conducted. Once these initial steps have been met, a group of experts in the law, technology and privacy go over all the submissions to verify the submission completeness and ask clarifying questions. This will ensure that privacy by design principles is built-in, the platform is legal and thought was given to the use of the platform (Cavoukian, 2010). Once approved, a limited proof of concept with oversight is conducted. This will ensure compliance and good practice. If the proof of concept is successful, then the platform can be scaled.

[3] A Privacy Impact Assessment is a document that assists in identifying risk, impacts to one's privacy and does the item in question comply with the legislation.

If the platform involves any biometrical data, then an additional step of an AI ethics board will need an approval process. This is not new in tech organizations. They are instituting external boards to ensure the responsible application of AI tools. One example is the *AI, Ethics, and Effects in Engineering and Research (AETHER)* Committee at Microsoft (Microsoft Corporation, 2020). It could be argued that the development of IP of big tech firms is more protected and valuable than the tools licensed for use by law enforcement. Based on this, an argument of secrecy and confidentiality by law enforcement to prohibit such transparency would not hold any merit.

Finally, training and education into the responsible application of technology and privacy law must be provided to our law enforcement community. They must be aware of the broader implications of the technology, the process to vet the technology and the ongoing scrutiny required to ensure full compliance. On an individual level and specific to Clearview AI, agencies can create a designation of 'Facial Recognition Specialist' to conduct searches. This is common practice with fingerprints, DNA, drug identification, breath technicians, etc. These recommendations are not a critique on law enforcement; it is instead a suggestion to ensure that the rights of the public are upheld, the very principle that law enforcement swears an oath to protect.

Conclusion

This is a complex subject matter. Technology may seem simple as we use it on a daily basis. Think about the last time you bought a new smartphone and went through the 'How-to-Guide'. Chances are that you do not have any recollection. The reason is simple; it does not come with a guide as it is meant to be intuitive. The design is elegant and simple, usually a screen with a few buttons.

Technology will continue to evolve; it is simple to reimagine the entire system, but asking a service to change an entire Records Management System or pivot on a new radio system may not be possible or practical. This is not a short-term plan that can be fixed overnight but will require several years and changes in management. This is a long-term strategy, but once implemented, it will start to provide value from the first day. This cannot and should not be done in isolation but needs to be a collaborative and transparent process. Policing is a single stakeholder in public safety. Leveraging partnerships and co-creating public safety should be the only model moving forward.

Technology is an enabler but can also be weaponized against the police and the community. Understanding the vulnerabilities, capacity issues and the convergence of crime will better prepare agencies to serve and protect the public.

Finally, technology can be used for good but can also be oppressive. To use online platforms is simple – click on a link and enter a username and password, and you now have access to the world's information. However, just because you can, should you? Law enforcement's role includes protecting rights in the physical world but also the virtual world. On the whole, the approach by the agencies in leveraging tech, data or algorithms may be narrow in scope – solving crimes. However, the approach needs to be broader and consider the legal, ethical and privacy lens of the platforms. Working with law enforcement to reimagine how cyber tools and platforms are used will prevent the unintentional violation of an individual's civil liberties.

Today the prominent discussion is on the use of facial recognition and its inaccuracy and bias within the algorithms. Tomorrow, it will be a new form of technology that we have not even grasped. We want to avoid the mistakes previously made. The suggested framework will provide guidance and will not delay the implementation of tech when leveraged for the benefit of society. The necessary oversight will ensure that individual rights are constantly protected. The use of technology in policing needs to be modernized as we cannot continue to keep using twentieth-century frameworks for twenty-first-century innovation.

References

Arthur, C. (2010, June 6). Why minority report was spot on. *The Guardian*. Retrieved from: https://www.theguardian.com/technology/2010/jun/16/minority-report-technology-comes-true

Beck, C., & McCue, C. (2014, March 13). Predictive policing: What can we learn from Wal-Mart and Amazon about fighting crime in a recession? *The Police Chief Magazine*. Retrieved from: https://controverses.minesparis.psl.eu/public/promo16/promo16_G16/acmcst373ethics.weebly.com/uploads/2/9/6/2/29626713/police-chief-magazine.pdf

Benner, K., & Nicas, J. (2020, January 7). F.B.I. asks Apple to help unlock two iPhones. *The New York Times*. Retrieved from: https://www.nytimes.com/2020/01/07/technology/apple-fbi-iphone-encryption.html

Bornstein, A. (2005). Antiterrorist policing in New York City after 9/11: Comparing perspectives on a complex process. *Human Organization, 64*(1), 52–61.

Cavoukian, A. (2010, May). *Privacy by design – The 7 foundational principles*. International Association of Privacy Professionals ("IAPP"). Retrieved from: https://iapp.org/media/pdf/resource_center/pbd_implement_7found_principles.pdf

CNN Business. (2020, March 6). *Clearview AI's founder Hoan Ton-That speaks out* [Extended interview] [Video]. Retrieved from: YouTube. https://youtu.be/q-1bR3P9RAw

Daskal, J. (2018). Microsoft Ireland, the CLOUD Act, and International Lawmaking 2.0. *Stanford Law Review, 71*, 9.

Dubinsky, Z. (2020, December 7). Genealogy buff delighted to find he helped solve Jessop cold case — But also learns he's killer's cousin. *CBC News*. Retrieved from: https://www.cbc.ca/news/christine-jessop-investigation-dna-tracing-cousins-1.5828034

Eyewitness News ABC7NY. (2019, April 25). *NYPD using VR to train for active shootings and real-life scenarios* [Video]. YouTube. Retrieved from: https://www.youtube.com/watch?v=VZyhQZSTIGQ

Gillespie, T. (2018, December 28). UK photographer captures image of Air Force One flying on secret trip to Iraq. *Sky News*. Retrieved from: https://news.sky.com/story/uk-photographer-captures-image-of-air-force-one-flying-on-secret-trip-to-iraq-11593001

Gov Tech. (2006, February 11). *NYPD real time crime center expands*. Retrieved from: https://www.govtech.com/dc/articles/NYPD-Real-Time-Crime-Center-Expands.html

Hill, K. (2020a, January 18). The secretive company that might end privacy as we know it. *The New York Times*. Retrieved from: https://www.nytimes.com/2020/01/18/technology/clearview-privacy-facial-recognition.html
Hill, K. (2020b, June 24). Wrongfully accused by an algorithm. *The New York Times*. Retrieved from: https://www.nytimes.com/2020/06/24/technology/facial-recognition-arrest.html
Liedka, M. (2019). CCTV and campus crime: Challenging a technological "fix". *Criminal Justice Policy Review, 30*(2), 316–338.
McGregor, C., & Bonnis, B. (2016, June). *Big data analytics for resilience assessment and development in tactical training serious games*. In 2016 IEEE 29th International Symposium on Computer-Based Medical Systems (CBMS) (pp. 158–162). IEEE.
Microsoft Corporation. (2020). *Responsible AI*. Retrieved from: https://www.microsoft.com/en-us/ai/responsible-ai
Ministry of Justice & The Rt Hon Sir Mike Penning MP. (2015, January 29). *Online tracking service launched for victims of crime*. Retrieved from: https://www.gov.uk/government/news/online-tracking-service-launched-for-victims-of-crime
Narayanan, M. (2020). Dark patterns: Past, present, and future. *Communications of the ACM, 63*(9), 42–47.
Nelson, K. (2011, December). *Daniel Solove's six general types of privacy. in propria persona*. Retrieved from: https://inpropriapersona.com/articles/daniel-soloves-six-general-types-of-privacy/
New York Times (2020 June 24). *Office of the Prosecuting Attorney of County of Wayne responding to the New York Times Article on 'Wrongfully Accused by an Algorithm'*. Retrieved from: https://int.nyt.com/data/documenthelper/7046-facial-recognition-arrest/5a6d6d0047295fad363b/optimized/full.pdf#page=1
Segall, L. (2014, August 1). Oops! Russian soldier Instagrams himself in Ukraine. *CNN*. Retrieved from: https://money.cnn.com/2014/08/01/technology/social/russian-soldier-ukraine-instagram/index.html
Stevenson, A. (2010). *Oxford dictionary of English* (3rd ed.). Oxford University Press.
The Police Chief Magazine. (2011, April). *Internet scanning and the use of social media for in-progress crime*. Retrieved from: https://www.nxtbook.com/nxtbooks/naylor/CPIM0411/index.php?startid=28#/p/16

Chapter 6
Increasing Gun and Community Violence in the United States: Causes and Analyses

James F. Albrecht

Introduction

Homicide rates and gun violence have dramatically increased nationally since 2014, and there is speculation that this upsurge is the result of a phenomenon generally referred to as the "Ferguson effect." The "Ferguson effect" involves "de-policing" or a decline in proactive enforcement by law enforcement personnel in cities and regions overwhelmingly impacted by over-sensationalized incidents in which police officers have been extensively criticized for their enforcement activity and specifically events that have involved the shooting by police of non-White criminal suspects. The police departments that have come under extreme scrutiny following sensationalized police-suspect encounters since 2013, i.e., the Baltimore Police Department, the Chicago Police Department, the New York City Police Department, and the Minneapolis Police Department, among many other across the nation, also align with the cities that have generally displayed discernible increases in murder and serious crime rates following those events. Other jurisdictions have exhibited, at the minimum, short-term homicide and crime increases following similar incidents. From a police practitioner perspective, this transition from proactive law enforcement to mainly reactive response appears to reflect a commonsense reaction to threats to job security and both professional and personal reputation. The increase in murder and violence rates across the United States since 2013 will be closely analyzed with an effort particularly made to determine the validity of the impact of the "Ferguson effect," the death of George Floyd, and the calls for defunding the police on American law enforcement strategies, from both individual and organizational perspectives.

J. F. Albrecht (✉)
Pace University, New York, NY, USA

J. F. Albrecht, G. den Heyer (eds.), *Understanding and Preventing Community Violence*, https://doi.org/10.1007/978-3-031-05075-6_6

The "Ferguson Effect"

The "Ferguson effect" stems from a police-involved shooting in Ferguson in Missouri in August 2014. The encounter involved a Ferguson Police Department officer stopping two robbery suspects shortly after the crime. Unexpectedly one of the suspects attempted to violently remove the firearm from the police officer's holster, resulting in the firearm discharging as the officer retained control of the weapon. For some unknown reason, the same suspect involved, who had been fleeing, turned directly at the police officer at full speed. Fearing for his life, the police officer discharged his firearm to stop the suspect and put an end to the violent assault. The suspect quickly succumbed to his injuries.

Although this sounded like a straightforward case of unfortunate yet justified use of force by police, there was a surprising twist to the narrative, as the second robbery suspect claimed that the suspect aggressor was actually raising his hands when the officer discharged his firearm at the suspect. This misinformation quickly transitioned across social media and ultimately to traditional media. Public outcry ensued, primarily from the African-American local and national communities. Ensuing demonstrations led to rioting and further violence. As a result, the Black Lives Matter movement was born. The group claimed that police officers consistently kill unarmed African-Americans due to endemic racism across the police profession in the United States. Ultimately the police officer involved was determined to have legally use justified and necessary force during the encounter separately by both federal and state prosecutors.

Compounding the matter was that another high-profile incident within New York City had taken place in July 2014, which involved the in-custody death of a suspect, Eric Garner, who opted to resist arrest rather than cooperate with police officers involved. In this case, the police officers involved were cleared criminally by the local prosecutor, including a Grand Jury investigation, and by federal civil rights investigators. Regardless of the findings in both cases, the group Black Lives Matter continued to promote the narrative that American police officers are all racists and that government entities should intercede to correct these injustices.

A Decline in Public Trust in American Police Officers

Both incidents resulted in numerous demonstrations, not all peaceful, orderly and without criminal incident, across many large cities across the country. As a result of the continuing allegations that the actions of police officers across the United States are prolifically discriminatory and unjustified, trust and confidence in the police declined across all sectors of the public. According to the Cato Institute (Ekins, 2016), public perception research had revealed that positive attitudes about the police vary by race. While 68% of Whites have a positive impression of the police, those sentiments were only 40% for Blacks and 59% for Hispanics. This actually is a decline from the 67% of Whites and 43% of Blacks in 1970 who had a favorable view of the police. On a good note, the same 2016 survey did note that the vast majority of participants had sufficient confidence in the police as, regardless of race, members of the public would generally report criminal incidents to the police.

While there is a common belief that public confidence in the police commenced its decline in 2014, this trend actually commenced in 2007 with a drop from the high of 64% in 2004 to 54% in 2007 (Jones, 2015). It had generally remained stable since then but declined to 52% in 2015. Racial differences have continued to be noted across decades, but this trend first became apparent in the 1970s. As such, one might have to question the event or phenomena that have cyclically resulted in notable decreases in public trust and confidence in the police. From another perspective, when the public were surveyed regarding trust in the criminal justice system as a whole (Ekins, 2016), only 17% of African-Americans believe that the criminal justice system treats all races the same (as compared to 49% of Whites and 27% of Hispanics). This lack of trust and confidence in rule of law in America appears to be a larger concern and apparently involves greater than just policing practices.

Contemporary Police Officer Perspectives

While surveys are often designed to gauge public perspective, a comprehensive evaluation of active American police officers (Morin et al., 2017) evaluated the impact of anti-police demonstrations on officer perceptions of their profession. About 86% of police personnel conveyed that fatal encounters between the police and Blacks have made policing harder, and 93% have expressed concerns about their safety. A strong indicator of police reservation to take proactive action was revealed when 72% of them stated that they have become less willing to stop and question criminal suspects even who appear suspicious. In contrast to the 67% of police officers who believe that fatal police-Black encounters are isolated, about 60% of the public believe that these events are indicative of a larger problem. And police view the public as holding contrasting perspectives of the law enforcement profession in that 79% of police officers report being thanked by the community, while 67% report being verbally abused by the public. The vast majority (92%) of police officers believe that anti-police are the result of long-standing bias against the police. When feelings about police work were evaluated, it was indicated that the vast majority of officers conveyed pride in their work (91%), felt frustration (93%), were fulfilled (84%), felt angry (71%), and expressed satisfaction with their agency (74%). About 83% of officers expressed that their respective agency did not have sufficient personnel to handle their responsibilities, and 84% believed that there is a personal responsibility to intervene when they believe that an officer may be prepared or is using excessive force, while 66% supported the use of police body cameras. About 97% of police officers recognized the importance of knowing the community to improve effectiveness, while the majority (56%) of officers believed that they had positive relations with the Black community that they serve. Overall, it would appear that police officers are satisfied with their jobs and believe that the demonstrations have strained public support for the police. Many of the negative sentiments possessed by the police are likely related to the decline in proactive police encounters that have been shown to support enhanced crime control. Can one conclude that there is support for the "Ferguson effect," even many years after the "trigger event" that initially provided support for the anti-police sentiment advocated and supported by many in the United States.

Recent Sensational Police Incidents

The most obvious incident that elicited further anti-police sentiment in the United States involved the death of George Floyd while being arrested in Minneapolis in May 2020. In this case, police officers stopped a vehicle since the occupants had reportedly just attempted to use counterfeit money to make a purchase in a store. Responding police officers saw three individuals seated inside a car, and George Floyd fit the description of the suspect involved in the earlier crime. When officers removed Floyd from the vehicle and attempted to place him under arrest, he violently resisted and continued the aggression when placed in the rear of the police car. One of the police officers removed Floyd from the police car and positioned him face down on the street and placed one knee on his shoulder to control the resistance. However, even after Floyd had discontinued his resistance, the arresting officer continued to apply his weight to Floyd's back for numerous minutes even after Floyd had apparently lost consciousness. As soon as the paramedics arrived, they did not detect a pulse and moved him to the ambulance and transported him to the hospital. George Floyd subsequently was declared dead.

Although the original incident was not filmed by bystanders, numerous individuals did record the police officers restraining the suspect on the street, including Floyd losing consciousness. The video was released to the press, which almost immediately reported the incident on traditional media. As a result, widespread demonstrations and eventually rioting took place in Minneapolis and other cities across the United States. Although the medical examiner did conclude that Floyd had died from a severe overdose due to his recent ingestion of Fentanyl and other illegal narcotics, prosecutors charged and eventually convicted the primary police officer involved of murder, as a result of his extended restraint of the suspect, which prosecutors contended had been reckless.

After this incident, Black Lives Matter and other groups routinely held demonstrations following police involved shootings that involved Black criminal suspects, alleging that the use of force was a sign of endemic racism, regardless of the circumstances and facts that had been revealed. Many large urban centers, particularly those with large minority communities, consequently called for the "defunding" of local police agencies and a transition of those funds to social programs in minority communities. The demand to "defund the police" continues to this day, even with the severe rise in violence, homicides, and gun crimes in most of those cities.

Police Shootings in the United States

While social and traditional media have been extoling that police officers in the United States overwhelmingly and unjustifiably shoot predominantly unarmed male Blacks due to endemic organizational racism, it would be best to undertake a comprehensive analysis of available related statistics. The SHOT database (Arlsan, 2019), housed at Western Connecticut State University, includes comprehensive statistics consisting of almost 5000 officer-involved shootings (OIS) that have occurred in all 50 American states between January 2000 and December 2019. While not all-inclusive, it documents all open-source OIS and additionally examined numerous variables that should permit a clearer understanding of these tragic phenomena.

Of the total OIS in the United States across two decades, 73.3% were fatal. From a gender perspective, 95.5% of the subjects being shot by police during these deadly encounters were male, and only 1.2% of the subjects were immigrants from various countries (Arlsan, 2019). Quite surprisingly, only a small percentage of the subjects (2.7%) had reported gang affiliations at the time of the OIS. Most of these police-suspect encounters lasted less than 3 min. Almost 20% of the incidents involved car pursuits, whereas another 18% resulted in police officers taking part in foot pursuits before the shooting. Sadly, almost 50% of either chase scenario ended up in a suspect fatality. A small number of OIS involved both a vehicle and a foot pursuit.

The distribution of OIS is almost equally distributed within all four seasons (Arlsan, 2019); however, Fall with 26% had the highest percentage, but minimally. The deadliest month for OIS is December, whereas the lowest months were revealed to be February and April. Similar to the seasons, there is not a single day of the week that strikes out significantly, which would surprise most police professionals, who likely would predict weekends as the most dangerous days for OIS.

The average age of all subjects involved in OIS was almost 34 years old (Arlsan, 2019). The mode for age is 25, and over half (60%) of all subjects were between the ages of 20–39. More than 70% of the subjects had documented no mental health issues with only few reportedly exhibiting unstable behavior at the time of the incident. About 11% of the incidents fit into the category "suicide by cop," a situation where the subject often acts erratically with the desired intent for the police to shoot them. Mental health concerns were present in 12% of the cases. Only 6% of the subjects had been reported to be under the influence of drugs, including many with multiple substances in their system.

Race stands at the center of the controversy. More specifically, a Black man killed by a White officer routinely stirs a considerable controversy as it relates to public trust and confidence in the police. Overall, White subjects made up 41% of all OIS, Blacks 30%, Hispanics 25%, and Asians 4% (Arlsan, 2019). In regard to age, young Black males (20–29) have a significantly higher fatality rate in OIS than any others. Whites, whether male or female, had higher rates of OIS deaths for subjects age 40 and older.

Regarding the officer's assignment at the time of the OIS (Arlsan, 2019), the vast majority (82.9%) were on-duty patrol officers. The remaining OIS were divided between tactical (e.g., Emergency Response Team and SWAT) officers 5%, state troopers 3.2%, plainclothes officers 3%, and vice and gang squads 1%. The remaining complement consists of a combination of various units and agencies. About 6% of the OIS cases involved more than one law enforcement agency. Federal law enforcement officers were involved in less than 1% of all OIS. In 65% of the incidents, only one officer fired his or her weapon. In 42.4% of the cases, the shooting officer was the only officer present; two officers were present in 31.8% of the cases. It should be highlighted that, as part of their training, officers target the body center mass when they fire their firearm in an effort to quickly stop the threatening actions of the subject. As a result, in 78.6% of the cases, police struck the subject in the torso and had effectively put an end to the threat.

There are 20 different call types during which most police shootings have taken place (Arlsan, 2019). Domestic disturbance cases involved 17% of OIS and were the most frequent police calls that officers responded to prior to an officer-involved shooting. This was followed by the traffic-related incidents with 12.8%, which often started merely as a simple traffic stop but escalated quickly to involve the use of deadly force. Other dangerous calls that resulted in OIS were welfare checks (7.1%) and person-with-a-gun calls (7%). However, it was revealed that uniformed patrol officers from local police departments are the police personnel with the highest risk for becoming involved in an OIS and particularly while responding to a family dispute or when making a vehicle stop. And most police officers involved in OIS had exhibited incredible restraint in firing their guns, as 50% of OIS involved the police officer firing only one bullet, with an additional 23% firing two rounds. In 93% of the cases, the police officer or police officers involved fired five or less bullets when involved in an OIS (Albrecht, 2021).

When analyzing the geographical location of OIS in America (Arlsan, 2019), most shootings (42%) occurred in the Western states. California and Nevada were the states in the West that had the highest ratio of OIS. The South had 34% of the OIS, with Texas and Florida being the top two states in that region. The Midwest was third with 14%, and then the Northeast region had 10%. The physical nature of the location of OIS varied widely. Most were outdoors, predominantly taking place on streets, highways, and parking lots (74.5%). Most indoor shootings took place in residential locations, such as apartment buildings and houses (40%).

While there is a strong perspective across the public, and more so within members of minority groups in the United States, that police officers routinely shoot unarmed Black suspects, OIS data has proven to show otherwise. In more than 50% of the cases (Arlsan, 2019), the subject possessed a firearm, and in an additional 25% of those scenarios, the suspect had both possessed and fired a firearm. In 17% of cases, the subject used or threatened a weapon other than a firearm. In 6% of the cases, the subject was physically attacking the police officer. In 11% of the cases, the subject was reportedly unarmed, but in some of those cases, the suspect had used a vehicle as a weapon or as a means to injure the police officer, i.e., dragging the officer with the car. It was very rare that the subject did not threaten or use a weapon or physically assault the police officer prior to an OIS taking place. Overall, only 2% of OIS could be identified as involving an unarmed suspect (Albrecht, 2021).

Race and Police-Involved Shootings

Research has revealed that the use of force by police officers in America is extremely rare and the use of deadly physical force by police is remarkably exceptional. The Bureau of Justice Statistics regularly surveys the public regarding contact with the police. According to the latest data (Bureau of Justice Statistics, 2020), the police made direct contact with 61.5 million individuals, or approximately 24% of the public in 2018. Whites (26%) were more likely than Blacks (21%), Hispanics (19%), or persons of other races (20%) to experience police contact. A higher percentage of Blacks (4%) and Hispanics (3%) than Whites (2%) or other races (2%) experienced threats or use of force. But it should be noted that the definition of use of force by police included grabbing, pushing, and all arrests, even if peaceful and not involving resistance. In addition, only 0.3% of all contacts involved the police officer drawing or pointing a firearm at them. Even more importantly, a police officer-involved shooting is extremely unlikely and occurred in only 0.0018% of police-public encounters (Albrecht, 2021). Overall, members of the public who engaged the police overwhelmingly conveyed that the police acted properly (90%) and respectfully (92%) during the contact (Bureau of Justice Statistics, 2020).

More compelling is the empirical evidence that has resulted from the evaluation of prosecutorial, judicial, and federal criminal investigations involving OIS in the United States. Of the more than 20,000 officer-involved shootings over the last two decades, it was determined that only 0.63% resulted in criminal charges and 0.22% resulted in criminal conviction (Albrecht, 2021). This should provide the most credible evidence that police officers have routinely and overwhelmingly engaged in legally justified actions when involved in situations that have involved the use of deadly physical force by police in America. And yet the criticism, apparently unwarranted and unsupported, continues to be over-sensationalized by community advocates, many government officials, and most of traditional media.

Latzer (2000) analyzed police-involved shooting data from 2019 and compared those statistics to arrest rates for violent crime committed by racial groups in the United States over the same time frame. Latzer's analysis showed that 49% of individuals killed by police were White, compared to 50% of arrests for violent crimes which involved White suspects. Similarly, 31% of individuals killed by police were Black, and 31% of arrests for violent crime involved Black suspects. And 17% of individuals killed by police were Hispanic, compared to 19% of arrests for violent crime committed by Hispanics. Latzer concluded that the racial/ethnic identities of those killed in police-involved shootings clearly bear a notable similarity to the identities of those involved in violent crime in America.

Latzer (2000) further explained that when police-involved shootings in Chicago, renowned for its high rate of violence and criminal homicide, from 2006 to 2014 were investigated, it was revealed that in 77% of the cases, police were responding to a report of a person involved in a violent crime or a suspect armed with a firearm and in 80% of those cases, the police reported a threat involving a gun. As such, in the overwhelming majority of police-involved shootings, the police officer did not initiate the confrontation but were responding to civilian reports of violence, and ultimately they were force to engage the subject in response to a direct threat of attack, usually involving a firearm.

Johnson et al. (2019) analyzed police-involved shootings in the United States from 2015 and determined that subject race did not play a role in determining whether a person of a certain race was more likely to be shot by police. In fact, comprehensive statistical analysis revealed that a person fatally shot by police was 6.67 times less likely to be Black than White and 3.33 times less likely to be Hispanic than White. As a result, in the typical police-involved shooting in American, there was no evidence of anti-Black or anti-Hispanic disparity. The primary predictor of the race of the subject involved in a police-involved shooting in the Unites States was the race-specific violent crime rate for that respective jurisdiction, supporting the findings of Latzer (2000).

Casselman (2015) found that fatal shootings by police tend to take place in neighborhoods that are more socioeconomically disenfranchised and have a higher percentage of Black residents than the United States as a whole. About 30% of police-involved shootings had taken place in communities that are in the bottom 20 percent nationally in terms of household income. And 25% of those killed by police died in neighborhoods with majority Black populations. It should be clarified that nationally, just 7% of the population live in majority Black areas.

Finally, Fryer (2019) found that police officers in New York City were more likely to use physical force against a Black suspect than a White suspect but interestingly concluded that Blacks were 27.4% less likely than Whites to be fatally shot by police. Therefore, it should now be obvious that the race of a subject has not been found to be as critical and relevant a variable as the racial breakdown of groups involved in violent crime within a specific jurisdiction in America. Even given the robust nature of related research, there are still many who continue to decry that police-involved shootings are racially motivated.

Serious Crime and Murder Spikes in the United States

American violent crime rates reached an unacceptable level in 1991 (7.58 per 100,000) but commenced a rather sharp decline in 1992 that continued until 2014 (361.6 per 100,000). In 2015, the violent crime rate suddenly reversed direction and has increased through 2021. The violent crime rate nationally has increased 16% to date in 2021, which follows a 3.3% rise in 2020 (Statistica, 2021a).

Since 2014, the violent crime rate in America has risen, but not at the astronomical rate that criminal homicide and murder have. The criminal homicide and murder rate in the United States stood at 10.4 (per 100,000) in 1980 and then declined to

9.4 in 1990 and 8.4 in 1995. From 2000 through 2008, the homicide rate remains stable at approximately 6.0 but thereafter declined to 5.1 in 2014. However from 2015 through 2021, the criminal homicide and murder rate across America began a continuous rise back to 6.2 per 100,000 (Statistica, 2021b), thereby erasing all of the gains in enhanced safety since the turn of the millennium. The national homicide rate increased 13% from 2014 to 2019 but has since skyrocketed another 30% in 2020 and continues to spike further in 2021 (approximately 15%). It should be apparent that the effective crime prevention and control measures have been dramatically and rather negatively impacted since 2014. There exists an obvious challenge and also a dilemma in explaining this significant and disturbing change of events.

Explanations for the Violent Crime and Murder Spike Since 2014

A number of theories have been proposed in an attempt to explain the significant increase in criminal homicides and gun crime in the United States since 2014. Much of the speculation has revolved around the apparent decline in trust and confidence in the police due to the over-sensationalization involving police-involved shootings and the unsupported claims that police officers act in an environment fueled by endemic racism. This unwarranted criticism of the police profession seemingly commenced in 2014 following the media coverage of the Garner death while resisting police in New York City and the police-involved shooting in Ferguson, Missouri.

Rosenfeld (2016) had proposed a number of theoretical explanations for this phenomenon. Rosenfeld first conveyed that the increase in gun violence was due to a decline in perceived police legitimacy. In lieu of requesting police to settle disputes between parties, many have opted to not notify the police of infractions and criminality. This was evidenced by a significant decrease in calls for service, i.e., 911 calls, in Black communities across the United States. This has thus permitted conflict to fester and criminality to continue unabated in many cases.

Rosenfeld (2016) also proposed that there is support for the "Ferguson effect," as the unfounded claims of police brutality and institutional racism have caused police officers to reevaluate their level of commitment to proactive policing strategies. With diminishing police engagement of criminal suspects, those individuals have become empowered to engage in heightened acts of violence as they no longer fear police interdiction and arrest. Rosenfeld further speculated that this lax atmosphere has permitted criminal gangs, particularly those who deal in drugs, to increase acts of violence against competing gangs without apprehension. Rosenfeld additionally posited that there has been a noteworthy increase in the number of gangs involved in the distribution of illicit drugs and this has resulted in increased competition and gang-related acts of violence. Rosenfeld cited the increase in gang-related homicide as support for this postulation.

Albrecht (2018) conducted a comprehensive and multifaceted examination of the increase of criminal homicides in the United States since 2014. Albrecht posited that the negative perceptions and sentiment of police officers across the United States (Morin et al., 2017) following numerous anti-police demonstrations provided strong support for the "Ferguson effect." Dramatic increases in homicides were routinely reported in cities in which sensational incidents involving police actions and large demonstrations and rioting had taken place. It is only rational and indicative of human nature that police officers have become overly concerned that they might face unjustified negative consequences, including prosecution, termination, or other punishment, if the "court of public opinion" determines that a police action, particularly if the criminal suspect is Black, has reportedly been the result of endemic racism across the police profession, even if these allegations are unsupported and without merit. This has been most apparent in jurisdictions where local and state politicians have openly and verbally supported anti-police sentiment and have often participated in related demonstrations. Police personnel, as a result, have therefore opted to limit engagements with criminal suspects, when possible, in an effort to reduce the likelihood that they will face allegations of criminality and brutality if the need to use physical or deadly physical force should arise. As such, career preservation has taken preference to public service. This is evidenced in the sharp decline in police stops, arrests, and case clearances in cities where the criminal homicide rates have generally risen the most.

Albrecht (2018), however, stated that the return to a reactive form of policing is only partially responsible for the increase in criminal homicides and gun violence in America. Albrecht opined that a number of factors have combined to create the dramatic increase in criminal homicides since 2014. These variables include the relatively new practice of classifying many opioid-related deaths, which formerly were classified as accidental overdoses, as criminal homicides. With opioid-related overdose deaths up 100% since 2014 and with these cases exceeding 50,000 annually, many police departments have elected to conduct more thorough criminal investigations with the intent to charge co-conspirators and opioid dealers with criminal homicide.

In addition, Albrecht (2018) further hypothesized that the legalization of marijuana has increased the likelihood of drug-induced conflict and driving while impaired vehicular fatalities. In line with this, advanced forensic technology and more thorough investigations following vehicle fatalities may have led to a slight increase in criminal homicide charges, particularly as it relates to criminally negligent and reckless driving and behavior. Many large cities in the United States have prioritized reductions in vehicle fatalities, and criminal investigations have become more commonplace.

Albrecht (2018) provided further explanation for the significant increase in criminal homicide rate in the United States by positing that the scrutiny placed on police-involved shootings has resulted in a small number of those cases being classified as criminal homicides in some jurisdictions, before the matter had generally resulted in acquittal within the criminal courts. In addition, since 2014, there have been between 1 and 2 million guns sold legally each year in the United States, which amounts to an almost 400% increase in firearms available across America. Couple this with a strong decline in incarceration as a general practice within State and federal governments and there are considerably more career criminals walking the streets. This has been compounded by the routine absence of pretrial detention due to pandemic restrictions placed on grand juries and criminal trials since March 2020 and the removal of bail in most cases, even when criminal charges involve serious felony charges, in many large urban settings, as part of criminal justice reform measures.

As such, the noteworthy, but undesirable, increase in criminal homicide and gun violence in the United States since 2014 is not the result of one factor but rather a combination of variables that unfortunately and tragically have led to the death of thousands more needlessly across America, of which many are unfortunately young Black males, particularly in large urban centers.

Conclusion

With criminal homicides and gun violence spiking across the United States since 2014, there clearly is the strong need for the reevaluation of policing strategies and the development of effective criminal justice reform that will ensure that crime control is again prioritized. It is critical to note that much of the increase in criminal homicides across America, and more so in large urban areas, involve Black victims. If "Black Lives Matter," then the effective prevention of violence must be immediately addressed to avoid needless death. Promoting the defunding of the police at a time that criminal homicides and gun violence are surging should be viewed as being clearly unacceptable and obviously irrational.

The obvious response is a prompt return to the highly successful and acclaimed proactive law enforcement and policing measures that emerged in the mid-1990s that fueled the dramatic reduction in all categories of serious crime. This was coupled with longer prison sentences, particularly for gun-related crimes. Keeping career criminals off the streets would require a reversal of the ineffective bail reform measures that have been implemented over the last 2 years in many metropolitan areas, which coincidentally align with many of the jurisdictions that are faced with the largest increases in serious crime and violence.

While misinformed politicians and community advocates openly condemn the police in America for endemic racism, there is little evidence to support these baseless allegations. Every noteworthy statistical analysis has revealed that race is not a major factor in police use-of-force scenarios and more specifically in police-involved shootings. The fact that more than 99.9% of police-involved shootings in America have consistently been found to be legally justified following intensive criminal investigation by state and federal prosecutors, often independently, also provides evidence that the police officers involved acted properly and lawfully.

There is, however, the need to address the diminished trust and confidence that portions of the public have for the police, and the return to enhanced community policing measures should strongly be contemplated. Enhancing police-community engagement and organizational transparency should coincide with any proactive crime prevention initiatives. Police administrators and policy makers should take the time to review Sir Robert Peel's principles of policing (Lee, 1901) that were developed when public policing was in its infant stages in the 1820s. These guiding tenets outlined the relevance of public input and scrutiny into law enforcement priorities and practices. Most critical is Peel's second principle, which posits that "(t) he ability of the police to perform their duties is dependent upon public approval of police actions." As the police are public servants, they must therefore strive to serve the public.

References

Albrecht, J. F. (2018). *Examining the Ferguson effect: Statistically supported or ideological speculation.* Presentation at the Annual Conference of the Homicide Research Working Group in Clearwater, Florida in June 2018.

Albrecht, J. F. (2021). *Understanding and investigating officer-involved shootings and in-custody deaths.* Presentation at the Annual National Sheriffs Association Conference in Phoenix, Arizona in June 2021.

Arlsan, H. (2019). The impact of police shootings in the United States on police-community relations. In *Policing and minority communities: Contemporary issues and global perspectives.* Springer Publications.

Bureau of Justice Statistics. (2020). *Contacts between the police and the public – 2018.* U.S. Department of Justice.

Casselman, B. (2015). Where police have killed Americans in 2015. In *FiveThirtyEight.* ABC News.

Ekins, E. (2016). *Policing in America: Understanding public attitudes toward the police. Results from a National Survey.* Cato Institute.

Fryer, R. G. (2019). An empirical analysis of racial differences in police use of force. *Journal of Political Economy, 117*(3), 1210–1261.

Johnson, D. J., Tress, T., Burkel, N., Taylor, C., & Cesario, J. (2019). Officer characteristics and racial disparities in fatal officer-involved shootings. *Proceedings of the National Academy of Sciences of the United States of America, 116*(32), 15877–15882. National Academy of Sciences.

Jones, J. M. (2015). *In U.S., confidence in the police lowest in 22 years.* Gallup.

Latzer, B. (2000). The facts on race, crime and policing in America. In *Law and order on June 18, 2000.* The Liberty Fund Network.

Lee, W. L. M. (1901). *A history of police in England.* Methuan and Company.

Morin, R., Parker, K., Stepler, R., & Mercer, A. (2017). *Behind the badge.* Pew Research Group.

Rosenfeld, R. (2016). *Documenting and explaining the 2015 homicide rise: Research directions.* U.S. Department of Justice, National Institute of Justice.

Statistica. (2021a). *Reported violent crime rate in the US 1990–2020.* Statistica Research Department.

Statistica. (2021b). *Death by homicide per 100,000 resident population in the U.S. from 1950 to 2020.* Statistica Research Department.

Chapter 7
The Impact of Community Conflict-Related Violence on Police Officer Mental Health and Well-Being

S. Hakan Can and Durmus Alper Camlibel

The Impact of Violence on Police Officer Mental Health and Well-Being

It is widely acknowledged that workplace stressors negatively affect the mental health and well-being of police officers. Recent studies have explored the causes of stress in policing and their associations with negative psychosocial outcomes consisting of anger, poor self-esteem, and conflict with romantic partners (Can & Hendy, 2014; Can et al., 2008; Gershon et al., 2009; Hall et al., 2010; Liberman et al., 2002; Stevens, 2008; Violanti, 2004). In these studies, sources of stress on the police officer frequently emphasized through the following general components such as department-related stressors, which include department politics, absence of police partner support, lack of recognition and trust, strict hierarchy, and alienation (House & Wells, 1978; LaRocco et al., 1980; Graf, 1986; Morris et al., 1999; Van Hasselt et al., 2008); workplace-related stressors, which include critical incidents, daily hassles, and work-family conflict (Maynard & Maynard, 1982; Headey & Wearing, 1989; Caulfield & Riggs 1992;Violanti & Aron, 1993; Hart et al., 1994; He et al., 2002; Liberman et al., 2002; Weiss et al., 2010); organizational characteristic of police agencies; (Monk, 1988; Rosa et al., 1989; Brown & Campbell, 1990; Violanti & Aron, 1993; Pilcher & Huffcutt, 1996); and availability of coping mechanisms (Gershon et al., 2009; Anderson & Lo, 2011; Ivie & Garland, 2011; Regehr

S. H. Can (✉)
Pennsylvania State University, Schuylkill Haven, PA, USA
e-mail: hakancan@psu.edu

D. A. Camlibel
University of Wisconsin, Oshkosh, WI, USA
e-mail: camlibed@uwosh.edu

J. F. Albrecht, G. den Heyer (eds.), *Understanding and Preventing Community Violence*, https://doi.org/10.1007/978-3-031-05075-6_7

et al., 2013; Yun et al., 2013; Can & Hendy, 2014). Although five decades of research have focused on identifying the associations between police stressors and negative psychosocial outcomes, relatively scant literature has been devoted to comparing workplace stressors and negative psychosocial outcomes perceived by police officers from police departments presently with and without community conflict directed at their department.

According to Anderson and Bauer (1987:381), there are three types of violence directed toward police officers: (1) violence toward community (e.g., assault or accident), (2) police violence that the officer directs toward community (e.g., civil unrest, or use of force), and (3) community violence directed the police officer (e.g., being verbally assaulted, shot at, or physically attacked).

The negative psychosocial impact of police workplace stressors may be expected to be worsened in the wake of the confrontation between police and citizen ending in violence. Mainly when community violence is directed at a police department, officers' mental health deteriorates as well as their psychological well-being (Johnson et al., 2005). Hence, in the current study, we hypothesize those police officers in departments confronted with community violence directed toward them will experience more severe mental health and psychological well-being problems than officers in departments without community violence against them.

Notably, during a civil unrest situation, the media and public closely monitor police officers' every action. While operating in a "fishbowl," police officers may feel anxious, powerless, and vulnerable, making them hypervigilant. Additionally, when the verbal or physical violence of community directed against the police officers triggers an increased level of workplace problems, it creates a conflict with colleagues and romantic partners, even causing doubts about their competencies and self-esteem.

Purpose of the Present Study

The present study took advantage of a unique opportunity to compare workplace stressors and negative psychosocial outcomes perceived by officers from police departments presently with and without community conflict directed at their department, with all variables measured *using identical instruments*. The officers with community conflict were from Istanbul, Turkey, sampled during a period of political unrest with community conflict and violence directed toward the police department (Body-Gendrot, 2016; Mendonça & Ercan, 2015). The officers without community conflict were from the northeastern US, sampled 2 years before the widely publicized incidents of community conflict toward police departments that occurred in New York City, Ferguson, MI, and Baltimore, MD (Body-Gendrot, 2016; Gamson & Sifry, 2013; Schwartz, 2011). Both samples of police officers completed anonymous surveys with the same measures of four types of police stressors and three psychosocial outcomes. The four types of police stressors considered were recently identified in the Law Enforcement Officer Stress Scale-Revised (Can et al., 2015), including critical incidents, departmental politics, daily hassles, and work-home conflict. The three negative psychosocial outcomes measured in both samples were those problems found associated with exposure to police stressors in past research (Can & Hendy, 2014; Can et al., 2008; Gershon et al., 2009; Hall et al., 2010; Liberman et al., 2002: Stevens, 2008): police partner conflict, romantic partner conflict, and poor self-esteem. While comparing the Turkish officers (with community conflict) and the USA officers (without community conflict) in their perceptions of these workplace stressors and psychosocial outcomes, we controlled for demographic variables that might differ between the two samples and that might be associated with their perceptions (such as age, gender, marriage, household size, years of police service).

Method

Participants and Procedures

Study participants began with 526 police officers from convenience samples in Turkey and the USA (250 from Turkey, 276 from the USA; 94.3% male; 47.0% under 30 years of age; 69.6% married; mean household size = 3.1, SD = 1.3; mean years of service = 11.5, SD = 8.3). Of these 526 officers, 440 (83.7%) completed information about their workplace stressors to be included in the present study (233 from Turkey, 207 from the USA; 95.7% male; 51.5% under 30 years of age; 69.5% married; mean household size = 3.1, SD = 1.2; mean years of service = 10.7, SD = 7.9).

Participants from Turkey originated with a sample from the large urban Istanbul Police Department, randomly selected from a list of all active-duty officers provided by the Istanbul Police Human Resources Department, and after permission was granted by the Turkish National Police (95.7% male; 87.3% under 30 years of age; 71.2% married; mean household size = 2.9, SD = 1.1; mean years of service = 6.9, SD = 5.3). Participants from the USA originated with a convenience sample of police officers from 18 urban and small-town police departments throughout Pennsylvania (95.7% male; 12.1% under 30 years of age; 67.6% married; mean household size = 3.2, SD = 1.4; mean years of service = 14.9, SD = 8.2).

For both samples from Turkey and the USA, anonymous surveys were distributed to officers by their department supervisors as paper copies with large sealable envelopes. Officers completing the surveys were asked to drop them into boxes located at specific locations within the police department, and then one of the authors of the present study collected them. The surveys asked for demographic information, reports of workplace stressors, and possible psychosocial outcome variables, including police partner conflict, romantic partner conflict, and self-esteem.

Measurement of Police Stressors

Police workplace stressors were measured with the Law Enforcement Officer Stress Scale-Revised (LEOSS-R, Can et al., 2015). The LEOSS-R is an 18-item measure of police stressors developed from factor analysis of the original 25-item LEOSS developed by Van Hasselt et al. (2008). Four subscales of police stressors measured by the LEOSS-R include critical incidents, departmental politics, daily hassles, and work-home conflict. The LEOSS-R presents items for which officers of the present study were asked to use 5-point ratings (1 = never, 2 = rarely, 3 = sometimes, 4 = often, 5 = always) to report both the "likelihood" and the "difficulty" of each scenario. These two scenario ratings were multiplied. Then scenario product scores relevant to each subscale were summed to serve as the score for that type of police stressor. Examples of items from **Critical Incidents** (α = .87 for Turkey, α = .84 for the USA) include "You are called to a burglary in progress, and the assailant may be armed" and "You respond to a motor vehicle accident with multiple injuries and possible fatalities." Examples of items from **Departmental Politics** (α = .74 for Turkey, α = .75 for the USA) include "You are engaged in a promotional process" and "You are recruited to investigate a fellow officer." Examples of items from **Daily Hassles** (α = .83 for Turkey, α = .74 for the USA) include "You are on your way to a high emergency call when the radio has interference" and "You are on a high pursuit chase in icy conditions." Examples of items from **Work-Home Conflict** (α = .80 for Turkey, α = .70 for the USA) include "You find work is taking up more time, leaving you with little left for family and recreation" and "Changing shifts has interfered with your sleep patterns."

Measurement of Psychosocial Outcomes

Police partner conflict was measured with the 6-item Verbal Aggression Subscale from the 12-item Revised Conflict Tactics Scale (CTS-R, Caulfield & Riggs, 1992). Officers were asked to use a 5-point rating (1 = never, 2 = rarely, 3 = sometimes, 4 = often, 5 = always) to report how often during the past year they displayed each behavior during the conflict with their present police partner, with the sum of these six ratings used as the score for romantic partner conflict displayed (α = .86 for Turkey, α = .73 for the USA). The CTS-R is the most widely used measure of conflict style because it includes displays of aggression that may apply in a variety of types of relationships (Schafer, 1997). Examples of scale items include "insulted or swore at the other," "did or said something spiteful," and "threatened to end the relationship."

Romantic partner conflict was measured with the same 6-item Verbal Aggression Subscale from the Revised Conflict Tactics Scale as described above for romantic partner conflict. Officers were again asked to use a 5-point rating (1 = never,

2 = rarely, 3 = sometimes, 4 = often, 5 = always) to report how often during the past year they displayed each behavior during the conflict with their "present spouse or romantic partner," with the sum of these six ratings used as the score for police partner conflict (α = .87 for Turkey, α = .82 for the USA). (Note: The remaining six items that make up the Violence Subscale of CTS-R were not included in the measure of conflict used for police partners or romantic partners because some police departments have a "zero-tolerance" policy concerning domestic violence, which would make officers reluctant to report it even on an anonymous survey.)

Self-esteem was measured using the 10-item Rosenberg Self-Esteem Scale (Rosenberg, 1965). Officers were asked to use a 5-point rating (1 = never, 2 = rarely, 3 = sometimes, 4 = often, 5 = always) to report how much they had each thought during the past year, appropriate items were reversed in their ratings, and then the sum of the ten ratings was used as the self-esteem score (α = .72 for Turkey, α = .87 for the USA). Examples of scale items include "I feel that I have a number of good qualities," "I certainly feel useless at times (reversed)," and "I can do things as well as most people."

Data Analysis

The first goal of data analysis was to identify demographic variables showing significant differences between the police samples from Turkey and the USA, so these variables could be statistically controlled in the later ANCOVAs planned to compare the two samples (with and without community conflict) in reported police stressors and negative psychosocial outcomes. Chi^2 analyses were used to compare the Turkish and US police samples in their percentages of officers who were male, under 30 years of age, and married. T-tests were used to compare the Turkish and US police samples in their household size and years of service.

The second goal of data analysis was to use ANCOVAs to compare the Turkish and US police samples (with and without community conflict) for their reported police stressors and negative psychosocial outcomes. The ANCOVAs would also include as covariates any of the demographic variables (gender, age group, marital status, household size, service years) found in the above analyses to be significantly different between the Turkish and US samples. One set of dependent variables for these ANCOVAs would include the four police stressors: critical incidents, departmental politics, daily hassles, and work-home conflict. Another set of dependent variables for these ANCOVAs would include the three psychosocial outcomes: police partner conflict, romantic partner conflict, and self-esteem. (Note: Sample sizes for these ANCOVAs were slightly reduced because some officers neglected to complete some of the study variables.)

Results

Demographic Differences Between Turkish and US Police Samples

The police samples from Turkey and the USA showed no significant differences in their percentages of males ($Chi^2 = .001$, $p = .977$) or officers who were married ($Chi^2 = .68$, $p = .411$). However, significantly more of the Turkish officers compared to the US officers were under 30 years of age ($Chi^2 = 245.66$, $p = .000$). Additionally, T-tests revealed that the US officers had larger households and more years of service than did the Turkish officers ($t = 2.76$, $df = 436$, $p = .006$; $t = 12.09$, $df = 430$, $p = .000$, respectively) (**see** Table 7.1).

Comparison of Turkish and US Police in Reported Police Stressors

To compare police stressors reported by officers from Turkey (with community conflict) and the USA (without community conflict), 2 × 2 ANCOVAs were used that also considered age group (under 30 years, 30+ years) and household size and

Table 7.1 Descriptive statistics for officers with community conflict (Turkey, $n = 233$) and without community conflict (USA, $n = 207$)

	Turkey	**USA**
Demographic variable	%	%
Male	95.7%	95.7%
Under 30 years of age***	87.3%	12.1%
Married	71.2%	67.6%
Demographic variable	***M (SD)***	***M (SD)***
Household size***	2.9 (1.1)	3.2 (1.4)
Service years***	6.9 (5.3)	14.9 (8.2)
Police stressors	***M (SD)***	***M (SD)***
Critical incidents	5.2 (4.4)	6.9 (3.8)
Departmental politics	4.5 (3.9)	4.8 (3.8)
Daily hassles	4.4 (4.1)	4.3 (3.2)
Work-home conflicts	10.4 (6.2)	7.5 (4.6)
Psychosocial outcomes	***M (SD)***	***M (SD)***
Police partner conflict	8.7 (3.6)	7.3 (2.2)
Romantic partner conflict	9.4 (4.0)	9.6 (3.5)
Self-esteem	3.8 (.6)	4.2 (.6)

Demographic comparisons made with Chi2 Analyses or T-tests (* $p < .05$, ** $p < .01$, *** $p < .001$)

service years as covariates because these demographic variables were found in above analyses to be significantly different for the Turkey and US samples. Results found that Turkish officers reported less intense critical incidents stressors ($p = .002$) and more intense work-home stressors ($p = .006$) than did US officers, with no significant differences found in their reported departmental politics ($p = .321$) or daily hassles stressors ($p = .884$) after controlling for demographic variables that differed between the two samples. Demographic variables significantly associated with police stressors included less intense critical incidents and daily hassles stressors for officers with more service years ($p = .008$; $p = .016$, respectively) (**see** Table 7.2).

Table 7.2 Results from 2 × 2 ANCOVAs to compare workplace stressors for police with and without community conflict (Turkey, USA, respectively), age groups (under, over 30 years), using household size and service years as covariates

Critical incidents				
Effect	*F*	*df*	*p*	*Effect size*
Community conflict	10.09	(1, 424)	.002	.023
Age group	.52	(1, 424)	.474	
Community conflict x age group	1.31	(1, 424)	.253	
Household size	.12	(1, 424)	.735	
Service years	7.00	(1, 424)	.008	.016
Departmental politics				
Effect	*F*	*df*	*p*	*Effect size*
Community conflict	.99	(1, 424)	.321	
Age group	2.88	(1, 424)	.090	
Community conflict x age group	1.43	(1, 424)	.233	
Household size	.53	(1, 424)	.469	
Service years	3.43	(1, 424)	.065	
Daily hassles				
Effect	*F*	*df*	*p*	*Effect size*
Community conflict	.02	(1, 424)	.884	
Age group	.36	(1, 424)	.550	
Community conflict x age group	2.16	(1, 424)	.143	
Household size	.05	(1, 424)	.819	
Service years	5.80	(1, 424)	.016	.013
Work-Home conflicts				
Effect	*F*	*df*	*p*	*Effect size*
Community conflict	7.50	(1, 424)	.006	.017
Age group	.01	(1, 424)	.940	
Community conflict x age group	1.39	(1, 424)	.239	
Household size	3.71	(1, 424)	.055	
Service years	2.70	(1, 424)	.101	

Table 7.3 Results from 2 × 2 ANCOVAs to compare psychosocial outcomes for police with and without community conflict (Turkey, USA, respectively), age groups (under, over 30 years), using household size and service years as covariates

Police partner conflict				
Effect	*F*	*df*	*p*	*Effect size*
Community conflict	5.48	(1, 381)	.020	.014
Age group	.22	(1, 381)	.636	
Community conflict x age group	1.09	(1, 381)	.297	
Household size	.21	(1, 381)	.648	
Service years	.20	(1, 381)	.652	
Romantic partner conflict				
Effect	*F*	*df*	*p*	*Effect size*
Community conflict	.38	(1, 399)	.539	
Age group	1.50	(1, 399)	.221	
Community conflict x age group	.20	(1, 399)	.652	
Household size	.00	(1, 399)	.953	
Service years	.19	(1, 399)	.662	
Self-esteem				
Effect	*F*	*df*	*p*	*Effect size*
Community conflict	13.24	(1, 401)	.000	.032
Age group	.14	(1, 401)	.705	
Community conflict x age group	2.52	(1, 401)	.113	
Household size	.10	(1, 401)	.758	
Service years	1.23	(1, 401)	.269	

Comparison of Turkish and US Police in Negative Psychosocial Outcomes

To compare negative psychosocial outcomes reported from Turkey (with community conflict) and the USA (without community conflict), 2 × 2 ANCOVAs were used that again considered age group (under 30 years, 30+ years) and household size and service years as covariates because these demographic variables were found in above analyses to be significantly different for the Turkey and US samples. Results found that Turkish officers reported more police partner conflict ($p = .020$) and worse self-esteem ($p = .000$) than did US officers, with no significant differences found in their reported romantic partner conflict ($p = .539$) after controlling for demographic variables that differed between the two samples (see Table 7.3).

Discussion

Results from the present study offer a unique opportunity to compare workplace stressors and negative psychosocial outcomes, *measured with identical instruments*, for two samples of police officers with one sample presently experiencing community conflict directed toward their department (233 Turkish officers from Istanbul) and one sample presently free of such community conflict (207 US officers from the northeastern USA).

Results revealed that the Turkish officers (with community conflict) reported less intense stressors from critical incidents than did the US officers, perhaps because the *atypical stressor* of community violence directed at their department reduced their focus and concern about more typical critical incidents of police work (burglaries, car accidents, barricaded suspects). This *atypical stressor* forces police department with community conflict to utilize their principal human resources to contain the violence during exposure to the unusual critical incident. Conversely, police administrators give their officers less time to focus on more typical critical incidents. Additionally, they become more tolerant toward their officers and put less pressure on them to identify criminals. Another potential reason for the less intense stressors from critical incidents might be caused by a significant increase in police presence at locations where public protests and community conflicts intensified. This would create a feeling of police omnipresence that would reduce *typical* critical incidents of police work in these areas. On the other hand, the typical critical incidents of police work shift from the areas where community violence is directed toward police officers' departments to areas where police departments are free of such community conflict. Therefore, this might be another reason why the Turkish officers (with community conflict) reported less intense stressors from critical incidents than did the US officers.

Furthermore, the harmful impact of this community conflict for their department may have also been evident in the greater work-home conflict reported by Turkish officers, as well as their reduced anger, reduced self-esteem, and increased reports of police partner aggression. The threat of possible violence from the community conflict, and the disruption it produces for their usual workplace tasks and environment, may have resulted in officers being more hypervigilant and critical of the actions of fellow officers, thereby increasing verbal conflict among peers.

Finally, the disruption caused by the community conflict could have "spilled over" to affect officers' private lives (Caligiuri et al., 1998), such as in the greater work-home conflict and worse self-esteem reported by the Turkish officers (with community conflict) than by the US officers (without community conflict). Hence, the increased risk of death and injury in critical incidents would bring "spillover effects" into married police couples' family and work lives, creating stress for spouses, affecting job performance, and creating additional stress for police officers (Can et al., 2015). This perception requires further investigation to validate whether the disruption by community conflict has "spilled over" to affect officers' private lives. However, because strong family support would show "compensation effects" in reduced concern about any work-home conflict, married police officers use more efficient coping mechanisms than single police officers when coping with stress (Zhao et al., 2003; Can et al., 2015).

Study Limitations and Directions for Future Research

This research is preliminary in nature due to the number of variables that have not been included in the data analysis reported here. One limitation of the present study is that broader cultural differences between the Turkish and US police samples could have explained differences in their officers' reported workplace stressors and negative psychosocial outcomes. Especially with the increasing number of US incidents of widely publicized community violence directed toward police departments, future research needs to clarify whether exposure to such community conflict is the variable most predictive of officer perceptions of workplace stressors and negative psychosocial outcomes. For example, future research could examine whether similar patterns as those of present results are found in comparisons of police departments matched in nationality, size, urban or rural region, ethnicity, and resources. Future research could also examine whether officer stressors and negative outcomes associated with community conflict lead to reductions in job performance, increases in workplace deviance, and more decisions to leave the police force.

References

Anderson, W., & Bauer, B. (1987). Law enforcement officers: The consequences of exposure to violence. *Journal of Counseling and Development, 65*(7), 381–384.

Anderson, A. S., & Lo, C. C. (2011). Intimate partner violence within law enforcement families. *Journal of Interpersonal Violence, 26*(6), 1176–1193.

Body-Gendrot, S. (2016). *Public disorder and globalization*. Taylor and Francis Group LLC.

Brown, J. M., & Campbell, E. A. (1990). Sources of occupational stress in the police. *Work and Stress, 4*, 305–318.

Caligiuri, P. M., Hyland, M. M., Joshi, A., & Bross, A. S. (1998). Testing a theoretical model for examining the relationship between family adjustment and expatriates' work adjustment. *Journal of Applied Psychology, 83*(4), 598–614.

Can, S. H., & Hendy, H. M. (2014). Police stressors, negative outcomes associated with them, and coping mechanisms that may reduce them. *Police Journal: Theory, Practice, and Principles, 87*, 167–177.

Can, S. H., Sever, M., & Mire, S. (2008). Police job stress and domestic violence in police families. *International Journal of Crime, Criminal Justice, and Law, 3*, 73–81.

Can, S. H., Hendy, H. M., & Karagoz, T. (2015). Law Enforcement Officer Stress Survey-Revised (LEOSS-R): Four types of police stressors and negative psychosocial outcomes associated with them. *Policing: Journal of Policy and Practice, 9*, 144–176.

Caulfield, M. B., & Riggs, D. S. (1992). The assessment of dating aggression: Empirical evaluation of the Conflict Tactics Scale. *Journal of Interpersonal Violence, 7*, 549–558.

Gamson, W. A., & Sifry, M. L. (2013). The# Occupy movement: An introduction. *Sociological Quarterly, 54*(2), 159–163.

Gershon, R. R. M., Barocas, B., Canton, A. N., Li, X., & Vlahov, D. (2009). Mental, physical, and behavioral outcomes associated with perceived work stress in police officers. *Criminal Justice and Behavior, 36*, 275–289.

Graf, F. A. (1986). Relationship between social support and occupational stress among police officers. *Journal of Police Science and Administration, 14*(3), 178–186.

Hall, G. B., Dollard, M. F., Tuckey, M. R., Winefield, A. H., & Thompson, B. M. (2010). Job demands, work-family conflict, and emotional exhaustion in police officers: A longitudinal test of competing theories. *Journal of Occupational and Organizational Psychology, 83*, 237–250.

Hart, P. M., Wearing, A. J., & Headey, B. (1994). Perceived quality of life, personality, and work experiences: Construct validation of the Police Daily Hassles and Uplifts Scales. *Criminal Justice and Behavior, 21*, 283–311.

He, N., Zhao, J., & Archbold, C. A. (2002). Gender and police stress: The convergent and divergent impact of work environment, work-family conflict, and stress coping mechanisms of female and male police officers. *Policing: An International Journal of Police Strategies & Management, 25*(4), 687–708.

Headey, B., & Wearing, A. J. (1989). Personality, life events, and subjective well-being: Toward a dynamic equilibrium model. *Journal of Personality and Social Psychology, 57*, 731–739.

House, J. S., & Wells, J. A. (1978, April). Occupational stress, social support, and health. In *Reducing occupational stress: Proceedings of a conference* (pp. 78–140). US Department of Health, Education, and Welfare.

Ivie, D., & Garland, B. (2011). Stress and burnout in policing: Does military experience matter? *Policing: An International Journal of Police Strategies & Management, 34*(1), 49–66.

Johnson, S., Cooper, C., Cartwright, S., Donald, I., Taylor, P., & Millet, C. (2005). The experience of work-related stress across occupations. *Journal Of Managerial Psychology, 20*(2), 178–187.

Kureczka, A. W. (1996). Critical incident stress in law enforcement. *FBI Law Enforcement Bulletin, 65*(213), 10–16.

LaRocco, J. M., House, J. S., & French, J. R., Jr. (1980). Social support, occupational stress, and health. *Journal of Health and Social Behavior, 21*(3), 202–218.

Liberman, A. M., Best, S. R., Metzler, T. J., Fagan, J. A., Weiss, D. S., & Marmar, C. R. (2002). Routine occupational stress and psychological distress in police. *Policing: An International Journal of Police Strategies and Management, 25*, 421–439.

Maynard, P. E., & Maynard, N. E. (1982). Stress in police families-some policy implications. *Journal of Police Science and Administration, 10*(3), 302–314.

Mendonça, R. F., & Ercan, S. A. (2015). Deliberation and protest: Strange bedfellows? Revealing the deliberative potential of 2013 protests in Turkey and Brazil. *Policy Studies, 36*(3), 267–282.

Monk, T. H. (1988). Coping with the stress of shift work. *Work and Stress, 2*, 169–172.

Morris, A., Shinn, M., & DuMont, K. (1999). Contextual factors affecting the organizational commitment of diverse police officers: A levels of analysis perspective. *American Journal of Community Psychology, 27*(1), 75–105.

Pilcher, J. J., & Huffcutt, A. I. (1996). Effects of sleep deprivation on performance: A meta-analysis. *Sleep, 19*(4), 318–326.

Regehr, C., LeBlanc, V. R., Barath, I., Balch, J., & Birze, A. (2013). Predictors of physiological stress and psychological distress in police communicators. *Police Practice and Research, 14*(6), 451–463.

Rosa, R. R., Colligan, M. J., & Lewis, P. (1989). Extended workdays: Effects of 8- and 12-hour rotating shift schedules on performance, subject alertness, sleep patterns, and psychosocial variables. *Work and Stress, 3*, 21–32.

Rosenberg, M. (1965). *Society and the adolescent self-image*. Princeton University Press.

Schafer, W. E. (1997). Religiosity, spirituality, and personal distress among college students. *Journal of College Student Development, 38*(6), 633–647.

Schwartz, M. (2011). "Pre-Occupied", *The New Yorker*, 28 November: 28–35.

Stevens, D. J. (2008). *Police officer stress: Sources and solutions*. Pearson/Prentice Hall Press.

Van Hasselt, V. B., Sheehan, D. C., Malcolm, A. S., Sellers, A. H., Baker, M. T., & Couwels, J. (2008). The Law Enforcement Officer Stress Survey (LEOSS): Evaluation of psychometric properties. *Behavior Modification, 32*, 133–151.

Violanti, J. M. (2004). Predictors of police suicide ideation. *Suicide and Life-Threatening Behavior, 34*, 277–283.

Violanti, J. M., & Aron, F. (1993). Sources of police stressors, job attitudes, and psychological distress. *Psychological Reports, 72*(3), 899–904.

Weiss, D. S., Brunet, A., Best, S. R., Metzler, T. J., Liberman, A., Pole, N., Fagan, J. A., & Marmar, C. R. (2010). Frequency and severity approaches to indexing exposure to trauma: The Critical Incident History Questionnaire for police officers. *Journal of Traumatic Stress, 23*, 734–743.

Yun, I., Kim, S. G., Jung, S., & Borhanian, S. (2013). A study on police stressors, coping strategies, and somatization symptoms among South Korean frontline police officers. *Policing: An International Journal of Police Strategies & Management, 36*(4), 787–802.

Zhao, J. S., He, N. P., Lovrich, N., & Cancino, J. (2003). Marital status and police occupational stress. *Journal of Crime and Justice, 26*(2), 23–46.

Chapter 8
Community Violence, Vigilantism, and Mob Justice in South Africa

Christiaan Bezuidenhout and Annalise Kempen

Introduction

During July 2021, crowds looting and setting alight shopping centers was a common scene in mainly two of South Africa's nine provinces, namely, KwaZulu-Natal and Gauteng. Isolated incidents occurred in three other provinces, namely, North West, Mpumalanga and the Northern Cape. At the time it was widely reported that the imprisonment of Mr. Jacob Zuma, the former President of South Africa, for contempt of court, had triggered the civil unrest (PMG, 2021). The reason why he had been held in contempt of court was because he had failed to attend the hearing of the Judicial Commission of Inquiry into Allegations of State Capture, Corruption and Fraud in the Public Sector including Organs of the State ("the Commission") to give testimony about corruption during his presidency. This resulted in the Secretary of the Commission approaching the Constitutional Court, the country's apex court, on an urgent basis for an order that would compel Mr. Zuma to cooperate with this Commission's objectives and investigations. In spite of the Constitutional Court's judgment and order earlier in 2021 that Mr. Zuma had to file affidavits and attend the Commission's hearings to give evidence before it, he did not comply with the court order. Instead, he reacted by first releasing a public statement claiming that he was victimized by both the Constitutional Court and the Commission. Thereafter, he published another statement levelling serious criticism against the Judiciary and confirming that he would neither obey the Constitutional Court order nor cooperate with the Commission. As a result of Mr. Zuma's failure to obey the court order, the

C. Bezuidenhout (✉)
University of Pretoria, Pretoria, South Africa
e-mail: cb@up.ac.za

A. Kempen
Editor: Servamus, Pretoria, South Africa
e-mail: annalise@servamus.co.za

J. F. Albrecht, G. den Heyer (eds.), *Understanding and Preventing Community Violence*, https://doi.org/10.1007/978-3-031-05075-6_8

Constitutional Court held him in contempt of court and ordered an unsuspended sentence of imprisonment for a period of 15 months when it delivered its judgment on 29 June 2021 (Constitutional Court of South Africa, 2021). On 8 July 2021, the Minister of Justice and Constitutional Development, Mr. Raymond Lamola, confirmed that in the early hours of that day, Mr. Jacob Zuma was admitted into the Estcourt Correctional Centre in KwaZulu-Natal in compliance with the Constitutional Court order to begin his sentence (Department of Justice and Correctional Services, 2021) which sparked several incidents of community violence.

Looting Should Have Been No Surprise

If one were to be honest and go back in time, the looting and community violence that happened in July 2021 should have come as no surprise as Zuma and his followers had implied in the past that all hell would break loose should his prosecution (or persecution, as they argued) proceed (Booysen, 2021). However, the extent and magnitude of the looting and the damage caused not only in terms of the physical destruction, but because so many people had lost their lives, were beyond belief. A few days after the violence had broken out, South Africa's current President, Mr. Cyril Ramaphosa, addressed the nation on 12 July 2021 noting that "over the past few days and nights, there have been acts of public violence of a kind rarely seen in the history of our democracy." At the time, the President mentioned that the violence may indeed have had its roots in declarations made by individuals with a political purpose, in the expression of anger and frustration, or by those who sought to agitate for disorder and violence along ethical lines. However, Mr. Ramaphosa expressed the view that this turned into opportunistic acts of criminality with groups of people institating chaos as a cover for looting in theft. The President made it clear that "no grievance or political cause could justify the violence and destruction that we have seen in parts of KwaZulu-Natal and Gauteng" during July 2021 (The Presidency, 2021).

The protests started in KwaZulu-Natal with the forceful blocking of main roads and highways, including the burning of trucks that transported goods between the province's harbor ports and Gauteng, the economic heartland of the country. It soon spread with threats made to economic keypoints such as the Port of Durban, the Port of Richards Bay, King Shaka International Airport, the offices of the South African Broadcasting Commission (the SABC), water and electricity infrastructure, and fuel depots. About a month after the violence broke out, the National Council of Provinces (NCOP) Committee on Security and Justice was informed by the Department of Police, the South African Police Service (SAPS), and the KwaZulu-Natal Provincial Government that vigilante groups had mushroomed in various areas resulting in brutal attacks and massacres. By mid-August 2021, 360 people had sadly lost their lives, while extensive damage was caused to 161 malls and shopping centers, 11 warehouses, eight factories, and 161 liquor outlets and distributors. More than 200 shopping centers and 300 shops were looted; at least 1400 ATMs were damaged, while 100 shopping malls suffered fire damage. In addition, 300 banks and post offices had been vandalized, 113 communication infrastructures were significantly damaged, and 1119 retail stores were damaged. The estimated impact on the country's GDP is R50 billion [about US $3.4 billion] as a result of the civil unrest (PMG, 2021).

However, these acts of violence and thuggery are not rare occurrences in South Africa. In fact, they are daily phenomena and manifest in different ways in different parts of the country. Community violence, vigilante justice, and mob violence are routine occurrences in most parts of South Africa. With an annual average of more than 600 000 cases of contact crime, which involved some form of violence against another person being reported to the SAPS (2020), it is clear that violence in general and community violence specifically are spiraling out of control across South Africa while mob justice attacks have become increasingly commonplace (Clark, 2018: 3). Many believe that these acts of violence in communities are the product of a social order in which violence has become normalized and entrenched on all levels of society. Because of South Africa's unique socio-political history, high rates of unemployment, and the large number of people living below the breadline, managing conflict and challenges through violence is engrained in South Africa's historical context (Naidoo & Sewpaul, 2014: 95). A "culture of violence" which implicates that violence is a means to an end or the only way to achieve success is common and enables one to either dominate others, deal with your own insecurities, or get what you want by means of violence (Bezuidenhout & Coetzee, 2017: 185). A significant dark figure exists regarding the type of crimes committed during mob attacks since mob violence is not quantified as a separate category in current South African legislation, and if a victim is killed during a mob attack, the motive for the murder cannot always be established.

Mob Justice and Mob Violence

According to the South African Police Service's annual crime statistics for the period from 1 April 2019 to 31 March 2020, at least 1202 people died as a result of vigilantism or mob justice. This type of violence resulted in a further 224 people who had been victims of attempted murder; 1867 people who had been the victims of assault with the intent to inflict grievous bodily harm (GBH), while another 595 people had been victims of common assault during this period (SAPS, 2020). This means that an average of three people lose their lives each day in South Africa due to mob violence or mob justice.

Mob justice is also referred to as instant justice or lynching (Sibanda, 2014). Others explain mob justice "as a situation where a crowd of people, sometimes several hundred, take the law into their own hands, act as accusers, jury and judge and punish an alleged criminal on the spot (Glad et al., 2010). This procedure often ends up with the victim being beaten to death or seriously injured." Sibanda (2014) adds that the person who is being accused of a crime has no chance of defending him- or herself or claiming his or her innocence. As a result the victim of mob "justice" is denied a fair trial and the right to life which violates the individual's human rights in terms of the Bill of Rights contained in the Constitution of the Republic of South Africa, 1996.

One of the many victims of mob violence and justice was the 28-year-old Thoriso Themane from South Africa's Limpopo province who had been dragged, assaulted, and stoned to death by a group of people, including high school students, in February 2018. The disturbing video depicting the brutal incident went viral on social media causing more trauma to those who had witnessed the attack, including the victim's family and friends. Following the arrest of nine teenagers for Themane's murder, the National Commissioner of the SAPS said that "any act of vigilantism is as much criminal as the action of the person accused of committing a crime" (Lancaster, 2019).

Another case that made headlines was when a former local football club player from Kaizer Chiefs, Lucky Maselesele, was killed for allegedly stealing electricity cables. On the night in question, the police received a complaint just before midnight that community members were assaulting an unknown male. Upon the police's arrival, the assailants ran away, but police could apprehend two suspects, who were charged with murder. At the time, the police spokesperson said that "it's alleged that the deceased was accused by the community of stealing electricity cables in the area. He was certified dead on the scene by the paramedics" (Fengu, 2021).

As is clear from the examples, these types of attacks are often cruel and extremely violent and perpetrated by a mob. The latter is defined as "a large crowd of people, especially one that is disorderly and intent on causing trouble or violence" (https://www.lexico.com/en/definition/mob). A popular act when mobs attack an alleged culprit is the so-called kangaroo court method during mob violence. This type of court is defined by the *Merriam-Webster Dictionary* as "a mock court in which the principles of law and justice are disregarded or perverted" and "a court characterized by irresponsible, unauthorized, or irregular status or procedures" (https://www.merriam-webster.com/dictionary/kangaroo%20court). What would typically happen is that a suspected transgressor will be accosted by an angry mob, prosecuted, and punished in public in a matter of minutes – usually with fatal consequences. In the majority of cases the assumed "guilty" suspect never gets the opportunity to state their own case or to defend themselves. Community members will hold unauthorized and fake "court" proceeding to settle a dispute or to punish an alleged perpetrator. As a result, the accused's due process rights to representation and a fair trial are disregarded, and the outcome give the impression to be predetermined. The punishment varies from being beaten, caned, bombarded with rocks and stones (Lancaster, 2019), kicked, beaten, dragged, or punished by means of a practice known as "necklacing." Clark (2018) informs us that "necklacing" refers to a brutal process when victims are burned to death in an act that reminds of the political violence that happened in South Africa during the late 1980s and early 1990s. During the necklacing process, the angry community members would force a vehicle tire doused in gasoline or another flammable liquid substance over the alleged transgressor's chest and arms and set it alight. Moyo-Kupeta (2021) agrees with Clark's comments and notes that these practices evoke memories of the apartheid-era style of dealing with impimpis (informers). Any person who was thought to share any information with the police or government was seen as an impimpi and was dealt with in this way. This painful death was not instant, and it also had a function to prevent others from becoming impimpis.

A Lack of Trust in the Authorities Contributes to Mob Justice

One of the alleged reasons why law-abiding citizens and children commit mob violence and heinous acts against fellow humans is their lack of trust in the police and the Criminal Justice System (CJS). Unfortunately, in most instances the inevitable consequence of community violence, mob justice, or vigilantism is that some sections of a community change over from largely law-abiding people into offenders (Lancaster, 2019). In the wake of mob justice killings, the question can rightly be asked how usually non-violent, law-abiding citizens become criminals overnight by committing such horrendous and macabre violent crimes (Moyo-Kupeta, 2021).

According to the findings of a survey conducted by Afrobarometer (2021) that were released on 8 October 2021, trust in South Africa's police was at an all-time low with 73% of respondents saying that they trusted the police not at all or just a little, and 26% claiming that they trusted the police somewhat or a lot. In cases when people intervene and stop crime in progress, they are most likely to hand over the perpetrators to the police or local authorities. Unfortunately, the lack of trust in the police contributes to cases where suspected perpetrators are caught and the community decides to also "punish" them (Lancaster, 2019) resulting in jungle or mob justice. In many cases the community also lack the incentive to hand the alleged criminals to the police or call them if they are of the opinion that nothing will happen to the alleged perpetrator. The community do not only want swift accountable justice when a perpetrator is arrested by the police, but need a guarantee that they will be prosecuted and convicted by the Criminal Justice System. Unfortunately, a variety of factors, including the conditions set during their bail proceedings, often result in the same arrested suspects being back on the streets in the same community within hours or days after their arrest. This makes people fearful, angry, and distrustful and as can be predicted, many South Africans, especially in rural and informal settlements, respond to this "lack of justice" by taking the law into their own hands resulting in mob violence.

Research conducted by South Africa's Centre for the Study of Violence and Reconciliation (CSVR) indicated that such violence often does not occur in a vacuum, but that community members would often have tried more peaceful ways of addressing the issues and problems prevalent in their communities. However, when the authorities, including the police, fail to address the community's grievances, they resort to violence, taking the law unlawfully into their own hands to deal with their own problems. Moyo-Kupeta (2021) from the CSVR denounces that this is what happened in the Zandspruit informal settlement area of Johannesburg where the community had reported crime and pointed out the criminals to the police without the latter taking any action.

Chumile Sali, a project officer with the African Policing Civilian Oversight Forum, a non-governmental organization that focuses on issues of police accountability and governance in Africa, echoed the CSVR's research findings. In his opinion, vigilantism has become normal in poor black communities where people feel they are not being serviced appropriately by the police. "The rate of violence will continue to rise unless we change how we police these communities," he said. He further used the example of Nyanga on the Cape Flats, an area which was regarded as South Africa's murder capitol between 2017 and 2019, where 597 murders were reported between 1 April 2017 and 31 March 2019. According to Mr. Sali, as many as 50 percent of these recorded murders could be connected to vigilante group actions (Clark, 2018).

Service Delivery Protests

The lack of trust in the police and the broader Criminal Justice System (which include the judiciary and correctional services) is not the only area where the community is unsatisfied with the Government. In South Africa, community violence often manifests due to poor service delivery and a lack of municipal utilities. Many towns, informal settlements, and rural areas experience regular power failures, a lack of fresh, running water, and basic municipal services such as sanitation (Geldenhuys, 2017a: 18)

South Africans have the right to protest, demonstrate, or strike in public in terms of section 17 of the Constitution of the Republic of South Africa, 1996, yet, this right may not infringe upon the rights of others, who opt not to participate in protests or to have their property destroyed. South Africa also has specific legislation in the form of the Regulation of Gatherings Act 205 of 1993 which allows for protests to be prohibited if they cause serious disruption. In such cases, the authorities, which include the police and the institution against which the protest is held such as the local government or municipality, should consult with the protestors before dispersing them. This legislation requires of the organizers to give notice of such gathering at least 7 days prior to the planned event and that the gathering can be prohibited if credible information is "brought to the attention of a responsible officer that there is a threat that a proposed gathering will result in serious disruption of vehicular or pedestrian traffic, injury to participants in the gathering or other persons, or extensive damage to property and that the SAPS and the traffic officers in question will not be able to contain this threat" (Geldenhuys, 2017a: 16).

In order to understand the meaning of "service delivery protest," Municipal IQ, a unique web-based data and intelligence service specializing in the monitoring and assessment of South Africa's municipalities, notes that it "describes a protest which is galvanised by inadequate local services or tardy service delivery, the responsibility for which lies with a municipality." It emphasizes that using this term makes it clear that similar protests occur across the country, of which many occur in informal settlement in the largest metropolitan areas. Allan and Heese (2021) further remind us that these metropolitan areas experience the highest population growth rates of all the localities and that there is a strong statistical link between high levels of migration and service delivery protests. These researchers also note that while the violence and criminality that are often associated with service delivery protests are unacceptable and should be condemned, “it is worth remembering that the communities living in informal settlements are essentially excluded from society – they have access neither to economic nor social opportunity and find themselves on the outside looking in” (Allan & Heese, 2021).

Even though many service delivery protests by communities are intended to be peaceful marches, they often turn into violent mob events where people are hurt, and property is damaged. For the period between 1 April 2019 and 31 March 2020, the SAPS recorded 8608 public order incidents of which 3636 or 42% were unrest-related (SAPS, 2020). In response to a Parliamentary question about service delivery protests, the Minister of Police, Mr. Bheki Cele, replied that 909 such protests took place between 1 August 2020 and 31 January 2021. These were reported as crowd management-unrest related incidents resulting in the arrest of 657 people (Martin, 2021).

The huge socio-economic disparities in South Africa also contribute to the frustrations among communities due to high levels of poverty, poor infrastructure, and the lack of adequate housing. As long as government, on local (municipal), provincial, and national levels fail to deliver these promised services, service delivery protests will remain a reality in the country. Examples that come to mind include when the residents of Soweto, Eldorado Park, and Freedom Park in Gauteng protested about the lack of housing, resulting in them blocking roads and burning tires in May 2017. The protests turned violent as the police had running battles along some of the major highways in the area, while several shops and a filling station were looted. Community members armed themselves with stones and petrol bombs and attempted to push the police back. During many of these protests, the police have to use water cannons, rubber bullets, or stun grenades to disperse the crowds when the latter resorts to violence (Geldenhuys, 2017a: 18).

The #FeesMustFall Student Protests

In 2015, a form of protests hit South Africa from an unexpected front. It resulted in so much publicity that it was even nominated at the Newsmaker of the Year for 2015 event. It started in October 2015 at the University of the Witwatersrand’s campus in Johannesburg, but soon spread to university campuses across the country as the students were protesting about the proposed student fee increases for the 2016 academic year. However, the fee structure, which quickly became known as the #FeesMustFall protests, was only one of the many issues that triggered the tertiary students’ disgruntlement. It had started earlier with #RhodesMustFall at the

University of Cape Town when students expressed their unhappiness about symbols of colonialism on the campus such as the statue of Cecil John Rhodes (Mavunga, 2019). The University of the Western Cape felt the brunt of the #FeesMustFall campaign in November 2015 when protesting students broke windows, looted dining halls, damaged a vehicle, and hurled stones at police. Students also congregated outside the residences, setting rubbish bins, couches, and tables on fire. One of the authors was a Head of a residence during this period and experienced the angry mobs of students, vandalism, and petrol bombs first hand. The students' anger was fueled further after the head of the university council had sent an e-mail to the Vice-Chancellor in which he allegedly criticized part of the #FeesMustMall campaign. According to the students, the e-mail had contradicted their agreement with the vice-chancellor which covered student debt, fees, the employment by the university of workers who worked on campus but were employed by private companies, and the private residence Kovacs. As a result of the violence perpetrated by the students in damaging infrastructure, they were met by the police who used rubber bullets, teargas, and stun grenades against the protestors (Furlong, 2015).

By January 2016, the students' protests included their unhappiness about their accommodation and language instruction policies at mainly the historically white universities, and the outsourcing of support staff such as gardeners, cleaners, and security officers. Sadly, the protests were very violent which led to the suspension of lectures and examinations, damage to property, as well as injury and arrest of some students at some universities (Mavunga, 2019). In March 2021, the #FeesMustFall 2.0 was catapulted back to the forefront of South African politics. In the process, a totally innocent bystander, namely, the 35-year-old Mthokozisi Ntumba, a civil servant who had just come out from a medical appointment in Johannesburg's inner city, became the innocent victim of stray rubber bullets. This happened after the police had fired the rubber bullets towards student protesters who had reignited the movement, which had raged across South African tertiary institutions since 2015, resulting in Mr. Ntumba being fatally wounded (Mpofu-Walsh, 2021).

Witchcraft and Mob Violence

Due to indigenous practices still prevalent in South Africa, individuals or mobs in the community sometimes identify witches in their neighborhood and if a witch is labelled as an evil person who caused any harm to someone or the neighborhood or caused poor harvests, he or she will be prosecuted and killed by the community members. According to Professor Theodore Petrus, an anthropologist at the University of Fort Hare in South Africa who has done extensive research on the topic of witchcraft, witches can be male or female, inherit their witchcraft powers and familiars from their mothers or their fathers. However, the majority of witchcraft suspects are elderly women (Geldenhuys, 2016: 24–25).

Witchcraft per se is not a crime in South Africa, but the Witchcraft Suppression Act 3 of 1957 stipulates that it is an offense to call someone a witch. The police will therefore not investigate witchcraft per se but rather the criminal acts that may be associated with witchcraft as defined by common and statutory law. This then results in those who accuse others of witchcraft who are arrested as well as those who perpetrate crimes against such persons suspected of practicing witchcraft, such as when they are assaulted or even killed. Numerous suspected witches have been the victims of mob justice as they have been shot, hacked, or stabbed to death. In the Eastern Cape village of Mlengana near Port St. Johns, a mob of youths abducted an elderly woman from her home after 15 people had died in a bus crash. The woman was taken to a mountain where she was interrogated about the crash, whereafter they hacked her to death with bush knives as they believed that she had bewitched the victims. In a case that happened in KwaZulu-Natal, a man was stoned and set alight by a group of vigilante community members after they accused him of raping and disemboweling his 14-year-old female cousin. The suspect allegedly confessed to his aunt that he had murdered the girl for her body parts on instruction from his traditional leader as the body parts were to be used in the making of a get-rich-quick magical potion (Geldenhuys, 2016: 26).

Nature of Mob Justice and Vigilantism in South Africa

Dr. Mary Nel, a lecturer in law at the University of Stellenbosch who wrote her thesis on South African vigilantism, is of the opinion that "vigilante groups by their very nature are sort of in that grey area between the law and crime and so it's very easy to overstep that mark. These groups often start with good intentions, then they get a bit of power and that power corrupts or is co-opted" (Clark, 2018). She explains that vigilantism can be understood as "the unlawful and intentional use of force by private citizens to punish someone who is the perpetrator of real or perceived forms of deviance. It is aimed (at least in part) at offering guarantees of collective security and social order in circumstances where there is a real or perceived absence of effective formal guarantees of order and security" (Nel, 2016). In addition, Bateson (2020) adds that vigilatism is more than a reaction to crime, it is an exercise in power as it creates and reinforces hierarchies that amplify some voices and silence others, stifling dissent. Simultaneously, by selectively punishing only certain offenses, vigilantes can draw attention to particular issues.

It is not always clear what mob violence entails in terms of the process of how a law-abiding individual transforms to a participant in a violent mob and the correlating emotional and instrumental factors of instigation and participation. Groups or mobs originate from different triggers in their environment and often have different motivations for their behavior. Mob violence is the consequence of a disorderly crowd of people that engage in lawless violence. There are at least three forms of mob violence, namely, riots, lynching, and vigilantism (Kempen, 1999: 8–15; Encyclopedia Britannica, [sa]). In criminal law, riots refer to a violent offense against public order, wherein three or more people gather for an unlawful purpose (Brittanica.com). The Arab Spring, a series of anti-government protests, uprisings, and armed rebellions that spread across much of the Arab world since 2010 (Abderrahmane, 2021) will fall into this category. The service delivery strikes and riots in South Africa will also fall into this category. Lynching is another form of violence which refers to an illegal execution of a presumed offender, often after inflicting torture and corporal mutilation, by a mob to maintain social control. This is done under the pretext of administering justice, but without a trial. Similarly, lynch law refers to a self-constituted "court" that imposes a sentence on a person without the process of law (Britannica.com). For example, the white supremacist group called Ku Klux Klan relied on violent tactics such as lynching to protect their privileged lifestyle compared to that of African Americans (https://www.bbc.co.uk/bitesize/guides/zq6csg8/revision/30). The kangaroo court and necklacing process in South Africa that have been discussed earlier in this chapter is relevant here.

Roelofse (2014: 18–19) informs us that vigilantism often stars as the result of a specific crime problem when the feeling among an entire community or a specific group is that the state is neglecting its duty to protect against criminals. It is therefore the reaction to a lack of public confidence and a reaction to what is perceived as poor policing. South Africa has two well-known vigilante groups, namely, PAGAD (People Against Gangsterism and Drugs) and Mapogo-a-Mathamaga, which were both formed during the 1990s. Mapogo-a-Mathamaga was established in the northern most province of South Africa by a group of local traders after local businessmen had been killed in separate incidents of violence. Their purpose was to root out criminal elements to ensure that justice was done. They later had memberships in other provinces and even among white farmers and businessmen and later organized and even registered themselves as a private security company. PAGAD's vision was to address certain problems in the community focusing on the scourge of gangsterism and drugs by raising the consciousness of the people, mass mobilization, and mass action. However, their noble cause turned criminal after group members took the law unlawfully into their own hands and hurled pipe bombs at people's homes in the wider Cape Town metropolitan area (Kempen, 1999: 10–13). Although vigilantism or "popular justice" occurs in most parts of South Africa, it is rife in the Western Cape Province among the different street gangs and in predominantly Black African townships and informal settlements. We believe that the reason for vigilante attacks in the Western Cape between the gangs is perhaps more in line with turf wars and establishing dominance while vigilantism in townships and settlements often have a torture and punishment component to it. However, in both instances vigilante justice or taking the law into your own hands is a challenge to the effectiveness of and belief in the South African Criminal Justice System.

Based on the different reasons why mobs and vigilante groups develop their motivations and why they participate, one can identify different types of mobs or groups.

Alvarez and Bachman state that there are four types of mobs:

- The aggressive mob targets people, property, or both. Violence is mainly motivated by emotion, and the group's existence is momentarily.
- The expressive mob utilizes violence as a means to voice their sentiments. Violence is viewed as a legitimate expression of collective emotions such as frustration, anger, and indignation.
- The acquisitive mob includes looters who plunder and steal because they are motivated by greed and a desire to obtain goods.
- The escape mob is characterized by panicked behavior. It is perhaps the only type of mob that can be instantly aroused into mindless violence.

The central theme in many cases of community violence or popular justice is the collective nature of the behavior. Several theories have been developed to explain these collective actions by a group or mob. In some cases, members of the group are not known to each other, but they unite as one when they have the same objective. The deindividuation theory stems from Gustave Le Bon's classic crowd theory as formulated in his book *The Crowd: A Study of the Popular Mind* (1895). Le Bon focused on the mob mentality as he attempted to explain how a person can transform from a law-abiding individual to a hysterical and violent person in the context of a mob who disregards breaking the law. He suggested that the mob develops a mind of its own and that individuals are susceptible to the collective group's will. Therefore, individuals' personalities cease to exist as it is substituted by a collective mind. Collective behavior plays a role in the instigation and perpetuation of violence and criminal activities, such as a necklacing incident (Bartol & Bartol, 2017: 127).

Herbert Blumer expanded on Le Bon's work by stating that a trigger that instigates mob violence must be present as well as a group of people converging on a common element as their emotions intensify. The deindividuation theory refers to the loss of a person's sense of individuality when they are in a group and, as a result, their uncoerced controls are removed and their internalized moral inhibitions are neutralized. It is closely related to the perception that one is not being scrutinized or accountable when operating as a group. Philip Zimbardo identified a chain of events that lead to deindividuation. He stated that the presence of other persons creates a sense of anonymity and non-accountability as the individual experiences a loss of identity when becoming part of the group (Bartol & Bartol, 2017: 123). Consequently, following the diffusion of the individual's identity into the collective identity, the person feels a loss of self-awareness, a disregard for the evaluation from others, and a limited focus of attention (Bartol & Bartol, 2017: 123). The collective identity facilitates collective thinking where several individuals think as one – a collective brain.

There are other factors that can also potentially explain why a person will participate in mob violence. Perhaps the concept of novelty suggests that bored individuals may view collective action as a viable option to break monotony and, in turn, produce excitement. Next, a person may be disinterested and unaffected by the collective group's grievance or cause; however, he or she may participate for the purpose of releasing a more general form of hostility and/or frustration. Furthermore, a desire for feelings of domination and supremacy can encourage an individual to participate in mob violence as it makes participants feel empowered by the violence and devastation that they cause. In some instances, the feelings of power as mentioned above can lead to justification considering that group members can experience a sense of righteousness and legitimacy. Lastly, people have an innate tendency to conform to a group's demands, especially considering that some forms of mob action such as riots tend to attack and victimize individuals who resist or do not choose to conform. In Blikkiesdorp (roughly translated to "Tin town" in English), on the outskirts of Cape Town, many residents initially supported the vigilantes whose targets were the leaders of a ruthless local gang called the Young Gifted Bastards (YGB). The YGB had terrorized the community with impunity for years, carrying out daily and sometimes deadly muggings, burglaries, and drug deals – often just to fund their own drug habits. As a result of the vigilantes' actions, many of the YGB's leaders were either killed, hospitalized, or went into hiding. However, the community's support for the vigilantes started to change when the latter apparently started "killing for fun," targeting those who allegedly did nothing wrong, such as Tashrieq Johnson. According to his father, Tashrieq was a soft-spoken 25-year-old man who had been burned to death in a brutal gasoline attack in September 2018. "Tashrieq didn't do anything wrong. He wouldn't harm a fly. Things can't go on like this," he said (Clark, 2018). What the real reason of Tashrieq's brutal death was is unclear, but that he was targeted by the vigilantes seems sure.

Xenophobic Attacks by Angry Mobs

Another area where community violence regularly occurs is violence against legal and illegal immigrants, also referred to as undocumented migrants, from neighboring or foreign countries. Immigrants are often the victims of local community mobs due to certain ill-informed perceptions towards them. Prejudice and feelings of threat and hopelessness fuel these xenophobic events. Xenophobia can be defined as an irrational fear, mistrust of, or an aversion to strangers, foreign nationals such as immigrants, or anything that is regarded as alien or different. Xenophobic attacks are usually perpetrated in a group that targets a single or a limited number of victim(s), and consequently, the targets are unable to defend themselves given their small ratio to the large number of perpetrators in the community (Bezuidenhout & Klopper, 2011: 216–217). People of neighboring African countries migrate to South Africa in search of a promising future when they flee from their countries of origin due to violence, poverty, and/or droughts (e.g., Zimbabwe, Mozambique; Lesotho) (Harris, 2001). Also, foreigners from countries such as China, Pakistan, Bangladesh, and India who open businesses in high-risk areas such as informal settlements, are often the targets of xenophobic attacks. An increase in xenophobic attacks occurred since South Africa underwent a transformation from an apartheid state to a democratic government in 1994. During the pre-1994 period, the expression of xenophobia was facilitated by laws and policy which enabled the strict control of anyone who was deemed different (Kempen, 2017: 28). Individuals who were non-white were labelled as the "other," and their claims to national rights and citizenship were controverted. It altered citizenship in a manner that gave rise to conflict and competition as it emphasized inclusion and exclusion (Zondi, 2008: 31). Following the abolition of apartheid, the hatred of foreigners substituted the divide between white and black South Africans (Kempen, 2017: 28). The occurrence of xenophobia in South Africa forms part of the challenge of reconstructing a state and society following colonial rule (Zondi, 2008: 31). Xenophobic violence is the result of a combination of factors such as South Africa's "culture of violence" that instigates and approves xenophobia. So-called black-on-black xenophobic violence has become the norm in South Africa with many Black South Africans believing that their actions and feelings towards immigrants are justified. They do not trust the police and harbor negative feelings towards the SAPS. Critique includes complicity in xenophobic violence, incompetence, and a lack of resources (Bekker, 2015: 239–240). For this reason and differently ill-informed prejudices, some South Africans see a need for mob justice against foreigners. Some communities believe that illegal or undocumented migrants are committing a high number of crimes in South Africa since there are no records of their fingerprints on the South African fingerprint database and they rarely have permanent home addresses (Chaskalson, 2017; Masiloane, 2010: 50). Mob violence towards immigrants is also complicated by current migration policy and careless border controls (Masiloane, 2010: 42). Politicians sometimes exaggerate the number of illegal and legal immigrants in the country which can also contribute to xenophobia. Many South Africans believe that immigrants are taking away their job opportunities, are willing to work for lower wages, work for longer hours, and are resistant to unionization. In short, the perceived influx of foreigners (true or not) poses a threat to the opportunities of local South Africans. In addition, some local males believe immigrants are more successful with local female partners. This belief apparently exists because the immigrants are at least earning an income to provide even if they are willing to work for lower wages (Bekker, 2015: 240; Kempen, 2017: 29). Another factor is poverty which facilitates an ongoing competition between poor people to fulfill their basic needs such as eating food and having a place to stay. Frustration stems from competition for housing and municipal services, which is exacerbated by service delivery failure on the part of the government (Bekker, 2015: 240). In this context, the realistic group conflict theory is relevant as the theory is based on the premise that competition between two groups for similar resources, whether real or perceived, can result in intolerance and prejudice. Muzafer Sherif maintained that intergroup conflict (i.e., conflict between groups) occurs when two groups are in competition for limited resources (Sherif, 1967). Resources in the rural areas and informal settlements in South Africa involve, among others, access to homes and jobs. If one group (immigrants) is willing to work for lower wages and longer hours to obtain resources, the other group (local South Africans) become frustrated. Consequently, adverse attitudes develop towards members from the other group while intergroup competition will also arise, resulting in xenophobic attacks where locals retaliate in response to the perceived threat posed by foreign nationals. Therefore, mob violence can be a product of both instrumental violence and expressive violence; the former goal-directed (such as to loot the shop of a foreigner to claim the goods in his shop) while the latter is emotionally satisfying (such as to necklace (brutally murder) the competition and feel they are no threat anymore) (Bruce, 2010: 14).

Competition for jobs is problematic since South Africa has an unemployment rate of 34.4 percent (Kumwenda-Mtambo, 2021). Mob attacks on immigrants are complicated by the fact that 60 percent of South Africans believe that immigrants take the job opportunities of local South Africans (Chaskalson, 2017). Consequently, foreigners become the scapegoat as they are being held responsible for the deterioration of South Africa and the lack of opportunities (Zondi, 2008: 28). Many South Africans experience relative deprivation as the economic strain within their social environment force them to compare themselves with the standards of living that are propagated by society. They lack resources to sustain a healthy diet, an average lifestyle, participate in social activities and enjoy amenities that are widely encouraged or approved in the society to which they belong (Maree, 2013: 70). Since some Black South Africans experience these frustrations that are facilitated by poverty, inadequate service delivery, and the failure to fulfill their expectations – which many consider as their entitlement – it cultivates a shared generalized anger towards their perceived direct competitors (immigrants) for scarce resources (Human Sciences Research Council, 2008 in Bekker, 2015: 244–245). The result of these perceptions and frustrations culminates in brutal xenophobic attacks on foreign individuals and their property by angry local mobs (Jansen van Rensburg & Mpuru, 2017: 27).

Addressing Community Violence, Vigilante Attacks, and Mob Violence

Isolated incidents of community violence are easier to manage through effective policing and an effective CJS. Unfortunately, in South Africa community violence or popular justice is rife, and the professionalism of the police and the CJS is being questioned. The SAPS's Public Order Policing (POP) Unit is the key component responsible for dealing with protests, especially where there is violence of a risk thereof. Over the past decade this has been one of the policing units which has been widely criticized following the Marikana incident in August 2012 during which the police shot and killed 34 striking miners and injured 76 others (Geldenhuys, 2017a: 21).

To address and tackle community violence, mob justice, and looting, the following needs to be considered:

- The state/government needs to re-establish its legitimacy by demonstrating its capacity to reduce the public's feelings of fear and insecurity. This requires of all the relevant government departments to deliver the required services (improve service delivery on all levels), deal harshly with crime (including vigilantism and community violence), and delegitimize the option that violence is a way to solve problems. For this to happen, Nel (2017) argues that the state must act in a way that it respects its citizens' human rights.

- Police members attached to the Public Order Policing (POP) Units in South Africa must undergo regular training to respond to public violence and crowd management (South African Police Service, 2018) more effectively. Calls have been made for police members to be trained to understand that the use of force in quelling violent public protests, should be avoided where possible, but that police members should rather be equipped with skills to negotiate with protest leaders and mobs (Geldenhuys, 2017b: 21–22). In cases where negotiations have failed to disperse the crowds, the protest gets volatile, and POP Unit members cannot control the crowd in another way, only then should they use smoke and stun grenades, the water cannon, and as a last resort, fire rubber bullets (Baloyi, 2017: 25). There is also an argument to be made that all frontline police officials (uniformed police members who are first responders from local police stations) should receive basic training in dealing with gatherings and protest actions which could result in community violence, at least until specialized policing units such as the POP Unit arrive at the scene.
- Mob violence needs to be identified as criminality rather than a social phenomenon. It must be dealt with and condemned accordingly by elected community leaders, politicians, the police and authorities, teachers, parents, and the mass media. This type of behavior needs to be rejected as repulsive, embarrassing, and shameful among neighbors and churches equally (Welner, 2011).
- Many South Africans have the perception that one can get away with crime, and, as a result, kangaroo courts, vigilantism, and mob justice often seem like a viable option to address lawlessness. Condemning the abovementioned mindset can act as a deterrent considering that punishment is just as applicable to vigilantes as to individuals who were murdered for allegedly engaging in illegal activities. Those who want to do something about crime and injustices in their community should join their local Community Police Forum to work closely with the police to eradicate crime (Geldenhuys, 2020), rather than taking the law unlawfully into their own hands.
- The media can learn to report in such a way that it evokes sympathy and empathy for the innocent victims of vigilantism and community and mob justice. This can be done by focusing on the vulnerability of the elderly whose shops or homes are damaged and as a result lose their livelihoods and shelter; or innocent bystanders who suffered life-threatening or lifelong injuries such as disabilities due to the violent actions of angry mob. This could contribute to evoking empathy for the unfortunate and innocent victims of such violence and mobilizing public outrage towards those who are responsible for unravelling the fabric of societal order (Welner, 2011).
- Restorative justice and the Ubuntu philosophy of "I am because you are" have the potential to address community violence in South Africa. The principles of restorative justice emphasize that crime concerns not only the harms committed

to individuals, but to the whole community. In the African traditions of justice, the community was involved as an alternative to the criminal justice system. Therefore, the philosophy of Ubuntu on which African communal cultural life is based has the potential for restorative justice as it focuses on the restoration of the victim, community, and the offender (Singh, 2005: 49; Elechi et al., 2010: 81). Nel (2017) is of the opinion that her research has shown that various community-driven restorative justice initiatives have been successful in the past, such as the Community Peace Programme which enabled community members to take peaceful ownership of their conflicts. The program was started in 1997 but was discontinued in 2009 due to a lack of state funding. Unfortunately, the effectivity of community involvement to end community violence is difficult as the lines are blurred due to the involvement of the same community in popular justice activities.

- A toll-free crime line that is accessible 24 h a day must be made available for the purpose of reporting mob violence. In addition, a mobile application should also be considered, especially since it can be installed on any smart device. The SAPS already has the MySAPS app, and it is suggested that the organization adds a specific button where mob violence or looting can be reported electronically or telephonically.
- One can consider forming an organized neighborhood watch or structure that allows trained community leaders and members to discourage crime and condemn violence, take the community's concerns seriously (Lancaster, 2019), supervise each other's property, and report incidents to the local police in their area. Simultaneously, such a structure can also be used as a reporting mechanism which can facilitate communication between authorities and communities. Take as an example when there has been a huge breakdown in basic services such as the disruption of water supply, regular communication and feedback about the extent of the problem and timelines when the service is likely to be restored could help to quell frustrations which could result in protest actions. Communication can be done using WhatsApp or Telegram groups and the like (Gould, 2021). Such community structures can also leverage pressure on authorities to sort out other problems in their area in an attempt to prevent future service delivery protests.
- Naming and shaming the instigators and looters is another option to consider in order to act as a deterrent for future perpetrators. This not only takes away the notion of anonymity of group violence but increases the risk for culprits to be exposed on public forums resulting in a greater possibility of prosecution. Naming and shaming is easier in areas with closed-circuit television cameras or where there is wide media coverage of the gatherings – provided that the owners of the footage is willing to share such. Few people will be brave enough to participate in community violence, mob justice, or looting if the group did not afford them anonymity (Welner, 2011).
- Resource allocation, training, and community education must form an essential part of the process because violence and nonconformist justice cannot be toler-

ated. A stable social order can be achieved by effectual informal social control and participatory justice (Singh, 2005: 49).

- Lastly, national public awareness campaigns are required to educate people and boost public awareness concerning mob violence. For instance, media campaigns must be conducted on social media, the radio, and/or television. In addition, educational programs and the school curriculum should be altered in a manner that advocates against mob violence and incentivize tolerance and inclusivity. According to a South African police officer who worked in an area in Gauteng where mob justice incidents were rife, people need to be educated and schooled into different ways of handling crime and conflict in society, through debate and discussions about crime, and the problems of mob justice (Geldenhuys, 2020: 15). *Dr. Michael* Welner *(2011), an American forensic psychiatrist, argues that* parents have to assume greater responsibility in controlling their children's behavior, while families need to reject any goods that enter their homes which had been stolen or bought as bargains from resellers because of its questionable origins (such as that they were the proceed of a looting spree).

Conclusion

Community violence cannot be understood without considering the plethora of dynamics in a specific community. One must also acknowledge the historical as well as the current factors at play in community violence. In addition, psychological and instrumental aspects are important in the manifestation of community violence. Community violence, mob violence, and vigilante justice, also broadly known as popular justice, highlight the fact that everyone in a certain situation is inherently susceptible to deindividuation and community violence. In South Africa, violence and collective action is ingrained in the moral fabric of society. The high unemployment rates, poverty, and fundamentally, the inadequacies and shortcomings of the current government fuel community violence. The latter is especially significant since a lack of trust of an incompetent police service seems to be an important contributing factor to collective community violence in general. In the South African context, xenophobic sentiments need to be addressed. Job creation, professional specialized policing units, a political will, as well as public condemnation of community violence are essential in addressing violence in general. Humans have been involved in wars and public violence since the earliest times, but we cannot use this as an excuse. Socialization, moral development, education, and awareness campaigns should be focusing on sensitization and address violence in general on all levels of society.

References

Abderrahmane, A. (2021, August 2). The Arab Spring struggle is far from over. *ISS Today*. Available from: https://issafrica.org/iss-today/the-arab-spring-struggle-is-far-from-over. Accessed 14 Oct 2021.

Afrobarometer. (2021). *South Africans' trust in police drops to new low, Afrobarometer survey finds*. Media statement dated 8 October. Available from: https://afrobarometer.org/press/south-africans-trust-police-drops-new-low-afrobarometer-survey-finds. Accessed 26 Oct 2021.

Allan, K. & Heese, K. (2021). *Understanding why service delivery protests take place and who is to blame*. Available from: https://www.municipaliq.co.za/publications/articles/sunday_indep.pdf. Accessed 27 Oct 2021.

Armstrong, J. (2017). *Hundreds of hooligans banned from following England abroad now free to travel to World Cup in Russia*. Available from: https://www.mirror.co.uk/sport/football/news/hundredshooligans-banned-following-england-11375791. Accessed 14 Oct 2021.

Baloyi, P. (2017). More "power" for public order policing units. *Servamus Community-based Safety and Security Magazine, 110*(7), 24–25. Pretoria: SARP Publishers.

Bartol, C. R., & Bartol, A. M. (2017). *Criminal behavior: a psychological approach*. Pearson Education.

Bateson, R. (2020). The politics of vigilantism. *Comparative Political Studies,* 54(6). Available from: https://journals.sagepub.com/doi/full/10.1177/0010414020957692. Accessed 27 Oct 2021.

Bekker, S. (2015). Violent xenophobic episodes in South Africa, 2008 and 2015. *African Human Mobility Review, 1*(3), 229–252.

Bezuidenhout, C., & Coetzee, L. (2017). Domestic violence in South Africa. In D. S. Peterson & J. A. Schroeder (Eds.), *Domestic violence in international context*. Routledge.

Bezuidenhout, C., & Klopper, H. (2011). Crimes of a violent nature. In C. Bezuidenhout (Ed.), *A South African perspective on fundamental Criminology*. Cape Town.

Booysen, S. (2021, July 30). South Africa's July riots and the long shadow of Jacob Zuma fall over party and state. *Daily Maverick*. Available from: https://www.dailymaverick.co.za/opinionista/2021-07-30-south-africas-july-riots-and-the-long-shadow-of-jacob-zuma-fall-over-party-and-state/. Accessed 26 Oct 2021.

British Broadcasting Corporation (BBC). [Sa.] International football. Available: http://news.bbc.co.uk/cbbcnews/hi/find_out/guides/sport/international_football/newsid_3089000/3089728.stm. Accessed 14 Oct 2021.

Bruce, D. (2010). Anger, hatred, or just heartlessness?: Defining gratuitous violence. *South African Crime Quarterly, 2010*(34), 13–22.

Chaskalson, R. (2017, September 18). Do immigrants "steal" jobs in South Africa? What the data tell us. *GroundUp*. Available from: https://www.groundup.org.za/article/do-immigrants-steal-jobs-south-africa-what-datatell-us/

Clark, C. (2018, November 29). South Africans are taking the law into their own hands. *Foreign Policy*. Available from: https://foreignpolicy.com/2018/11/29/south-africans-are-taking-the-law-into-their-own-hands-vigilantism-extralegal-justice-police-apartheid-anc-private-security/-. Accessed 14 Oct 2021.

Constitutional Court of South Africa. (2021). Secretary of the judicial commission of inquiry into allegation of state capture, corruption and fraud in the public sector including organ of state v Jacob Gedleyihlekisa Zuma CCT52/21. Post judgment media summary. Available from: https://www.concourt.org.za/index.php/judgement/398-secretary-of-the-judicial-commission-of-inquiry-into-allegation-of-state-capture-corruption-and-fraud-in-the-public-sector-including-organ-of-state-v-jacob-gedleyihlekisa-zuma-cct52-21. Accessed 30 July 2021.

Department of Justice and Correctional Services. (2021, July 8). *Statement by minister of justice and correctional services, ronald lamola outlining correctional services processes*. Available from: http://www.dcs.gov.za/wp-content/uploads/2021/05/Statement-by-Minister-of-Justice-

and-Correctional-Services2c-Ronald-Lamola-outlining-Correctional-Services-Processes-at-Estcourt2c-KwaZulu-Natal2c-08-July-2021-1.pdf. Accessed on 26 Oct 2021.

Deriemaeker, A. & De Maere, D.P. (2016). *Football hooliganism in England: is football hooliganism still as active now as it was during the 'English Disease'?*. Available from: https://www.researchgate.net/publication/298789337_Football_Hooliganism_in_England. Accessed 14 Oct 2021.

Education Risk Management. [Sa]. Managing fan and player violence at sporting events. Available from: file:///C:/Users/downi/Downloads/Managing%20Fan%20and%20Player%20 Violence%20at%20 Sporting%20Events.pdf. Accessed 14 October 2021.

Elechi, O. O., Morris, S. V. C., & Schauer, E. J. (2010). Restoring justice (Ubuntu): An African perspective. *International Criminal Justice Review, 20*(1), 73–85.

Encyclopedia Britannica. [Sa]. Riot. Available from: https://www.britannica.com/topic/riot Accessed 14 May 2019.

Fengu, M. (2021, October 17). Mob kills Maselesele for 'stealing cables'. *City Press*. Available from: https://www.news24.com/citypress/news/maselesele-runs-out-of-luck-as-mob-kills-him-for-stealing-cables-20211016. Accessed 17 Oct 2021.

Furlong, A. (2015, November 11). UWC students clash with police. *GroundUp*. Available from: https://www.groundup.org.za/article/uwc-students-clash-police_3496/. Accessed 27 Oct 2021.

Gauteng Department of Community Safety. [Sa]. Sector policing. Available from: http://www.gauteng.gov.za/government/departments/community-safety/Pages/SectorPolicing.aspx. Accessed 14 Oct 2021.

Geldenhuys, K. (2016). When cultural beliefs turn into crime: The witchcraft issue. *Servamus Community-based Safety and Security Magazine, 109*(6), 24–31. Pretoria: SARP Publishers.

Geldenhuys, K. (2017a). A language called violence. Violent protest actions. *Servamus Community-based Safety and Security Magazine, 110*(7), 16–20. Pretoria: SARP Publishers.

Geldenhuys, K. (2017b). Policing public violence. *Servamus Community-based Safety and Security Magazine, 110*(7), 21–23. Pretoria: SARP Publishers.

Geldenhuys, K. (2020). Mob justice serves not justice at all. *Servamus Community-based Safety and Security Magazine, 113*(11), 10–15. Pretoria: SARP Publishers.

Glad, R., Strongberg, A. & Westerlund, A. (2010). *Mob justice – A qualitative research regarding vigilante justice in modern Uganda*. Social Work Program dissertation University of Gothenburg. Available from: https://gupea.ub.gu.se/bitstream/2077/23084/1/gupea_2077_23084_1.pdf. Accessed 26 Oct 2021.

Godobo-Madikizela, P. (2006). *A human being died that night: forgiving apartheid's chief killer*. Portobello Books.

Gould, C. (2021, May 4). Lessons in preventing violent protest in South Africa. *ISS Today*. 4 May. Available from: https://issafrica.org/iss-today/lessons-in-preventing-violent-protest-in-south-africa. Accessed 28 Oct 2021.

Gow, P., & Rookwood, J. (2008). Doing it for the team – Examining the causes of hooliganism in English football. *Journal of Qualitative Research in Sports Studies, 2*(1), 71–82.

Harris, B. (2001). *A foreign experience: violence, crime and xenophobia during South Africa's transition*. Violence and Transition Series. Available from: http://www.csvr.org.za. Accessed 14 Oct 2021.

Hoffman, P. (2012, November 19). *Vigilantism: The last resort of the unprotected*. Institute for Accountability in Southern Africa. World Justice Project. Available from: https://worldjusticeproject.org/news/vigilantism-last-resort-unprotected

https://www.bbc.co.uk/bitesize/guides/zq6csg8/revision/30

https://www.lexico.com/en/definition/mob

https://www.merriam-webster.com/dictionary/kangaroo%20court

Independent Online News. (2019). *Mob violence condemned as another boy is killed*. Available from: https://www.iol.co.za/news/south-africa/north-west/mob-violence-condemned-as-another-boy-iskilled-19520804. Accessed 14 Oct 2021.

Jansen Van Rensburg, S., & Mpuru, L. (2017). Xenophobia in South Africa: is violence the answer? *Servamus Community-based Safety and Security Magazine, 110*(7), 26–27. Pretoria: SARP Publishers.

Kempen, A. (1999). Vigilantism: a question of jungle justice because of a lack of justice? *Servamus Policing Magazine, 92*(10), 8–15. Pretoria: SARP Publishers.

Kempen, A. (2017). Xenophobia – Serious prejudice against foreigners… with violent consequences. *Servamus Community-based Safety and Security Magazine, 110*(7), 28–32. Pretoria: SARP Publishers.

Kennedy, H. (2004). *Just law: the changing face of justice – And why it matters to us all*. Chatto & Windus.

Kumwenda-Mtambo, O. (2021, August 24). South Africa's unemployment rate hits new record high in second quarter. *Reuters: Economic News*. Available from: https://www.reuters.com/article/safrica-economy-unemployment/south-africas-unemployment-rate-hits-new-record-high-in-second-quarter-idUSJ8N2KH000. Accessed 14 Oct 2021.

Laing, J. (2010). *Why does football violence happen?*. Available from: http://news.bbc.co.uk/local/devon/hi/people_and_places/newsid_9176000/9176519.stm. Accessed 14 Oct 2021.

Lancaster, L. (2019, March 5). Is mob violence out of control in South Africa? *ISS Today*. 5 March. Available from: https://issafrica.org/iss-today/is-mob-violence-out-of-control-in-south-africa. Accessed 14 Oct 2021.

Longman, J. (1998). *World cup '98; Iran vs. America: Political football*. Available from: https://www.nytimes.com/1998/06/18/sports/world-cup-98-iran-vs-america-political-football.html. Accessed 14 Oct 2021.

Maree, A. (2013). Criminogenic risk factors for youth offenders. In C. Bezuidenhout (Ed.), *Child and youth misbehaviour in South Africa: a holistic approach* (3rd ed.). Van Schaik.

Martin, G. (2021). 900 service delivery protests in South Africa over six months. *DefenceWeb*. 20 April. – Available from: https://www.defenceweb.co.za/featured/900-service-delivery-protests-in-south-africa-over-six-months/. Accessed 26 Oct 2021.

Masiloane, D. (2010). Dealing with an economic crisis: the difficulty of policing illegal immigrants in South Africa. *South African Journal of Criminal Justice, 23*(1), 39–54.

Mavunga, G. (2019). #FeesMustFall protests in South Africa: A critical realist analysis of selected newspaper articles. *Journal of Student Affairs in Africa, 7*(1), 81–99.

Moyo-Kupeta, A. (2021, May 30). *Mob justice is a language in South Africa*. Centre for the Study of Violence and Reconciliation. Available from: https://www.csvr.org.za/mob-justice-is-a-language-in-south-africa/. Accessed 26 Oct 2021.

Mpofu-Walsh, S. (2021, June 16). Fallism's faultlines: The paradoxes of "Fees Must Fall". *African Arguments*. Available from: https://africanarguments.org/2021/06/fallisms-faultlines-the-paradoxes-of-fees-must-fall/. Accessed 27 Oct 2021.

Naidoo, L., & Sewpaul, V. (2014). The life experiences of adolescent sexual offenders: factors that contribute to offending behaviours. *Social Work/Maatskaplike Werk, 50*(1), 84–98.

Nel, M. (2016). *Crime as punishment: A legal perspective on vigilantism in South Africa*. University of Stellenbosch. (Doctoral Dissertation).

Nel, M. (2017, February 17). How South Africa can turn the rising tide against vigilantism. *The Conversation*. Available from: http://theconversation.com/how-south-africa-can-turn-the-rising-tide-against-vigilantism-72986. Accessed 26 June 2018.

Netshitomboni, S. (1998). *Ubuntu: Fundamental constitutional value and interpretive aid*. University of South Africa. (MA Dissertation)

Parkinson, J. (2016, June 15). Five ways to stop football hooliganism. *BBC News Magazine*. Available from: https://www.bbc.com/news/magazine-36516017

Parliamentary Monitoring Group (PMG). (2021, August 13). *Extent of recent unrest: SAPS and KZN briefing; with Minister and Deputy*. NCOP Security and Justice. Available from: https://pmg.org.za/committee-meeting/33357/. Accessed on 26 Oct 2021.

Phokeer, A., Densmore, M., Johnson, D. & Feamster, N. (2016). *A first look at mobile internet use in township communities in South Africa*. Available from: http://pubs.cs.uct.ac.za/archive/00001154/01/aphokeer_acmdev_mobileusage_paper.pdf. Accessed 26 Oct 2021.

Roelofse, C. (2014). Vigilantism, mob action and policing. *Servamus Community-based Safety and Security Magazine, 107*(7), 18–19. Pretoria: SARP Publishers.

Sherif, M. (1967). *Group conflict and co-operation: their social psychology*. Routledge.

Sibanda, M. (2014). *Contextualising the right to life and the phenomenon of mob justice in South Africa*. North-West University. Available from: https://repository.nwu.ac.za/handle/10394/15653. Accessed 26 Oct 2021.

Singh, D. (2005). Resorting to community justice when state policing fails: South Africa. *Acta Criminologica: Southern African Journal of Criminology, 18*(3), 43–50.

South African Police Service (SAPS). (2018). *Welcoming address General Sitole: launch of the public order policing reserve units*. Available from: https://www.saps.gov.za

South African Police Service (SAPS). (2020). *Crime situation in Republic of South Africa*. Twelve (12) months (April 2019 to March 2020). Available from: www.saps.gov.za/services/april_to_march_2019_20_presentation.pdf. Accessed 1 Nov 2021.

Spaaij, R. (2006). *Understanding football hooliganism: A comparison of six Western European football clubs*. Amsterdam University Press.

Stott, C., Livingstone, A., Adang, O., & Schreiber, M. (2008). Tackling football hooliganism: A quantitative study of public order, policing and crowd psychology. *Psychology, Public Policy, and Law, 14*(2), 115–141.

The Presidency, Republic of South Africa. (2021, July 12). *Address by President Cyril Ramaphosa on acts of violence and destruction of property*. Available from: http://www.thepresidency.gov.za/speeches/address-president-cyril-ramaphosa-acts-violence-and-destruction-property. Accessed on 24 July 2021.

Welner, M. (2011, August 11). Mob violence: psychological myths, facts, solutions. *ABC News*. Available from: https://abcnews.go.com/Health/london-riots-2011-psychological-myths-facts-solutions/story?id=14276532. Accessed 28 Oct 2021.

Wood, V. (2016, June 16). Watch: Korean police show France how to stop a riot with ancient military masterclass. *Express*. Available from: https://www.express.co.uk/news/world/680360/french-police-southkorea-riot-formation-tactic-ancient-military-euros

Young, K. (1986). The killing field – Themes in mass media responses to the Heysel Stadium riot. *International Review for the Sociology of Sport, 21*, 252–264.

Zondi, S. (2008). Xenophobic attacks: towards an understanding of violence against African immigrants in South Africa. *Africa Insight, 38*(2), 26–35.

Chapter 9
Canada and the USA: Community Violence and the Police Use of Deadly Force in Bordering Nations

Rick Parent and Catherine Parent

Canada and the USA: Neighbouring Nations

Canada and the USA are geographically proximate, sharing similar social and economic experiences. The population of Canada in 2021 is roughly 38 million within a nation comprised of 9,985 million square kilometres. Canada is the second-largest country in the world, located in the upper half of North America. The nation is vast and rugged. To the south, Canada shares 8,890 kilometres of land border with the USA, the longest international border in the world. Canada's largest cities and the bulk of the nation's populous live within a few hundred kilometres of the US/Canadian border (Statistics Canada, 2021). The nation is highly developed with an advanced economy and membership in several international institutions and groupings that include NATO, the G7 and the World Trade Organization. The nation is also a bilingual parliamentary democracy providing universal health care for all citizens.

The USA is the fourth largest country in the world within a nation comprised of 9,834 million square kilometres. In 2021, the population of the USA is estimated to be roughly 332 million making it the third most populated nation in the world (World Factbook, 2021). It is considered a federal republic with three separate branches of government having one of the world's largest economies. Internationally, the USA is seen as a leader in areas that include human rights, education, economic freedom and quality of life. It is a founding member of the United Nations with membership in several international institutions and groupings that also include NATO, the G7 and the World Trade Organization.

R. Parent (✉)
Simon Fraser University, Vancouver, BC, Canada
e-mail: rparent@sfu.ca

C. Parent
Medical and Police Researcher, Vancouver, BC, Canada

J. F. Albrecht, G. den Heyer (eds.), *Understanding and Preventing Community Violence*, https://doi.org/10.1007/978-3-031-05075-6_9

Both Canada and the USA reflect nations founded upon democratic principles and high qualities of life, enjoying a GNP that is one of the highest in the world. Canada and the USA also administer national Uniform Crime Reporting (UCR) programmes that are based upon police reported data thus allowing for limited comparisons of crime rates.

Policing in Canada

Policing is the largest component of the Canadian criminal justice system with a budget of over $14 billion (Whitelaw and Parent, 2018:21). There are approximately 200 police agencies and 69,000 police officers in the nation reflecting a rate of police strength of 183 officers per 100,000 population (Statistics Canada, 2019). Sixty percent of all police officers are employed within five Canadian police services – the Royal Canadian Mounted Police (RCMP), the Toronto Police Service, the Ontario Provincial Police (OPP), the Sûreté du Québec (SQ) and the City of Montreal Police Service (Service de police de la Ville de Montréal, or SPVM). Stand-alone municipal police services in Canada represent the remaining 40 percent of the police personnel. In 2015, there were a total of 176 municipal police services of which 117 police services had fewer than 25 staff. In the far north, Nunavut, the Northwest Territories and the Yukon utilize the services of the federal RCMP for policing (Statistics Canada, 2017).

Police officers carry out their tasks within several legislative frameworks that define their roles, powers and responsibilities. Policing in Canada is carried out at four levels: municipal, provincial, federal and First Nations (Indigenous). Most police work is performed by services operating at the municipal level. Across Canada, municipal police services range in size from three officers to more than 5,000 officers (the Toronto Police Service has 5,366 plus an additional 2,818 civilian personnel, and the Montreal Police Service has 4,583 and an additional 1,364 civilian personnel) and have jurisdiction within a city's boundaries (Statistics Canada, 2016).

A unique feature of the Canadian policing landscape is the evolution of "autonomous" Indigenous police forces occurring within the context of a broader movement leading towards Indigenous self-government. Under the First Nations Policing Policy (FNPP), Indigenous policing is implemented across Canada through tripartite agreements negotiated among the federal government, provincial or territorial governments, and First Nations. In 2015, there were 186 First Nations policing programme agreements in place in Canada, providing policing services to roughly 65 percent of First Nation and Inuit communities nationwide. A total of 1,299 police officer positions receive funding under the FNPP, serving a population of approximately 422,000 in 453 communities. Officers in Indigenous police forces generally have full powers to enforce the *Criminal Code* and federal and provincial statutes, as well as band bylaws on reserve lands (Whitelaw and Parent, 2018:24).

In Canada, the police are responsible for the services they provide to the community as well as for their conduct within the community. There are both legislative and administrative frameworks for holding Canadian police officers accountable for their actions. The Canadian Charter of Rights and Freedoms has had a significant impact on police work. Since its enactment in the early 1980s, a number of major decisions by the Supreme Court of Canada (so-called Charter cases) have further defined the role and powers of the police. Police officers can be held accountable under the Criminal Code as well as under civil and administrative law for their actions. For example, the police have been held civilly liable for negligent investigations and both negligent supervision and negligent retention of employees. Furthermore, the various provincial police acts set out mechanisms and procedures for overseeing and reviewing the actions and decisions of police officers. One of the most significant recent developments is the Supreme Court of Canada's decision in *R. v. McNeil* (2009), as a result of which police services must now release a police officer's disciplinary records to defence counsel prior to a criminal prosecution. Police services and their employees are also held accountable by coroner's inquests or fatality inquiries and by human rights boards and commissions. Freedom of information legislation has also established a heightened level of accountability in relation to police records and their management.

Every Canadian province has established an office whose task is to receive and review general complaints against police officers. The role of each oversight body varies, ranging from reviewing complaint investigations and making recommendations to conducting the investigation itself. In addition, there has also been the establishment of policing oversight bodies to review specific issues related to the police use of force. For example, in Canada's most populated province of Ontario, the Special Investigations Unit (SIU) provides external civilian review of police activities. The SIU specifically investigates cases involving serious injury, sexual assault, or death that may have been the result of criminal offences committed by police officers. The SIU is independent of any police service and operates directly under the provincial attorney general. It has the authority to investigate municipal, regional and provincial police officers. The director of the SIU has the authority to decide whether charges are warranted in a case, and he or she reports this decision directly to the attorney general. This model of external civilian review has also been established in other provinces. In the western province of Alberta, the Alberta Serious Incident Response Team (ASIRT) has a similar but broader mandate in that it also investigates sensitive matters involving police conduct (Whitelaw & Parent, 2018:28).

Policing in the USA

In the USA there are approximately 18,000 separate police agencies and a wide variety of governmental agencies that have police powers (e.g. United States Postal Service). Together these various law enforcement agencies employ roughly 700,000 sworn law enforcement officers serving approximately 330 million people (USCB, 2021). These numbers reflect a rate of police strength of roughly 212 officers per 100,000 population. In contrast, Canada has fewer officers per capita at a rate of 183 per 100,000 population.

Policing in the USA is complex. Although the Tenth Amendment to the US Constitution reserves police powers for the individual states, law enforcement agencies have evolved at the local, state and federal levels, each having unique operational responsibilities. For example, the national government has police agencies such as the FBI and the Secret Service, but they are authorized to enforce only those laws prescribed under the powers granted to Congress. The FBI, part of the Department of Justice, is responsible for the investigation of all violations of federal laws. The FBI has jurisdiction over fewer than 200 criminal matters, including offenses such as kidnapping, extortion, interstate transportation of stolen motor vehicles and treason (Cole, 1987). In addition, the FBI is responsible for the Uniform Crime Reporting (UCR) system that collects national statistics on crime, criminals and criminal justice agencies.

For the most part, law enforcement in the USA is a function of state and local agencies. Within this setting, there are 52 separate criminal law jurisdictions in the USA. Of these 52 jurisdictions, one exists in each of the 50 states, one in the District of Columbia and one represents the Federal jurisdiction. Each of these jurisdictions has its own criminal law and procedure as well as its own law enforcement agencies. Although the systems of law enforcement among the 50 states are quite similar, there are frequently substantial differences in the penalties for similar offences. Furthermore, a given jurisdiction in the USA may be policed by several law enforcement agencies: a city police department, a sheriff's department, a state police organization and several federal agencies (e.g. the Federal Bureau of Investigation, the Drug Enforcement Administration and the Bureau of Alcohol, Tobacco and Firearms).

Along with federal police agencies, each state operates their own law enforcement agency that may include a state police or a state highway patrol agency. Historically, state police agencies were created for a variety of reasons that included the need to provide law enforcement in rural or undeveloped areas, the need to investigate criminal activities occurring outside of city or county jurisdictions and to provide assistance to local police agencies if need be (Gaines and Kappeler, 2015).

There are also local police agencies in the USA. These local police agencies include city, municipal, college, university and county agencies. County police departments include sheriff's departments and county police agencies. In addition, Tribal governments operate over 200 local police departments. Combined, these local police agencies employ the largest number of police officers in the USA and account for the vast majority of police services provided (Gaines and Kappeler, 2015).

Community Violence and Policing

While the societies of Canada and the USA are similar in many ways, there are significant differences in the rates of extreme violence between the two nations. Crime rates between Canada and the USA, for the year 2020, indicate that the USA has much higher rates of violent crime per capita. Despite the differences in crime rates, previous research suggests that trends in crime between the two countries have been quite similar during the 1980s and 1990s. Both countries administer national Uniform Crime Reporting (UCR) programmes but use different offence definitions and techniques to record and count crimes (Statistics Canada, 2001). Canada and the USA also have very different regional variations in crime and varying economic and socio-demographic characteristics. Nonetheless, it is possible to examine selected acts of community violence that include the rates for homicide, justifiable homicide, the police use of deadly force and the murder of police officers.

For example, in Canada, there were 743 homicides in 2020 resulting in a national rate of 1.95 homicides per 100,000 population. In comparison, there were 21,570 homicides in the USA in 2020, resulting in a national rate of 6.5 per 100,000 population – *a figure that is more than three times higher than Canada's*. It is interesting to note that, in the USA, private citizens (non-police) "justifiably" kill roughly 350 individuals each year. Certain wilful killings are considered to be justifiable or excusable. In the USA, justifiable homicide is defined as, and limited to, the killing of a felon by a law enforcement officer in the line of duty, or the killing of a felon by a private citizen during the commission of a felony (UCR, 2021). Since these killings have been determined to be justifiable by way of a law enforcement investigation, they are tabulated separately and apart from murder statistics.

The vast majority of these individuals are shot and killed with a handgun. In contrast, private citizens in Canada rarely, if ever, are involved in a "justifiable" shooting incident largely due to the unavailability of handguns as well as the restriction of firearms in general. In those extremely rare incidents where a member of the Canadian public has discharged a firearm to prevent a crime, the individual discharging the firearm is often charged with a firearm offence or other Criminal Code offence, resulting in a judicial examination of the incident (Parent and Parent, 2018).

Noteworthy is that the homicide rate in general has been rising in the USA with recent UCR data indicating nearly a 30% increase in homicides from the year 2019 to 2020. This is the largest single-year increase since the 1960s. The increase in homicides is believed to be based upon a recent spike in gun violence highlighting that 77% of reported murders were committed with a gun (UCR, 2021). Overall, violent crime in the USA was up 5.2% in 2020 with 1,277,696 incidents reported. The 2020 statistics reflect a rate of violent crime as 398.5 offenses per 100,000 inhabitants. The estimated rate of property crime was 1,958.2 offenses per 100,000 inhabitants, reflecting a decline of 8.1 percent (UCR, 2021).

In contrast, Statistics Canada noted that the homicide rate in Canada increased 7%, from 1.83 homicides per 100,000 population in 2019 to 1.95 in 2020. Canadian police agencies reported higher rates of all three violent firearm violations: discharging a firearm with intent (+21%, 1,850 incidents in 2020), pointing of a firearm (+14%, 1,670 incidents) and using a firearm in the commission of an indictable offence (+3%, 617 incidents). However, robbery, and the act of violence or threat of violence during the commission of a theft, was down sharply.

Crimes that are more serious but not specifically related to firearms, such as homicide, robbery, assault and sexual assault, may also involve the use or presence of a firearm. In 2020, there were 8,344 victims of violent crime where a firearm was present during the commission of the offence, or a rate of 29 per 100,000 population. This rate was unchanged when compared with 2019. In sum, there were over 2 million police-reported *Criminal Code* incidents (excluding traffic) in 2020, about 195,000 fewer incidents than in 2019. At 5,301 incidents per 100,000 population, the police-reported crime rate – which measures the volume of crime – decreased 10% in 2020 with a recorded 5,301 incidents per 100,000 population (Statistics Canada, 2021a, b).

The Police Use of Deadly Force

When police officers in western society use firearms against individuals, it may be assumed that they are using lethal force. Generally, officers who discharge a firearm or utilize other forms of potentially deadly force are attempting to immediately incapacitate a perceived lethal threat to themselves or another individual. This decision-making process will usually transpire at a time when the individual officer is under considerable stress and perceived danger, leaving him or her open to the influence of a variety of physiological and psychological factors.

In both Canada and the USA, police shootings and the use of deadly force tend to generate the most media attention, public interest and controversy regarding police misconduct. However, in terms of volume, the police use of deadly force is more of an issue in the USA than in Canada. Proportionately, and in absolute numbers, far more people die by legal intervention in the USA. One possible explanation for this difference relates to the availability and use of handguns by the public in the USA as well as the American Constitutional provision to bear arms. Possession of a handgun is both highly regulated and restricted in Canada. Furthermore, Canada has no provision within the *Canadian Charter of Rights and Freedoms* enshrining the right to possess firearms (Parent and Parent, 2018).

While policing within Canada and the USA is similar in many ways, there are also differences between the two nations. For example, the Canadian province of Newfoundland remained the last bastion of "unarmed policing" on the continent of North America until as recently as 1998. This was due to the fact that Canada's most eastern province entered into a confederation with Canada in 1949, becoming the nation's tenth province. Prior to 1949, Newfoundland was under the guidance of

Great Britain and distinct from the rest of North America in many ways, including that of policing. The former British Colony created an independent police force using the Royal Irish Constabulary as a model thus drawing upon the best features of Irish and British Policing. When joining with Canada, Newfoundland maintained their tradition of having an unarmed police force while the rest of North America had armed their police. For over 120 years, the "Royal Newfoundland Constabulary" (RNC) continued to be the only policing jurisdiction within Canada and the USA where day-to-day street level policing was conducted without police having immediate access to firearms. This was a fact that was long considered to be a source of pride by the local population of Newfoundland. While the police had access to firearms that were kept either secured in the trunk of their vehicles or at their police station, members of the RNC rarely, if ever, utilized firearms. A review of police shootings revealed that RNC personnel had been involved in only one shooting incident during the 20-year period from 1978 to 1998. This single shooting incident was non-fatal (Parent, 2004).

However, owing to changes within society and the influx of visitors from the USA and the rest of Canada, members of the Royal Newfoundland Constabulary lobbied to have immediate access to firearms like their Canadian and American counterparts. In June 1998, the RNC was granted its request, and shortly after being equipped with firearms, the RNC became involved in two shooting incidents underscoring the complexities associated with deploying an armed police service.

Other differences between US and Canadian police exist. For example, Canadian police officers rarely, if ever, carry their issued police service firearm on their days off. Most Canadian police agencies require that police personnel secure their firearm at their place of employment when not working. In contrast, it is not uncommon for "off-duty" police personnel in the USA to be involved in a shooting incident. One study noted that, in some instances, off-duty police officers were the first to attend the scene of a crime in progress and could be the first to confront an assailant with their police issued firearm in hand (Parent, 2004:290). Typically, these off-duty US officers were dressed in civilian attire and were somehow alerted to shots fired outside their personal residence, or at a commercial centre. The attendance of off-duty and non-uniformed police personnel to the altercation further added to the dynamics of the shooting incident.

Research has revealed that overall there are relatively few differences in relation to the dynamics and circumstances of police use of deadly force in the USA and Canada. The issues pertaining to police use of deadly force are for the most part very similar. The major differences between these two nations are reflected in the frequency of incidents rather than the individual characteristics of a police shooting (Parent, 2004:281-219).

Frequency and Risk

It is within this setting that approximately 1000 individuals are shot and killed by American law enforcement personnel each year. In 2015, the *Washington Post* first estimated that police agencies in the USA fatally shot 987 individuals. Reporting a population of 320 million people, this number reflects a frequency rate of roughly three fatal police shootings per 1 million individuals. The Washington Post continues to monitor and document fatal police shootings within the USA reporting that there were 999 fatal shootings in the year 2019 and 1021 fatal shootings in the year 2020 (Washington Post, 2021).

In stark contrast, there were 30 fatal police shootings in Canada in 2017 and 21 fatal police shootings in 2019. Researchers have documented 376 fatal police shootings in Canada during the 25-year period from January 01, 1990, and December 31, 2014 (Parent & Parent, 2018). This number equates to approximately 15 fatal police shootings per year during this time period, reflecting a rate of one fatal shooting per 1.85 million individuals (Parent & Parent, 2018). Upon adjusting for population figures, the number of deaths by legal intervention within the USA is roughly *five times greater* than the corresponding number of legal intervention deaths within neighbouring Canada (per capita).

Researchers suggest that the police use of deadly force in Canada and the USA typically occurs when police personnel, or a member of the public that they are protecting, are facing the immediate risk of being murdered or suffering grievous bodily harm at the hands of an assailant. The use of a police firearm is often the only means available that will immediately incapacitate the perceived lethal threat and prevent harm (Parent & Parent, 2018).

Police use of deadly force in Canada: 1990–2014 (n=376)

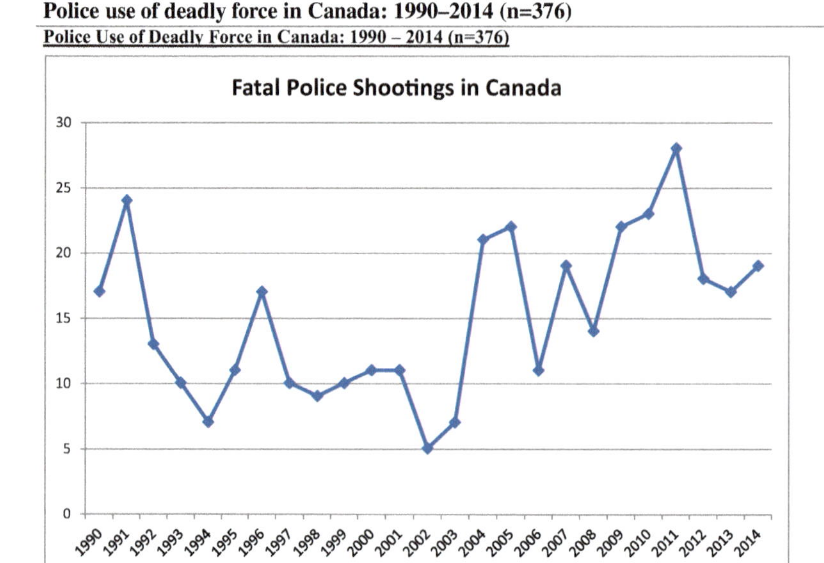

Frequency of fatal police shootings in relation to relative population in Canada

1990: 17 fatal/27,691,000 = Roughly 1 fatal shooting per 1.62 million people
2000: 11 fatal/30,685,000 = Roughly 1 fatal shooting per 2.8 million people
2005: 22 fatal/32,242,000 = Roughly 1 fatal shooting per 1.47 million people
2009: 22 fatal/33,628,000 = Roughly 1 fatal shooting per 1.53 million people
2011: 28 fatal/34,342,000 = Roughly 1 fatal shooting per 1.25 million people
2014: 19 fatal/35,543,000 = Roughly 1 fatal shooting per 1.85 million people

Note:
*The frequency of fatal police shootings per population in Canada has slightly increased over the past 25 years. Since 2004, there is a noticeable increase in fatal police shootings in Canada
From 2004 through to 2014, a total of 214 fatal shootings occurred in Canada during the 11-year period of analysis reflecting a rate of roughly **19.5 fatal police shootings per year (n = 214/11 = 19.45). *This high average is higher than the previous decade*
In contrast, police agencies in the USA fatally shot an estimated 1,000 individuals in 2015, within a nation of 320 million people. This reflects a frequency rate of roughly three fatal police shootings per one million citizens. (The Washington Post media source estimates that police agencies in the USA fatally shot 987 individuals in 2015.) The frequency rate of fatal police shootings in the USA is roughly ***five times greater than the frequency of fatal police shootings in Canada (per capita):
2014 – Canada: Roughly 1 fatal shooting per 1.85 million
2015 – USA: Roughly 1 fatal shooting per 320,000
Source: Parent, Richard and Parent, Catherine (2016)

Added to the circumstances surrounding police shootings are numerous documented incidents where law enforcement personnel in Canada and the USA have faced a potentially lethal threat, but the death of a suspect *did not* occur. This category includes those incidents in which a police officer utilized potentially deadly force by discharging his or her firearm, but death did not result. In these instances, the suspect either survived his or her wounds or, in other instances, the police missed, so the suspect was not shot.

It must be emphasized that in both Canada and the USA there are also countless incidents of lethal threats to law enforcement personnel that are resolved each year without the discharge of a firearm. During these instances, the officers utilized alternate tactics or less-lethal compliance tools such as pepper spray or Taser guns to subdue the individual who was posing a lethal threat. Often, this method of resolution has occurred with an increased risk to the police officer. This increased risk to police officers has at times resulted in their deaths. Indeed, there is no other occupation in society like policing that places the risk of murder or grievous bodily harm during day-to-day duties as a condition of employment. Owing to the very nature of their day-to-day duties, operational police personnel routinely face the real possibility of being assaulted or murdered.

On average, approximately 50 police officers are murdered each year within the USA (B.J.S., 2021, O.D.M.P. 2021). In Canada, during the 11-year period from 2010 through to 2020, an assailant has murdered a total of 13 police officers reflecting a rate of roughly 1 police murder per year (P.P.M.R.S., 2021). In both Canada and the USA, the police death typically occurs due to gun shot. *These figures illustrate that the risk of a police officer being murdered by an assailant is roughly four times greater in the USA than in Canada.*

Due to the precarious nature of their work, police also face the risk of death due to accidental circumstances. Accidental on duty police deaths are typically due to mishaps that include automobile and motorcycle crashes as well as being struck by a vehicle while directing traffic or standing on a highway. In this regard it was noted that approximately 50 police officers are accidentally killed each year in the USA (B.J.S. 2021, O.D.M.P, 2021). In Canada, roughly 2 police officers will die each year, accidentally in the line of duty (P.P.M.R.S., 2021).

Theories and Research Surrounding the Police Use of Deadly Force

Most empirical research surrounding the police use of deadly force is grounded in theory that police behaviour is influenced by the social dynamics of police-public encounters. This line of inquiry has directed an analytical focus upon the structural characteristics of situations in which the police and public interact. These structural characteristics include age, race, social class, gender, attitude, sobriety and demeanour of suspects; the seriousness of the offence; the number of police officers present; and the characteristics of the community in which the encounter takes place. It is within this theoretical framework that these "situational factors" serve as cues to influence and direct police officers to form judgements on how to react to a given situation (Alpert and Fridell, 1992; Geller and Scott 1992).

Due to the nature of their duties, front-line police officers may react to violent encounters, often within moments of arriving at a situation. As such, research has often also focused upon the related theories of violence and victimology in an attempt to understand the complex situational factors that confront police officers (Geller and Scott, 1992; MacDonald et al., 2001; White, 2001).

Research literature provides theories to explain the changing patterns of extreme violence (such as homicide) among community members, across time and geography. These theories adopt an integrated approach in that it is assumed that a combination of social and psychological factors cause persons to commit violent crimes (Geller and Scott, 1992; MacDonald et al., 2001; White, 2001; Best and Quigley, 2003). To help explain the varying levels of violence against police, it is necessary to explore possible variations in the nature of police shootings.

One of the most widely cited explanatory theories of violence is the "subculture of violence" concept pioneered by Wolfgang and Ferracuti (1967). They posit that, within different communities, there exist "subculture(s) with a cluster of values that support and encourage the overt use of force in interpersonal relations and group interactions". These authors further argue that this subcultural system is normative and localized within the lower social class of society (Wolfgang and Ferracuti, 1967:11).

Wolfgang's and Ferricuti's hypothesis may offer some insight regarding police shooting frequencies. Within the subculture of violence theory, one may theorize that individuals predisposed to violent criminal activities will engage in contact with the police more frequently. Increased contact with police, combined with a disposition towards violence, may precipitate the actions of a police officer, resulting in greater frequencies of deadly force.

Geller and Scott (1992) add that the "structural theory" of violence asserts the influence of "broad-scale social forces such as lack of opportunity, institutional racism, persistent poverty, demographic transitions, and population density all combining to determine homicide rates. These forces operate independently of human cognition and do not require individual learning to explain their impact".

Fyfe (1980) and other researchers have suggested that police personnel are more likely to shoot and kill individuals who are disproportionately involved in violent crimes. The police use of deadly force is best explained by the exposure of police personnel to dangerous persons and places. Jacobs and O'Brien (1998) refer to this concept as the "reactive hypothesis", while MacDonald et al. (2001) refer to this concept as the "danger-perception" theory. This suggests that the number of criminal homicides and extreme violence in a community is correlated with the police use of deadly force. The ratio-threat represents police officers' defensive stance towards the danger of their work. Put simply, police officers are more likely to use deadly force during situations in which they encounter greater levels of violence, or when they perceive their situation to be dangerous. In this regard, Fyfe's (1986) examination of criminal homicide in New York City revealed that an area with a high rate of criminal homicide would also experience a high rate of police use of deadly force. Fyfe noted that there exists a high correlation between the police use of deadly force and threats to police and general public safety.

Stress and the Use of Deadly Force

Murray and Zentner (2001, p. 257) define *stress* as a physical and emotional state that is always present in people, but can be intensified when an environmental change or threat occurs to which an individual must respond. The individual's survival depends upon constant negotiation between environmental demands and their own adaptive capacities. Experimentation and observational examination of threat, stress and anxiety suggest that extreme elevated stress levels negatively affect any performance. In addition, physical and social settings can heighten anxiety; stress is intensified in relation to dark or poorly lit places, high crime and violence areas, angry or upset people and non-supportive social structures. While these factors affect all individuals, police officers are likely to experience even higher levels of anxiety as they often have few choices regarding entrance into a dangerous situation.

Skolnick (1966) suggests that "in reaction to the pressures they face, police officers develop a perceptual shorthand" to identify certain kinds of people as "symobilic assailants". These symbolic assailants are individuals who use specific gestures and language and wear attire that the officer has come to recognize as a possible prelude to violence. In other words, the characteristics of a person's presentation (physical and behavioural) may be associated with individuals that engage in criminal actions. Their characteristics may be grounds for suspicion but are not necessarily conclusive of criminal activity or intent (Pate, 2012). This may also apply to symbolic settings and types of encounters, associated with communities, neighbourhoods and locations that officers have come to recognize as having potential for danger. The responding officer's arousal level may be heightened upon confronting a perceived symbolic setting. This recognition and arousal pattern may serve to "trigger" the use of force, whether it is actually required or not. An officer's preconceived expectation may serve to alter facts, thereby creating an improper situational assessment and response. Symbolic situations may additionally provoke fear within an individual officer, including the fear of serious injury, disability or death. These noted levels of stress may serve as explanatory variables of why individual officers use force. An individual that perceives a serious threat will act on that perception. In sum, physiological and psychological changes that occur to officers under stress may also serve as important factors in an officer's decision to deploy their firearm.

Further influences of stress may also include the community environment. As a result of inadequate community resources for the mentally ill, homelessness and increased availability/use of hallucinogenic drugs such as PCP (phencyclidine) and cocaine, there is greater potential for law enforcement officers to encounter and deal with disturbed, irrational and perhaps violent individuals. Methamphetamine-type drugs, which are often used by this population, frequently cause the user to be aggressive and violent when confronted by law enforcement personnel.

In many instances, officers must be able to assess and interpret the cues of an individual (often within seconds) to ascertain the correct procedure in dealing with them. The behaviour exhibited by a person with a mental illness can easily be misinterpreted as an aggressive act, indicating the need for the use of force. A mentally distressed individual waving a knife in the air while shouting and raging may be "talked down" by one officer using verbal communication techniques; however, another officer who encounters this individual may perceive that their life is in danger and decide that resolving the situation requires the use of a firearm. Police officers are at times placed in the precarious situation of being required to assess and instantaneously confront people in various community settings, including on the street and in residences or workplaces. Skolnick and Fyfe (1993) suggest that these factors create increased stress levels for police officers.

In sum, modern-day law enforcement agencies deal with both contemporary crime problems and a public that often expects immediate solutions to problems that are deeply rooted within society. These solutions need to be achieved within the parameters of legislation, constitutional guarantees and the complexities of the criminal justice system. In addition, the public expects law enforcement personnel to maintain an exemplary level of service, professional and accountable to all individuals within society. The various theories and empirical studies surrounding the police use of deadly force and potentially deadly force provide some insight into why police shootings occur. Throughout these explanations, it is clear that no single theory serves to fully explain why the police use of deadly force occurs. In many instances, organizational, psychological and sociological forces combine to influence and direct the individual police officer in the deployment of deadly force.

Discussion

The reason for the disparity in crimes and behaviour associated with violence between the two neighbouring nations of Canada and the USA is varied and complex. Unique to the USA is a culture of firearms and the widespread availability of handguns. This situation suggests that the perceived threat and calculated risk for police officers in the USA is substantially higher than for police officers in Canada and in many other nations. This may partially explain why police officers in the USA utilize deadly force in greater frequency than in most western nations.

Due to the nature of their duties, police in both nations are often required to confront society's systemic failures that are manifested within community settings. On a daily basis police may respond to domestic violence, mental illness, homelessness, drug addiction and other complex social issues. As first responders, they are often criticized for failing to completely resolve complex situations that may be dynamic and violent. In the USA, law enforcement personnel may be quicker to respond to these issues with deadly force as a pre-emptive means in dealing with greater perceived threats of violence.

Also unique to the USA is a policing structure that creates additional challenges due in part to the vast array of police agencies and national differences. As stated, there are over 18,000 different police agencies in the USA, spread over 50 states, with few national guidelines or policies to ensure consistency in the police response. In contrast, Canada has far fewer police agencies per capita, operating within national frameworks that include one national Criminal Code and one national use of force model that regulates and directs the use of force by police personnel. Furthermore, Canada has only 10 police training centres scattered across the country, sharing information and techniques, thereby providing similar training to police personnel on a national basis. Added to these features are recruiting standards and pay/benefit scales that are comparable throughout the roughly 200 police agencies in Canada (Parent & Parent, 2018).

Furthermore, Canadian policing emphasizes community values incorporating problem-solving responses that involve community partnerships. High public expectations have also ensured that officers are held accountable for their actions. Canadian police agencies have responded to this demand by developing organizational policies and procedures that are reinforced by internal processes and mechanisms. Several external factors, including evolving case law and designated police oversight agencies, provide checks to ensure police transparency and accountability in the use of force (Parent & Parent, 2018). In contrast, civilian oversight in the USA can vary greatly from county to county.

In sum, community attitudes towards firearms, violence and crime appear to be closely related to the rates of justifiable homicide by the police. Social, cultural and historical forces of a geographic area may also influence and direct the associated levels of violence. Further research of extreme violence and the risk of violence perceived by police personnel in their policing jurisdiction may assist in understanding the patterns of police shootings from both a national and an international perspective.

References

Alpert, G. P., & Fridell, L. A. (1992). *Police vehicles and firearms: Instruments of deadly force*. Waveland Press.

Best, D., & Quigley, A. (2003). Shootings by the police: what predicts when a firearms officer in england and wales will pull the trigger? *Policing and Society, 13*(4), 349–364.

Bureau of Justice Statistics. (2021). *Sourcebook of criminal justice statistics – 2000*. U.S. Department of Justice.

Cole, G. (1987). United States of America. In H. G. Cole, S. Frankowski, & M. Gertz (Eds.), *Major criminal justice systems: A comparative survey*. Sage Publications.

Fyfe, J. J. (1980). Geographic Correlates of Police shootings: A Microanalysis. *Journal of Research in Crime and Delinquency., 17*(1), 101–113.

Fyfe, J. J. (1986). The split-second syndrome and other determinants of police violence. In A. Campbell & J. Gibbs (Eds.), *Violent transactions*. Basil Blackwell. Reprinted in Roger G. Dunham and Geoffrey P. Alpert (eds.), *Critical Issues in Policing: Contemporary Readings*. Prospect Heights, IL: Waveland Press (1989).

Gaines, L. K., & Kappeler, V. E. (2015). *Policing in America* (8th ed.). Anderson Publishing.

Geller, W. A., & Scott, M. S. (1992). *Deadly force: What we know - A practitioners desk reference on Police-involved shootings*. Police Executive Research Forum.

Jacobs, D., & O'Brien, R. (1998). The determinants of deadly force: A structural analysis of police violence. *American Journal of Sociology., 103*(4), 837–862.

MacDonald, J., Kaminski, R., Alpert, G., & Tennenbaum, A. (2001). The temporal relationship between police killings of civilians and criminal homicide: A refined version of the danger-perception theory. *Crime & Delinquency, 47*(2), 155–177.

Murray, R., & Zentner, J. (2001). *Health promotion strategies through the lifespan* (7th ed.). Pearson.

Officer Down Memorial Page (2021). *Fallen officers*. Retrieved from: https://www.odmp.org/

Parent, R. (2004) *Aspects of Police Use of Deadly Force In North America: The Phenomenon Of Victim-Precipitated Homicide*. Burnaby, BC: Simon Fraser University. (Doctoral Dissertation).

Parent, R., & Parent, C. (2018). *Ethics and Canadian law enforcement*. Canadian Scholars' Press.

Pate, M. (2012, March 31). Seeing danger through tinted windshields. *Hawaii Tribune Herald*. Retrieved from http://hawaiitribune-herald.com/sections/commentary/their-views/seeingdanger-through-tinted-windshields.html

Police and Peace Officers Memorial Ribbon Society (2021) *Honour roll*. Retrieved from: https://www.memorialribbon.org/honour-roll/

Skolnick, Jerome (1966) Justice without trial: Law enforcement in a democratic society. : Wiley and Sons, Inc.

Skolnick, J., & Fyfe, J. (1993). *Above the law: Police and the excessive use of force*. Maxwell MacMillan.

Statistics Canada. (2001) *Crime comparisons between Canada and the United States*. Cat. No. 85-002 – XPE Vol. 21, No. 11.

Statistics Canada. (2016). *Police Resources in Canada, 2015*. Cat. No. 85-002-X. Ottawa. Retrieved from: https://www.statcan.gc.ca/pub/85-002-x/2016001/article/14323-eng.htm

Statistics Canada. (2017). *Police resources in Canada, 2016*. Cat. No. 85-002-X. Ottawa: Retrieved from: http://www.statcan.gc.ca/pub/85-002-x/2017001/article/14777-eng.htm
Statistics Canada. (2019). *Police resources in Canada, 2019*. Retrieved from: http://www.statcan.gc.ca/pub/85-002-x/2017001/article/14777-eng.htm
Statistics Canada. (2021a). *Canada's population estimates: Age and sex, July 01, 2020*. Retrieved from: https://www150.statcan.gc.ca/n1/daily-quotidien/200929/dq200929b-eng.htm
Statistics Canada (2021b). *Police-reported crime statistics in 2020*. Retrieved from: https://www150.statcan.gc.ca/n1/pub/85-002-x/2021001/article/00013-eng.htm
Uniform Crime Reports. (2021). *FBI releases 2020 crime statistics*. Retrieved from: https://www.fbi.gov/news/pressrel/press-releases/fbi-releases-2020-crime-statistics
United States Census Bureau. (2021). *U.S. and World Population Clock*. Retrieved from: https://www.census.gov/popclock/
Washington Post. (2021). *Fatal force*. Retrieved from: https://www.washingtonpost.com/graphics/investigations/police-shootings-database/
White, M. D. (2001). Controlling police decisions to use deadly force: Reexamining the importance of administrative policy. *Crime & Delinquency, 47*(1), 131–151.
Whitelaw, B., & Parent, R. (2018). *Community-based strategic policing in Canada*. Nelson.
Wolfgang, M. E., & Ferracuti, F. (1967). *The subculture of violence: Towards an integrated theory in criminology*. Tavistock.
World Factbook (2021). *The United States*. Retrieved from: https://www.cia.gov/the-world-factbook/

Chapter 10
Commodification of Kidnapping and School Insecurity in Nigeria: Appraisals and National Challenge

Amos Oyesoji Aremu and Abisoye Priscilla Aremu

Introduction

Globally from time immemorial, the subject of crime has always been detested and condemned. This makes any act of crime absolutely outside social norms and antithetical to the dictates of criminal justice system. Crime, is therefore, not socially sanctioned. It is also culturally disapproved and legally disowned. Pakes and Pakes (2009) define it as harmful acts committed by individuals who are, to a certain degree, culpable, i.e. blameworthy. One simple explanation of this definition is that, there are behaviours that are not worthy and which stand condemned. Again, another perspective therein the definition is that crime is a function of a doer and the environment it occurs. Thus, crime being a socially disapproved behaviour is manifested in a context (environment) and by a significant person.

The last few months have been harrowing in Nigeria in respect of internal insecurity which continues to defy military solutions. This has continued to attract national discourse and global attention. National insecurity has assumed a serious challenge since 2009, when Boko Haram promoters took the nation by storm. The aftermath of this has led to many insecurity challenges like insurgency, terrorism, banditry, kidnapping, and Fulani-famer's conflict. Thus, national insecurity comes under different labels. And with this, the national toll of mayhems ranging from brutal killings, arsons, kidnappings, abductions of school children, and farm rustlings have not only defied military solutions, it has also continued unchecked. While all the mayhems and heinous crimes perpetrated by insurgents and bandits are very dastardly and emotionally disturbing, abduction/kidnapping of school children which is assuming a norm is getting stakeholders and international communities worrying. This comes under school insecurity. Affirming this, Nwosu et al. (2019) note with concern that the effect of school attacks has further exacerbated the

A. O. Aremu (✉) · A. P. Aremu
University of Ibadan, Nigeria, Ibadan, Nigeria

J. F. Albrecht, G. den Heyer (eds.), *Understanding and Preventing Community Violence*, https://doi.org/10.1007/978-3-031-05075-6_10

fragile school system which is antithetical to national development. Nwosu et al. (2019) are not only noting the obvious, the fear expressed by them in 2019 has even become rife and worrying in recent times as a result of resurgence and orchestrated attacks on schools. Within a spate of 3 months (December 11, 2020, and March 12, 2021), there were five cases of school attacks and abduction from Government Science Secondary School, Kankara, Katsina State, over 300 boys; Government Science College, Kagara, Niger State, 27 boys excluding staff and family members; Government Girls Science Secondary School, Jangebe, Zamfara State, 31 students; National Institute for Construction Technology, Uromi, Edo State, one lecturer and a student kidnapped on March 10; and over 200 people (students and staff) of Federal College of Forestry Mechanisation, Kaduna, Kaduna State abducted on March 12, 2021. And on the same day, troops of Quick Response Force of 1 Division, Nigerian Army, foiled an attempt by bandits to abduct students of Turkish International Secondary School, Rigachikun, Kaduna State. Days after this, the spate of abductions of students and faculty members continued, especially in Kaduna and Ogun states. Prior to this, timeline of school abductions included the popular 276 Chibok girls from Borno State on April 14, 2014; May 25, 2017, kidnapping of six boys from Igbonla Model College, Epe, Lagos State; and February 19, 2018, abduction of 110 students from Government Girls' Science and Technical College, Dapchi, Yobe State. Governments in (Federal and states) in Nigeria have reportedly said to have paid $2.099 million (#800 million) to bandits as ransom to free the kidnapped school children. Given this alarming spate, the US Government has offered to assist Nigeria in stemming the spate. Similarly, the Secretary-General of the United Nations expressed sadness by the spate of abduction of school students in Nigeria (Punch Newspaper, March 13, 2021). This timeline excluded kidnappings and killings of students and members of faculties of higher institutions in Nigeria, especially in the North East part of the country. According to Global Watchdog Report (2021), an arm of Amnesty International, over 640 students were abducted between December 2020 and March 2021 from the Northern part of the country. From another account credited to Peace Corps of Nigeria, 1,179 students were reported to have been abducted in 7 years in Nigeria (Punch Newspaper, April 21, 2021).

The scourge of abductions of school pupils, students, and staff is not only defying solutions, it is assuming an alarming proportion. For example, the following timeline was also recorded, abduction of twenty students from Greenfield University in Chikun Local Government Area, Kaduna State, on April 20, 2021. Five of the students were later killed on account of nonpayment of ransom. Another abduction of 200 students from an Islamic school in Niger State occurred on May 30, 2021. 136 pupils of another Islamic school in Tegina, Rafi Local Government Area of Niger State, were also kidnapped on June 2, 2021. And recently, scores of students and four teachers from the Federal Government College, Birnin Yauri, Kebbi State, were kidnapped on June 17, 2021.

Given the avalanche of school children abductions and payment of ransoms, Nigeria currently has the world's highest rates of school-children's abduction for ransom cases globally. This is not only disturbing and worrying, it portends grave danger to education and manpower sustainable development. Incident of cases of school insecurity is, however, not peculiar to Nigeria as this paper would later unveil.

School insecurity, in the context of this paper and in reference to cases cited above, refers to any external aggression unleashed on school children and personnel with the intention of killing, maiming, abducting, and causing maximum emotional and physical traumas. Thus, school insecurity, here, does not refer to natural hazards or human-motivated actions like bullying (emotional or physical) and cyber actions. School insecurity itself is a reflection of the general insecurity in the country. Nigerian nation is presently fractured as a result of the failure of her internal insecurity orchestrated by Boko Haram since 2009 and banditry in the North West which has become more pronounced, and assumed a more dangerous trend since 2017. Other than this, kidnapping and farmer-herder clashes have also contributed to the ranking of Nigeria on Insecurity Index globally. Nigeria has consistently ranked number three in the last few years after Iraq and Afghanistan. For example, Nigeria accounted for 13% of all terrorist-related deaths globally in 2018 with a 33% rise in the number of fatalities compared to the year 2017 (Global Terrorism Index, 2018). The latest ranking by the Global Terrorism Index still ranks Nigeria as *numero trois*. Although several indices of internal insecurity accounted for the continued ranking of the country, the dimension and spate of abduction of school children for ransom by Boko Haram elements and bandits underscores the state of schools (especially primary and secondary) in Nigeria. On this, government, stakeholders, and international communities have come to express concerns and anxieties.

Commodification of Kidnappings

In literature, three forms of kidnappings have been identified. These are the ritual-oriented, politically motivated, and business-related (Osumah & Aghedo, 2011). In recent times (especially from 2010 till date), there has been another form of kidnapping that has to do with insecurity, and it is driven by bandits and targeted at students (most especially those in secondary schools). Although Nigeria fares better on Global Kidnapping Index in 2020, this record may plummet in subsequent ratings given series of cases of reported kidnappings in recent times. As earlier reported in this paper, the rate of kidnapping especially of school-children has increased exponentially from December 2019 till date. This in effect has made bandits to turn kidnappings into 'business ventures'. The commodification of kidnapping in Nigeria with respect to school children and students is not only worrying, the speed of the rate and huge ransoms paid are also very alarming. From December 2019 till date, about 969 students have been kidnapped across the country with bulk of this in the following states: Zamfara, Kaduna, Niger, and Katsina. And between March 2020 and June 2021, about $18.34 million has been paid to bandits as ransoms (SBM Intelligence, 2021). This figure excluded the sum of about #200 million paid to bandits for the release of Greenfield University, Kaduna State, in May 2021. A further breakdown indicated that Zamfara State Government spent #970 million on payment of various ransoms in the first quarter of the year 2021. The state, according to its Commissioner of Information, has more than 100 different camps with over 30,000 bandits. These bandits, the Commissioner further reported, had killed 2,619 and abducted 1,190 people (including students) during the same period. In the same line, the Minister of Information in Nigeria, Lai Mohammed, had also volunteered that the Federal Government of Nigeria paid the sum of #800 million to secure the release of Kagara Government Science Secondary School students in Niger State.

More than what is officially reported in terms of ransom payments, there are other payments made by parents and guardians of the victims of kidnappings in Nigeria. This further underscores the commodification of kidnapping in Nigeria. Writing on business dimension of kidnappings, Briggs (2001) submits that it is not as visible as it used to be in Britain and in the Middle East. He further reiterates that it hardly now makes the headlines. He, however, submits that in many areas of the world, kidnapping is now big business, and kidnappers are motivated by profit rather than principle. Briggs (2001) might not have mentioned Nigeria; it is instructive to infer that kidnappings in Nigeria fall in the dimension of its claim. Briggs (2001) estimates it that kidnappers globally take home well over $500 million every year. He notes that the business is centred on Latin America, notably Colombia, Mexico, and Brazil, and with pockets of it in the Philippines and some parts of Soviet Union and Africa. Here, the increasing rates of kidnapping, especially abductions of school children, might justify the inclusion of Africa although it wasn't as rife as this when Briggs came to that conclusion in 2001.

Drawing some inferences from above, there are not only concerns for wellness of the citizenry, there are as well for intelligence and strategies especially given the poor state of many public schools (primary and secondary) in Nigeria. According to the Commandant of the Nigeria Security and Civil Defence Corps, Ahmed Audi in the Punch Newspaper of June 8, 2021, there are 81,000 *registered* (emphasis mine) primary and secondary schools in Nigeria out of which 62,000 are government owned. This portends some worrying signals.

Emerging Concerns

Presently, of utmost concern to the Federal Government of Nigeria and many states is the question of internal security. Aremu (2015) argues that the greatest contemporary challenge to national security in Nigeria is the insurgency orchestrated by Boko Haram. He notes further that the internal security concerns have made human life unsafe and unpredictable. As earlier provided in this paper, the evolution of *Boko Haram* militants group which has now splintered into other groups, which started in 2009, opened the floodgates of insecurity in Nigeria. *Boko Haram* is an Islamic fundamentalist group which abhors provision of Western Education in the core Northern part of Nigeria. The sect group formed and led by Mohammed Yusuf in 2002 in Maiduguri, Borno State, later became deadly by attacking Nigeria Police

Force's formations. That was after the extrajudicial murder of its founder in 2009 in the police custody. Upon the death of Mohammed Yusuf, the leadership of the sect fell on Abubakar Shekau who was more daring and deadly. Shekau himself was reported to have been killed on May 19, 2021, inside Sambisa Forest, North East, Nigeria, his stronghold, through explosive self-detonation when the Islamic State West Africa Province laid a siege on him. Aremu (2015) submits that the Federal Government of Nigeria did not take interests in the activities of the group in spite of the intelligence reports of the danger it portended on the society. At the onset, the asymmetric warfare of *Boko Haram* elements incapacitated the Nigerian Police (the agency primarily constituted to safeguard internal security), and this necessitated the Federal Government to draft the military into the field. And while the warfare continues, especially in the North East, the dimension of school-children's abduction in the North generally has brought about new narratives on the counterinsurgency warfare in Nigeria. And, the seeming unabated spate of abductions of school-children and other school personnel indicate a serious national problem that has to be addressed before it gets out of hand. Other than this, there are also insecurity concerns such as banditry in the North West and farmers-herders conflict in the North Central. In a way, therefore, banditry and other criminal activities are continued to impact on school safety. One of the theories advanced for the continued siege on schools is that schools are seen as soft targets for criminals. Unlike conventional kidnapping that occurs mostly on the roads or highways and of which adults (men and women are targets), abduction of school-children and students in higher institutions attracts more incentives and deep emotions. Given this, the cases of abduction of school children may continue for a long time.

The above have serious implications for schooling and security of students, school personnel, and parents/guardians. The school system is, therefore, under a siege. This siege, which seems unending, has implications. Generally in the Northern part of the country, there are about 13.2 million out of-school children the highest in the world. According to United Nations International Children's Emergency Fund (UNICEF) (2020), most of these children are from Borno, Yobe, Bauchi, Zamfara, Kebbi, Gombe, Taraba, and Adamawa states, where *Boko Haram* and other forms of insecurities have disrupted academic activities. The account of Bakar and Rabiu (2018) further laid credence to the depletion secondary and primary schools may face on account of terrorism and abduction. According to them, they aver that the *Boko Haram* crisis serves as a serious constraint to education especially with the girl-child education which could result in low record of attendance and poor enrolment figure. This would not only be exponential in a few years to come, it will also become frightening as a result of insecurity in the school system in Nigeria. This is one of the emerging concerns in view of the dangerous implications it portends on manpower development, sociocultural activities, and inbreeding insecurities. It is also of great concerns that orchestrated school insecurity as being unleashed by bandits and criminals could decimate school attendance resilience. This could engender poor attitude to schooling as a result of morbid fear of being attacked or abducted by bandits. This could further impact on fragile schooling behaviour, especially in Northern part of the country.

Insecure school environment generally is antithetical to academic performance. Thus, school insecurity, especially as a result of kidnaping and abduction, could impact negatively on academic performance. This is an emerging concern of which stakeholders (school personnel, educational, and counseling psychologists) are beginning to interrogate. Affirming this, Ojukwu (2017) reported a positive relationship between school insecurity and academic performance. This, more or less is as a result of perceived insecurity by the students. This could be a result of psychological dispositions of the students to schooling most especially after abduction cases. Here, it is instructive to note that school psychological environment is correlated positively to academic activities. More often, emphases are always on the physical environment of the school to the detriment of the psychological dispositions of the students. The latter concerns, psychological dispositions, could gravitate to something more serious if not handled properly and checked, that is, mental health challenges, which could be as a result of a long-held abduction in the dens of the bandits could be inevitable.

Till date, some abducted girls from Chibok and recently, too, many abducted students spent days in the dens of abductors. Affirming this, Norris et al. (2002) report that many survivors show transient symptoms of distress, sadness, and anxiety after attacks. These can be likened to Post-traumatic Stress Disorder (PTSD). Writing on PSTD of former abductees in Uganda, Pfeiffer and Elbert (2011) submit that abductees continue to suffer from severe mental ill-health.

Future of School

As a result of the increase in insecurity which collocates with rising spate of school-children abduction in Nigeria, the consequences may lead to more out-of-school children. This may also lead to increase in other forms of criminality. Ordinarily, the principles of schooling, among other things, are to provide a safe haven for teaching and learning and empowerment of pupils/students for an inclusive sustainable future. These presuppose that schooling and its associated activities can only thrive in a physically and emotionally secure environment. According to the Ministry of Home Affairs of India in a publication, *Safe School* (2004), it is remarked that no task is as important as creating safe learning environment for school-children. Here, it stands to reason that safety in schools should be of paramount concern to all stakeholders including the government, whose primary responsibility to the citizenry is safety of life and properties by ensuring absolute internal security. Schools are also in loco parentis. School personnel have the duty and responsibility to ensure maximum security of the students. This, in recent times in Nigeria, is a tall dream going by the avalanche of abduction cases especially in the Northern part of the country. This gory incident is raising some questions as to the future of schools in Nigeria.

While several scenarios (technology, COVID-19 new normal, re-schooling, and de-schooling) are shaping the future of school globally, the question of terrorism is fast depopulating schools and making learning uninteresting among some students.

Thus, the future of schools looks more precarious and disturbing. Efforts should, therefore, be made to ensure the future of the school. This is because the current insecurity scenario especially in respect of school safety is having its toll on the question of national cohesion. Education, right from the colonial period, is one of the bonds through which Nigerian nationhood is made cohesive. This is now being threatened through insecurity that now ravages the sector. The general atmosphere of public space insecurity is rubbing on the future of the school in Nigeria. If this continues, Nigerian schools may witness a gross desertion which may lead to the increase in statistics of out-of-school children across the country, and crime rate. The latter could fuel threat to public safety in the country. Fallouts of this are being witnessed in the Southern part of the country, with the upsurge in the migration of children, adolescents, and youths; and with different colonies of these different populations, signals here may be dangerous for national cohesion and safety of schools.

Nigeria is fast losing grip of some parts of the country (especially in the North East and West) to *Boko Haram* and Islamic State West Africa Province to terrorists and bandits. While other parts of the country are being ravaged by Fulani herders, it is the act of terrorism and banditry which culminated in school abductions that are becoming rifer and vociferous. Across the North West, North East, and North Central, many states are groping with insecurity in many schools. For example, in Zamfara State, 130 Junior Secondary schools have been closed down for lack of patronage. The State has 340 secondary schools. Similar to Katsina State, the government has reduced the number of boarding schools to nine. While in Kebbi State, seven schools were shut down on account of insecurity and inability of the government to guarantee security.

As it stands, the gross insecurity and its incursion into the school space has added to the local and global rating of the country. Nigeria is classified by the Fund for Peace (2020) in its Fragile States Index of the year 2020 as a failed state. The country is rated Number 14 globally with a score of 97.3. One of the indicators of fragile states as enunciated by the Fund for Peace (2020) is security threat. This Nigeria and schools in Nigeria are not immune from. The rating may, therefore, go worse in the coming years, given the deluge of insecurity in recent times in Nigeria. The reason is that the current insecurity which breeds banditry is defying military solutions given the fact that the challenge is much more asymmetric than the conventional approaches which the Nigerian Army personnel are used to. The *Boko Haram* war which started in Borno State in the North East is now more than a decade and has spread to other parts of the country, the North West and the North Central.

Strategic Policies and Practice for Safeguarding Schools

Nigerian educational system is now in danger arising from insecurity and abductions cases in many public and private schools, primary, secondary, and tertiary. With the increase in the scourge of abductions of school students, it is instructive for government and stakeholders to put up strategies to halt the scourge with a view to returning schools to the path of safety. Some strategic safety policies have been put in place prior to this period of security uncertainties in Nigeria. A good example was the Safe Schools Initiative (SSI) launched at the World Economic Forum on Africa in Nigeria in May 2014 after the country witnessed the first mass abduction of 276 girls from a secondary school in Chibok, Borno State. The SSI was championed by the Global Business Coalition for Education led by the former British Prime Minister, Gordon Brown. The SSI was based on the world standard promoted to secure schools from attacks. The overall objective of SSI was to develop practical measures to make schools safer in Nigeria. With the SSI measures which the Federal Government embraced, it becomes much more essential to interrogate further strategies through which Nigerian schools can be safeguarded against 'external' aggressions. Here, the SSI policy should be reappraised by the Federal Government and the International agency, the Global Business Coalition for Education, with a view to having another look into its operations. Recent cases of abductions and porousness of many schools (especially governments' schools) have revealed why many of the schools have become soft targets for the criminals. It is also instructive for the government (federal and states) to consider transfer of students in the highest-risk areas to other safer schools in safer parts of the country. This is aligned with the SSI policy of 2014.

Arising from the above, Aremu (2021) contends that in ensuring safety of Nigerian schools, governments (federal and states) should initiate solution-based proactive policies and strategies. Here, Security Education Agenda through which strategic measures can be developed and recommended for the security of Nigerian schools. Community Intelligence, which has to do with the understanding of the community the school is located, is strategic to curbing incidents of abduction. Through this, the school management, personnel, and students should be schooled on the geography and made to understand the culture and social-religious life of the community. They should also try to integrate significant others in the community to the school culture and vision. In doing this, community intelligence will be better facilitated between the school and the community it is located. Through the information sharing, intelligence would be collected, analysed, and shared. Innes and Roberts (2008) allude to the efficacy of information in the delivery of community safety. They argue that it is information and the analysis of the data that enable the contours of the risks and threats to which a community is exposed to be calibrated, and the ways of effectively and efficiently targeting the causes and consequences of these risks and threats to be identified. Since schools are based in the community, it is expedient that community should be involved in ensuring their safety.

Beyond this and given the increasing scourge of school insecurity in Nigeria, it will not be out of place to deploy non-conventional security personnel to protect Nigerian schools. Aremu (2021) notes that this was the practice in the late 1970s when soldiers were part of school personnel during the administration of President Olusegun Obasanjo. Then military personnel who were approaching retirement were deployed to schools as a means of facilitating their retirement adjustment to the civil populace. Aremu (2021) then canvasses for a revisit of the policy by deploying personnel of Nigeria Civil Defence Corps and Nigeria Security Network

(*Amotekun*), Eastern Security Network (*Ebubeagu*), and others. *Amotekun* translated to leopard is a regional security network created by Development Agenda for Western Nigeria (DAWN). It is a registered organisation put together by the Executive Governors in Southwest, Nigeria (Aremu, 2020). The DAWN Commission is a dedicated technocrat organisation whose main objective is the development of the Southwest Region of Nigeria, and it is one of the six regions in Nigeria. Aremu (2020) submits that *Amotekun*, a code name for regional security outfit, is the Yoruba name for leopard in English language. Leopard is a strong carnivorous animal, which is very strong, deft, confident, rugged, and intelligent. The philosophy of adoption of codenaming WNSN after leopard informed the motto of the outfit, which is zero tolerance for crime.

These personnel can be complemented with that of the Nigerian Army and the Police in hotbed states in the Northern part of the country. This will require strategic broad coalition network and support in which appropriate funding should be made available for logistics and motivation of the joint forces. This would ensure seamless response contingency proactiveness. Alluding to this, Klingman (1978) contends that in response to repeated terrorist attacks on Israeli communities, there should be four phases of strategic responses, preventive interventions (pre-disaster), impact phase, short-term adaption phase, and the long-term adaption phase.

It will also not be out of place if the Federal Government of Nigeria can seek international strategic support to fight terrorism and banditry with a view to securing our schools and return them to normalcy. Similarly, the trying period should also call for the need to establish schools' specialised security. This is because the Nigerian Army which are now in charge of internal security are being overwhelmed and, in a way, abdicating their primary responsibility, which is security against external aggression. The Nigerian Police are equally 'fatigued' and not properly motivated to secure the internal space against criminals. In this wise, it is only then instructive to tinker with the idea of another form of security whose personnel would be trained mainly on school security and intelligence.

Conclusion

The current security challenge which has snowballed into abduction of students and pupils for commodification in Nigeria has reached a crescendo in which parents/guardians, stakeholders, and internal community take a swipe at the leadership of President Mohammed Buhari. This calls for some appraisals of the present security and education policies. With these, the paper has been able to articulate by interrogating the national security challenge as it affects education. As evident in the paper, the Federal Government nay state governments should review the Safe School Initiative (SSI) policy with a view to making it more impactful. The SSI policy launched in 2014 provides for absolute school security through a number of approaches like school perimeter fencing, movement of students and other school personnel from high-risk schools to safer schools, and other practical safety measures should be reviewed with a view to appraising its gains (if any). Given the increasing rate of abductions, the SSI policy could be made much more impacting through provision of funds. The spate of unending attacks on Nigerian schools is worrying and disturbing. Its continuation could also affect the future of education in Nigeria. Similarly, the current school insecurity should beget the need to review some aspects of education policy to accommodate security education. This could be through incorporation of basic security tips in the curricula. School personnel (including administrators, teachers, and others) should also be trained in some pro-active and rapid counter-security measures. Here, the Federal Government of Nigeria should declare a state of emergency in the sector. This, itself, may not achieve the desired outcome unless more and better proactive measures are deployed to tackle the increasing menace of insecurity. Although the Nigerian Army now takes over policing duties in ensuring national security, this is an aberration mainly because primary responsibility of internal security is that of the Nigeria Police Force which has been serially decimated by *Boko Haram* group and other bandits. Thus, ensuring state of emergency in education sector would have to be preceded by guaranteed national security of which would require interagency collaboration.

References

Aremu, A. O. (2015). Police planning to curb insurgency in Nigeria: The need for a strong and effective police-public partnership. In J. F. Albrecht, M. C. Dow, D. Plecas, & D. K. Das (Eds.), *Policing major events: Perspectives around the world* (pp. 115–123). Taylor & Francis.

Aremu, A. O. (2020). Indigenous community policing for a seamless security through West Nigeria security network (*Amotekun*). *Nigerian Journal of Social Work Education, 19*, 23–30.

Aremu, A.O. (2021). *Promote security, teach security education*. News Agency of Nigeria. Retrieved from https://newsdiaryonline.com/promote-security-teach-security-education-expert-advises-govts-schools on May 07, 2021.

Bakar, Z. A., & Rabiu, D. K. (2018). The development of post-traumatic stress disorder among secondary school students in Borno State Nigeria: A systematic review. *International Journal of Engineering and Technology, 7*, 32–38.

Briggs, R. (2001). *The kidnapping business*. London: The Foreign Policy Centre, Mezzanine Floor, Elizabeth House, 39, York Road, London, SE1 7NQ

Innes, M., and Roberts, C. (2008). *Community intelligence in the policing of community safety*. Retrieved from http://theupsi.squarepace.com on May 08, 2021.

Klingman, A. (1978). Children in stress: Anticipatory guidance in the framework of the educational system. *Personnel and Guidance Journal, 57*, 22–26.

Ministry of Home Affairs. (2004). *School safety*. A Handbook for Administrators, Education Officers, Emergency Officials School Principals and Teachers. Ministry of Home Affairs, Government of India, National Disaster Management Division.

Norris, F. H., Friedman, M. J., Watson, P. J., & Byrne, C. M. (2002). 60,000 disaster victims speak: Part 1. An empirical review of the empirical literature, 1981-2001. *Psychiatry, 65*(3), 207–239.

Nwosu, C., Chukwuka, E., Ukwunna, G, & Ukwuna, J. (2019). *Insecurity and the nigeria school system: The securitisation option for sustaible development*. Paper delivered at 2nd International Conference of Unizik Business School, Unizik, Awka, Anambra State.

Ojukwu, M. O. (2017). Effect of insecurity of school environment on the academic performance of secondary school students in Imo State. *International Journal of Education & Literary Studies, 5*(1), 20–28.
Osumah, O., & Aghedo, I. (2011). Who wants to be a millionaire? Nigerian youths and the commodification of kidnapping. *Review of African Political Economy, 38*(128), 277–287.
Pakes, F., & Pakes, S. (2009). *Criminal psychology*. Willan Publishing.
Pfeiffer, A., & Elbert, T. (2011). *PSTD, depression and anxiety among former abductees in Northern Uganda*. Confi Health. Retrieved from http://creativecommons.org/licenses/by/2.0 on May 03, 2021
SBM Intelligence. (2021). *Nigeria's kidnap problem. The economics of the kidnap industry in Nigeria*. SB Morgen
The Fund for Peace. (2020). Retrieved from fragilestatesindex.org on May 13, 2021.
UNICEF. (2020). *Zamfara State Commissioner of Information* (https://www.channelstv.com/2021/04/02/2619-killed-1190-abducted-by-bandits-since-2011-in-zamfara-govt/

Chapter 11
American Policing Strategies to Prevent Community Violence

Theresa C. Tobin

Introduction

Feeling safe and secure in one's home, work space, in school, and on the street should be a given, but many Americans are threatened by violence every day. A major threat to the health and safety of all Americans is gun-related violence. Three hundred and sixteen people are shot in the United States every day. Among those, 106 people are shot and killed and 210 survive gunshot injuries (Brady Campaign to Prevent Gun Violence, 2021). According to the Centers for Disease Control and Prevention (CDC) based in Atlanta, Georgia, in 2020, more Americans died to gun-related injuries (45,222) than in any other year on record (CDC, 2021). The human suffering caused by gun-related violence is unmeasurable; however, the cost of medical care, public service, and work-loss costs each year are significant. A national priority for the United States must be to reduce gun-related injuries and deaths. There is not one cause of gun violence, and therefore at all levels of government, Federal, State, and local, there must be comprehensive strategies that address not only the consequences of gun violence, but the underlying causes as well. There are many innovative responses to gun violence that involve police, prosecutors, judges, probation and parole officers, mayors, school officials, and other leaders. It requires that jurisdictions recognize gun violence as a problem, devising solutions and collaborating with others to implement them. Gun violence is an epidemic in the United States, and communities are looking for effective solutions to their gun violence problems. The intent of this chapter is to describe three of the successful solutions that some cities and towns have already implemented.

T. C. Tobin (✉)
Molloy College, Long Island, NY, USA
e-mail: theresa.tobin@nypd.org

J. F. Albrecht, G. den Heyer (eds.), *Understanding and Preventing Community Violence*, https://doi.org/10.1007/978-3-031-05075-6_11

New York City's Ceasefire Program

NYC Ceasefire aims to decrease group-involved violence without increasing arrests or incarceration rates. It proactively delivers a strong, face-to-face message to high-risk populations—including gangs, street crews, drug sets, etc.—because of their disproportionate likelihood of becoming victims or perpetrators of violence. The NYPD, in partnership with local, state, and federal law enforcement agencies, clergy and community leaders, and social service providers, launched Ceasefire in Brooklyn in December 2014. The program has since expanded into parts of the Bronx, Manhattan, Staten Island, and Queens. The Ceasefire messages touch upon the following points:

- The NYPD wants to keep high-risk people alive, safe from violence, and out of prison.
- Violence is unacceptable and must stop.
- Continued violence will be met with swift and certain consequences.
- Services and support are available for anyone who needs help.

The NYPD builds the capacity of community members who want to be involved in the NYC Ceasefire partnership as speakers or volunteers. They may include clergy, people who have lost loved ones to violence or incarceration, and people who were once involved with group violence or were incarcerated.

The NYPD also engages local supportive service providers to ensure that these same high-risk people receive affirmative outreach. This outreach is multifaceted and includes services such as assistance with preparing for the TASC (Test Assessing Secondary Completion), enrollment in certification programs, job training and placement, housing needs, and counseling.

Operations

Ceasefire follows the Group Violence Intervention model developed by David Kennedy, a professor of criminal justice at John Jay College of Criminal Justice in New York City and the director of the National Network for Safe Communities at John Jay College of Criminal Justice in New York City. The most fundamental premise of the work comes from research findings from major cities, including New York: that less than half of a percent of the population—people in groups—gangs, crews, and drug sets—are responsible for 50 to 75% of the homicides. These group members are not only most likely to be shooting others and committing homicides, they are also most likely to be shot or killed themselves. Ceasefire focuses on the people in these groups—the **point five percent**—to reduce group violence. In many ways, it uses the peer pressure and group dynamics that lead to violence, to stop it.

There are four elements:

- Direct communication with those most involved in violence
- Collaboration with community members to reinforce that communication
- Targeted enforcement directed at individuals after acts of violence
- Social services for every member of a group who wants it

Ceasefire's most important goal is to reduce violence. First and foremost, it is a public safety strategy, and success can be obtained with fewer arrests and less incarceration. Second, direct communication about expectations and consequences—and then delivering on those consequences—results in a greater sense of fairness. Third, by engaging the community and by speaking with one voice and offering help to those who want it, builds trust and increases legitimacy. In Ceasefire, the rules of engagement, and every time action is taken, the NYPD explains why the action is being done. The NYPD makes it clear that police actions are based on individuals' behavior.

In order to launch Ceasefire an unprecedented partnership of 10 law enforcement agencies, 13 members of the clergy, and 5 social service providers was created. As Ceasefire expanded, new law enforcement partners and new community partners joined the initiative.

The entire partnership is engaged in multiple ways. All partners communicate directly with group members. The participants are told that the priority is to have them alive, safe, and out of prison.

The participants are also told the new rules:

- You make the choice: don't kill anyone, don't shoot anyone, and don't stab anyone.
- It is explained to them that when the next group member commits a homicide, the person who pulled the trigger will still be prosecuted, **but every member of that group will also feel consequences** through an enforcement action. In addition, every member of the group identified as the **most violent group at that time** will also be subject to an enforcement action. They are then given actual examples of actions taken against other group members so they can visualize what those consequences might be.
- A genuine offer of help to all group members is presented. Services and support are available for any group member.

In many ways Ceasefire is a communications strategy. There are four ways the Ceasefire Message is delivered: Call-ins, Custom Notifications, No Retaliation Notifications, and Enforcement Actions.

Call-Ins

The goal for a call-in is to have direct communication with several group members at once. An examination of the NYPD's list of group members in the catchment area is conducted. Selected are people who are **over 18 and on probation or parole so they can be mandated to attend**. Also invited are people not on supervision. No one invited or mandated has a warrant or is wanted. This is important because it is made clear that everyone is going to go home after the meeting. **Group members are encouraged to bring a family member** with them so they can also hear what is being said during the call-in. Others in the community are also invited to observe.

Speakers include high-ranking law enforcement officials, a **voice of redemption** (someone who has been in a gang or crew and changed his ways), a **voice of aspiration** who encourages them to change (usually a minister, but has also been a former high school principal), a social service provider who offers assistance, and a **voice of pain** (a mother who lost her son from gang violence). It is made clear that they are responsible for bringing the Ceasefire message back to their groups; in the call-in the speakers are not just talking to them—they are talking to their group through them. The message is clear: Stop the violence.

Custom Notifications

For those the Ceasefire initiative wants to reach who cannot be mandated to attend a call-in, or do not come voluntarily, there are custom notifications. This means the team goes to them, usually to their homes. A team from the NYPD and another law enforcement agency (either ATF or the Sheriff) and a community member, usually a minister, deliver the Ceasefire message, along with a letter with language from the District Attorney which explains the group member's personal exposure.

No Retaliation Notifications

Ceasefire messages are also given when the NYPD is trying to prevent retaliation for a shooting or homicide. After a shooting, the same team (NYPD, Sheriff or ATF, and a minister) visits "Impact Players" from the victim's group. They explain Ceasefire with an additional urgent message: "We're watching. Don't retaliate or there will be consequences." The goal is to reach members of the victim's group within 48 hours.

Enforcement Actions

Enforcement actions are not only a critical part of Ceasefire's communication strategy, they are part of Ceasefire's promise. When someone in a group kills someone or a group is particularly violent, an enforcement action is launched. Essentially, Ceasefire's enforcement partners meet and review every legal vulnerability that every member of a group has, and take every action available. Each time an enforcement agency takes action, the group member is told, "We are doing this because of Ceasefire and because your group committed a homicide."

In that way, Ceasefire is not only keeping the promise that if they continued to be violent, there would be consequences; it is also making it clear that the enforcement actions are a direct result of their behavior. Anyone who has no levers to pull are visited anyway and put them on notice that if they violate the law in any way, there will be action taken.

To meet its full potential, Ceasefire needs to become part of how law enforcement does business. This means creating legitimacy within the community by keeping promises. Law enforcement do want group members alive, safe, and out of prison. The focus of the law enforcement partnership is on the next group that commits a homicide and the most violent group at that time. Law enforcement, with the help of social services agencies and non-profits, will help any group member with whatever they need. As Ceasefire has developed within the NYPD, partners have found increasingly more creative ways to reach group members during enforcement actions, and more effective ways to offer and provide social services.

Cure Violence Model

Gary Slutkin, a physician trained in infectious diseases, developed the Cure Violence model at the University of Illinois at Chicago. He is an epidemiologist and a physician who worked abroad in Somalia, Uganda, Rwanda, Tanzania, and several other African nations for over 10 years, battling infectious diseases. Like tuberculosis and cholera, he believes that violence directly imitates these infectious diseases. Believing in that assumption, Slutkin suggests that the treatment should also replicate the treatment applied to infectious diseases: go after the most infected and stop the infection at its source. In analyzing the data in Chicago, Slutkin saw a clustering of violence as it had been seen with infectious disease, and the same was true when it was mapped out. The basic question he asked was, "what predicts a case of violence?" The answer is the greatest predictor of violence is a preceding case of violence.

Slutkin believes applying the same three elements to reverse epidemics would also work to stop the transmission of violent behavior. The first is to interrupt transmission; in order to do this, one needs to detect and find the first case. Second, one needs to prevent further spread, and lastly, change the norms. Doing all three will create group immunity. The program tries to interrupt the next event, the next transmission, the next violent activity (Kotlowitz, 2008). This is done by preventing retaliatory shootings, mediating ongoing conflicts, and continuing to follow up to keep conflicts from simmering up.

In the 2000s, Cure Violence created new categories of workers. The first were violence interrupters who were hired from the same group surrounding the violence, and they had credibility, trust, and access. Slutkin compares them to the health workers in Somalia, who were part of the refugee camp and then became the workers. The violence interrupters are trained in persuasion, cooling people down, buying time, and reframing. Another category of workers is the outreach workers to keep people on "therapy" for 6 to 12 months, with the objective being behavior change. Changing group norms involves many community events with the goal of educating the public that violence is harmful to everyone, it is unacceptable behavior, and it can be stopped.

The program targets a small population: members of the community with a high chance of being shot or being shooters in the near future. The members recruited to receive the treatment of Cure Violence must meet at least four of the seven criteria:

1) Gang-involved
2) Major player in a drug or street organization
3) Violent criminal history
4) Recent incarceration
5) Reputation of carrying a gun
6) Recent victim of a shooting
7) Between 16 and 25 years of age

After the participants are identified, a three-pronged approach is applied to prevent the violence:

A. Detection and Interruption—Data obtained from a multiple of sources, including street knowledge, identifies the areas where to focus efforts, concentrate resources, and intervene in violence. The data identifies communities most impacted and finds those individuals at the highest risk for violence.
B. Behavior Change—Cure Violence intervenes in crises, mediates disputes between individuals and groups, and intercedes in group disputes to prevent violence. There are two sets of workers: the violence interrupters who directly engage with participants on the street, working to stop a retaliatory violence after a violent incident, and the outreach workers whose main function is to connect participants to services and provide counselling.
C. Changing Community Norms—Cure Violence aims to change the thinking about violence, both at the community level and society at large. To accomplish this, Cure Violence uses public education, community-building activities, and motivational interviewing with participants. This allows for introducing new ways of resolving conflicts without violence.

The Cure Violence Model currently has active programs in more than 25 cities in eight

countries. According to the National Gang Center (2021), an independent study showed that six of the seven Cure Violence sites in Chicago found significantly reduced homicides and shootings. In Baltimore there were statistically significant reductions in their four program sites. Although many of the evaluations of the Cure Violence Model point to many limitations and claim the evaluations are inadequate, no one would argue that prevention strategies are key in reducing gun violence.

New York City's Gun Violence Strategies Partnership

Recently begun in New York City, the Gun Violence Strategies Partnership (GVSP) is a multi-agency effort to reduce gun violence in New York City. The partnership brings local, state, and federal law-enforcement stakeholders together in a shared workspace facilitated by the High Intensity Drug Trafficking Area (HIDTA) to develop intelligence and protocols that can better analyze and enhance gun violence and gun trafficking cases as well as arrests among the most violent and dangerous offenders and groups in the city.

The goal of this partnership is to utilize data-driven analytics and partner agency resources and intelligence to achieve a multi-tiered approach to reducing gun violence. This methodology has several processes for the partnership to develop:

- Identify the highest priority individuals, groups, and cases to be enhanced by the GVSP for investigation and prosecution on an ongoing basis.
- Improve the process and timeliness for inter-agency information sharing and dissemination.
- Develop intelligence streams held by individual agencies into shared and accessible resources that partner agencies can access and utilize to enhance gun-related investigations and prosecutions.
- Improve the processes for integrating available intelligence into open investigations and long-term cases.
- Provide local and federal prosecutors with timely and comprehensive intelligence to enhance bail packages, improve prosecutions, and ensure violent and multi-incident offenders are off the street.
- Coordinate multi-jurisdictional and cross-borough gun violence and trafficking cases to reduce overlap of resources and improve available intelligence and timeliness of information sharing.

Each agency dedicates resources and personnel to the GVSP, who are located at NY HIDTA office. The GVSP began in the summer of 2021. Agencies meet collectively for a daily information-sharing briefing where new arrests, high-priority cases, intelligence leads, and investigative issues are discussed. Agency representatives are then able to work cooperatively in real-time with partners to quickly gather and investigate case information, develop leads, and analyze shared data in order to strengthen cases and take immediate steps to keep those driving violence in custody.

The following core group of agencies have dedicated personnel to the GVSP:

- New York City Police Department (NYPD)
- New York City Probation
- New York City Special Narcotics Prosecutor (SNP)
- New York City Department of Corrections (DOC)
- District Attorney's Offices (Manhattan, Queens, Staten Island, Brooklyn, Bronx)
- New York State Department of Corrections and Community Supervision (DOCCS)
- New York State Police (NYSP)
- NY/NJ High Intensity Drug Trafficking Area (HIDTA)

- Federal Bureau of Investigation (FBI)
- Homeland Security Investigations (HSI)
- US Customs and Border Protection (CBP)
- US Probation (USPO)
- US Postal Inspection Service (USPIS)
- Drug Enforcement Administration (DEA)
- Bureau of Alcohol, Tobacco, Firearms and Explosives (ATF)
- United States Attorney's Offices (EDNY, SDNY)

Strategy

The GVSP is unique in that it houses law-enforcement agencies and prosecutors in a shared space, eliminating silos and barriers to timely information and intelligence sharing. This allows partners to work cooperatively to better prepare cases to meet prosecutorial deadlines, take investigative actions in a more focused and timely manner, and ensure that the right information is in the hands of the agency that needs it, when they need it.

Agencies agreed to initially focus efforts on specific subjects who have been identified as trigger pullers and major drivers of gun violence in New York City. Through the NYPD's Gun Recidivist Investigation Program (GRIP), approximately 970 initial subjects were identified following specific criteria, with over 700 of them currently out of custody and on the streets. These criteria target the most recently active violent shooting recidivists who will receive the focus of the partnership to identify vulnerabilities, prioritize new arrests, and revisit or refocus open cases in an effort to ensure subjects receive high or no bail at arraignment and are prosecuted fully. The criteria are as follows:

1. Active GRIP subject
2. At least two shooting incidents total (FS, NFS, Shots Fired) since January 1, 2018
3. At least one of the shooting incident (FS, NFS, Shots Fired) since January 1, 2020

The GVSP meets for a daily strategy session to discuss priority cases from the GRIP list. New arrests of GRIP list subjects from the past 24-hour period take precedence, and agencies focus on immediate actionable intelligence and investigative steps that can be leveraged to ensure the best possible bail package, indictment, and prosecution. A follow-up on the status of the previous day's subjects is conducted to ensure agencies received what they needed, and outcomes will be evaluated to better develop internal processes and track success. Prosecutors will have the opportunity to directly communicate their needs to law-enforcement to ensure necessary evidence is collected and prosecutorial concerns are addressed early, to enhance the chances of a positive outcome in the investigation, arraignment, and indictment.

During the daily strategy session, partners also have an opportunity to focus discussion on cases of high value to their agencies, sharing details and findings that may benefit the investigative focus of the team. Representatives are also able to share strategies and programs their agencies can bring to the partnership as a resource, and work together on streamlining data sharing processes and tools. This includes the opportunity for GVSP partners to additionally connect with previously difficult-to-access resources now available to them through the HIDTA partnership such as federal partner programs, databases, and investigative tools that can be worked into the gun violence investigation and prosecution strategy. There are currently thirty-six (36) local, state, and federal agencies who are all housed within the shared HIDTA space that contribute to investigations and provide access to criminal justice information that may have otherwise been difficult to obtain in a timely manner.

Operations

The GVSP is led by a multi-disciplinary team of NYPD executives and investigators who serve several functions within the structure of the team including oversight, identification of target subjects, facilitating the sharing of intelligence and investigative findings with partners, and improving internal processes and communication around gun violence investigations and cases. The team works to coordinate efforts and investigations between agencies to enhance arrests, build stronger long-term and trafficking cases, and improve prosecution outcomes at the state and federal level.

The executive team has built and will maintain the Crime Gun Intelligence Center (CGIC) infrastructure to support the work of this group. The NYPD updates and maintains the current list of GRIP subjects that meet the GVSP program criteria and shares the list with partner agencies weekly as it is updated. Investigators review new gun arrests, shooting incidents, and open gun violence investigations involving GRIP list subjects to prepare daily briefings for the partnership on priority subjects and cases. The briefings highlight the following priority cases:

1. New arrests of GRIP list subjects (whether related to a firearm/shooting or not)
   a. Special attention to GRIP subjects with open Criminal Possession of a Weapon cases
2. Newly added subjects to the GRIP list (presence/participation in recent shooting events)
3. Upcoming GRIP list subject court dates (priority to court dates in the next 2 weeks)
4. New intelligence or evidence related to high priority GRIP list subjects (DNA match, ballistic evidence, gun trace results, jail calls, social media, etc.)
5. Gun violence cases involving GRIP subjects that cross borough boundaries

NYPD investigators additionally generate and forward daily GVSP arrest reports and shooting incidents involving GRIP subjects from the past 24 hours to ensure partners have the most up-to-date information on new arrests and incidents. An early notification system for all new firearm and shooting/shots fired arrests is also being developed within the NYPD so that the GVSP can be notified in real-time. This allows the NYPD team to compile and forward the perpetrator's background, case details, and arrest enhancements to prosecutors quickly, in an effort to improve bail and arraignment packages. This will also allow the team to have additional time to review new arrests for Triggerlock eligibility—program which specifically targets individuals who are arrested for criminal possession of a weapon. The case is immediately referred to the Bureau of Alcohol, Tobacco and Firearms, which reviews it and, if accepted, refers it to the federal prosecutor. The rationale is that gun violators, when convicted in federal court, are given far stiffer jail penalties than they would face for the same conviction in state court. The team also has the opportunity to review parole or probation violations and also provides additional intelligence that District Attorney's (DA) require to request remand or higher bail.

District Attorney's Offices are asked to review GRIP list subject's open cases and flag any issues where law-enforcement partners can enhance cases. Priority is given to new arrests and cases where upcoming impactful court dates are pending (i.e., bail hearings). This can include additional evidence needed such as results of firearm testing, National Integrated Ballistics Information Network (NIBIN) and DNA hits and leads, social media data, video and body camera footage, etc. that may give prosecutors leverage to ask for higher bail or remand in court.

Federal prosecutors identify any GRIP list members who are the subject of a federal investigation or indictment, and share this information with partners. DAs and law-enforcement partners are able to work with their federal partners, the Eastern District of New York (EDNY) and the Southern District of New York (SDNY) to identify cases for federal prosecution and to de-conflict overlapping investigations in order to identify the strongest prosecution angle.

Federal partners (ATF, CBP, USPIS, HSI, etc.) are also available to law enforcement and prosecutors to enhance investigations and lend resources, intelligence, and insight into cases. This also gives law-enforcement and prosecutors access to the new Gun Violence Dashboard (developed in partnership with the NYPD and ATF) where shootings, shots fired incidents, NIBIN leads, and gun traces are mapped to aid agencies in identifying leads, gun trafficking, and links between gun cases and shooting incidents. The ATF is available to confer with partners daily to run gun traces, discuss case findings, and enhance trafficking investigations as well as expedite traces when necessary in priority cases.

Although in its infancy, the GVSP shows very promising results. It is through the collaboration of everyone sitting at the table on a daily basis that gun violence will be reduced. Given that we know a small percentage of individuals commit the majority of violent crime, the GVSP laser focus on individuals who are driving violence in the community will result in a reduction in violence in New York City.

Conclusion

Violence reduction strategies across the nation are focused on ending the tragedy of gun violence. It requires a sustained effort at all levels of government and society. So many programs not described here, whether it be gun buybacks, strategies to interrupt sources of illegal guns, which has gotten much harder since the advent of ghost guns, to education initiatives, all aim to reduce violence. Gun violence is an epidemic in the United States. All institutions, including education, public health, and criminal justice systems, must work together to reduce violence and save lives.

References

Butts, J. A., Bostwick, C. G., & Porter, J. R. (2015). Cure violence: A public health model to reduce gang violence. *Annual Review of Public Health, 36*, 39–53.

Foley RJ. (2016, December 9) *New CDC data understate accidental shooting deaths of kids. USA Today*.

Global Health Data Exchange. (2016). *Global Burden of Disease Study 2016 (GBD 2016) data input sources tool*. http://ghdx.healthdata.org/gbd-2016/data-input-sources.

Gorman-Smith, D., & Cosey-Gay, F. (2014). *Residents' and clients' perceptions of safety and CeaseFire impact on neighborhood crime and violence*. School of Social Service Administration, University of Chicago.

Government Report Centers for Disease Control and Prevention. (2021). *National center for health statistics 2020*. Centers for Disease Control and Prevention.

Kegler, S. R., Stone, D. M., Mercy, J. A., & Dahlberg, L. L. (2022). Firearm homicides and suicides in major metropolitan areas – United States, 2015-2016 and 2018-2019. *MMWR Morb Mortal Wkly Rep, 71*, 14–18. https://doi.org/10.15585/mmwr.mm7101a3externalicon

Kotlowitz, A. (2008, May 4). *Blocking the transmission of violence*. New York Times Magazine: New York: 52-59,100-102.

Meszaros, J. (2017). Falling through the cracks: the decline of mental health care and firearm violence. *Journal of Mental Health, 26*(4), 359–365. https://doi.org/10.1080/09638237.2017.1340608

Ransford, C., Kane, C., Metzger, T., Quintana, E., & Slutkin, G. (2010). An examination of the role of CeaseFire, the Chicago police, Project Safe Neighborhoods, and displacement in the reduction in homicide in Chicago in 2004. In R. J. Chaskin (Ed.), *Youth gangs and community intervention: Research, practice, and evidence* (pp. 76–108). Columbia University Press.

Ransford, C. L., Kane, C. M., & Slutkin, G. (2013). Cure violence: A disease control approach to reduce violence and change behavior. In E. Waltermaurer & T. Akers (Eds.), *Epidemiological criminology*. Routledge. Google Scholar.

Skogan, W. G., Hartnett, S. M., Bump, N., & Dubois, J. (2008). *Evaluation of CeaseFire-Chicago*. Final Report to the National Institute of Justice. Northwestern University. Retrieved from http://www.ncjrs.gov/pdffiles1/nij/grants/227181.pdf.

Slutkin, G. (2013). *Violence is a contagious disease*. The Contagion of Violence. Institute of Medicine. Retrieved from http://www.cureviolence.org/wp-content/uploads/2014/01/iom.pdf

Slutkin, G., Ransford, C., & Decker, R. B. (2015). Cure violence: Treating violence as a contagious disease. In M. Maltz & S. Rice (Eds.), *Envisioning criminology*. Springer. https://doi.org/10.1007/978-3-319-15868-6_5

The Geneva Declaration on Armed Violence and Development (2006). http://www.genevadeclaration.org/home.html.

The Global Burden of Disease 2016 Injury Collaborators. (2018). Global Mortality From Firearms, 1990-2016. *JAMA*. 2018;320(8):792–814. https://doi.org/10.1001/jama.2018.10060

Tracy, M., Braga, A. A., & Papachristos, A. V. (2016). The transmission of gun and other weapon-involved violence within social networks. *Epidemiology Review, 38*(1), 70–86.

Webster, D. W., Whitehill, J. M., Vernick, J. S., & Curriero, F. C. (2013). Effects of Baltimore's safe streets program on gun violence: A replication of Chicago's CeaseFire program. *Journal of Urban Health, 90*, 27–40.

Chapter 12
Communal Complexity Conflict and Security in Gambia

Perry Stanislas and Ebrima Chongan

Introduction

This chapter examines the sources of possible tension in Gambia that contribute to communal conflict and their policing and security implications. The chapter will first briefly explore some important concepts and theories that help explain and understand communal conflict, before going on to outline the demographic and geographical features of Gambia and Gambian society. Thirdly, it examines how many of the issues rooted in the early post-independence period, where the security of the country is concerned, structure the contemporary policing and security problems of the country and its relationship with its neighbour Senegal. Fourthly, the chapter will examine some of the complex issues around economic, and foreign policy, and migration and its potential contribution to current communal conflict with significant policing implications. One dimension of this problem is the role of the Chinese in Gambia, and Africa more broadly. Some of the issues addressed in the chapter will be examined in greater depth in a forthcoming book on policing and national security in Gambia.

P. Stanislas (✉)
Canterbury Christ Church University, Canterbury, UK
e-mail: perry.stanislas@canterbury.ac.uk

E. Chongan
Gambia Police Department (ret.), Banjul, Gambia

J. F. Albrecht, G. den Heyer (eds.), *Understanding and Preventing Community Violence*, https://doi.org/10.1007/978-3-031-05075-6_12

Theories of Communal Conflict

Understanding communal and societal conflict has long antecedence across many disciplines ranging from sociology, anthropology, history, war, and peace studies inter alia (Galtung, 2003; Keegan, 1993; Malervic, 2010). Most of the sources of inter and intra communal conflict are well-known in the social sciences. Structural conflict lay at the heart of Marx's theory of social change (Malervic, 2010, p. 23). The counter use of violence by the impoverished working classes according to his view is seen as a critical precondition for transformation and the establishment of a new order. Racial and ethnic differences, as a potential potent source of communal conflict and instability, were identified by Machiavelli as early as the sixteenth century, along with tactics to ameliorate many of the problems associated with ruling territories characterized by ethnic and racial differences (Machiavelli, 2019; Stanislas, & Sadique, 2019). Linked to ethnicity is religious difference, which can be another factor among a plethora of others, and is a potential source of conflict which demonstrates the complexity of human social identity.

African societies provide some excellent examples of the complexity of social identities and their capacity to contribute to a range of serious conflicts. In Nigeria and Kenya ethnic, religious, geographical, and economic inequalities have resulted in communal conflicts (Mkutu & Stanislas, 2017; Jatto & Stanislas 2017; Aremu & Stanislas, 2019). The Turkana people of Northeast Kenya have been in a protracted conflict with a foreign oil producing company, whose activities adversely impact on the pastoralists' traditional grazing land. Not only do oil pipes and other structures impede on the Turkana's and their cattle's movement, but chemical run offs from the oil production process damages land and affects drinking water of people and livestock. To exacerbate matters much of the anticipated benefits of oil production for the Turkana in the poverty-stricken Northeastern region, which was critical in persuading tribal elders to support oil production on their land, has not materialized in the forms of jobs inter alia (Kim & Mkutu, 2021).

Galtung's (2003) theory details the multiple variables that can contribute to communal conflict and demonstrates the complex challenges involved in the maintenance of peace. According to his view violence is always latent in society and reflects a pattern of human behaviour which manifests once a particular breach or threshold has been reached. Peace for Galtung is simply not the absence of direct physical violence brought about consciously by social actors but is also preconditioned on the absence of what he describes as structural violence which can consist of several factors that can include political, cultural, economic, historical grievance, prejudices, and beliefs, sentiments or inflammatory behaviour that contribute to an environment that can fuel communal conflict.

In this regard, Galtung shares important similarities to Marx and authors such as Fanon (1967) and Freire (1973) where the subordinate group is constantly subjected to different forms of violations and emotional harms, until a critical tipping point is reached that culminates in communal violence. Common to the theories of Marx, Fanon, and Freire is the notion of violence as facilitating individual and collective transformation in identity terms of how subordinate groups view themselves. Communal violence according to these authors empowers the hitherto oppressed, helping to form new more confident and assertive identities, representing a distinct break from the past.

Demography of Gambia

Gambia is a west African country located between both sides of the River Gambia, within the territory of Senegal and facing the North Atlantic Coast. The boundaries of Gambia are totally artificial and drawn by British colonialists, as they did elsewhere, and bears no relationship to the ethnicity of the people who live there (Hughes & Perfect 2008). Gambia is one of the smaller countries in Africa consisting of 11, 300 square kilometres (CIA Fact Book, 2021) and has a population of 2,221,301 people who are made up of eight ethnic groups, with the Mandinka being the largest (34.4%), Fula (30.1%), Wolof (16%), Sera (9%), and Jola (9%) inter alia. Approximately 90 percent of Gambians are Muslim, in terms of religious beliefs, with the remainder being Christians. Religion is not a general source of tension within the country, which is largely tolerant with a long history of peaceful coexistence between those of different faiths. However, more recently the influence of Wahhabi Islam has begun to emerge which is a worrying development given its association with extremism and terrorism (Drammeh, 2021). By means of comparison Senegal has a population of 16,082,442 (CIA Fact Book, 2021) and in terms of size is 192,530 square km.

An important feature of West African societies is the existence of caste identity and groupings (Dilley, 2000). The term caste usually applies to occupational craft specialists within society which individuals are born into, and are particularly prevalent in Senegal, Gambia, and Mali who share strong cultural and ethnic similarities among the Wolof and Serer inter alia. Occupational castes, such as artisans, craftsmen, singers, and musicians, are common within these ethnic communities (Dilley, 2000, p. 150). Because members of the same ethnic and caste groups exist within Gambia and Senegal, communal conflict in one country may have significant impact on other group members living in the neighbouring country. 1n 2019 The National Human Rights Commission Gambia (NHRCG) published a press release[1] condemning caste-based discrimination among the Sarahule tribe in Koina and Fatoto. The NHRCG criticized the unlawful behaviour among some groups within the Sarahule caste who viewed themselves as 'nobles', and their treatment of others within the tribe deemed as inferior 'slaves'. These attitudes have led to clashes with people being wounded and threatened to escalate. Such conflicts occur among other tribes over land disputes or due to inter-caste marriages inter alia.

[1] Beakanyang – Posts | Facebook. Accessed 24 August 2021

The History of Policing and Security in Gambia

In 1843 Gambia was removed from the administration of Sierra Leone and granted administrative autonomy and its own colonial Governor. The first formal police organization in Gambia was the 10-man Gambia River Police (GRP) formed in 1855. The role of the River Police was to control smuggling, enforce taxation, and prevent the waterways to be used for anything that threatened white rule and the colonial order (Andrade, 1985). Prior to the establishment of the GRP policing was carried out by British soldiers, including members of the West Indies Regiment, and local militia drawn from white traders and freed slaves (Colonial Annual Report 1905). The Gambia Constabulary was formed in 1866 and headed by a Superintendent and an Assistant Superintendent (Colonial Annual Report 1905) and was a typical colonial paramilitary force similar to those found in other colonized countries at the time. The Gambian Constabulary absorbed the Frontier Police which was formed in 1895, to become part of the unified police organization after independence from Britain in 1965.

After the Gambia Regiment (a Company of the West African Frontier Force[2]) rescinded its security responsibilities in 1958, these were taken over by the police (Andrade, 1985). In structural terms, the Gambian Constabulary consisted of a Criminal Investigation Department, a Traffic Department, and Immigration Department and Fire Department. The Police Field Force was a 200-person paramilitary capability, who could be deployed in the event of major incidents. In geographical terms the Gambia Police had four divisions, with the majority of the 80 noncommissioned officers based in what today is the capital Banjul.

Early Communal Conflict

One of the earliest manifestations of communal conflict in Gambia which threatened the colonial order was rumours of a plot to kill all whites in Bathurst (contemporary Banjul) on Christmas Eve in 1865. This news reached the attention of the Governor, who quickly mobilized soldiers in preparation for the expected attack. The alleged leader of the planned attack was an Igbo (Nigerian) Methodist and successful trader Harry Finden (Mahoney, 1963, 218; Hughes & Perfect 2008). The anxiety caused by this plot was exacerbated by the events in Morant Bay, Jamaica, earlier in the same year led by Baptist Deacon Paul Bogle that shook the colonial administration and grabbed attention back in Britain (Robotham, 1981). A significant source of grievance among Africans in Gambia was the dominance of the Legislative Council by British merchants and their agents at their expense,

[2] Despite the name Gambia Regiment being used to describe the soldiers of the African Frontier Forces, colonial reports describe them as a company which is more in keeping with the actual number of soldiers deployed.

marginalizing issues of concern to them, which contributed to further galvanization of black opinion and mobilization. This is seen in the formation of the Committee of Black Inhabitants, who dispatched representatives to London to lobby the British government. The political, economic, and other forms of dominance and structural violence (Galtung, 2003) experienced by Gambians was symbolized by the white-led police, military, and militia. Prior to the scare of 1865, the most significant communal conflict in Gambia was what historians have dubbed the Soninke-Marabout wars of the 1850s, caused by the clash of an expansionist Islam with religious traditionalists.

While the country has experienced little significant and sustained periods of violence compared to many West African countries, the various indices of serious conflict as identified by Galtung, have always been present in Gambia. Deliberate efforts to reduce potential communal tension in the form of tribalism, which has crippled countries such as Nigeria and Kenya (Aremu & Stanislas, 2019), were taken by the founding father of independence Sir Dawda Jawara, whose People's Progressive Party came to power in 1965. The popular Jawara, who remained in power for nearly 30 years, adopted an inclusive approach to government and administration to reduce the dominance of the Mandinkas. Prior to coming into power, Jawara transformed the PPP from a Mandinka dominated organization, to one which represented the diverse ethnic communities in Gambia (Perfect, 2010; Hughes & Perfect, 2008).

Nepotism and corruption became issues of concern under Jawara, primarily due to the conduct of some of his ministers. The President's success and dominance of politics contributed to the exclusion of many voices and minor political parties, which was exacerbated by the marginalization of young people and the lack of opportunities. This was to reach a crisis point with a drastic decline in the economy in the early 1980s, compounded by drought and poor harvests, in conjunction with financial scandals that brought the country to the type of tipping point in the slide towards conflict elucidated by Galtung.

The changing environment led to the emergence of radical and militant political formations, in the form of the Movement for Justice in Africa-Gambia (MOJA-G) launched in 1979, which was Marxist and Pan African in orientation and the Gambia Socialist Revolutionary Party (GSRP), who were both forced underground after being declared illegal in 1980. Acts of political vandalism and the militant tone of the publications of these organisations served to potentially threaten the political status which had developed under the Jawara administration. To make matters worse, an internal plot within the security forces to seize power, driven by personal and group rivalries, was thwarted with the assistance of the Senegalese authorities, not before a senior leader of the Field Force was assassinated (Hughes & Perfect 2008, p. liii). The superior security capabilities of Senegal and Gambia's ability to call on it in critical instances has been a key characteristic of their post-independence relationship (Chongan, 2009).

Other new political organizations begun to operate in a clandestine manner, to include established ones such as National Liberation Party (NLP) who unsuccessfully contested previous elections. The growing dissatisfaction with the government spread to the security services, and within the Field Force in particular, where many of its personnel begun to evolve a plot to overthrow the government with GSRP leader Kukoi Samba Sanyang (Hughes & Perfect 2008, p liv). Perceptions of tribalism and its twin cousin nepotism were a particularly inflammatory issue for the conspirators. The resulting coup attempt led to several hundred people being killed, before it was squashed by the Gambian Police under Inspector General of Police Abdoulie Mboob, with the assistance of neighbouring Senegal. This was not before a last-ditch attempt by Sanyang to rally his tribesmen when he realized the forces against him, and the coup was not going according to plan. These events brought to the fore the lack of preparation of the Jawara administration for security challenges of this nature, and reflected the President's focus on leading a peaceful democracy which can be seen by his lenient attitude towards the conspirators involved in the 1980 plot. Important changes to the country's security capabilities were introduced, as a matter of priority in the wake of the attempted coup, but as Chongan (2009) highlights these improvements were inadequate. These concerns were ignored by government, which contributed to a successful coup 13 years later.

Policing and Security Reform

One of the problems with evaluating the effectiveness of the Gambian police service is that for 23 years from 1994 to 2017 its power was stymied under the administration of dictator President Yahya Jammeh, who seized office via a coup. Many of the top leaders in the police either fled at the start of the coup, or like the coauthor (Assistant Inspector General of Police Ebrima Chongan), were detained in the notorious 2 Mile Prison where they underwent torture and deprivation (Chongan, 2009). The police institution during this period was reduced to largely a shell organization, in favour of the military, intelligence services, and foreign appointed judges who were introduced to carry out the will of the new President. It is very difficult to ascertain the character of the police force of the newly independent Gambia, given the lack of available information. Some of the characteristics of former colonial police organization during the early days of independence are high levels of patriotism and sense of public service (Stanislas, 2020; Stanislas 2017, Sinclair, 2010), with newly appointed police leaders being acutely conscious of expectations and their responsibilities in what were low crime societies. Given the popularity of the First Republic under Jawara, and his commitment to democratic accountability (Hughes & Perfect, 2008), these values in all likelihood were reflected in the workings and ethos of the police.

The few studies on the police in Gambia (*Jobarteh,* 2013*;* Perrot, 2013a, b; Davidheiser & Hultin, 2012) were all carried out under the abnormal conditions of a violent dictatorship (see M'bai, 2012; Yeebo, 1995) and a largely emasculated and compliant police organization. The key findings of these studies highlighted many of the traditional features of former colonial police in Caribbean and African countries, but in more extreme form (see Mkutu et al., 2017). Absent in the literature was any notion of public service, crime prevention, or law enforcement as the overriding ethos and raison detre of the police. Closely related to this was a culture of nepotism and incompetence, particularly in the selection of police leaders and as Perot (2013a, pg. 142) observed a concern for the trappings of authority, as opposed to authority based on professional competence rooted in police work. He also found micromanagement of subordinates by managers and leaders in rather mundane matters took precedence, over focusing on effectively running the activities or departments they were responsible for, highlighting a clear lack of priorities (see Adebayo, 2005). In resource terms, the number of police personnel is small with 5, 000 police officers in 2018 (Interpol, 2018), consisting largely of individuals lacking the most elementary education, with poor levels of training in many aspects of contemporary policing.[3] The police lacked vehicles and basic equipment, such as radios and computers to carry out rudimentary functions (see Stanislas, 2020).

The research findings are reinforced by more recent testimony of police officers.[4] A key feature of police, and other branches of the security services, during Jammeh's era was that many unqualified and unsuitable personnel were recruited, on the sole basis of their loyalty to the regime. In addition, continuous professional training was abandoned which resulted in large turnover of senior police leaders and personnel who tried to accommodate the incumbent administration as best as they could. The police were essentially politicized and not much has changed.

Since the return to democracy with the election of President Adama Barrow in 2017, his government has instituted Security Sector Reform (SSR), where the police figure largely, which is funded by international governments and agencies (Mutangadura, 2020). However, since the launch of SSR there has been no production of a report outlining any planned policing reforms, or any discernible visible changes in the police organization, and how it operates. Moreover, there are still senior police officers who served Jammeh's violent regime in post, along with significant number of clearly unqualified personnel of questionable character.

The extraordinary slow pace of change is highlighted by Mutangadura (2020). Important factors in producing this outcome are the political weakness of President Barrow's coalition government, and his own apparent indecisiveness. The policing demands in Gambia are also changing, with the increasing numbers of black people from the Diaspora (primarily the UK and USA) choosing to visit, relocate, and invest in the country in supporting its economic development (Essa, 2018).[5] One of the authors was invited to address a meeting held by the Council of African Descent in February 2021 in Gambia, attended by people from the Diaspora who lived in or were visiting the country, including local Gambians, on the issue of personal security and crime prevention given the increasing concern about these matters. The key issues aired at the meeting were:

[3] The quality of police human resources was confirmed in a meeting Dr. Stanislas had with the Inspector General of Police in May 2021.

[4] Information ascertained through verbal and written communications with former Gambian police officers

[5] See Blaxit YouTube Channel.

- Poor police response to public request for assistance.
- High levels of burglaries, repeat victimization, and the targeting of new arrivals.
- Concerns about women's safety (the potential of burglaries turning into rapes or other assaults)[6].
- Road safety.
- Poor levels of professional competence.
- Police soliciting money or accepting money from the public.
- Cybercrime and its potential impact on new businesses, given the poor levels of technological capacity within the police.

There is a need for baseline research to capture the actual crime rate in Gambia, and to establish the perception of citizens and visitors to the country of police performance, which can be used to inform and drive police reform.[7] The police do not regularly publish crime statistics and clearance rates, which is usually a sign of government trying to mask the real levels of crime and poor police performance.[8] In the Gambian instance, the absence of crime data enables government, the tourism industry, and others to promote the image of the country being a safe and peaceful place because the true level of crime is hidden. The publication of crime statistics and clearance rates should be a statutory requirement.

Crime and Communal Conflict

The increasing concerns around crime within the country serves as a potential flashpoint of intercommunal tensions and violence (Jallow, 2021). Several examples can be provided to illustrate this. The first was the attack on an Immigration Officer at a new Immigration office at the seafront in Gunjur, where the attackers purportedly had guns and were believed to be migrants. Due to the establishment of several Chinese fish meal factories on the west coast seafront,[9] the location has drawn prospective migrant workers from the entire west Africa region, but primarily Senegal, Mauritania, Guinea Bissau, Guinea, and Mali. This influx of migrants has caused tensions between local Gambians and the established Senegalese who work in the fishing industry. For example, the lack of toilet facilities for such large numbers of people adversely impacts on the tourism industry, with people fouling the environment, and those who traditionally work and live there. The violence against Immigration officials further intensifies deep-seated sentiments among those

[6] This video illustrates how confident criminals are in breaking into property with no fear of being caught by the police, and the fear that women have. https://youtu.be/5rqTTOwZgp4

[7] Dr. Stanislas wrote the new Inspector General of Police and raised his concerns about the lack of baseline research to support his ideas of reform after they met in May 2021 to discuss SSR. To date he has received no reply.

[8] Caribbean countries, such as St Lucia, stopped publishing the crime rate for similar reasons.

[9] https://youtu.be/Yipf1nU9Lf8

adversely affected and Gambians at large. The swift police response to this crime mirrored the impact this inflammatory act had on sections of society (Galtung, 2003).

The second incident occurred in Sanyang (another fishing town) and involved the killing of 33-year-old Gibril Ceesay, who lost his life after his home was broken into by an armed burglar in March 2021 (Jallow, 2021). The loss of life was made worse by the fact that Ceesay had become a father less than a month earlier. The victim's brother was also injured in the machete attack. Information about the incident quickly spread, and young men in significant numbers arrived at the Sanyang police station. One reason provided for this response was to prevent the assailant, who was believed to be in police custody, from escaping. This fear was shaped by the relatively recent incident of a Senegalese national suspected of murder escaping, after being held by the authorities twice in short succession, either due to corruption or incompetence or both. On hearing the assailant was not in police custody, the angry crowd stormed the police station destroying property before setting it on fire.

The orgy of violence then escalated taking on an anti-Senegalese tone and became focused on the Senegalese fishing community who are well-established in Sanyang, with the destruction of buildings and structures, fishing boats, machinery, and other equipment. Information that the suspected killer was a fish worker who was employed by a Chinese company led to mob attacks on the equipment and premises of the Chinese company; resulting in burning down the buildings, along with company vehicles and living quarters; not before large amounts of money held on the premises was stolen. The latter's presence has been a source of much communal grievance given its impact on fish stocks, an important source of food, and the local indigenous fishing industry and tourism (Hunt, 2021). Another concern is the impact of the Chinese company's work practices on the environment, which affects the quality of life of residents. The events escalated into a full-scale riot, and a special unit of paramilitary police was dispatched to Sanyang. However, given the scale of the ferocity and sheer number of rioters, the police were forced to withdraw. The attack on domestic dwellings of the Senegalese workers forced over 200 of them having to seek refuge outside of Sanyang, assisted by the Red Cross and the National Disaster Management Agency (Hunt, 2021).

The riot at Sanyang is extremely important for several reasons. Gambians pride themselves and seen by many outsiders as a peaceful and accommodating people, which is illustrated in the nickname of the country as the 'smiling coast' of Africa (see Janko, 2018) and an important factor in its popularity as an international tourism destination and for Diasporan migration. Crime and collective acts of violence are rare in this largely law-abiding society and requires adequate explanation.

As Galtung (2003) postulates, public and communal violence is caused by multiple structural and other factors. In this instance, the dissatisfaction of the wider community at the poor police response in reducing crimes, such as burglary, is a longstanding grievance[10] which is on the increase due to the structural poverty that has increased given the economic impact of the Covid pandemic on the small poor country which is heavily dependent on tourism; and symbolized by the burning down of Sanyang Police Station. The national sensitivity to the increase in crime can be seen by the fact that 'Operation Zero', a joint task force involving the police, immigration services inter alia, had just concluded a major operation resulting in the arrest of 881 individuals for a range of offences days before the disturbance at Sanyang (Kandeh, 2021).

The perpetrator of the killing in Sanyang, being an immigrant, intensified the sense of injustice and the perception of Gambians being second class citizens in their own country and government indifference to the treatment of its people, which emboldens outsiders in their ability to kill citizens. Finally, the association between the killer and the Chinese presence in Gambia, as in other African countries, is unwelcomed and viewed as an exploitative and racist presence (Sul, 2020, Pilling and Wong, 2020). One element of the structural nature of the violence that occurred is cited by a respondent in an interview in the *Freedom* newspaper (2021):

> Is a buildup of frustration upon frustration. Chinese do whatever they want to do, and they are getting away with it, and then we have this fishing agreement with Senegalese, where Senegalese can come in any number, using any kind of net and fish in our ocean and sell directly to the Chinese, ignoring the locals and the Chinese are paying them in Francs. The locals are seeing this, they feel that the country is being taken over by foreign nationals.

Adopting the viewpoint of Marx, Fanon, and others discussed earlier, the violence which occurred at Sanyang is indication of changes in the Gambian population, which the government needs to take serious note of. The riot witnessed the abandonment of the traditional image of Gambians, and in its place emerged violent and fearless people who were prepared to attack and destroy traditional symbols and agents of authority and target the source of their grievances. The specter of Wahhab Islam and its capacity to feed off the frustration and discontent sections of the population in small countries has been documented in the case of Trinidad and Tobago and elsewhere (Stanislas & Sadique, 2019; see Counter Extremism Project. ND). The attack against predominantly Senegalese workers is particularly important, given its ramifications for Senegalese people in Gambia, and Gambians in Senegal, and possible reprisals and something appreciated by the governments of both countries.[11] As has already been highlighted, the Gambia nation-state is literally a false construct, created by the British in establishing another country within Senegal. Thousands of Senegalese live in Gambia, and people travel there for business or shop to buy goods and services and vice versa. The relationship between Gambia

---

[10] Dr. Stanislas spoke at a meeting held in Gambia in February 2021 about policing and crime attended by black people from the Diaspora and Gambian returnees many of whom had bought property who reported the large numbers of burglary and break in being experienced as new target groups for criminals. However, it was reported that local Gambians are also subject to these types of crimes. Given the poor policing and record keeping, the real level of crime in Gambia is unknown.

[11] https://youtu.be/hu9uNiUPQzY

and its closest neighbour is a complex one. But more importantly the poor leadership and policymaking of Gambian government in taking decisions which adversely impact on their own citizens and their livelihoods, with little realistic alternatives, creates the deeply held perception among Gambians that they are the perennial losers in their special relationship with their larger and more powerful Senegalese neighbours.

Conclusion

One of the important paradoxes of Gambia is despite the apparent peaceful and welcoming nature of this society it is currently a potentially very fragile society, where many of the structural and nonstructural factors detailed by Galtung are present and can coalesce with violent consequences for this poor small country. The two considerations of size and lack of resources are clearly evident in the weakness of the police and state security institutions resulting in government historically struggling to contain major violent incidents, be it attempts to seize power by the aggrieved, without the assistance of its larger and more powerful neighbour Senegal. By the same token, the police's inability to control collective violence as seen in the Sanyang riots is troubling. While a weak police organization may be less of a concern in a low crime and content society, however, the changing character of the country increases the levels of instability and potential insecurity. One of the key legacies of President Jammeh's rule has been a severely weakened and compromised police and security institutions which has not been remedied under the current leadership of President Adama Barrow.

Barrow's government has also been responsible for important policy decisions which appear to have the potential to undermine the peace, so highly valued by citizens and visitors alike, which is crystallized in the presence of the Chinese fishing industry and its partnership with Senegalese fishermen that is impoverishing local Gambians; at a time when an already poor country is struggling under the economic effects of the Covid pandemic. Ironically, despite all the negatives associated with the Jammeh regime, one of his qualities valued by citizens was his patriotism in terms of not allowing outsiders disrespect or undermine Gambia and its citizens which shaped how foreign businesses operated in Gambia. How these matters develop is closely linked to the oncoming general election in December 2021, which will decide if the current administration is removed or remains in power. Either way, unless there is significant policy change in Gambia, the likelihood of communal violence is high.

References

Adebayo, D. (2005). Perceived workplace fairness, transformational leadership and motivation in the Nigeria police: Implications for change. *International Journal of Police Science and Management, 7*(2), 110–122.
Andrade, J. (1985). *World police and paramilitary forces*. Palgrave Macmillan.
Aremu, A., & Stanislas, P. (2019). Police strategies for dealing with tribal conflicts in Nigeria. In G. Den Heyer, P. Stanislas, & J. F. Albrecht (Eds.), *Policing minority communities: International perspectives*. CRC Press.
Chongan, E. (2009). *The Price of Duty 994 days in The Gambian Junta's Dungeon: A Memoir* (Self Published).
Davidheiser, M., & Hultin, N. (2012). In D. Francis (Ed.), *Policing the post-Colony: Legal pluralism, security and social control in the Gambia*. Policing in Africa, Palgrave-Macmillan.
Dilley, R. (2000). *The question of caste in West Africa with special reference to Tukulor Craftsmen*. Nomos Verlagsge sellschaft.
Drammeh, B. (2021, April 6). *Wahhabi Henchmen, Stop meddling in the affairs of Islamic organisation*. www.voicegambia.com. Accessed 30 Aug 2021.
Essa, A. (2018, January 18). *Why some African Americans are moving to Africa*. www.aljazeera.com. Accessed 23 Aug 2021.
Fanon, F (1967). *The wretched of the Earth*. Binding Paperback.
Freire, P. (1973). *Pedagogy of the oppressed*. ELT Reprint Edition.
Galtung, J. (2003). *Positive and negative peace*.
Hughes, A., & Perfect, D. (2008). *Historical dictionary of the Gambia* (4th ed.). The Scarecrow Press.
Hunt, L. (2021, April 29). *A fatal stabbing sends a Gambian fishing village into turmoil over fishmeal www.mongbay.com*. Accessed 18 Aug 2021.
Jallow, M. (2021, April 19). *Gambia: 408 People Arrested Since Establishment of 'Operation Zero Crime'*. www.allafrica.com. Accessed 17 Aug 2021.
Janko, S. (2018). *Why the Gambia is known as 'The Smiling Coast' (theculturetrip.com)*. Accessed 17 Aug 2021.
Jatto, A., & Stanislas, P. (2017). Contemporary territorial, economic, and political security in Edo state, Nigeria. *Geopolitics, History, and International Relations, 9*(2), 118–140.
Jobarteh, P. (2013). Gambia. In M. Nalla & G. Newman (Eds.), *Community policing in indigenous communities*. Taylor and Francis.
Kandeh, J. (2021, May 20). *Operation Zero Crime Arrests 881 Suspected Criminals in 2 Months*. wwwthepointgm.com. Accessed 18 Aug 2021.
Keegan, J. (1993). *The history of warfare*. Hutchinson.
Kim, H., & Mkutu, K. (2021). *Oil extraction and public attitudes: A conjoint experiment in Turkana*. Extractive Industries and Society (In Press).
M'bai, P. N. (2012). *The Gambia: The untold dictator Yahya Jammeh's story*. I Universe Inc.
Machiavelli, N. (2019) *The Prince*.
Mahoney, F. (1963) *Government and opinion in Gambia 1861–1901*. PhD Thesis School of Oriental and Studies, University of London.
Malervic, S. (2010). *The sociology of war and violence*. Cambridge University Press.
Mkutu, K., & Stanislas, P. (2017). Corruption and procurement fraud in the south Saharan African extraction industries: The cases of Turkana, Kenya, and Mtwara, Tanzania. In P. Gottschalk & P. Stanislas (Eds.), *Public corruption, regional, and National Perspectives on procurement fraud*. CRC Press.
Mkutu, K., Stanislas, P., & Mogire, E. (2017). Book conclusion: State and non-state policing: The challenge of postcolonial political and social leadership: Building inclusive citizenship, safety and security in East Africa. In K. Mkutu (Ed.), *Security governance in East Africa a view from the ground*. Wilmington Press.

Mutangadura, C. (2020) *Security Sector Reform in the Gambia*. What is At Stake? Institute for Security Studies.
Perrot, S. (2013a). Predatory leadership as a foil to community policing partnership: A west African case study. In A. Verma, D. Das, & M. Abraham (Eds.), *Global community policing: Problems and challenges*. CRC Press Bacon Raton.
Perrot, S. (2013b). Reforming policing of sex tourism in the Philippines and the Gambia. In S. Caroline Taylor, D. J. Torpy, & D. K. Das (Eds.), *Can we avoid confusing messages policing global movement: Tourism, migration, human trafficking, and terrorism*. CRC Press Boca Raton.
Pilling, D. Wong, S. (2020, April 13) *China-Africa relations rocked by alleged racism over Covid-19*. Financial Times.www.ft.com. Accessed 16 Aug.
Robotham, D. (1981). *The notorious riot: The socio-economic and Political Base of Paul Bogle's revolt*. Institute of Social and Economic Research, University of West Indies.
Sinclair, G. (2010). *The end of the line: Colonial policing and the Imperial end game 1945–1980*. Manchester University Press.
Stanislas, P. (2017). Interview with commissioner Ellison Greenslade of the Royal Bahamas Police. In B. Baker (Ed.), *Trends in policing, interviews with police leaders across the globe* (5th ed.). CRC Press.
Stanislas, P. (2020). *The changing perceptions of St Lucian Policing: How St Lucian police officers view contemporary policing*. Police Research, and Practice (Vol 2,1 Issue 3).
Stanislas, P., & Sadique, K. (2019). International police attitudes to teaching religion and faith and the policing of minority communities. In G. De Heyer, P. Stanislas, & J. Albrecht (Eds.), *Policing minority communities: International perspectives*. CRC Press.
Sul, C. (2020, April 13). *Chinese racism is wrecking its success in Africa*. Chinese Racism Is Harming Africans (foreignpolicy.com). Accessed 16 Aug.
Yeebo, Z. (1995). *State of fear in paradise: Military coup in Gambia and It's implication for democracy*. Africa Research & Information Bureau.

Links

CIA Factbook. (2021). Department of Justice, United States.
Sanyang crisis: Identity of stabbed man revealed (gunjuronline.com) March 15, 2021. Accessed 16 Aug.
The Gambia 2020 Crime & Safety Report (osac.gov) Accessed 16 Aug.
Countering Extremism Project (ND). The Gambia: Extremism and Terrorism | Counter Extremism Project. Accessed 30 August.
www.interpol.int/ Accessed 23 Aug 2021.

Chapter 13
Crime Prevention and Complementary Law Enforcement in Hungary

László Christian and István Jenő Molnar

Introduction

In the twenty-first century, the issue of security and safety as a fundamental need, which is becoming increasingly valued, is at the heart of the everyday life of modern societies, as the fear of crime, and especially terrorism, permeates everyday life. Therefore, the need for crime prevention and the closely related complementary law enforcement has become unquestionable. The former is so crucial that some experts believe we live in a crime-prevention-based society (Garamvölgyi, 2015).

The twentieth century saw a real breakthrough in crime prevention when the representatives of the Chicago School (Sutherland, Park, Burgess, etc.) conducted hundreds of studies on the criminal processes at the individual and community levels and investigated how effective crime prevention interventions could be made. In countries where urbanization, which began in the nineteenth century and culminated in the first half of the twentieth century as a result of the industrial revolution, fundamentally changed the way communities of urban populations lived together, particularly in the first half of the twentieth century, the need for this was naturally a public necessity. New crimes and hitherto unknown problems emerged, requiring much more concerted and conscious action than previously.

However, the development of crime prevention in Hungary has been different. While the overseas, researchers were looking for appropriate prevention measures in city-wide research, in Hungary, even before the change of regime (1989), crime prevention had to be brought to life from a more distant perspective. First of all, everyone had to become aware that the socialist conception of the state, according to which the victory of the proletariat would end class struggles and thus the crime

L. Christian (✉) · I. J. Molnar
National University of Public Service, Budapest, Hungary
e-mail: Christian.Laszlo@uni-nke.hu; molnar.istvan.jeno@uni-nke.hu

J. F. Albrecht, G. den Heyer (eds.), *Understanding and Preventing Community Violence*, https://doi.org/10.1007/978-3-031-05075-6_13

would become causeless, was not correct. Although many attempts have been made to stress the need to prevent crime, they have been unsuccessful. In socialist criminal law, crime prevention, or "war on crime" as it was called at the time, was seen as part of law enforcement and policing, a specific synthesis of these two areas, and was identified with deterrence (Gratzer-Sövényházy, 2014:8). The crime-prevention organizations of the socialist system served to protect the system and ideological education (e.g., Youth Guard, Labor Guard, and Voluntary Police).

The First Period (1989–2003): The Birth of Crime Prevention Organizations

The system of crime prevention in Hungary could only really emerge after the change of regime. The first step was the establishment of the Crime Prevention Department of the National Police Headquarters almost at the moment of the regime change, in 1989, and in 1990–1991 crime prevention departments were established at the county police headquarters.

1995 is the next important milestone in the history of domestic prevention. In that year, the Nationwide Crime Prevention Council (hereinafter: NCPC) was established, which played a role of reconciling interests, preparing decisions, and making proposals, but even more important was the National Crime Prevention Program it developed and its adoption in 1997. The National Crime Prevention Program can be considered as the first crime prevention strategy whose basic objective, as stated in its introduction, was to establish a "network of state and social control over crime and the circumstances that give rise to it, which can prevent a further increase in crime" (Molnár, 2020:28–29).

Stopping the growth of crime became a cardinal issue in the post-change period, when the collapse of the socialist system suddenly saw a multiplication of crimes, and unprecedented and unforeseen reckonings became commonplace and had to be faced unexpectedly.

The same year saw the creation of the National Public Security and Crime Prevention Foundation, whose primary task was to support the crime prevention activities of local authorities, NGOs, and citizens through grants and to assist victims. According to the founding charter of the Foundation, the aim is "to support the performance of public tasks necessary for the consolidation and improvement of public safety and the prevention of crime, to support the establishment and the professional and financial conditions for the operation of voluntary associations of citizens for crime prevention and self-defense, to prepare and assist potential victims, to support education, training, information and propaganda, to organize conferences, exhibitions and events, and to promote cooperation in crime prevention" (Molnár, 2019:84).

The creation and establishment of the above bodies is an excellent illustration of how crime prevention became part of the thinking in the first decade of the regime change and also shows how prevention tasks were transferred quite quickly and smoothly outside the world of policing and law enforcement. Unfortunately, the pace of progress slowed down around the turn of the millennium, with several seemingly premature measures being taken.

In addition to the above tasks, the NCPC continued to coordinate the implementation of the National Crime Prevention Program, to manage tasks related to the protection of victims; to analyze and evaluate social, economic, and crime trends; to monitor international trends; to promote crime prevention; to provide methodological support to civil society organizations; and to carry out drug education activities for young people. The workload of the secretariat of the NCPC – which was incorporated into the Ministry of the Interior organizational structure – continued to grow, and in 2001 the mentioned Foundation was abolished. Although its place has been taken by the Public Foundation for a Safe Hungary, but it took time to set up the system. According to the new Public Foundation's statutes, the Foundation continued the work of its predecessor, but the protection and compensation of victims of crime and their relatives was given a much more important task.

Unfortunately, from 2001 to 2003, problems of competence made it difficult to organize crime prevention work. At the same time, crime prevention was dealt with in principle by the Ministry of Justice and in practice by the Ministry of the Interior.

So, the wheels of administration were grinding in two mills at the same time, unfortunately without any consistency. Perhaps it was the lack of coordination that led to the adoption of Government Decision 1066/2003 (18.VII.) amending Government Decision 1002/2003 (8.I.) on certain government tasks necessary to increase the effectiveness of crime prevention, which abolished the NCPC, which had been in operation for just 8 years, and created the National Crime Prevention Committee as its successor.

The Second Period (2003–2011): The First Hungarian Crime Prevention Strategy

One of the Committee's key tasks was to draw up Hungary's first crime prevention strategy, so Hungary became one of those countries that have adopted their own community crime prevention strategy[1]. In the new strategy, "the principles and objectives set out new priorities and required a new approach not only from professionals but also from society as a whole" (Gönczöl[2], 2004:6). According to the Strategy, the modern social crime prevention is a professional and civic program, directed and supported by the government and enhances the self-defense capabilities of the society. The Strategy also declared that more police, more

[1] National Strategy for Social Crime Prevention, Annex to the Parliamentary Resolution No. 115/2003. (X.28.)

[2] Katalin Gönczöl was the first ombudsman in Hungary, and she was the Head of the National Crime Prevention Committee between 2003 and 2010 and commissioner for crime prevention and criminal policy, Ministry of Justice.

penalties, and more prisons do not solve the major problems of crime (Gönczöl, 2010:99).

The Strategy contained the following key principles:

1. **Avoiding "stigmatization":** Crime prevention is a responsible activity within a regulated framework, which must respect human rights and the principles of the constitutional rule of law. Clear lines of responsibility and clearly defined roles should be established to reduce crime and victimization. "All crime prevention activities are in one way or other interventions into the life of the individuals and their communities. Therefore, it is not permissible to undertake coercive interventions that could lead to stigmatization. Crime prevention is to stigmatize certain types of behavior and not certain types of people. It must also be borne in mind that crime related problems have different effects on women, men, young and elderly people" (Gönczöl, 2013:336–337).
2. **Application of the proportionality principle:** The choice of intervention should respect and follow the principle of proportionality, striking a balance between individual autonomy and community control. Crime prevention measures must be implemented with due respect for human rights, the rights of potential victims, offenders, and the freedoms of third parties, taking into account the principle of proportionality. In the pursuit of community security, a balance must be struck between often conflicting interests.
3. **Avoiding exclusion:** Reducing crime is a socially accepted goal. Measures taken to achieve this, and the fear of crime, can lead to increased exclusion of certain groups. It can contribute prejudice against young offenders, prisoners, drug addicts, the homeless, the poor, and members of Roma community. The social crime prevention system is based on the principle of social justice.
4. **Wide-ranging involvement of stakeholders:** *Social and situational crime prevention considerations must be incorporated into every social and economic policy action that has a direct or indirect influence on crime and victimization. There is a need for continuous cooperation among ministries and representatives of various sciences, and must include NGOs, the private sector, churches and individuals. Effective crime prevention means interdisciplinary cooperation at governmental and local level* (Gönczöl, 2013:336–337).
5. **Creating synergies between strategies:** The social crime prevention strategy contributes to the improvement of the quality of life, the development of the economy, and the reduction of moral and material damage caused by crime if it is linked to the national strategy against drugs and alcohol, the government program to reduce segregation, the inter-ministerial coordination for the integration of the Roma population, the anti-discrimination and national public health programs, and the government policy for the protection of the natural and built environment in order to achieve common goals. *Social and situational crime prevention considerations must be incorporated into every social and economic policy action that has a direct or indirect influence on crime and victimization. There is a need for continuous cooperation among ministries and representatives of various sciences, and must include NGOs, the private sector, churches, and individuals.*

6. **Subsidiarity:** Local crime prevention is a local public matter, says the Strategy. The social crime prevention strategy and the government action plans for its implementation can only become an integrated part of local social policy with the involvement of local authorities. Municipalities, in cooperation with the local police, should play an active and leading role in the preparation of plans for the safety of the local community. They have a proactive role in organizing local signposting systems, various forms of cooperation, coordinating and implementing local crime prevention programs, and evaluating them on an ongoing basis.

In Hungary this Strategy was the first document to identify areas of intervention in crime prevention, thus creating a framework for crime prevention measures. The authors of the Strategy have paid particular attention to ensuring that the areas of intervention include effective and institutionalized responses at national and local level to all phenomena that threaten public safety and public perception of safety. The five priorities were the following:

- Reducing child and juvenile delinquency
- Increasing urban safety
- Prevention of domestic violence
- Prevention victimization, supporting and compensating of victims
- Prevention of recidivism

The target areas listed above have been classified according to which sectoral actors in crime prevention can act most effectively. In this way, the authors of the Strategy have grouped the tasks into three types: those of law enforcement and criminal justice actors, those of community crime prevention, and those of sectoral cooperation.

The first group of actors included the police, the prosecution, the prison service, and the probation service. The second group included local authorities, economic operators, civil associations (NGOs), neighborhoods, and individuals. The third group included education, health, social, youth, sport, and employment policies as special policy levels.

Those tasks were destined to succeed which were backed by a strong political or professional will. These included the creation of the highly significant Victim Protection Act (Act CXXXV of 2005 on Assistance to Victims of Crime and State Compensation), closely linked to which was the establishment of the Victim Support Service in 2006, the 24-hour victim support dispatch service and the National Crisis Management and Information Telephone Service (https://www.okit.eu/). Another outstanding achievement was the modernization and organizational reform of the Probation Service.

The Strategy has also achieved results in its activities to prevent recidivism, notably the introduction of reintegration methods in prisons, in cooperation with prison mission, church, and civil society organizations.

It is also worth mentioning the tendering system, which, by providing resources of varying amounts, has made it possible to tackle local problems at local level by the people concerned themselves. This practice continues to this day.

It is important to emphasize that the effectiveness of Hungarian prevention efforts must be assessed in the context of the state and social system of the period before the regime change. In this context, the fact that we had an independent crime prevention strategy in 2003 was a major achievement. In Western European countries and on the international scene, crime prevention bodies and organizations had existed long before. Denmark in 1971 (Det Kriminalpræventive Råd), Sweden in 1974 (Brottsförebyggande rådet – Brå), the United Nations in 1981 (European Institute for Crime Prevention and Control – HEUNI), and Finland in 1989 (Rikoksentorjuntaneuvosto) established their own crime prevention councils and institutes.

The Third Period (2011–Present): The Establishment of the National Crime Prevention Council and the Development of the New Strategy

After another 8 years, the National Crime Prevention Committee has been abolished and replaced by the National Crime Prevention Council. By Government Decree 1087/2011 (12.IV.) on the National Crime Prevention Council (hereinafter referred to as the "NCpC"), the Government established a proposal, opinion, and advisory body whose tasks include, inter alia, developing a national strategy for social crime prevention in the light of the latest scientific findings, formulating proposals for the Government, and preparing effectiveness studies and methodological studies to support the theoretical basis of criminal policy and crime prevention.

The NCpC is an interdepartmental organization, but its Secretariat, which carries out the operational work, is a department of the Ministry of the Interior. The Secretariat of the NCpC is responsible for the following:

- To harmonize the implementation of the National Crime Prevention Strategy, to take part in the development of action plans and monitor their implementation
- To draw up proposals for the Government in order to disseminate and apply all the resources aimed at implementing crime prevention programs and tasks
- To initiate and encourage measures against the causes of committing crimes and processes that promote crime
- To initiate the drafting of legislation in the field of crime prevention and to give its opinion thereon
- To harmonize the actions of the central public administration bodies and the law enforcement agencies in the field of crime prevention and to support the activities of the local crime prevention bodies
- To cooperate with foreign and international crime prevention organizations
- To coordinate cooperation between the Hungarian public administration and law enforcement bodies, local crime prevention organizations, and foreign or international organizations

- To contribute to the creation of a coherent national crime prevention information system
- To disseminate good practices in social and law enforcement crime prevention in Hungary and abroad and to help to put professional know-how to good use in law enforcement education and training
- To contribute to law enforcement crime prevention and victim support and to the crime prevention activities of scientific and educational institutions
- To help to achieve the Government's goals in public security with efficacy and methodological studies
- To contribute to the granting of subsidies to crime prevention projects from the available resources

The current national strategy of social crime prevention drawn up by the NCpC came into force on 18 October 2013 by Government Resolution No 1744/2013 on the National Crime Prevention Strategy (2013–2023).

The Strategy sets out the necessary legislative, organizational development and training tasks for 10 years as well as public awareness programs and the possibilities of promoting societal actions in the area of crime prevention. The priorities, measures, and areas of intervention specified in the Strategy are designed to help achieving the objectives of criminal policy, reducing the vulnerability of children and youth, reducing victimization, and avoiding repetition of offenses.

The strategy has a clear view of actions to be taken; it contains a detailed action plan. Its aim is to be clear and acceptable for experts working in the field of crime prevention as well as for partners and citizens. The strategy takes into account those policies that have common interfaces with crime prevention, such as health, family, youth, child protection, sport, education, and cultural policy, combating the use of drugs and alcohol, social policy, employment policy, municipal policy, nature conservation policy, social inclusion and the integration of minorities, cybercrime, and the fight against corruption and domestic violence (www.bunmegelozes.info).

The new Strategy has almost the same priorities, as the previous one:

- Urban security
- Protection of minors and children
- Assistance to victims of crimes and prevention of victimization
- Prevention of repeated offenses

Urban Security: The first Strategy has previously identified this as a priority to "increase urban safety," based on the criminological finding that the vast majority of crimes are committed in urban environments. This is particularly true when it comes to assessing the public safety of several (geographical) areas and municipalities with different characteristics and populations, and in many cases with different socio-economic development. Focusing only on cities can therefore easily overlook problems affecting smaller municipalities which may undermine the general sense of security of the population.

Following the entry into force of the strategy in 2013, crime prevention programs aimed at increasing urban safety have been extended not only to cities, but also to smaller settlements and even to sparsely populated, rural areas.

CPTED (crime prevention through environmental design) was also introduced as a new prevention method and has since become a key tool for crime prevention. Large-scale programs, promotional campaigns, and information sites (e.g., www.safecity.hu) have been developed, and more and more municipalities are interested in the method.

Other priority actions include various measures to promote the importance of property protection, bicycle registration programs, and the development of Mobile Crime Prevention Centers[3], which allow the police to reach the target audience themselves.

Protection of Minors and Children: According to the new Strategy child and youth protection, educating young people to become useful members of society, is one of the most important and fundamental tasks and values of society and the state as a whole. In the field of child and youth protection, the so-called educational and cultural arenas play a key role, as they are essential for the protection of young people, the development of their protective mechanisms, the transmission of moral standards, the development of humanity, and the development of law-abiding behavior. These are the family, educational establishments, and leisure activities.

Accordingly, the Strategy supports the implementation of activities that address young people in one of the previous areas. It is important to note that there has been a paradigm shift in the preventive approach to children and young people, with the replacement of deterrence-based education sessions by sessions developing personal competences and self-protection mechanisms. Sport, art, and other creative activities have become important tools for crime prevention.

Completely new initiatives have also emerged, including the production of crime prevention tales for kids. These are now available not only in printed form but also electronically, online, some of them in English.

Assistance to Victims of Crimes and Prevention of Victimization

Hungarian criminal policy has now recognized that, in addition to respecting the fundamental human rights of offenders, the rights of victims must also be guaranteed. The concept of restorative justice means accepting the legitimate claim of persons who have been victims of crime to receive help in their changed life situation. From now on, the victim is no longer just a special witness with direct

[3] The Mobile Crime Prevention Centers are well-equipped buses that can be used to target specific groups of all ages.

knowledge of the case, but a person whose emotional, psychological, physical, and ultimately financial rehabilitation and social integration is in the interest of the whole community.

The new strategy declares the importance of the implementation of victim protection efforts and calls in particular for cooperation between the NCC and the Ministry of Justice. Partly as a result of this work and the government's Year of Victim Protection 2020 program, new victim protection centers were opened in 2020 and 2021 in nine cities.

Of course, the focus of this theme is essentially on vulnerable groups, including young people and the elderly. For both groups, it is important to identify appropriate communication channels. Recently, the theatre and then the Internet have become such a tool, with a proliferation of educational videos.

Prevention of Repeated Offenses: We have long known that the effectiveness of repressive, retaliatory measures is questionable. Punishment can never be an end; even under criminal law it is only necessary to prevent anyone from committing a crime to protect society. The restorative justice method is optimal in that it makes the offender take responsibility, relieves the burden on the state justice system, and promotes the need to strengthen the community and the importance of individual responsibility.

Naturally, the restorative approach first had to be introduced among prison staff, which is why part of the resources in the first years of the new Strategy implementation were devoted to staff training. At the same time, however, a large number of sensitivity training, art therapy, and other competence-building courses for prisoners were launched. One of the most important of these is "right-brain drawing," which develops the prisoner's self-esteem and concentration by giving him a sense of achievement in a short time.

The government's central objective for the prison service is to extend employment to a wider prison population, which not only promotes reintegration but also contributes significantly to achieving self-sufficiency in the prison service. A further objective is the internalization of prison staffing and participation in public work programs.

It is legitimate to ask why the new strategy did not address the prevention of drug-related crime. The explanation is that the Government has identified drug prevention as such a specific area that a separate Strategy[4] has been adopted to deal with the problem. It is unfortunate that the strategic planning document expired in 2020, and since then the issue of drug treatment has been somewhat relegated to the background, although various forums are still in place and the Institute for Drug Research was established in 2020.

There are of course shortcomings in the Hungarian crime prevention system that need to be addressed in the future. Nevertheless, the extremely high crime rate of the post-change period has been reduced, the attitude of law enforcement and crime

[4] Parliamentary Resolution 80/2013 (X. 16.) on the National Anti-Drug Strategy (2013-2020)

prevention personnel has changed, and more modern, open and service-oriented solutions are being developed by the actors involved.

Hungary won the European Crime Prevention Award for the first time in 2021 with its Ask for Help program[5], which is a testament to the effectiveness of their work.

The main objective of the Ask for help! project is to raise awareness on the seriousness and extent of bullying behavior, as well as the harm it can cause towards the victims, perpetrators, and bystanders. This project therefore provides four pillars containing various art, pedagogical, and educational tools (e.g., professional guided videos, music and drama pedagogy, and a peer-to-peer education program) that help to discuss bullying in all its perspectives and to address attitude formation. Minors often go through challenging social and emotional experiences which is why the project utilizes the power of opinion forming to encourage minors to follow positive examples set by their peers. A second aspect of the Ask for help! project is discussion sessions in order to facilitate dialogue between youngsters, teachers, and parents. These sessions allow for the development of a peer network that can discuss issues and explore effective anti-bullying responses.

Complementary Law Enforcement

Crime prevention, as already mentioned in the introduction to the Strategies, cannot be successful without the broad involvement of stakeholders. Security, including public security, is a social issue that cannot be achieved by the public authorities alone through the mandatory provision of services. There is a need for complementary initiatives, some of which are mandatory and some of which are voluntary, to support prevention efforts.

Some members of the complementary law enforcement, whose position is becoming more and more sophisticated, are important custodians of these efforts, but this was not always the case. But what is meant by complementary law enforcement?

The law enforcement is part of the public administration, and its mission is to maintain the internal order of the State and public order and security, to protect the members of society and their fundamental values by preventing, deterring, and disrupting offenses that violate or threaten them, even by the legitimate use of physical force. This is an extremely complex and multifaceted task which cannot be expected to be carried out exclusively by a single public body, which happens to be the police. Fulfilling the mission of policing, creating security, is the result of social cooperation and collective work, in which, in addition to law enforcement agencies and the bodies responsible for law enforcement, local authorities, private security companies, and civilian self-defense organizations also play an important role. This can be

[5] Summary of the program: https://www.youtube.com/watch?v=v8bCC_ZuF8I

described as a complementary law enforcement system, in which the activities of state bodies are complemented, supported, and assisted by market and civil organizations (Christián, 2018a).

Complementary law enforcement bodies:

- Municipal police, police forces with specific police functions
- Voluntary associations for the prevention of crime in society, in particular the Civil Self-Defense Organization
- Private security (protection of persons and property, armed security guards)

Prior to the change of regime, the police alone were responsible for public safety and were the embodiment of crime prevention. There was no system of complementary law enforcement and its actors. After the change of regime, the dismantling of the state police model became an immediate necessity, partly because of this perceived shortcoming and because of the crime rate that was on the rise. Demilitarization, decentralization, and depoliticization were the main guiding principles behind the demand for change, but there was also a strong demand for the police to be professionalized. The possibility of reviving the municipal police, in line with the development of the municipal system, was then raised. The latter, however, did not take place, and in fact, the 1990 Act LXV of 1990 on Local Self-Government and Article 8 of the Act, which is relevant to our topic, merely stated that it was the duty of local government to provide for local public security within the scope of local public services (Christián, 2018b:34–35).

The role of local authorities and the development of local policing the first crime prevention strategy contained interesting and forward-looking findings. However, in many respects it was not in line with the legislation in force in the years following the millennium, when it stated that local crime prevention was a local public matter.

Two clearly identifiable results of this brief and all the more puzzling legislation and contradictions were the following:

- Local public order and public safety protection bodies with very different names, appearances, and structures were set up in the various municipalities, and their operation also varied greatly.
- The majority of local authorities simply did not recognize their responsibility but resorted to the simplest solution and passed on responsibility and the management of the tasks to the police.

While this attitude of local authorities has changed a lot in a positive direction in recent years, there is still room for improvement and a lot of work to be done. According to the results of a previous survey[6], only 1/3 of municipalities have a law enforcement organization or staff. It is a sad fact that 65.49% of the municipalities surveyed have no police presence, but the situation is even worse (86.62%) with regard to Public Space Supervision. Unfortunately, the fact that hardly any of the municipalities surveyed employ a public safety officer reflects the systemic lack of

[6] National Laboratory for Security Technologies (National University of Public Service, 2021)

a security conscious attitude. In less than ¼ of the municipalities alone, such a person is employed. It is worrying that not only in practice, but even at the level of strategy formulation, local authorities do not pay much attention to crime prevention and public safety. A study written in 2020 summarizes this as follows: "perhaps one of the most worrying figures is that 84.62% of those who completed the questionnaire did not have any crime prevention strategy or concept. 79.75% of the public target group respondents have no crime prevention concept or strategy" (Christián, 2020:61–62).

There are several reasons for the lack of complementary law enforcement on the side of municipalities:

- *local governments are underfunded, they do not have sufficient resources to establish and properly operate local governmental law enforcement organizations,*
- *the present legal framework is not sufficient to establish local governmental law enforcement organizations that can operate efficiently and are based on standardized foundations.* (Bacsárdi & Christián, 2016:88–89)

Note that the above statements are not in themselves the problem or difficulty. The operation of local governmental law enforcement organizations is hampered by problems concerning the organizational system, the management, the staff, and the legal and administrative environment (Bacsárdi & Christián, 2016:96).

But the effectiveness of complementary law enforcement depends not only on the efficiency of local authorities. Civil initiatives play a key role, and the Nationwide Civil Self-Defense Organization, which celebrated its 30th anniversary this year, is a prominent example in Hungary. The organization was basically modelled on the Neighborhood Watch movements abroad, established in Hungary in the 1990s as a loose civil initiative, later as a professional organization. The Civil Self-Defense Organization carries out patrolling activities in public premises, watch activities, signaling activities at traffic accidents and in the area of day nurseries, kindergartens, elementary, and secondary schools in order to participate in the safeguarding of public order and security, as well as crime prevention. The social recognition of these activities is also indicated by the fact that a law was enacted in relation to the Civil Self-Defense Organization that is unique among European countries (Madai, 2015:29–30). So, the organization has a separate law[7] and a specific line in the state budget to ensure its secure and continuous operation.

Today, the organization has over 60.000 members and more than 2.000 associations countrywide. "Civil Guards" has become a dominant actor to maintain public order and security, and it is an important strategic partner for the Government and for the Hungarian Police as well. This civilian organization is deeply rooted in the society, and they have an important role to strengthen the subjective sense of security. The volunteers, as the name suggests, perform unpaid public tasks, supporting the efforts of the professional bodies, with strictly limited liabilities. A significant

[7] Act CLXV of 2011 on the Civil Guard and the Rules of Civil Guard Activity

mission is to take part in crime prevention and maintain the subjective sense of security. Anyone above the age of 18 with no criminal record may take the oath, after completing a training course and passing an exam. The organization has a three-level structure including the local, regional, and national civil volunteer associations (Christian, 2017:136).

Last but not least, we must mention the private security actors. Before the change of regime, neither individuals nor companies were or could be engaged in such activities. In the 1990s, however, a succession of companies were set up to offer personal and property protection services. Although still a big question today, in the early days it was more a question of whether only the police could keep order. If not, what framework should be set up for civil society players to intervene.

It took time for the sector to be seen as a service provider, and even more so as an actor involved in maintaining public safety. The existence and growth of the security sector is proof that the citizen is taking the responsibility for his security into his own hands, taking back from the state what was previously the responsibility of the state (Kerezsi & Pap, 2017:573). Private security includes the protection of persons and property and private investigation, services through which the individual contributes to the maintenance of public order and security by protecting his or her personal rights more effectively. It is not an exaggeration to say that without private security there is no balanced public security, and therefore the state has a responsibility to create the regulatory and operational conditions for private security. In 2005, the sector was regulated, and Act CXXXIII of 2005 was adopted, which set the legal framework for the performance of this activity.

There are a few relevant numbers about the Hungarian private security sector worth considering: 127.000 licensed security guards, 1700 private detectives, and 3000 companies deal with private security. Obviously, it is quite an important and relevant part of the economy. Compared to other countries' figures, it is an outstandingly high number, one of the highest in the EU (Christián, 2017:138). This makes it clear that we can regard private security as a part of public security, because the private security is taking over more and more responsibilities from the state. Moreover, it is important to stress that while the private security focuses on prevention, the public law enforcement agents focus greatly on reaction.

Conclusion

During the period of regime change in our country, the number of crimes started to increase rapidly due to the disintegration of the former law enforcement system and the redistribution of markets. In 1989, the number of crimes brought to the attention of the authorities rose to 225,000, in 1990 to 341,000 and in 1995 to 502,000.

András Túrós himself, who headed the National Police Headquarters in 1989 and 1990 as Deputy Minister of the Interior, recalls those times in this way: "In 1989, the previous 'balanced' crime rate began to rise and there was a very significant increase in crime, which was almost unbelievable. We police leaders were left scratching our heads as to what to do about this new situation" (Christián, 2018a, b:35).

Over the past 30 years, our country has had to build a system that can create synergies between public action, civil initiatives, and the potential of the for-profit sector, almost from scratch. The system has begun to work, if not without fail, and both old and new actors have actively contributed to making Hungary a safe place to live in 2021.

We cannot, of course, sit back and relax; crime prevention needs constant renewal and attention. There are so many challenges in the online world, we need to step up the policing role of local authorities, and we need to further increase the contribution of civil society and volunteers. So, there is a lot to do, but the goals and the means are clear.

References

Bacsárdi, J. & Christián, L. (2016). Local governmental law enforcement in Hungary. In: Meško, G. & Lobnikar, B. (edit.) *Criminal justice and security in Central and Eastern Europe: safety, security, and social control in local communities: conference proceedings* (pp. 84–98). Ljubljana, Slovenia: University of Maribor. https://doi.org/10.32577/mr.2018.4.3

Christián, L. (2017). *The role of complementary law enforcement institutions in hungary. Efficient synergy in the field of complementary law enforcement? A new approach* Pagalbinės Teisėsaugos Institucijos Vengrijoje - Teisėsaugos Institucijų Sinergija. Visuomenės Saugumas ir Viešoji Tvarka: Mokslinių Straipsnių Rinkinys = Public Security and Public Order: Scientific Articles, ISSN: 2335-2035, (pp. 132–139).

Christián, L. (2018a): *Rendészeti szervek* In: JAKAB András – FEKETE Balázs (szerk.): Internetes Jogtudományi Enciklopédia (Alkotmányjog rovat, rovatszerkesztő: BODNÁR Eszter, JAKAB András, https://ijoten.hu/szocikk/rendeszeti-szervek, date of download: 14/12/2021

Christián, L. (2018b). A *helyi rendészeti együttműködés rendszere* Iustum Aequum Salutare XIV., ISSN 1787-3223, (pp. 33–62).

Christián, L. (2020). *A helyi önkormányzatok felelőssége a települések közbiztonságának megteremtésében* Magyar Rendészet, 2020/3. ISSN: 1586-2895, (pp. 55–78). DOI: https://doi.org/10.32577/mr.2020.3.4

Garamvölgyi, L. (2015). *Bűnmegelőzés-alapú társadalom – Prevenció a XXI. században*. Budapest, Studium Plusz Kiadó, ISBN: 9786155463839

Gönczöl, K. (2004). *Partnerség a közbiztonság javításáért. Nemzeti stratégia és cselekvési program a hatékonyabb közösségi bűnmegelőzésért* Belügyi Szemle, 52. évfolyam 10. szám, Budapest, ISSN: 1218-8956, (pp. 5–14).

Gönczöl, K. (2010). *Strategy of community crime prevention in practice as an integrative part of public policy* Annales Universitatis Scientiarum de Rolando Eötvös Nominatae Sectio Iuridica, 51., Budapest, ELTE, (pp. 99–112).

Gönczöl, K. (2013). *War on Crime or Community Crime Prevention?* In book: Kriminologie - Kriminalpolitik - Strafrecht. Festschrift für Hans-Jürgen Kerner zum 70. Geburtstag, Herausgegeben von Klaus Boers, Thomas Feltes, Jörg Kinzig, Lawrence W. Sherman, Franz Streng und Gerson Trüg, Thübingen, Mohr Siebeck, ISBN: 978-3-16-152216-1, (pp. 333–344).

Gratzer-Sövényházy, G. (2014). *A bűnmegelőzés rendszere* Biztonságpiac Évkönyv 2013, Budapest

Kerezsi, K. & Pap, A. L. (2017). *A bűnözés és a bűnözés kontroll jövője*. In: Finszter–Sabjanics (edit.): Biztonsági kihívások a 21. században, Budapest–Pécs, Dialóg Campus

Madai, S. (2015). *The Hungarian Civil Self-Defence Organisation* European Police Science and Research Bulletin, Issue 12, Luxembourg, European Police College (CEPOL), ISSN: 1831-1857, (pp. 29–31).

Molnár, I. J. (2019). *A bűnmegelőzés értelmezése és magyarországi fejlődése* In: *A bűnüldözés és a bűnmegelőzés rendészettudományi tényezői Edited by: GAÁL Gyula, HAUTZINGER Zoltán,* Pécsi Határőr Tudományos Közlemények XXI., ISSN 1589-1674, (pp. 77–89).

Molnár, I. J. (2020). *A magyar bűnmegelőzési stratégiák alakulása* In: Kriminológia MA, Edited by: BARABÁS A. Tünde, Budapest, Dialóg Campus, (pp. 27–39).

Chapter 14
New Zealand's Dirty Secret: Family Violence

Garth den Heyer

Introduction

Exposure to violence and its effects has been a topical area of research since the early 1980s, with thousands of studies having been completed in various aspects of domestic and family abuse and violence (Smith-Stover, 2005). A literature search undertaken by Smith-Stover (2005) identified that there were more than 15,000 articles published on these topics between 1995 and 2005. Domestic abuse can also be called 'domestic violence' or 'family violence' or 'intimate partner violence' (IPV) (United Nations, n.d.). The most widespread form of domestic or family violence found in society is that of intimate partner violence (IPV) (Smith-Stover, 2005).

Domestic or family violence exists in every society and 'can be defined as a pattern of behavior in any relationship that is used to gain or maintain power and control over an intimate partner' (United Nations, n.d.). 'Domestic abuse can happen to anyone of any race, age, sexual orientation, religion, or gender' and can occur within any form of relationship, such as 'couples who are married, living together or dating' (Rollè et al., 2019; United Nations, n.d.). It can affect people of any social, economic and cultural status or background and educational level (Rollè et al., 2019; United Nations, n.d.). Such violence can be considered a violation of human rights and includes physical, sexual, economic, religious and psychological abuse threats of actions that influence another person (Rollè et al., 2019; United Nations, n.d.). These actions can include 'behaviors that frighten, intimidate, terrorize, manipulate, hurt, humiliate, blame, injure, or wound someone' (United Nations, n.d.).

A recent change in the definition of domestic or family violence has been its amendment to emphasize the term family rather than an individual. As noted by the

G. den Heyer (✉)
Arizona State University, Phoenix, AZ, USA
e-mail: garth.den.heyer@asu.edu

J. F. Albrecht, G. den Heyer (eds.), *Understanding and Preventing Community Violence*, https://doi.org/10.1007/978-3-031-05075-6_14

Social Policy Evaluation and Research Unit (2013), the amendment 'encapsulates a number of forms of violence including sibling abuse, elder abuse, child abuse and domestic violence' (p. 16). However, some researchers have argued that the emphasis on the term, family, detracts from the domestic violence aspect and obscures the fact that the majority of violence in the home is perpetuated by men (Lievore & Mayhew, 2007; Social Policy Evaluation and Research Unit, 2013).

Domestic or family violence is not a recent phenomenon (Social Policy Evaluation and Research Unit, 2013), and although men experience it, the rate of violence and death amongst women is much higher than that is of men (Rollè et al., 2019). According to Rollè et al. (2019), recent research has found that between 13% and 61% of women (15–49 years old) have been physically abused at least once by an intimate partner. As a result, violence against women, in particular, has been recognized 'as a serious and pervasive phenomenon affecting women's lives and health, and a violation of their rights' since the development of the United Nations Declaration on the Elimination of Violence against Women and the 1995 Beijing Platform for Action (World Health Organization, 2021).

One of the main problems with domestic or family violence is the impact that it has on the victim. European research found that victims of such abuse can lack self-esteem, have feelings of shame and guilt, have difficulties in expressing negative feelings and feel hopeless and helpless, which, in turn, can lead to difficulties in using appropriate coping strategies, self-management and mutual support networks (Rollè et al., 2019). Other research has found that domestic or family violence has significant short-, medium- and long-term effects on the physical and mental health and wellbeing of women, children and families (World Health Organization, 2021). According to the World Health Organization (2021), it can cause negative social and economic consequences for countries and societies.

Witnessing, or being a victim of family violence during childhood, can result in being a victim of family violence later in life (Lievore & Mayhew, 2007). Research has also highlighted that those children who have experienced family violence may perpetrate violence when they become adults. Wider research on the prevalence of domestic and family violence has examined the effects of children being exposed to such violence and their emotional and behavioural development and their relationships with family, friends and the wider world (Davies & Cummings, 1994; Edleson, 1999; Rollè et al., 2019; Smith-Stover, 2005). An analysis of research data has found that continual exposure to violence during childhood is associated with behavioural and psychiatric problems (Augustyn et al., 1995; Grych et al., 2002; Holden & Ritchie, 1991) and that such problems can also affect the cognitive functioning, initiative, personality style, self-esteem and impulse control of a child (Pynoos & Nader, 1989). However, research has not been able to clarify whether the experience of violence in childhood causes violent behaviour later in that person's life, or whether a person becomes violent due to a complex correlation of social and experiential factors (Lievore & Mayhew, 2007).

Research has also suggested that couples who are violent towards each other are between three and nine times more likely to abuse their own children (Moffitt &

Caspi, 2003). Violent parents are also more likely to instil violent norms and contribute to behavioural problems in their children (Lievore & Mayhew, 2007).

Another problem with domestic and family violence is that it is often under-reported by the victim. This can be traced to a number of factors, including the fear of reprisal from the perpetrator, a hope that it will stop, 'shame, loss of social prestige due to negative media coverage, and the sense of being trapped with nowhere to go' (Rollè et al., 2019).

In a United States Department of Justice 2017 report, domestic or family violence was described as having a significant impact, not only on those that had been abused, but also on other family members and friends, and on people, such as work associates of both the abuser and the victim. Early studies established that between 60% and 75% of relationships that suffer from intimate partner violence have children who are also battered or neglected, and this is usually from the same abuser (Bowker, 1988; McKibben et al., 1989; Smith-Stover, 2005; Straus & Gelles, 1990). Children that live in homes where family violence occurs are physically abused and neglected at a rate 15 times higher than the national average (Osofsky, 2003).

Research on family violence that is conducted in New Zealand may adopt a different perspective than other countries. Studies in New Zealand have often used the public health approach (Contesse & Fenrich, 2008), which may include a cost-benefit analysis, and as a result, emphasizes the economic costs of responding to family violence (Snively, 1995). The economic costs include the well-being of women and their children who have been victims of family violence and 'the costs associated with political and social instability through intergenerational transmission of violence' (The Secretary-General, 2006). Another approach that is used by other researchers is the socio-ecological approach, which examines the complex interplay between individual, relationship, social, cultural and environmental factors to understand family violence (Heise, 1998, 2011). This approach is important in identifying risk and protective factors associated with the occurrence of family violence and for the development of prevention strategies, as it is based on the assumption that changes in contributing factors can potentially lead to changes in the prevalence of family violence (Heise, 2011).

Another perspective uses an international human rights framework to review family violence. According to Contesse and Fenrich (2008), this perspective reviews 'a state's response to violence against women as a form of discrimination and the existence of larger structures of subordination' (p. 1803).

This chapter examines the problem of family violence in New Zealand. It does not use any of the perspectives that have been discussed above, but takes a critical perspective of literature to review the family violence prevention strategies that have been adopted in New Zealand to identify possible future approaches to the problem. The first section examines the level of crime in New Zealand and sets the context for understanding the seriousness of family violence in New Zealand. The second section introduces family violence and child abuse in New Zealand, and the following sections discuss each of these topics. The concluding sections analyse the whole-of-government approach and discuss options for improving the current response framework.

Crime in New Zealand

New Zealand has some of the highest levels of crime of the 36 Organisation for Economic Co-operation and Development (OECD) countries. It is 13th highest for homicides, third highest for the offence of rape, second highest for burglaries, 21st for robberies, first for theft of vehicles and 32nd for assaults that result in an injury to the victim (Civitas Crime, 2012).

In 2000, there were 427,230 recorded crimes. This figure then fluctuated between a low of 406,363 in 2004 to a high of 451,405 in 2009. Following the high 2009 number, the number steadily declined to 350,389 in 2014, and increased again to 414,854 in 2017 (den Heyer, 2020). The problem with comparing this period with more modern, recorded crime levels is that in 2015, the New Zealand Police changed the way that they recorded reported crime.

In 2008, the New Zealand Police introduced a National Recording Standard (NRS) that was based on the National Crime Recording Standard (NCRS) that was used in Australia. Previously, crime statistics in New Zealand counted one offence for each offence that was recorded in a Police Offence Report. However, some of the offences could have more than one victim, and as a result, the new recording system counted each victim separately if an offence involved more than one victim. The crime statistics that were previously recorded included all offences recorded by the police, even if they were the same type of crime that had been committed against the same victim. It also included offences that the police used later for the purpose of laying charges. The new recording system counts each broad type of crime against a given victim that has been included in the same report once on any given day that the crime was reported and excludes any offence that the police add later for laying charges. Nor are multiple offences of the same type that are experienced by the same victim that has been reported to the police at the same time counted separately (New Zealand Police, 2016). This means that the total number of crimes that were recorded each year prior to 2015 cannot be compared with the figures for the years after 2015, but individual crimes can.

When examining the period 2015–2020, the level of recorded crime fluctuated between 256,768 in 2015 and 264,238 in 2020. However, the highest level was recorded in 2019 at 282,143. The number of reported crimes for homicide, violence and sexual assault for 2015 to 2020 has been presented in Table 14.1. The number of crimes per 10,000 population has been presented in brackets in the table.

The table clearly shows that although total crime has fluctuated over this period, the number of crimes per 10,000 population has decreased. It can also be seen that the number of recorded violence offences and sexual assault offences has increased between the 2015 and 2020 period. The table indicates that homicides decreased, but sexual assaults increased significantly. The number of violent crimes cannot be analysed over this period because of the way that it was recorded, as the way that it was defined was altered in 2015. Homicides and related offences increased from 59 in 2000 (0.15 per 10,000 population), to 81 (0.19 per 10,000 population) in 2009 and decreased again to 57 (0.11 per 10,000 population) in 2020. In relation to sexual

Table 14.1 Reported crime in New Zealand 2015–2020 – total and per 10,000 population (in brackets)

Crime type	2015	2016	2017	2018	2019	2020
Violence	20,744 (45.1)	21,575 (45.9)	21,874 (45.6)	22,937 (46.9)	23,451 (47.0)	26,223 (51.5)
Sexual assault	5707 (12.4)	5619 (12.0)	5940 (12.4)	6189 (12.7)	6400 (12.8)	6705 (13.2)
Homicides	48 (0.10)	58 (0.12)	40 (0.08)	50 (0.10)	43 (0.09)	57 (0.11)
Total	**256,768 (558.3)**	**268,339 (571.4)**	**265,593 (553.8)**	**258,656 (529.17)**	**282,143 (565.5)**	**264,238 (519.2)**

Source: New Zealand Police (2021)

Table 14.2 Reported crime in Scotland 2015–2020 – total and per 10,000 (in brackets)

Crime type	2015	2016	2017	2018	2019	2020
Violence	6272 (11.7)	6737 (12.5)	7164 (13.2)	7251 (13.3)	8008 (14.7)	9316 (17.1)
Sexual assault	9557 (17.8)	10,273 (19.1)	11,092 (20.5)	12,487 (23.0)	13,547 (24.8)	13,364 (24.5)
Homicides	62 (0.12)	59 (0.11)	62 (0.11)	59 (0.11)	60 (0.11)	64 (0.12)
Total	**256,350 (477.2)**	**246,243 (455.6)**	**238,921 (440.5)**	**244,504 (449.6)**	**246,480 (484.1)**	**246,516 (451.0)**

Source: Scottish Government (2021)

assault, there were 3839 (9.95 per 10,000 population) offences in 2000, 4826 (11.2 per 10,000 population) in 2009 and 6705 (13.2 per 10,000 population) in 2020 (den Heyer, 2020).

To appreciate the level of crime in New Zealand, the same type of offences and the annual total number of crimes were compared with those that were recorded between 2015 and 2020 in Scotland. Both countries have similar sized populations, and the police in both countries are national forces. New Zealand experiences more violence and has more total crime but has less sexual assaults than Scotland. The number of reported crimes for homicide, violence and sexual assault in Scotland between 2015 and 2020 have been presented in Table 14.2. The number of each type of crime per 10,000 population has been presented in brackets in the table.

As with most countries, the crime figures recorded in New Zealand need to be viewed with caution. According to the Parliamentary Library (2018), a number of crimes, especially sexual crimes and violence, go unreported and consequently do not appear in the official statistics. This claim was supported by the Social Policy & Parliamentary Unit (2019), in their State of the Nation Report, that observed that there was a lack of reliable data about criminal offending in New Zealand, particularly for domestic violence (Johnson, 2019). Furthermore, the level of confidence held in the police, by the public, and changes in media reporting may have also had an effect on the reporting of crime (Parliamentary Library, 2018).

Family Violence in New Zealand

New Zealand has one of the highest recorded rates of child abuse and domestic violence amongst the Organisation for Economic Cooperation and Development countries (Gammon, 2016). New Zealand law defines family violence to include intimate partner violence and violence against other family members, including children and extended family, as well as people living together in the same household (Fanslow et al., 2021). New Zealand has the fifth worst child abuse record out of 36 Organisation for Economic Cooperation and Development countries with one child killed, on average, every 5 weeks (New Zealand Police, 2021). Most children that are killed are under 5 years old, and 90% are killed by someone they know. Studies have estimated that one in four girls aged under 15 have been touched sexually, or made to do something sexually that they did not want to do (New Zealand Police, 2021).

In 2020, there were 155,338 incidents of family violence or harm incidences recorded in New Zealand. The attendance of the police at these incidents accounted for 16% of all police activity (New Zealand Police, 2021). According to the New Zealand Police (2021), family violence events have increased by 60% over the past 5 years and are predicted to increase by a further 35% by 2025. Research indicates that over 67% (Ministry of Justice, 2021) of family violence events are not reported to the police. As a result, there is a lack of reliable data pertaining to the actual level family violence in New Zealand (Johnson, 2019).

New Zealand has an appalling record of the occurrence of family violence (Social Policy Evaluation and Research Unit, 2013), and it is a major, social problem (Fanslow, 2005; Lievore & Mayhew, 2007). A commonly agreed prevalence rate of family violence in New Zealand is that 14% or 1-in-7 families experience such trauma annually (Snively, 1995). The country also has a high rate of domestic murders and high rates of children being maltreated (Social Policy Evaluation and Research Unit, 2013). During the period 1978–1996, there was an average of 11 adult deaths from family violence per year, and between 1988 and 1993, 40% of all homicides were the result of domestic violence (Snively, 1995).

The 2001 National Survey of Crime Victims (NSCV) was the first survey to ask respondents questions pertaining to family violence. It found that 26% of women and 18% of men reported experiencing some form of family violence. More women than men are killed by their partners, with an average of nine women per year being killed. Two men are killed each year in a family violence event. One estimate is that 50% of female victims of a homicide are killed by a partner or ex-partner (Lievore & Mayhew, 2007). Higher rates of homicide were found however, in a study that was conducted by the University of Auckland. According to this research, 36% of women experienced some form of family violence (Fanslow & Robinson, 2004).

Acts of family violence are not distributed equally across New Zealand society, with Maori and people from deprived neighbourhoods being over-represented as both victims and perpetrators of family violence (Lievore & Mayhew, 2007). Family violence has been found to cause harm across generations (Family Violence Death Review Committee, 2017).

The numbers of incidents and offences responded to and recorded by the police as family violence events have substantially increased since the mid-1990s. It is not clear, however, whether recording changes have influenced this increase. Family violence events increased by 140%, from about 11,300 in 1995 to 27,165 in 2005. The number of offences from these events increased by 87%, from about 14,600 to 27,343, with many incidents and offences being repeat calls (Lievore & Mayhew, 2007). In 2006, there were 32,675 family violence related offences recorded by the New Zealand Police (Families Commission, 2009). During the same period, the proportion of male assaults female offences that were included as being a family violence event was high, and had risen from being 68% in 1995 to being 83% in 2005 (Lievore & Mayhew, 2007).

Other researchers found that the total number of family violence offences had increased by 54% between 2000 and 2006, while violent family-related offences had increased by 49%. Serious assaults contributed the most to the increase over the period, and in 2006, accounted for more than 55% of all family-related violent offences. Similarly, drugs and anti-social offences comprised of more than 20% of all family-violence-related offences. However sexual offences were relatively low in number, comprising of approximately 1% of family-violence-related offences (Families Commission, 2009).

In more modern research, it was found that 1 in 3 New Zealand women, who had a partner, reported having experienced physical or sexual interpersonal violence in their lifetime (New Zealand Family Violence Clearinghouse, 2017). However, when psychological or emotional abuse is included, 55% of women reported having had experienced this type of violence in their lifetime (Fanslow & Robinson, 2011). The research also found that between 2009 and 2015, there were 92 interpersonal, violence-related deaths, and in 98% of these deaths, there was a recorded history of abuse, that women were the primary victim and that they had been abused by their male partner (Family Violence Death Review Committee, 2017). Later research noted that there were 33 intimate partner violence deaths between 2016 and 2018 (Family Violence Death Review Committee, 2019b) and that approximately half of all homicides and reported violent crimes were family violence related (Ministry of Justice, 2021). The Ministry of Justice (2021) also claimed that one in four females and one in eight males experience sexual violence or abuse in their lifetimes, many before the age of 16.

Responding to family violence offences accounts for 41% of a frontline police officer's time (SCOOP Independent News, 2015). The police have conducted more than 100,000 investigations into family violence offending every year since 2015 (Ministry of Justice, 2021).

In 2016, there were 5461 applications for protection orders following a family violence incident. Of these, 5072 (89%) were made by women and 550 (10%) by men, while 4940 (89%) of the orders were against men and 560 (10%) were against women (New Zealand Family Violence Clearinghouse, 2017).

Prevalence of Harm to Children in New Zealand

The number of children that are victims of family violence and trauma or sexual assault in New Zealand is also worrying. According to the New Zealand Family Violence Clearinghouse (2017), between 1 in 311 and 1 in 512 New Zealand women and 1 in 1011 men have experienced child sexual abuse. Furthermore, 20% of female and 9% of male secondary school students reported having experienced unwanted sexual contact in 2013 (Clark et al., 2013). Female children and young people are far more likely to identify as victims of sexual assault or a related offence and account for approximately 86% of all reported sexual assaults and related offences for people aged under 20 (Oranga Tamariki – Ministry for Children, 2021). Unfortunately, there is no single data source that gives a holistic and exact understanding of the harm that has been inflicted on children in New Zealand. Data is collected from Oranga Tamariki (Ministry for Children), the police, the Ministry of Health and the University of Otago's Injury Prevention Unit (Oranga Tamariki – Ministry for Children, 2021).

In 2016, the police recorded 10 homicides of children and young people under 20 years of age perpetrated by a family member, and 63 children, aged 16 years or under, were hospitalized for an assault that was perpetrated by a family member (New Zealand Family Violence Clearinghouse, 2017). In the majority of the deaths that involved children under 5 years of age, two-thirds of the deaths resulted from physical abuse or grossly negligent treatment events (Family Violence Death Review Committee, 2017). During the same year, 63 children under the age of 15 died of injuries from a violent assault (Oranga Tamariki – Ministry for Children, 2021) and 2163 children, aged 16 years or under, were victims of a sexual assault (New Zealand Family Violence Clearinghouse, 2017). Between 2009 and 2018, there were 70 child abuse and neglected deaths in New Zealand (Family Violence Death Review Committee, 2019a).

In more recent research that was undertaken in 2020, 12,861 children were found to be abused or neglected after an investigation or assessment was completed by Oranga Tamariki (Ministry of Children). A large number of children had also experienced neglect or emotional, physical or sexual abuse. In addition, during 2020, 282 children required hospital treatment as a result of an assault, and 31,300 children were hospitalized from injuries that occurred during a family violence or harm incident (Oranga Tamariki – Ministry for Children, 2021).

In an analysis of Coroners' inquest files from 1980 to 2003, Moore (2005) found that very young children were at the greatest risk of being killed and that boys (61%) were more likely to be killed than girls (39%). The majority (84%) of children killed by adults were killed by their parents or parent figures and that the offender was as likely to be a female as a male (Moore, 2005).

Intimate Partner Violence (IPV) in New Zealand

Intimate partner violence (IPV) is 'the most common form of violence experienced by women globally' (United Nations, 2006). It includes physical and sexual violence, psychological and economic abuse and controlling behaviour (Fanslow et al., 2021; Hashemi et al., 2021). According to the World Health Organization, violence results from the complex relationship between individual, and social, cultural and environmental factors (Dahlberg & Krug, 2008). Intimate partner violence affects a women's physical, mental, sexual and reproductive health, and can include fatal and non-fatal injuries, HIV and sexually transmitted infections, induced abortion, depression, anxiety and suicide (Sanz-Barbero et al., 2019; World Health Organization, 2013).

Research has established the prevalence of intimate partner violence amongst women, involving physical and sexual violence (Fanslow & Robinson, 2004; Kazantzis et al., 2000; Koziol-Mclain et al., 2002; Lievore & Mayhew, 2007; Whitehead & Fanslow, 2005). However, the figures vary across studies, as there is a lack of consistent and reliable data that can be used to monitor the changes in the prevalence of this form of family violence over time. The figures may reflect the difference in the way that the offences have been measured (Fanslow et al., 2021). Furthermore, previous research has been based on an analysis of homicide data, or similar forms of data from agencies such as health providers, the police or courts (Kangaspunta & Marshall, 2012). While this type of data may provide some insight into the levels of violence, it does not reflect the size of the problem, as a number of people who are victims of violence often do not report an event to the authorities (Gulliver & Fanslow, 2012). Nor has earlier research examined how any changes in environmental and social norms influence the perpetuation of violence, or how society accepts or tolerates this type of violence (Fanslow et al., 2021).

Similar to other forms of family violence, intimate partner violence affects people in all levels of New Zealand society, but the highest rates of occurrence 'tend to be found among young, cohabiting adults of low socioeconomic status, particularly when they have children' (Moffitt et al., 2001). Most female victims are between 16 and 40 years old, are not married but live with the abuser (Lievore & Mayhew, 2007).

An analysis of the 92 intimate partner violence deaths that occurred between 2009 and 2015 found that males were the predominant aggressor in the abusive relationship. Ninety-eight percent of death events included a woman with a recorded history of abuse (81 deaths) and involved men who had abused their female partners. Of the deaths, women comprised of more than 66% of those killed, and males comprised of more than 75% of the offenders (Family Violence Death Review Committee, 2017).

The level of physical and sexual intimate personal violence in New Zealand was examined by using population-based surveys in 2003 and 2019. The research found that the prevalence of physical intimate personal violence remained relatively unchanged between 2003 and 2019, with almost one-third of women in both surveys reporting that they had experienced at least one act of physical violence in their lifetime. Despite the actions taken to address the occurrence of family violence, there has been no change in the level of family violence. The actions taken have included the introduction of legislation and the establishment of new violence prevention campaigns. Many of the new programmes concentrated on the importance of those experiencing violence seeking help (Fanslow et al., 2021).

The results of the surveys were similar to the results of surveys that were conducted in the European Union (33%) (Goodey, 2017) and the United States (31%) (Smith et al., 2018). The findings were also similar to the global average (World Health Organization, 2013) and comparable to high-income countries (Ansara & Hindin, 2010), but were high in comparison to low- and middle-income countries (Leonardsson & San Sebastian, 2017; Linos et al., 2014).

The Early Response to Family Violence in New Zealand

Since the early 1980s, the approach that government agencies in New Zealand take to reduce family violence has changed significantly (Social Policy Evaluation and Research Unit, 2013). These changes have taken place for a number of reasons. The country had experienced extensive economic and social change during the 1980s, resulting in large increases in the rate of unemployment of unskilled workers and large decreases in household incomes (Social Policy Evaluation and Research Unit, 2013), social change and an increase in the level of crime (den Heyer, 2016). However, the primary reason for the change in approach pertained to the high-profile murders of two women in the early 1980s, and has raised the spectre of intimate partner violence and the government's response to its occurrence (Newbold & Cross, 2008).

Following the murders, the government introduced the Domestic Protection Act 1982, which gave the police the power to detain persons who had breached non-molestation and non-violence orders (Social Policy Evaluation and Research Unit, 2013). The introduction of the legislation was followed by the development and implementation by the New Zealand Police, in 1987, of the first family violence policy and the issue of specific guidelines explaining to officers how to use the strategy (Herbert, 2008).

In 2001, Serious Abuse Teams, also known as Child Abuse Teams, were established, and these comprised of police officers and staff members of the Child, Youth and Family (now Oranga Tamariki – Ministry for Children). The role of the teams was revised in 2003 (Waldegrave & Coy, 2005) and again in 2010 in order to concentrate on child protection (Child, Youth and Family & New Zealand Police, 2010). Later in 2010, the police revised their family violence response policies and procedures further (New Zealand Police, 2012) to ensure that they aligned with the new Australasian family violence policing strategy (Australian Federal Police & New Zealand Police, 2008).

Recent Family Violence Initiatives

The New Zealand response to family violence has been varied and is reflective of the changing demographics of the country (Social Policy Evaluation and Research Unit, 2013) and the increasing awareness of the long-term impact that this type of harm has on society. However, it is difficult to quantify and identify changes in societal attitudes towards the occurrence and reporting of family violence incidents or to identify when the change occurred. This is despite family violence being more likely to be reported to the police and actioned by them than was the case in the 1980s (Spier, 2002). Changes in police practice are also difficult to quantify, especially when comparing when the crime was discovered by the police to when the crime was reported to the police (Lash, 2005). In recent years, the majority of family violence policy initiatives have been based on a coordinated or whole-of-government approach. A summary of initiatives and the year that they were introduced has been presented in Table 14.3.

In 2002, the first whole-of-government family violence prevention strategy was introduced. This strategy was called Te Rito: New Zealand Family Violence Prevention Strategy, and was defined as 'an integrated, multi-faceted, whole-of-government and community approach to preventing the occurrence and reoccurrence of violence in families/whanau' (Ministry of Social Development, 2002). The

Table 14.3 Summary of recent New Zealand Family Violence Initiatives

Year	Initiative
2002	Introduction of the first whole-of-government Te Rito New Zealand Family Violence Prevention Strategy
2005	Establishment of Taskforce for Action on Violence with Families
2008	Australasian Policing Strategy for Family Violence developed and adopted
2010	1. Introduction of a new New Zealand Family Violence Policy and Procedure by the police 2. Provisions introduced for issuing Police Safety Orders (PSOs). PSOs assist police staff in providing safety for victims and their children where the police believe that family violence has occurred or will occur, but no offence can be identified
2011	1. The introduction of a new system for recording family violence offences by the police. This provided a way to describe the relationship between the perpetrator and the victim 2. The Prevention First strategy is launched, which shifted the focus from offenders to victims of crime. It included the development of an IT system that allowed repeat and high-risk offenders and victims to be identified
2012	The Ontario Domestic Assault Risk Assessment tool (ODARA), the Intimate Partner Vulnerability Factors (IPVF) tool and the Child Risk Factor (CRF) tool are introduced (Nimmo, 2012)
2013	Police officers are provided with tablets to facilitate the retrieval of information from their database and for the recording of case notes while attending an occurrence
2021	Introduction of 'Te Aorerekura' – a 25-year strategy to eliminate family violence and sexual violence. The strategy coordinates the activities of 10 government agencies

Sources: Australian Federal Police and New Zealand Police (2008), New Zealand Police (2011, 2012, 2013), Nimmo (2012), Radio New Zealand (2021)

strategy defined family violence as '[A] broad range of controlling behaviours, commonly of a physical, sexual and/or psychological nature which typically involve fear, intimidation and emotional deprivation. It occurs within a variety of close interpersonal relationships, such as between partners, parents and children, siblings, and in other relationships where significant others are not part of the physical household but are part of the family and/or fulfilling the function of family' (Families Commission, 2009, p. 8).

The development and implementation of Te Rito was guided by a set of nine principles, which were based on five key goals and objectives that were to be implemented within a 5-year timeframe. The strategy also highlighted 18 areas of action, which directed its implementation and stressed improving 'inter-agency co-ordination, collaboration and communication' (Ministry of Social Development, 2002). Most of the areas of action to respond to family violence emphasized a need for culturally and ethnically based approaches with specific reference to Maori and Pacific peoples.

In June 2005, the Taskforce for Action on Violence within Families was established to provide advice to the government 'on how to make improvements to the way family violence is addressed, and how to eliminate family violence' (Taskforce for Action Against Violence Within Families, 2006). The role of the Taskforce was to 'lead and co-ordinate interagency action to address family violence' (Taskforce for Action Against Violence Within Families, 2013). The Taskforce was a joint initiative that brought together governmental and nongovernmental agencies, independent Crown entities and the judiciary 'to work together and provide leadership to end family violence and promote stable, healthy families' (Taskforce for Action Against Violence Within Families, 2009).

The Taskforce developed specific family violence prevention programmes for Maori and Pacific peoples, as well as initiatives to address child abuse (Taskforce for Action Against Violence Within Families, 2007). It also introduced a number of initiatives, including the 'It's not OK' campaign and the establishment of the Family Violence Death Review Committee (Taskforce for Action Against Violence Within Families, 2013) and it oversaw the training of the police in investigating and assessing the risk in family violence (Taskforce for Action Against Violence Within Families, 2007).

Each of these initiatives was designed to not only provide a framework for a more coordinated approach to preventing family violence, but they were also designed to specifically improve the services delivered by the police for the victims of family violence as the police are the entry point for criminal action and for the victim. The more recent initiatives were also expected to improve the quality of information gathered by police on family violence events. It was hoped that the improvement in data would assist with understanding the basis for family violence and provide a basis for the development of future policies. Historically, the police recording of a family violence event was inconsistent, and the initiatives were designed to provide a structured direction for the police to minimize the variation in their reporting and the way that they responded to the perpetrator and the victim (Fanslow & Robinson, 2010).

The initiatives have provided the police with a platform to improve their policies and procedures to respond to family violence. What is recorded as a family violence offence has been affected by changes to police forms, technological systems and the refining of definitions pertaining to which relationships are relevant to family violence (e.g. the inclusion of people in shared residential arrangements). New police family violence policies were also established under the Prevention First strategy. These included Police Safety Orders, intimate partner risk assessments (ODARA) and child risk assessments. As family violence incidents are significantly under-reported to the police, changes in approaches to public education and awareness may impact on the likelihood of reporting these offences (Families Commission, 2009; Stats New Zealand, 2013). These changes and the initiatives should add to our understanding of how the police make decisions rather than just the incidence or prevalence of family violence (Social Policy Evaluation and Research Unit, 2013).

Analysis of the New Zealand Approach to Family Violence

Family violence is a significant social issue in New Zealand, and despite the concerted effort to address its occurrence, it remains a problem. In an effort to respond to the problem, the New Zealand Government has been a signatory to international law to secure equality for women and to act with due diligence to prevent, investigate or punish acts of family violence and to provide for effective remedies for the victims of family violence (Contesse & Fenrich, 2008). It has also enacted legislation and overseen the development of whole-of-government strategies that aim to prevent and eliminate family violence (Radio New Zealand, 2021).

A number of government agencies have also created public media and educational campaigns calling on people to stop family violence and seek to increase the community's understanding of this form of violence (Contesse & Fenrich, 2008; Fanslow et al., 2021). Family violence was also the major theme of the widely acclaimed movie, *Once Were Warriors*, which included a depiction of an urban Maori family's involvement in gangs, alcohol, drugs and abuse. However, even with an increase in awareness, the level of family violence remains high, with all sections of society being affected, but with Maori communities suffering higher rates than the general population (Fanslow et al., 2021).

According to Contesse and Fenrich (2008), there are a number of other practical reasons as to why the family violence prevention strategies have not been successful. The first is that the prevention programmes only require attendees to complete a specific number of sessions. Attendees are not actually assessed as to whether, and how, the programme has helped a person deal with violence. The second reason is more practical and relates to Protection Orders. These are often not served or enforced adequately by the police, and victims often have little knowledge on how to obtain such an order. The third reason is that a family violence incident often does not meet the standards of being a criminal offence.

The Family Violence Death Review Committee (2017) claimed that there are six reasons why intimate personal violence and child abuse cannot be reduced effectively. According to the committee, six reasons need to be addressed simultaneously, and they are:

1. Intergenerational violence requires an intergenerational response.
2. The decision to abuse a child's parent is a harmful, unsafe parenting decision.
3. 'Failure to protect' approaches fail to respond to both child and adult victims' safety needs.
4. Protecting children means acting protectively towards adult victims.
5. To prevent family violence, we must work with the people using violence.
6. Victims' safety is a collective responsibility: it cannot be achieved by individuals or individual agencies acting alone (adapted from Family Violence Death Review Committee, 2017).

The six reasons provide a framework for the development and implementation of a new, coordinated organizational response that acknowledges the complex nature of intimate personal violence and child abuse. The reasons re-focus resources 'from assessing the protectiveness of adult victims to assessing the level of risk and danger' that a person's abusive behaviour poses to both child and adult victims (Family Violence Death Review Committee, 2017, p. 10). This focus ensures that responding agencies concentrate on protecting vulnerable infants, their siblings and their mothers (Family Violence Death Review Committee (2017).

Internationally, there is consensus that New Zealand has sound legislation in place for responding to family violence (Contesse & Fenrich, 2008). However, there are a number of practical areas in which improvement should be made that would strengthen the implementation of the whole-of-government strategies. These include:

1. Improved access to family violence prevention programmes for abusers
2. Improved access to legal aid for victims and abusers
3. Increasing the training given in government departments to ensure a coordinated response to family violence
4. Improve the collection of the appropriate data to inform the development of policy (adapted from Contesse & Fenrich, 2008; Fanslow et al., 2021)

Conclusion

Research to date on the prevention of recidivism of family violence has identified that the strategy has not been effective (Smith-Stover, 2005; Fanslow et al., 2021). Studies have found that that recidivism rates in family violence cases are high with some estimating 40–80% or more of perpetrators repeating their violent abuse (Garner et al., 1995; Goodey, 2017). Although gains have been made in our understanding of how family violence affects families and communities, there is still a need to understand how to implement effective interventions that reduce the occurrence family violence and improve the outcomes for children and families. Furthermore, the prevention of inter-generational violence requires an inter-generational response to break the cycle and to stop the problem repeating itself in each new generation (Family Violence Death Review Committee, 2017). This means that the most important area for further study is the evaluation and identification of appropriate and effective family violence prevention strategies.

Our understanding of the problem of family violence and what works in preventing its occurrence has advanced greatly since the early 1990s. The review of the New Zealand response to the occurrence of family violence provides information on the effectiveness of the strategies, what aspects are most important and what needs to be considered in relation to future policy and strategy development.

The size of the problem of family violence in New Zealand means that the development of prevention strategies and the response to incidents cannot remain the responsibility of a few government departments and non-government organizations. Future strategies need to be inclusive and include approaches that are 'whole-of-family and -whānau,[1] whole-of-organisation and whole-of system responsiveness' (p. 3) (Family Violence Death Review Committee, 2017).

References

Ansara, D., & Hindin, M. (2010). Formal and informal help-seeking associated with women's and men's experiences of intimate partner violence in Canada. *Social Science & Medicine, 70*, 1011–1018.

Augustyn, M., Parker, S., Groves, B., & Zuckerman, B. (1995). Children who witness violence. *Contemporary Paediatrics, 12*, 35–57.

Australian Federal Police & New Zealand Police. (2008). *Prevention and reduction of family violence: An Australasian policing strategy*. The Commonwealth of Australia.

Bowker, L. (1988). On the relationship between wife beating and child abuse. In K. Yllo & M. Bograd (Eds.), *Feminist perspectives on wife abuse* (pp. 11–26). Sage.

Child, Youth and Family & New Zealand Police. (2010). *Child protection protocol between New Zealand Police and Child, Youth and Family*. Child, Youth and Family, & New Zealand Police.

Civitas Crime. (2012). Comparisons of Crime in OECD Countries. https://www.civitas.org.uk/content/files/crime_stats_oecdjan2012.pdf

Clark, T., Fleming, T., Bullen, P., Denny, S., Crengle, S., Dyson, B., Fortune, S., Lucassen, M., Peiris-John, R., Robinson, E., Rossen, F., Sheridan, J., Teevale, T., & Utter, J. (2013). *Youth'12 overview: The health and wellbeing of New Zealand secondary school students in 2012*. The University of Auckland.

Contesse, J., & Fenrich, J. (2008). It's not OK: New Zealand's efforts to eliminate violence against women. *Fordham International Law Journal, 32*(6), 1770–1871.

Dahlberg, L. & Krug, E. (2008). *Violence a global public health problem*. http://www.scielo.br/scielo.php?script=sci_arttext&pid=S1413-81232006000200007&nrm=iso

Davies, P., & Cummings, E. (1994). Marital conflict and child adjustment: An emotional security hypothesis. *Psychological Bulletin, 116*, 387–411.

[1] Means an extended family or community of related families who live together in the same area.

den Heyer, G. (2016). Ghosts of policing strategies past: Is the New Zealand Police 'prevention first' strategy historic, contemporary or the future? *Public Organization Review: An International Journal, 16*(4), 529–548.

den Heyer, G. (2020). Police strategy development: The New Zealand Police prevention strategy. *Police Practice and Research: An International Journal, 22*(1), 127–140.

Edleson, J. (1999). Children's witnessing of adult domestic violence. *Journal of Interpersonal Violence, 14*, 839–970.

Families Commission. (2009). *Family violence statistics report*. Research report 4/09.

Family Violence Death Review Committee. (2017). *Fifth report data: January 2009 to December 2015*. Health Quality & Safety Commission.

Family Violence Death Review Committee. (2019a). *Supplementary detail: Child abuse and neglect death information sheet*. Health Quality & Safety Commission.

Family Violence Death Review Committee. (2019b). *Supplementary detail: Intimate partner violence death information sheet*. Health Quality & Safety Commission.

Fanslow, J. (2005). *Beyond zero tolerance: Key issues and future directions for family violence work in New Zealand*. A report for the Families Commission. Research report no. 3/05.

Fanslow, J., & Robinson, E. (2004). Violence against women in New Zealand: Prevalence and health consequences. *The New Zealand Medical Journal, 117*(1206), 1173.

Fanslow, J., & Robinson, E. (2010). Help-seeking behaviours and reasons for help seeking reported by a representative sample of women victims of intimate partner violence in New Zealand. *Journal of Interpersonal Violence, 25*(5), 929–951.

Fanslow, J., Hashemi, L., Malihi, Z., Gulliver, P., & McIntosh. (2021). Change in prevalence rates of physical and sexual intimate partner violence against women: Data from two cross-sectional studies in New Zealand, 2003 and 2019. *BMJ Open, 11*. https://doi.org/10.1136/bmjopen-2020-044907

Fanslow, J., & Robinson, E. (2011). Sticks, stones, or words? Counting the prevalence of different types of intimate partner violence reported by New Zealand women. *Journal of Aggression, Maltreatment & Trauma, 20*, 741–759.

Gammon, R. (2016). *Family violence: New Zealand's dirty little secret*. https://www.massey.ac.nz/massey/about-massey/news/article.cfm?mnarticle_uuid=C61AEFE4-B1D7-0794-48A1-CFA90FEDDEFF

Garner, J., Fagan, J., & Maxwell, C. (1995). Published findings from the spouse assault replication program: A critical review. *Journal of Quantitative Criminology, 11*, 3–28.

Goodey, J. (2017). Violence against women: Placing evidence from a European Union-Wide survey in a policy context. *Journal of Interpersonal Violence, 32*, 1760–1791.

Gulliver, P., & Fanslow, J. (2012). *Measurement of family violence at a population level: What might be needed to develop reliable and valid family violence indicators?* New Zealand Family Violence Clearinghouse.

Grych, J., Jouriles, E., Swank, P., McDonald, R., & Norwood, W. (2002). Patterns of adjustment among children of battered women. *Journal of Consulting and Clinical Psychology, 68*, 84–94.

Hashemi, L., Fanslow, J., Gulliver, P., & McIntosh, T. (2021). Relational mobility and other contributors to decline in intimate partner violence. *Journal of Interpersonal Violence, 0*(0), 1–24.

Heise, L. (1998). Violence against women: An integrated, ecological framework. *Violence Against Women, 4*(3), 262–290.

Heise, L. (2011). *What works to prevent partner violence? An evidence overview STRIVE research consortium*. London School of Hygiene and Tropical Medicine.

Herbert, R. (2008). *Learning our way forward: Implementation of New Zealand's family violence strategies*. Master's Dissertation. Victoria University of Wellington.

Holden, G., & Ritchie, K. (1991). Linking extreme marital discord, child rearing, and child behavior problems: Evidence from battered women. *Child Development, 62*, 311–327.

Johnson, A. (2019). *Are you well? Are we safe? State of the Nation Report*. The Salvation Army Social Policy & Parliamentary Unit.

Kangaspunta, K., & Marshall, I. (2012). Trends in violence against women: Some good news and some bad news. In J. van Dijk, A. Tseloni, & G. Farrell (Eds.), *The international crime drop: New directions in research* (pp. 103–155). Palgrave Macmillan.
Kazantzis, N., Flett, R., Long, N., Macdonald, C., & Millar, M. (2000). Domestic violence, psychological distress, and physical illness among New Zealand women: Results from a community-based study. *New Zealand Journal of Psychology, 29*(2), 67–73.
Koziol-Mclain, J., Davies, E., Crothers, C., Casey, C., Fanslow, J., & Hassall, I. (2002). *Evaluation of Te Rito: A national reporting index*. Ministry of Social Development.
Lash, B. (2005). *Young people and alcohol: Some statistics to 2003 and 2004 on possible effects of lowering the purchase age*. Ministry of Justice.
Leonardsson, M., & San Sebastian, M. (2017). Prevalence and predictors of help-seeking for women exposed to spousal violence in India – A cross-sectional study. *BMC Womens Health, 17*(1), 99–114.
Lievore, D., & Mayhew, P. (2007). *The scale and nature of family violence in New Zealand: A review and evaluation of knowledge*. Ministry of Social Development.
Linos, N., Slopen, N., Berkman, L., Subramanian, S., & Kawachit, I. (2014). Predictors of help-seeking behaviour among women exposed to violence in Nigeria: A multilevel analysis to evaluate the impact of contextual and individual factors. *Journal of Epidemiol Community Health, 68*, 211–217.
McKibben, L., Devos, E., & Newberger, E. (1989). Victimization of mothers of abused children: A controlled study. *Pediatrics, 84*, 531–535.
Ministry of Justice. (2021). *Addressing family violence and sexual violence*. https://www.justice.govt.nz/justice-sector-policy/key-initiatives/addressing-family-violence-and-sexual-violence/
Ministry of Social Development. (2002). *Te Rito New Zealand family violence prevention strategy*. Ministry of Social Development.
Moffitt, T., & Caspi, A. (2003). Preventing the inter-generational continuity of antisocial behaviour: Implications of partner violence. In D. Farrington & W. Coid (Eds.), *Early prevention of adult antisocial behaviour* (pp. 109–129). Cambridge University Press.
Moffitt, T., Robins, R., & Caspi, A. (2001). A couple's analysis of partner abuse with implications for abuse-prevention policy. *Criminology & Public Policy, 1*(1), 5–36.
Moore, E. (2005). *No sun has shone. Child homicide in New Zealand: An analysis of a small scale sample of cases 1980–2003*. Masters Dissertation. Victoria University of Wellington.
Newbold, G., & Cross, J. (2008). Domestic violence and prearrest policy. *Social Policy Journal of New Zealand, 33*, 1–14.
New Zealand Family Violence Clearinghouse. (2017, June). *Data summaries 2017: Snapshot*. www.nzfvc.org.nz
New Zealand Police. (2011). *Prevention first: National operating strategy 2011–2015*. New Zealand Police.
New Zealand Police. (2012). *Statement of intent: 2012–2014*. New Zealand Police.
New Zealand Police. (2013). *Mobility rollout shifts work from desk to community*. https://www.police.govt.nz/featured/mobilityrollout-shifts-work-desk-community
New Zealand Police. (2016). *The transformation of NZ Police crime statistics: New measures and trends*. New Zealand Police.
New Zealand Police. (2021). *Unique victims (demographics)*. https://www.police.govt.nz/about-us/publications-statistics/data-and-statistics/policedatanz/unique-victims-demographics
Nimmo, B. (2012). *Stakeholders information sheet: New police family violence*. National Family Violence Unit, New Zealand Police.
Osofsky, J. (2003). Prevalence of children's exposure to domestic violence and child maltreatment: Implications for prevention and intervention. *Clinical Child and Family Psychology Review, 6*, 161–170.
Oranga Tamariki – Ministry for Children. (2021). *At a glance: Prevalence of harm to children in New Zealand*. https://library.nzfvc.org.nz/cgi-bin/koha/opac-detail.pl?biblionumber=6904

Parliamentary Library. (2018). *From offences to victimisations: Changing statistical presentations of crime in New Zealand 1994–2017*. Research Paper. Parliamentary Service.

Pynoos, R. S., & Nader, K. (1989). Prevention of psychiatric morbidity in children after disaster. In D. Shaffer, I. Philips, & N. Enzer (Eds.), *Prevention of mental disorders, alcohol and other drug use in children and adolescents* (pp. 225–271). US. Department of Health and Human Services.

Radio New Zealand. (2021). *Government unveils 25-year plan to tackle violence in New Zealand homes*. https://www.newshub.co.nz/home/politics/2021/12/government-unveils-25-year-plan-to-tackle-amount-of-violence-in-new-zealand-homes.html

Rollè, L., Ramon, S., & Brustia, P. (2019). Editorial: New perspectives on domestic violence: From research to intervention. *Frontiers in Psychology: Gender, Sec and Sexualities.*. https://www.frontiersin.org/articles/10.3389/fpsyg.2019.00641/full

Sanz-Barbero, B., Barón, N., & Vives-Cases, C. (2019). Prevalence, associated factors and health impact of intimate partner violence against women in different life stages. *PLoS One, 14*(10), e0221049.

SCOOP Independent News. (2015, August). *Q+A: Justice Minister Amy Adams on domestic violence law*. https://www.scoop.co.nz/stories/PO1508/S00009/qa-justice-minister-amy-adams-on-domestic-violence-law.htm

Scottish Government. (2021). Recorded crime in Scotland, 2015–2020. https://www.gov.scot/publications/recorded-crime-scotland-2015-2020/

Smith, S., Zhang, X., Basile, K., Merrick, M., Wang, J., Kresnow, M., & Chen, J. (2018). *National intimate partner and sexual violence survey: 2015 data brief – Updated release*. National Center for Injury Prevention and Control, Centers for Disease Control and Prevention.

Smith-Stover, C. (2005). Domestic violence research: What have we learned and where do we go from here? *Journal of Interpersonal Violence, 20*(4), 448–454.

Snively, S. (1995). *The New Zealand economic cost of family violence*. Department of Social Welfare.

Social Policy Evaluation and Research Unit. (2013, December). *Family violence indicators*. Families Commission.

Social Policy & Parliamentary Unit. (2019). State of the nation 2019. Salvation Army New Zealand.

Spier, P. (2002). *Reconviction and reimprisonment rates for released prisoners*. Ministry of Justice.

Stats New Zealand. (2013). *Overview of recording and counting crime*. http://www.stats.govt.nz/tools_and_services/tools/TableBuilder/recorded-crime-statistics/overview.aspx

Straus, M., & Gelles, R. (1990). How violent are American families? Estimates from the national family violence resurvey and other studies. In M. Straus & R. Gelles (Eds.), *Physical violence in American families* (pp. 95–112). Taylor & Francis. Transaction.

Taskforce for Action on Violence within Families. (2006, July). The first report. .

Taskforce for Action on Violence within Families (2007). *The ongoing programme of action: Summary*. http://www.msd.govt.nz/documents/about-msd-and-our-work/work-programmes/initiatives/action-family-violence/taskforce-ongoing-programme-of-action-summary.pdf

Taskforce for Action on Violence Within Families. (2009). *The Taskforce*. http://www.msd.govt.nz/about-msd-and-our-work/workprogrammes/initiatives/action-family-violence/taskforce-info.html

Taskforce for Action Against Violence Within Families. (2013). *The work of the Taskforce*. http://www.msd.govt.nz/about-msd-andour-work/work-programmes/initiatives/action-familyviolence/taskforce-work.html

The Secretary-General. (2006, July). *In-depth study on all forms of violence against women: Report of the Secretary-General*. United Nations document A/61/122/Add.1.

United Nations. (n.d.). *What is domestic abuse?* https://www.un.org/en/coronavirus/what-is-domestic-abuse

United Nations. (2006). *Secretary-General's in-depth study on all forms of violence against women*. Report of the Secretary-General. Document A/61/122/Add.1.

Waldegrave, S., & Coy, F. (2005). A differential response model for child protection in New Zealand: Supporting more timely and effective responses to notifications. *Social Policy Journal of New Zealand, 25*, 32–48.

Whitehead, A., & Fanslow, J. (2005). Prevalence of family violence amongst women attending an abortion clinic in New Zealand. *Australian and New Zealand Journal of Obstetrics and Gynaecology, 45*, 321–324.

World Health Organization. (2013). *Global and regional estimates of violence against women: Prevalence and health effects of intimate partner violence and non-partner sexual violence*. World Health Organization.

World Health Organization. (2021). *Violence against women prevalence estimates, 2018*. United Nations Inter-Agency Working Group on Violence Against Women Estimation and Data.

Chapter 15
Afterword and Final Thoughts

James F. Albrecht

Understanding Violence

The goal of this book has been to examine violence through multifaceted lenses. And furthermore to articulate the mechanisms that the police and criminal justice can implement to deter and detect acts of violence and serious criminality and more effectively identify and apprehend perpetrators and suspects.

Is Violence Innate or a "Career Choice"

Violence has plagued humanity since the infancy of mankind. In fact, the proclivity to harm another being may be an innate behaviour inherent in all animals as a survival mechanism. As such, one could state that violence may be a natural reaction to stress, and this aggression may manifest itself when an animal or person feels threatened. So one can engage in violence as a method of self-defence, which may be construed as being reasonable in many situations, but, on the other hand, it may be an action in response to life's or societal pressure. Could it be that crime is a natural reaction to the absence of equitable opportunity and the drive for survival and that street violence is a mere option in the modern era for ensuring the greater success of those actions? Or do certain individuals make a rational choice to engage in violence and acts of deviance in order to attain their personal objectives, which often involve material gain? Criminological and sociological theories do point in competing, and even overlapping, directions.

J. F. Albrecht (✉)
Pace University, New York, NY, USA

J. F. Albrecht, G. den Heyer (eds.), *Understanding and Preventing Community Violence*, https://doi.org/10.1007/978-3-031-05075-6_15

Criminality and Violence

Criminality can take many forms, such as theft through simply stealing or through use of force. However, once violence is involved, it elevates the level of immorality to a higher magnitude. When one generally thinks of violence, one envisions a criminal brutally pummelling an innocent victim in a desolate and dark alley way. However, violence does not only take place outdoors, but also in the privacy of one's home. And it does not necessarily have to involve the direct interaction of two or more individuals. Violence can be transmitted through technology, and these injuries can be just as dramatic and traumatic, as evidenced by acts of child pornography and cyber-bullying.

Crime and Violence Targeting and Involving Children

Randall in Chap. 1 examines the trauma of abuse and violence perpetrated through the Internet, particularly targeting children and juveniles. On one hand, while this can take the form of bullying on a social media platform, it can also be as severe as live online exploitation of children being sexually abused by adult predators. The Internet has made life easier for people across the globe, but it has also permitted criminals the opportunity to support extreme forms of criminality, including the trafficking of human beings and the sexual manipulation of both children and adults often from the safety of their homes. Randall has outlined these disturbing phenomena in comprehensive detail and assesses the impact that these practices have had on society.

Glomseth and Aarset in Chap. 2 evaluate the challenges that violent crime perpetrated by or targeting children and younger individuals poses for police professionals. The chapter extensively examines these variables and then proceeds to analyse organizational leadership options to best develop effective strategies to address these difficult responsibilities. In particular, police commanders in Norway outline their concerns and tactics in an effort to provide guidance to law enforcement colleagues across the globe.

Limiting the Use of Violence to Control Violence

In the modern era, there has been substantial criticism on the use of force by police. It should be obvious that, at least in established democracies, the use of force by law enforcement officials, while legally permitted, is strongly controlled through legislation and organizational policy. It is generally mandated that use of force by police be reasonable and minimal and this strict guideline is regularly reiterated in training and instruction. Cotton in Chap. 3 describes in detail the tactics and training options that many professional police agencies have implemented with the intention of minimizing violent encounters between police officers and suspects, subjects and ordinary citizens. Hendy in Chap. 4 conducts an even more comprehensive analysis of efforts at conflict resolution, verbal de-escalation and inter-personal cooperation between police and encountered individuals. Albrecht in Chap. 6 examines the complex interaction of police use of force and suspect race, particularly as it relates to officer-involved shootings. Many may be astonished to read that the actual statistical data in the United States does not align with the sensationalized perspectives portrayed by traditional and social media in America and that also have been used by many misinformed politicians to inappropriately call for the defunding of the police.

Using Technology to Prevent Violence and Apprehend Violators

It is well acknowledged that random patrol did little if anything to impact street crime and community violence. While policing had remained generally reactive since the inception of the profession in the 1820s, a number of developments were introduced in the mid-1990s that have dramatically reformed the tactics and strategies implemented in the field. Not only was there a substantial shift toward proactive measures, but the introduction of real-time statistical analysis and crime mapping permitted law enforcement leaders to deploy personnel and resources where and when they are most needed. As such, the use of technology has resulted in more effective and highly strategic deployment, real-time awareness and the ready availability of critical information and intelligence in the field. Kotak in Chap. 5 explores the benefits of technology to law enforcement policy makers in particular detail.

The Emotional Toll of Community Violence on Police Personnel

Can and Yenigun in Chap. 7 examine the role that exposure to community violence plays on police officer psychological and emotional wellbeing. As a major part of their job responsibilities, police officers globally are routinely exposed to criminal acts of violence targeting crime victims, and there are limited scenarios in which law enforcement officials are placed in scenarios when they must use (or threaten to use) force as an option to gain control of a suspect or mentally disturbed individual or to act in self-defence or defence of others. There are, however, circumstances when police officers themselves become victims of community violence, often during mass demonstrations and riots. Each of these scenarios impacts law enforcement officers, individually and collectively, to a varying level. Can and Yenigun additionally point out that police practitioners across the globe are impacted differently to these work stressors and that these factors could also have negative consequences on private relationships and lifestyle.

Global Perspectives on Community Violence

Community violence and criminality take on different perspectives as one navigates across the globe. Bezuidenhout and Kempen in Chap. 8 highlight the higher incidence of violent crime across South Africa. Given the general inefficacy of the South African Police Service (SAPS), the public unfortunately often resorts to vigilantism, at times at the mob level, to address threats and criminal encounters. These extrajudicial activities can only be deterred if members of the SAPS can elevate their professionalism and service delivery to the content of the communities being served.

Parent and Parent in Chap. 9 examine the dramatic differences in community violence existing between two neighbouring democracies, Canada and the United States. In this context, community violence was measured by looking not only at homicide rates, but also at the use of force by police officers and civilians against criminal suspects, as well as the incidence of violence targeting police officers. Even though the democratic practices in both nations do not vary greatly, there is a significant difference in the quantity and extent of violent encounters, with the United States exhibiting significantly higher levels of criminal homicide and violence targeting law enforcement officials. This has resulted in police officers in the United States perceiving a higher level of apparent threat from the public and specifically from criminals, which is evidenced through the more routine use of force by American police officers against criminal suspects when compared to their Canadian counterparts.

Aremu and Aremu in Chap. 10 analyse the concept of community violence in another nation, Nigeria, on the African continent. Due to the discovery of oil and a thriving port, Nigeria has a generally stable economy. However, tribal conflict and socio-economic differences have supported an environment enabling criminality and organized crime. More troubling is the existence of Boko Haram and groups that support the radicalized ideology promoted by the Islamic State. Not only is the north-eastern region of Nigeria plagued by terror incidents and armed conflict, one strategy used by Boko Haram has been to attack local community schools and kidnap students. In many cases, young female students are held for ransom, and some are forced to marry combatants. Clearly the Nigerian government has been forced to develop strategies to counter these attacks. As a result, specific strategies to strengthen the security at schools and in local communities across the nation have been designed and have now been effectively implemented.

Albrecht in Chap. 6 conducts a thorough analysis of the extreme increase in violence and serious crime in the United States since 2014 and provides criminological and practical reasons for this undesirable scourge on society. Given the success that proactive and more stringent enforcement measures have had on crime rates prior to 2014, it should be obvious that a return to strategic, proactive, and intelligence-led and data supported deployment of police personnel and resources should be strongly reconsidered in an effort to regain the grasp and control of, at times, unfettered violence and criminality.

As a follow-up, Tobin in Chap. 11 extensively examines the phenomenon of gun violence in the United States and subsequently outlines and investigates specific tactics that law enforcement agencies in America have implemented in an effort to deter these tragic incidents. With the dramatic rise in street violence and the proliferation of firearms across the country, there is a need for strategic coordinated action. Multi-jurisdictional collaboration is apparently warranted and has been shown to effectively deter firearm and other forms of violence.

Stanislas and Chongan in Chap. 12 continue the global perspective by assessing communal violence and crime control measures in Gambia, a western African country. While the people of Gambia are generally acknowledged for their generally peaceful demeanour, there have been recent instances of intercommunal violence. The police response has been less than adequate in many of these circumstances, and unfortunately that has led to death, vandalism and community instability. In addition, inter-ethnic differences, even if mere perception, have created an atmosphere of indifference, competition and sense of inequality across different sectors. There are clear policy and training implications as it relates to the police in Gambia, but it is incumbent on the Gambian government to address societal issues that may be in need of future remedy.

Christian and Molnar in Chap. 13 transition the discussion to Hungary in eastern Europe. The Hungarian government has prioritized crime prevention for many decades. Given that Hungary possesses a federal police, the nation has opted to create numerous national crime prevention councils and subsequent comprehensive strategies that include not only police organizational measures but also address underlying causes at the local level. While street and community violence are not at the overwhelming levels experienced in the United States or South Africa, Hungarian authorities have taken violence and crime prevention seriously and have included and incorporated the community and victims of criminality at all stages of planning and action.

When one imagines violence, one often envisions a criminal threatening a victim with a weapon in order to retrieve the possessions of another. However, violence does not always take place on the streets. A portion of that criminality takes places indoors in the form of domestic abuse. Den Heyer in Chap. 14 analyses violence from the perspective of the family. While violence is generally limited in Australia and New Zealand, those incidents occurring behind closed doors provide an added challenge to law enforcement personnel on that continent (and also at the global level). Specifically intimate partner violence and child abuse are two traumatic forms of serious crime that result in long-term, negative consequences. The police in New Zealand have designated family violence as organizational priorities and have outlined specific strategies for prevention and needed societal support. However, recidivism remains high in New Zealand, so revised policies and tactics appear warranted. It should be clear that this predicament should involve more than mere police response, which is often reactive. The extensive involvement of medical and mental health professionals and social services agencies should be incorporated into any future comprehensive strategies.

Final Thoughts

Efforts to prevent and contain violence, whether targeting an individual, a community or a police official, have generally been the responsibility of local police representatives. Given the traumatic impact that acts of violence have on their victims, and also witnesses, law enforcement agencies and criminal justice officials globally have normally taken these incidents and actions seriously. There has been a transition since the mid-1990s to take a more proactive approach with a move from what had been merely a reactive documentation of instances. These strategic approaches, coupled with higher and longer incarceration rates, did dramatically reduce crime for decades. However, a more liberal approach to criminal justice and calls for police reform and actual defunding, even though that efforts at crime control had been highly successful, have resulted in exactly the opposite effects. Serous crime and particularly violence in the United States has increased drastically, as detention and incarceration rates have plummeted.

In addition, two options for perpetrating violence, namely, domestic abuse and via technology (i.e. cybercrime), continue to present challenges to law enforcement agencies. It would appear that developing strategic options to deter street crime are less overwhelming to law enforcement policy makers, but this does not eliminate the need to comprehensively evaluate the underlying roots and causes of these troubling criminal trends and to develop stronger collaborations with other organizations, outside of the criminal justice realm, to enhance the likelihood of safer livelihoods and co-existence for all people globally. All persons should feel comfortable and safe within the confines of their homes. Stronger efforts have to be made by government agencies and officials to improve the health and wellbeing of all persons, regardless of gender, race, ethnicity, immigrations status and social status, among other socio-demographic variables.

It has been the goal of the editors and authors to thoroughly evaluate the concept of violence from multifaceted perspectives. In addition, analyses of strategic responses and attempts to control violence and other forms of serious crimes, specifically by law enforcement professionals, have been outlined through a global prism. Successes, failures, challenges and obstacles have been identified with the hope of improving future tactics and developing more effective responses through experiential learning. Ultimately, the key observation is that preventing the proclivity to violence will require a complex, multidimensional approach where not only criminal justice agencies, but also medical, educational, mental health, social services, employment and other related altruistic public service and private organizations, must play critical roles in enhancing opportunity, safety, security, health and welfare for all.

Index

J. F. Albrecht, G. den Heyer (eds.), *Understanding and Preventing Community Violence*, https://doi.org/10.1007/978-3-031-05075-6

Printed by Printforce, the Netherlands